Eric Marshall-Hardy 1894-1965

ANGLING WAYS

By

E. MARSHALL-HARDY

Revised and edited
by
LEN CACUTT

BARRIE & JENKINS
LONDON

Barrie & Jenkins Ltd.,
24 Highbury Crescent,
London. N5 1RX

ISBN 0 214 66870 3

First published 1934
Second Edition 1934
Revised and Enlarged . . . 1944
Fourth Edition 1945
Revised and further Enlarged . 1947
Reprinted 1948
Revised and Reprinted . . 1950
Revised and Reprinted . . 1956
Revised and again Enlarged . 1960
Reprinted 1963
Ninth Edition, Revised and Re-edited 1973

Printed in Great Britain by
Redwood Press Limited
Trowbridge, Wiltshire

DEDICATION

THIS BOOK IS DEDICATED
TO MY LATE FRIENDS
ALBERT VINCENT EARLE
AND
CORRIE IVIMEY
SPORTSMEN AND GENTLEMEN
WITH WHOM IS JOINED
RICHARD WALKER

. . . not because he caught the largest freshwater fish yet taken on rod and line in the United Kingdom, and is an outstandingly skilful angler; but because of the author's appreciation of Walker's always thoughtful and persevering approach to angling problems. That, coupled with his unwillingness to accept rule-of-thumb methods unchallenged has put him in possession of, knowledge which he has translated into improved coarse-fishing techniques to an extent that has not been equalled for several decades. And having so done, he has disseminated his hard-earned findings with remarkable generosity via the spoken word and a facile pen, for the general weal.

CONTENTS

7

8   CONTENTS

LIST OF PLATES

EDITOR'S FOREWORD

THIS, the ninth edition of *Angling Ways*, was in course of preparation by Eric Marshall-Hardy when he died. His partial amendments have been incorporated into the text wherever possible. I am responsible for a number of changes, some of which correct minor sins of omission or commission, and others reflect changing views, improvements in the tools and techniques of the sport following the passage of time; other alterations have arisen where ichthyological research has arrived at conclusions perhaps contrary to statements made in all faith in earlier editions, when fish ecology was in its infancy.

My work on this book has been guided by a sincere desire to perpetuate everything in *Angling Ways* that is right and of lasting benefit to the angler.

I am most grateful to the author's son, Richard Marshall-Hardy; to a devoted friend in Mr. N. J. ('Sam') Weller, and to Mrs. Dorothy Chilman, of Birchington-on-Sea, Kent, all of whom have been most kind and cooperative in allowing me access to Mss. and papers.

Finally, any credit for the continuing popularity of *Angling Ways* must remain with its author Eric Marshall-Hardy; any criticism of this edition must rest with myself.

LEN CACUTT

Streatham, London, 1973

11

BIOGRAPHICAL NOTE: ERIC MARSHALL-HARDY

ERIC Marshall-Hardy, born in Bognor Regis, Sussex, on February 27 1894, the son of a Wesleyan minister, was educated first at Kingswood School, Bath, Somerset and later, at Bradford School of Art, Yorks. At the outbreak of the First World War Marshall-Hardy enlisted in the Royal Flying Corps, to be discharged in 1918 with the rank of sergeant. The war over, he began his business career by founding the firm of Marshall-Hardy Advertising, in Bradford, selling out to his partner and moving to London in 1924.

It was perhaps during this period that Marshall-Hardy's deep and life-long interest in fishing developed, following visits to Highgate Ponds, Hampstead Heath, in North London. But these minor waters did not provide enough scope for Marshall-Hardy's rapidly developing prowess with rod and line; neither were there the necessary sizeable fish. He was therefore fortunate (through his business activities) in being able to travel extensively throughout the British Isles, fishing such well-known waters as the Huntington Ouse, Slapton Lea (Dorset), and Bedfont Gravel Pits, where fine bream, pike and perch fell to his now considerable talents as an angler, and many other rivers, lakes and ponds, this varied experience of widely differing waters enabling him to accumulate a great deal of background knowledge of angling throughout the country.

The Thames also was fished regularly by Marshall-Hardy, but the waters of the south did not claim his undivided attention. He roamed the innumerable lochs of Scotland and learned to understand the Highlander's predilection for salmon and trout, and his almost total lack of interest in any fish of lesser species.

Marshall-Hardy did not allow his great love for freshwater fishing to blind him to the world of sea angling, but—in common with many devotees of fine freshwater tackle—the saltwater species and the heavier tackle needed to allow the angler to cope with them (plus the likelihood of strong tidal currents and deep water) did not hold his concentration as did the roach, bream, chub and other river and lake fish.

It is a tribute to Eric Marshall-Hardy's integrity that he never claimed a complete working knowledge of all the styles and methods of fishing he discussed so eloquently in his books and articles. He claimed nothing but that he had gathered together facts, figures and anecdotes concerning fishing and fishermen and their associated problems, presenting them in an interesting and readable fashion in order that all anglers could gain both pleasure and profit from them.

13

His many correspondents supplied him with innumerable 'new' ideas, all invariably guaranteed by the sender to bring instant angling success. They would be always considered and sometimes introduced into his features and articles; put up to be shot down or applauded as the case may be. (My own term of office in the Editorial chair of angling publications brought the same fascinating but perilous experience.)

Angling Ways was of course Eric Marshall-Hardy's most famous book. Soon after its launch in 1934 it was sold out, an immediate success. A reprint was in fact necessary before twelve months had passed, this in itself something of a phenomenon in angling literature. Since then, nine reprints and revised editions have appeared, and the author was working on a further edition at the time of his death in 1965.

Together with his books, Marshall-Hardy wrote fishing articles for the London *Evening News* and the *Daily Herald*; his name also appeared infrequently under articles and letters in the *Fishing Gazette*. His professional expertise as Advertising Manager of the port and sherry firm of Sandemans, plus his wide personal knowledge, enabled him to write one or two books on wines. His liking for long hours and hard work also gave him the ability, among all his business, writing and social activities, to hold the Editorial chair of the magazine *Angling*, a position which he held with distinction from 1936 to 1954.

Coupled with his writings, Marshall-Hardy was a great and tenacious campaigner: one of his successfully fought battles was waged to close the unreasonable rift between the London Anglers' Association and the Anglers' Cooperative Association. The L.A.A. had instructed its members that they were not at liberty to become members of the A.C.A., on the (unfounded) grounds that the latter body had commercial interests in fishing. During the term of office of his great friend Mr. N. J. ('Sam') Weller as President of the City of London Piscatorial Society, Marshall-Hardy sent a donation to the A.C.A., and then (in January 1952) published the fact in *Angling*. This was tantamount to defying the L.A.A. (to whom also the C.L.P.S. were affiliated) to do anything about it. For some time after this the C.L.P.S. were one of the few angling bodies having official and recognised affiliations to both the L.A.A. and the A.C.A. Now, as is well known, wiser counsels have prevailed and the once-ridiculous attitude of the L.A.A. has changed. The A.C.A. co-exist at peace and harmony with the L.A.A.—which is right and proper when one realises that both bodies have identical concepts: the preservation of our fishing heritage and the betterment of the sport in general.

Eric Marshall-Hardy was not competitive in spirit, preferring to fish for pleasure in leisurely fashion, rather than to attempt to catch more fish, or a greater total weight, over a given length of time, than the next man. His ability as an angler, however, was considerable. An instance of his technique makes the point. In July 1932 he entered a

British Fly and Bait Casting Association competition (held that year at Thorney Weir, Middlesex) and won a silver medal for casting a float the remarkable distance of 98 ft. 8 in.

Prior to his retirement from Sandemans, Marshall-Hardy became a Freeman of the City of London, under the sponsorship of W. D. Spittle. He was also for some years a Fellow of the Zoological Society of London, being introduced by the angling author H. Chapman Pincher.

Eric Marshall-Hardy died at Margate General Hospital on January 9 1965, aged 70. He left this book *Angling Ways* and other works as his lasting contribution to the literature of a fascinating and hugely rewarding sport.

LEN CACUTT

CHAPTER I

TO FISH OR NOT TO FISH

AS a prelude to this work, I propose to digress from matters of strict angling technique and to offer the reader what I hope will prove useful general information on matters pertaining to the art of angling. The law with regard to fishing is as ancient and elaborate as any lawyer could wish. The average fisherman, however, while desiring to know what he may and may not do, has neither the time nor the inclination to scratch around among the law books like a hen in a farmyard, searching for the necessary information.

Oke's *Fishing Laws* contains this disquieting passage: 'Although public fisheries may and do exist in law, yet it is only in very few localities that the public have any right of fishing, and in the majority of instances when persons angle they do so on sufferance, and are in law liable to be proceeded against.'

Where non-tidal waters are concerned, the position of the fisherman is comparatively clear. You have no *right* to fish a river or stream from either a boat or the shore purely in your capacity as a member of the general public. The river may be free for boating and a public right-of-way may run along its banks—neither fact gives the right to fish the said river. In practice it is seldom that facilities for fishing are withheld in such circumstances. Nevertheless, though anyone has enjoyed the freedom of fishing in such waters as long as memory serves, a ban can be enforced on the fishing at any time by either the land-owners, River Authority, or other competent body in the district concerned. It is well known that long and unrestricted use of a road or footpath once constituted such road or footpath a right-of-way after a given period—this is not the case with a fishery, however.

You can, of course, acquire the right to fish in various rivers or over certain stretches of water, in a number of ways. If your forbears have fished from the dim and remote past in a given stream, you are entitled to fish there also. You may, moreover, acquire the right to fish in connection with the ownership of a house. If you and the previous owners have fished a stretch of water without anyone's permission and quite openly for thirty or more years, then you may fish that water and catch and take from it sufficient fish to supply your household

17

needs, but no more. The most usual and complete right to a fishing is, of course, ownership of the bank of a river or stream. Unless the landowner (riparian owner) sells or otherwise disposes of the right to fish the water abutting his land, this right is his exclusively. In this connection he is deemed in law to own the fishing rights from his shore to the centre of the water between his and the opposite bank.

You may also acquire by properly drawn agreement the right to fish in common with the owner for any or only certain fishes which inhabit his water.

Several persons may have the joint right to fish a water by agreement with the owners. Similarly, a stretch of water may be leased by the owner in sections to a number of people. You may secure the right to fish for coarse fish only or game fish only in a water. The permutations of such arrangements are considerable. Personal permission, either verbal or in writing, granted by the owner of a fishery is quite usual and satisfactory, especially the latter. I believe it is correct to say that when verbal permission is given, this permits you to catch fish but not to kill and take them away. Written permission, on the other hand, implies both privileges. It boils down to this: apart from fishing from a boat in tidal waters, you are beholden to someone or other for the privilege you enjoy when fishing any river or stream. Bad behaviour or unsportsmanlike conduct on the part of anglers is liable at any time to provoke an otherwise willing owner to close his fishery to all-comers. It behoves us, therefore, not to take for granted, or to abuse, the pleasures we have been accustomed to enjoy for years, on any given stretch of any river which is privately owned.

This applies also to fishing in lakes, ponds, reservoirs, and artificial waterways. You have no right to fish in any of these of your own volition. It must always be by specific permission (direct or indirect, as through a club which leases the water) of the owner of the land surrounding, or the authority controlling such waters, or by their courtesy in that while they do not grant specific permission to fish, they do not, on the other hand, prohibit it, which they have the right to do.

Should you acquire a fishery by any of the various means at your disposal, see to it that the right to fish includes the right to enter upon the banks for the purpose of fishing. These two rights are not synonymous.*

All these rights are, in turn, governed in some respect by Act of Parliament and Bye-laws made by Fishery Authorities or other bodies, having power within the area where the water is situated. The owner of a fishery cannot himself fish when and by whatever means he thinks fit.

For example, the times and seasons of fishing for freshwater fishes

* If either you or your club join the Anglers' Co-operative Association, 76 New Oxford St., London W.C.1, the Association's legal experts will, should you so desire, prepare or vet your fishing lease, for a very reasonable charge, in such a way as to ensure that it is both easily understandable and legally watertight.

are controlled. Coarse fish, as an instance, must have a closed period for spawning of not less than ninety-three days. The usual period prescribed by the authorities is from 15th March to 15th June, both days inclusive. These dates may, however, be varied by bye-law, providing the total period of respite is not curtailed. In some cases, bye-laws are made which authorize relaxations to permit the taking of certain fish to be used as bait, either alive or as spinners, for the capture of game fish in the same waters. One may, for example, catch bleak for use as bait for Thames trout when the latter are in season and the former are not.

As to restrictions on the time of day during which one may fish, be he owner or otherwise, I give this example from the Bye-laws of the Thames Conservancy:

> No person shall, between the expiration of the first hour after sunset and the commencement of the last hour before sunrise, fish for, take, or attempt to take, any fish by any means whatsoever in that part of the Thames as lies above the City Stone at Staines nor when on any vessel on that part of the Thames which lies below the said City Stone.

In short, night fishing is prohibited, except, it would seem, from the bank below the said City Stone.

Law and bye-law govern also the appliances and methods whereby one may or may not take fish. Here are further examples of this control from the Bye-laws of the Thames Conservancy:

> No person shall use or attempt to use any night hook, fixed hook, night line, hand line, or fixed line in the Thames.

And, again:

> No person on any vessel under way in the Thames shall draw or cause or suffer to be drawn in the direction in which such a vessel is proceeding any line with hook or bait attached thereto, whether such line be attached to a rod or otherwise.

Similarly, such contrivances as otters, wire snares, spears, gaff or tailer (except as an auxiliary to a rod and line) are prohibited—neither must any light be used to aid in luring fish.

No sportsman will ever run foul of such provisions.

Mention of the word foul reminds me that it is illegal to 'foul hook' or 'snatch' fish deliberately, whether with a rod and line or otherwise. Another aspect of illegality is not, however, quite so well known, and a sportsman might be in error under its provision without realizing the fact. This applies especially at the close and beginning of the season:

> It is illegal *to kill* a fish which is about to spawn, has recently spawned, or has not recovered from spawning.

If such a fish is caught, as must be the case quite often, it must be returned to the water unharmed. Here, again, any decent sportsman would comply most willingly, for the obvious benefit of himself and other fishermen. To kill one fish in spawn means the death of countless numbers of fish. With pollution so rife and growing as it is, no precaution of this kind could be irksome to any decent and thoughtful angler, but care is required to note the conditions to which this provision refers.

It is also illegal to take immature fish. The term 'immature' is interpreted through the bye-laws of the district authority concerned with any given water, and often means lamentably small fish.

While the provisions of the Salmon and Freshwater Fisheries Act, 1923, remain constant, the Bye-laws of district or local authorities may vary considerably. Every angler should secure a copy of the regulations which govern the district in which he fishes, and acquaint himself with its details. The foregoing is but a ruffling of the surface of the law in respect of fishing and fisheries, but it gives, I hope, sufficient data to provide the reader with a healthy respect for the rights of others as applying to his fishing. As between sportsmen and gentlemen there is seldom need to resort to the law; which it is, indeed, well to avoid. If, however, litigation with regard to fishing or a fishery becomes imperative, secure sound and well-considered advice before you embark upon it. Someone has said: 'The law is an ass.' That may or may not be a statement of fact. It is, however, indisputable that law is expensive.

CHAPTER II

WHILE record fish are beyond the dreams of the average angler, all may hope at some time to catch a 'whopper.' These big fellows usually find their way to the taxidermist to be 'set up,' and there the fun begins. I have peeped behind the veil of the taxidermist's craft, and what I saw amazed me. Generally speaking fish do not give the impression that their appetites are on a large scale. There are, however, exceptions. Pike and trout appear to hold the records for strange and prodigious feeding. Fish sent 'for setting up' are opened and skinned—it is then that their latest meals come to light. Here are a few: An Avon pike of 30½ lb. was found to contain a 10 lb. pike, a 1 lb. pike a 4 oz. dace, and a 2½ oz. gudgeon. Another pike of 14 lb. had swallowed a roach of 1 lb. 9 oz., and another of 27 lb. had consumed a tench, the tail of which measured 6¾ in. vertically. I am sure these details will give pike anglers food for thought. What fisherman, for instance, would use a large tench or a 10 lb. pike as a bait? Stranger even than this was a butcher's hook 3½ in. in depth which one of these fish had swallowed. Whether it had mistaken the hook for a small eel, it is impossible to say, but that it had swallowed it I assure my readers is an authentic fact. Moorhens, water rats, eels and perch are commonly found in the bellies of pike.

What size livebait for pike? This depends to a great extent on the size of pike you know inhabits the water you intend to fish. Those great pike fishermen of the Broads, the Vincent brothers, well aware of the 30 lb.-plus *Esox* monsters that rule the murky, reedy expanses of Hickling and other Broads, are reported as having used jack pike of 3 lb. as livebait—and with considerable success.

In a dimly lit workroom I made the acquaintance of very rare fish. How many anglers have seen a golden roach? The body of these fish is almost identical with that of the well-known goldfish, while all the fins are brilliant red. There before me was the only one of its kind of which I know, a splendid specimen weighing 1 lb. 5 oz., which was caught at Mapledurham in Oxfordshire in 1927. Yet another rarity was a perfect specimen of the 'silver pike,' weighing 3½ lb., not large but so scarce that it is hardly known; as truly silver as the most brilliant roach and with the most delicate pink fins. There also was a fine example of the rare golden eel caught in the Trent in 1898.

'How many stripes has a perch?' asked my taxidermist friend. Five was the number which came spontaneously as my reply. But I was to learn a most interesting fact, namely, that small perch have seven stripes and only the larger ones five, the two extras merge into the second and third stripes from the head as the fish mature. To prove this he showed me fish of different sizes and his statement became a demonstrated fact.

Surprises and angling mysteries are everywhere in the taxidermist's den. If ever the opportunity comes your way to enter the 'setter's' holy of holies, don't hesitate.

My angling expeditions have taken me over hundreds of miles of country, and I have visited many hotels and club-rooms where anglers' trophies in the shape of cases of specimen fish adorn the walls. Here a fine case of tench, there a splendid barbel. In one room I found no fewer than five pike all taken by the same angler and all weighing well over 20 lb. One feature of most of these 'settings' struck me very forcibly, namely, their lack of artistic merit and the unnatural appearance of the fish.

CHAPTER III

SOME FISHY QUESTIONS ANSWERED

Can fish taste?

THIS is a question of high importance to the angler. In fishes the sense of taste, being closely connected with the olfactory system, is a more complex function than that which exists in human beings, where taste is confined to areas of the tongue. The taste sense in fishes is carried beyond the tongue, even extending to areas outside the mouth. The barbules of carp and other cyprinids, catfish, as well as the widespread cod family, carry concentrations of taste buds, extending in some species to the ends of paired fins.

However, in fishes taste is experienced as part of the environment and not so much as a selective feeding mechanism, although it is wise to assume that fish find certain flavours repellent and avoid tobacco, oil, petrol and similar substances which anglers might handle, thus passing the taint to the bait and terminal tackle.

The sense of smell

Why do chub favour a knob of ripe cheese? Why are roach so partial to fresh wasp-grubs, which are still fragrant with honey of these insects? Why does the bream fisher use brewers' grains or oil cake in his groundbait? This excellent example of sense of smell in fish is taken from *Shark! Shark!* the fascinating work by Captain William E. Young, published by Gotham House, Inc., N.Y.: 'Havana dumps its garbage out to sea four or five miles off shore several times a day. Native fishermen go out to the dumping grounds and lie in wait for the keen-smelling brutes which come up from the deep blue to eat. Harpoons flash, and when the captive is drawn to the boat, the fisherman wields a swift knife. One slash across the backbone and the shark is paralysed. . . . I frequently went to watch this shark hunting, for it promised great possibilities. On one such occasion I noticed a large tiger shark come up to the surface from far below, and head straight for a burlap sack. He grasped it with a snap of his great incisors and shook it as a terrier would a rat. It ripped open, exposing to view a dead mother cat and four kittens. We rowed over to get an iron shot and scared off the brute, but not before it had gulped down the cat whole. Such a perfect

23

example of trailing by scent is not frequently observed, yet the shark had gone straight as a die for the only bit of animal meat in the garbage.'

There can be no doubt that all fish have a more or less highly developed sense of smell. In 1653 Izaak Walton wrote: 'And now I shall tell you that which may be called a secret. I have been a-fishing with old Oliver Henly, now with God, a noted fisher for trout and salmon . . . but he has been observed, both by others and myself, to catch more fish than I, or any other body . . . especially salmons . . . the box in which he put these worms was anointed with a drop, or two or three, of oil of ivy berries . . . by the worms remaining in that box an hour, or a like time, they had incorporated a kind of smell that was irresistibly attractive . . . to force any fish . . . to bite.'

Fish which feed at night and in 'thick' water must rely on their senses of smell and taste to find their food. Most exacting experiments have proved the keenness of these senses in fish—not the least interesting of which was performed by Mr. Gregg Wilson, who found that the introduction of water which had been flavoured with worms into a tank containing fish set them actively in search of food.

Two inferences may be drawn from the foregoing. Experiments with new baits and flavourings may well repay a thoughtful and constructive angler, while the necessity for scrupulous cleanliness and care in preventing unsavoury odours contaminating baits cannot be overemphasised. Even predatory fish like pike, which feed to a great extent by sight, will turn away after following a pickled spinning bait which has not been sufficiently cleansed from the smell of formalin or other preservatives.

The sense of touch

Barbel, gudgeon and carp exhibit the most apparent form of touch organ in their barbules. The illustration shows the disposition of the beards of a barbel which are typical of the highly sensitive feelers, by the aid of which the fish detects food on the bottom. Some fish have other organs of touch, but I will mention only one. Every angler is familiar with what is termed the 'lateral line' in the fish he catches; that clearly defined line running from the gill cover along the length of the fish to the caudal fin. What is the function of this 'elaborate sensory system'

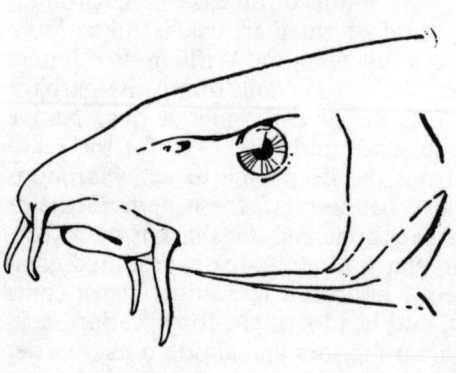

Organs of touch—Head of barbel, showing the four sensitive barbules.

described as such by Dr. P. H. Greenwood, in his book *A History of Fishes*? We know the lateral line organs respond to pressure waves transmitted through the water from moving objects; we also are aware that these organs are able to register the passage of water past the fish, thus giving the fish information on its attitude to its surroundings.

Do fish feel pain?

The answer to that question is debatable, particularly if degree is considered. The trouble is that in general we tend to consider pain and the body's reaction to it in human terms. This is not surprising, since we shall probably never know exactly how the brain of a fish interprets a nervous impulse received by it, following damage or injury to part of the body. I am, however, anxious to give all fish the benefit of any doubt. To this end some lines dealing with hooking devices for live bait have been added to the pike chapters, to which I urge the reader's careful attention. Perhaps most convincing are the actual experiences of anglers themselves. I have hooked, played and landed a pike, weighed and measured it, and returned the fish to the water, only to hook and play it again within five minutes. I was able to identify this friendly fish by certain deformities which were immediately recognisable. Then there is the classic experience of the late Mr. H. Cholmondeley Pennell, who wrote in his work, *The Angler Naturalist*: 'A very singular, if not unparalleled, instance of the voracity of the perch occurred to me when fishing in Windermere. In removing the hook from the jaws of a fish, one eye was accidentally displaced, and remained adhering to it. Knowing the reparative capabilities of piscine organisation, I returned the maimed perch, which was too small for the basket, to the lake, and, being somewhat scant of minnows, threw the line in again with the eye attached as a bait, there being no other of any description on the hook. The float disappeared almost instantly; and on landing the newcomer, it turned out to be the fish I had the moment before thrown in, and which had thus been actually caught by *his own eye*. This incident proves, I think, conclusively, that the structure of cold-blooded animals enables them to endure very severe injuries and wounds without experiencing material inconvenience. . . .' More injury can, I think, result from handling the fish with dry, hot hands or a dry cloth, a procedure which removes their protective slime.

As this is a subject which quite rightly exercises the minds of many anglers, some amplification is merited of the view that fish are not very sensitive to pain.

Frankly I am driven to the conclusion that fish do not experience pain to anything like the same extent as humans, if at all.

Perhaps it should be left to Dr. P. H. Greenwood, Curator of Fishes at the British Museum (Natural History) to have the last word. In his revised edition of *A History of Fishes* (originally by J. R. Norman), Dr. Greenwood says: 'The great difficulty in deciding whether or not under normal circumstances fishes feel pain lies in the fact that it is only possible to judge the matter by our own standards . . . the fact that all fishes possess an elaborate system of nerves and sense organs suggests that they must at times experience feelings of this nature, although it is impossible to obtain any finite information as to the extent of their sufferings . . . it would seem as though some fishes are much less sensitive to pain than others, or at least that they lose their sensitivity to pain under the stress of some emotional excitement. . . .' Dr. Greenwood then went on to describe the familiar story of shark feeding while suffering mortal injury.

No angler is however absolved from taking every possible precaution to avoid causing unnecessary discomfort to the providers of his greatest pleasure. Never for example allow a fish to gasp to death. If for any reason you want to retain a fish, kill it by a hard blow on the back of the head with either a priest or other suitable instrument.

Do fish hear?

Fish have no external evidence of the organs of hearing, but do possess inner ear structures. Most fish have elaborate organs for the detection of sound which are adapted to receive low-frequency tones. One experimenter carried out a series of tests by firing a gun immediately above fish which were visible—he reported that there was no effect upon them. On the other hand, we have the evidence of another who kept fish which he was able to collect to be fed at the sound of a bell. A third investigator found that fish would collect to be fed when they saw a person, whether the bell was rung or not, while they took no notice of the bell if rung by a person out of sight. Experiments have gone to show that fish took no notice when objects were beaten together under water; yet every angler knows from practical experience that the smallest pebble rolling into the water will cause fish which he is stalking to disappear in a flash. It has been noted that the detonations of blasting at a distance from the water produced a marked reaction in some fish and not in others.

Otoliths or ear-stones of the roach (From the collection of G. Allan Frost.)

Showing age rings of a five-year-old fish.

I must mention those truly marvellous bones known as 'otoliths' or ear-bones, which are connected with the auditory organs of fish. The illustration shows the otoliths of a roach. These tiny bones enable the fish to preserve its balance in the water, and volumes have been written regarding them by such great authorities as G. Allan Frost, to whom I am much indebted for access to his collection of otoliths, which is probably the finest in existence.

The small illustration shows clearly how the age of fish may be determined by taking a section of the otolith—each concentric ring representing one year of life and growth.

My study of a number of highly scientific pronouncements on the subject of hearing in fish has given me a wholesome respect for the auditory powers of these animals. It would seem clear, however, that the aural faculty varies in its acuteness in different species. H. Muir Evans, in his interesting and learned work, *Sting-fish and Seafarer*, says: 'In a carp the area (of the brain) that is supposed to represent hearing and called the central acoustic area is small, while fish like the bleak ... that live on the surface and are plankton feeders, have a large central acoustic area.'

In the same book, chapter 13, pp. 107–8, Dr. Muir Evans gives further evidence of hearing in fish: 'A very common catfish in Borneo, known to the natives as "ikan baong," is a scavenger, but gives a lot of sport to both natives and the officials of the islands. ... The methods of catching these bearded animals are interesting to those who are inclined to doubt the hearing powers of fish. If when bottom-fishing with worms the fish fail to bite, the native fisherman puts the closed fist into the water and, suddenly opening the hand, produces a squeaking noise; this is quite sufficient to attract the fish. ...'

Perhaps the most interesting and convincing findings in respect of hearing in fishes have resulted from the experiments of Prof. K. von Frisch, of the University of Munich.

I have always made a practice of moving quietly when either wading, rowing a boat, or walking on the bank, being satisfied that whether fish hear as we understand hearing or not—they are sensitive to vibration.

I did not, however, believe that coarse fish could hear external, i.e. air sounds—and said so without equivocation. But Professor Frisch has left no margin for error in this matter and as the subject is one of considerable importance to anglers, I will give my reader a brief resume of the salient points made by him in a lecture at University College, London, and set down at length in *The Weekly Journal of Science Nature* (Vol. 141, Jan. 1938, p. 8, Macmillan).

An American catfish (*Ictalurus nebulosus*) had its eyes removed surgically. It lived in a small earthenware pipe at the bottom of an aquarium. When food was placed in the mouth of the pipe, by means of a glass feeding tube, the fish came out, being attracted by its chemical sense. At each emergence, von Frisch whistled with his lips. Within a few days, the fish could be brought out of the tube by the whistling alone—*even from the other side of a long room*. Dr. Stetter, one of von Frisch's collaborators, continued these experiments using a minnow (*Phoxinus phoxinus*) surgically blinded. The fish could be conditioned quickly to sounds made by tuning forks and whistles. The upper limit for the minnow being between D and A in the fifth octave, i.e. about 5,000–7,000 vibrations a second. *Ictalurus*, the catfish, gave responses to considerably higher notes—up to 13,000 vibrations per second. A minnow was trained to E in the second octave (frequency 660) and the intensity was reduced to a low value. *Positive reactions were obtained at a distance of* 200 *feet from the tank*. A man was submerged in the tank and tested in the same manner as the fish; *and the best fish were slightly better at hearing than the man*.

Other fish were trained to a feeding sound and negatively to another sound by giving them a light blow with a glass rod. This latter sound the experimenters called the warning sound, because it entailed a punishment; and most fishes can be trained in this way to distinguish between two sounds at an interval of not less than an octave.

In *A History of Fishes* Dr. P. H. Greenwood has this important statement to make concerning hearing and sound production in fishes:

> During the last 25 years an impressive body of evidence has been drawn together concerning sound perception in Bony Fishes. From all these studies one clear fact has emerged: the Ostariophysine fishes have the best developed sense of hearing particularly with regard to the frequency range of the sound and the discrimination of pitch. The conclusion is inescapable that hearing has considerable biological significance to these fishes. The ability to hear and to produce sounds also suggests, at least for certain species, that some form of sound communication exists between individuals.

Fishy vision

Is there any subject more important to the angler than that of the vision of fish? The acuteness or otherwise of fish vision is always a subject for conflict when experts in these matters express opinion. One fact is certain—all our freshwater fish can see. It is most interesting, in considering this subject, to note the effect of environment on the vision of some fish which do not come under the direct purview of the British angler.

There are, for instance, blind fish, of which the Cuban blind fish may be taken as an example. The young of this species have eyes, but these disappear as the fish matures. There can be no doubt that this fact is due to their cave or underground stream existence, where sight would be of no value to them in their search for food. As in the case of human beings who are afflicted with blindness, the maximum compensation is given by nature in the sharpening or heightening of other senses.

More fortunate are the four-eyed fish—a Central and South American species. The illustration opposite shows how this multivision is arranged. The lower eyes are constructed for observation below water, while the upper eyes operate above water and are able to detect insects, flies, etc., which may serve as food. There are many other modifications of fish vision, but these extremes must suffice in passing to the angler's immediate problem—what can the fish for which I angle see? Experts appear to agree that the formation of a fish's eye indicates that they are short-sighted. Nevertheless, within the effective range of their vision—which I believe varies with the species—the sight of fish is sufficiently acute to warrant the angler's careful attention. A valid comment has been made by H. Chapman Pincher who says:

It is very significant that fishes which are themselves hunted, e.g. roach and dace, have eyes set well on the side of the head giving a wide field of vision, whereas predatory fishes like the perch, trout and pike have the eyes set forward giving a wise binocular field at the expense of the range of total vision. 'Pike,' he says, 'pay little attention to baits passing at their side, but react to those passing through their binocular field.' This binocular field he describes as 'an area immediately in front of the fish which is visible simultaneously to both eyes.'

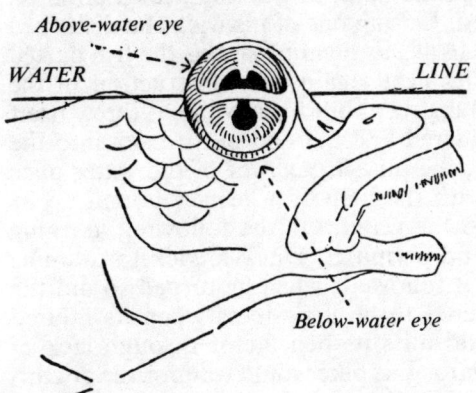

Above-water eye

WATER · · · ➤ LINE

Below-water eye

To sum up, the vision of fish, especially in clear water on a calm day, is most acute; it is certain that fish are often able to see an angler or detect his movements when he is quite unable to see them. Chub will sink from sight at the slightest movement—the flash of a rod or the flight of a bird over the surface of the water is sufficient. To be as invisible as possible is a cardinal rule of good anglers, leaving the biologists and comparative anatomists to settle their intricate disputes at will.

Do fish think?

Anticipation, gratitude and thought would almost seem to be faculties possessed by some fish! What angler has not spoken of 'educated' fish, when his skill, fine tackle and dainty baits have proved of no avail on some well-fished water?

Nevertheless men of science assure us that fish are not intelligent, but that they are creatures of conditioned reflexes. Kenneth Tomlinson, B.Sc., F.R.I.C., writing in *Angling* (No. 37, Vol. VIII), explains the term 'conditioned reflex' this way:

A pike and perch were kept in a large tank divided in two by a movable glass partition. At first the pike was on one side of the glass partition and the perch on the other. As soon as the pike saw the perch it made a dash towards it and received a sharp blow on the nose from the glass partition. This went on for some time until the pike began to associate attacks on the perch with sharp blows on the nose and presently gave up the practice. At this stage the glass partition was removed and the pike was enabled to swim freely with the perch; but it never touched it because of its 'conditioned reflex' that attacks on perch equal blows on the nose.

I subscribe to the reflex theory and believe that a hooked fish may head toward a reed bed or a submerged tree root, not because it reasons that by so doing it will free itself from the angler's tackle, but because an ingrained conditioned reflex causes the fish to associate the weed or tree root with safety. This subject could be much extended and developed but the exigencies of space must prevail.

Are fish grateful?

I have in mind the alleged experience of one Dr. Warwick, who, when resident in Dunham, was in the habit of walking near a pond on the estate of the Earl of Stamford. During one of his walks he disturbed a pike which was lying near the bank; as he approached the fish darted away, and in doing so struck its head against an obstruction in the water, and was injured. After plunging about for a while, it threw itself on to the bank. The doctor rendered first aid and put it back into the pond. In a short time, however, the pike leaped out of the water once more, whereupon the doctor, with the help of a keeper, bound up its injuries and again returned it to the water. On the following morning the fish swam to the banking and permitted Dr. Warwick to examine its injuries. As he moved away it followed; when he turned so did the fish, exhibiting what he considered to be uneasiness when its injured eye was shoreward, lest it should miss its benefactor through lack of vision in that eye. Always afterwards this pike would wait for the doctor, and in due course was taught to feed from his hands.

These considerations have a considerable bearing upon the respect anglers should pay to fish by way of their being silent and as invisible as possible when pursuing their sport; it pays to give fish the benefit of any doubt which may exist as to whether they associate a fisherman and his gear with possible disaster to themselves. Thoughtful interest in these matters pays good dividends in better sport. For lucid information on these subjects I recommend *A History of Fishes*, by the late J. R. Norman, as revised by P. H. Greenwood, D.Sc.

Do fish sleep?

There is no doubt that fish do sleep; some of them even lie down on their sides when sleeping. They do not always sleep on the bottom but may sleep suspended at any depth.

Every angler knows that small boys and some who are not so small, are able to extract trout from streams by what is known as 'tickling' or 'guddling.' I well remember one youth who was thrashed regularly for this practice by his father, who was an employee of the owner of the fishery. Neither fact however spoiled father's appetite for these ill-gotten gains—but let me not digress too far.

The point I wish to make is, that trout taken in this way are almost certainly sleeping fish.

Are fish travel sick?

It is I think more than likely that one of the causes of death among fish during transport from one water to another is travel-sickness.

Dr. Percy O. Jones (The Wellcome Foundation) writing in *The New Scientist*, Vol. 2, No. 36, p. 11, says:

> Like man, most animals which lead a sedentary life are prone to this disorder. . . .
>
> Curiously enough, even animals whose natural habitat is the sea are not totally immune. Seasickness has occurred in trained seals travelling from England to America, *and in fish being taken from the Pacific Islands to the New York Aquarium.*

(The italics are mine. M-H.)

That freshwater fish do vomit and that psychological factors play their part in producing this unpleasant condition is well known.

An English pike of 37 lb. 8 oz. vomited several large roach before it was weighed. And I remember the late J. S. Rigby telling me of a case where large roach while being netted from one of the Metropolitan reservoirs threw up quantities of sticklebacks, which odd though it may seem appeared to be their principal food.

Holding fish too tightly or submitting them to unaccustomed motion in transport may well produce this effect, *verb sap.*

CHAPTER IV

ROACH HYBRIDS—THE PAGE THEORY

EARLY editions of *Angling Ways* carried this chapter, which introduces and describes the Page Theory, a system of roach identification based on a scale count which claimed to enable the investigator to give positive identification to a fish after an evaluation of a triangle of scales near the base of a pectoral fin. The progenitor of the theory was a taxidermist, Mr. F. Page, and Eric Marshall-Hardy carried this man's banner, bearing at the same time the criticisms—and there were not a few—that were launched at the system. In order to put the matter in a proper perspective Marshall-Hardy, in a letter published in June 1959 in the *Fishing Gazette*, said '. . . such criticisms and comment should be addressed to the organ-grinder not the monkey. Anyone who was not familiar with the subject would . . . assume that the theory was mine. . . . Let it not, however, be assumed that I am running away from the theory after giving it so much credence and publicity. I shall not do that until Mr. F. Page, its author, abandons his findings and tells me why.'

In his original attempts to give prominence to the Page Theory Marshall-Hardy gave what he called later a 'bad expression' of the concept and in the 1960 edition (the eighth) of this book—also reprinted in 1963—he said 'That it (the theory) aroused a great deal of interest is certain, and that I expressed it badly is now apparent to me.'

The interest thinking anglers showed in the Page system can be found from articles and letters in the *Fishing Gazette*, beginning in November 1957, and carrying on through the following issues. Harvey Torbett, well known for his books, articles and broadcasts on angling, had been contributing a series of features on the identification of coarse fish and devoted a whole article to the Page theory. It was unfortunate that Mr. Torbett used the original version of the theory as the basis of his comments, but he did finish his feature by saying that he did not ask his questions in a spirit of levity; if someone could produce a trouble-free method of identifying roach he was anxious to make use of it. In the meantime he would resort to orthodox methods. Basically the worth of the Page Theory depends on whether an evaluation of the five-scale count can without doubt and to the satisfaction of scientific opinion truly identify a true roach from the bream × roach, dace × roach, chub × roach and rudd × roach hybrids. Richard Walker affirmed that Harvey Torbett was motivated by a desire to arrive at the truth of the matter; the point that the 5–5–5 triangle of scales demanded by the Page test will only be satisfied by a count of four scales between the ventral fin and the lateral line.

Marshall-Hardy replied to the Walker and Torbett correspondence but the letters did not really achieve more than to illustrate how touchy authors can be when their theories are criticized.

I can do no more than quote one of the country's most eminent ichthyologists, Dr. Alwyne Wheeler, of the Department of Zoology, British Museum (Natural History) and author of *The Fishes of the British Isles and N.W. Europe* (Macmillan, 1971), with whom I conducted a brief but enormously worthwhile correspondence on the subject of the Page theory. Dr. Wheeler described himself as a person whose job it is to identify fishes, and to evaluate methods of doing this. The major drawback to the Page theory, explained Dr. Wheeler, was that the evidence was not published. 'If Marshall-Hardy was so convinced (the theory) was correct he should have produced the evidence of correlation between the Page counts and other diagnostic features, such as pharyngeal teeth counts, scale and fin ray counts. This would enable everyone to judge the validity of the figures. . . . I believe that this formula is useful to a degree. In general it can be a useful field character for checking whether a fish is a hybrid or not, but that it cannot be taken to be proof of the authenticity of large suspect roach on its own, without recourse to meristic and morphometric features. It all boils down to the fact that you cannot confidently identify a roach using the Page system and nothing else. Fish identification is always based on agreement in several characters, there is rarely one character alone that suffices.'

The following chapter, a shortened version of the one that appeared in previous editions of *Angling Ways*, gives the story of the Page theory as seen by Eric Marshall-Hardy. It is published in fairness to the author of the theory which was formulated as the result of factual (sic) data observed and compiled by him over a period of twenty-five years. If the accumulated data, with detailed accounts of the researches, and properly kept records of Mr. Page's work exist and have not been published I would be most interested to receive them in order for scientific opinion to give a considered evaluation of the place the Page theory should hold in fish identification.

LEN CACUTT

IN his capacity as a taxidermist Mr. Page has been able to examine large specimens from all parts of the country. Moreover, the reader should note that he was in a position to examine these fish both internally and externally: *a fact of great importance*—the pharyngeals, otoliths, fins, scales, colour of the eyes and general form of each fish being compared and contrasted with meticulous care. Large specimens are not the only objects of Mr. Page's diligent study, by any means. Hundreds of smaller fish received his careful scrutiny. Only after identical phenomena had been observed in 100 per cent of cases did he care or dare to propound the theory which has now emerged. I am not unmindful that there is little which may be regarded as inevitable and unfailing when natural phenomena are under examination. Time and again scientific theories have been exploded. My present purpose is, therefore, to record a specific finding which should stand acceptable until reasoning, based upon scientific data, shall prove the hypothesis improbable or impossible. I urge the reader to believe that my only desire is to make a clear statement of the details concerned, in such a manner as will obviate any misunderstanding.

If not, what is lost?

Illustration A opposite is reproduced from an unretouched photograph of a cast of the largest true roach which Mr. Page has been able to find, in a search extending over a quarter of a century. Objections have been raised against the use of a cast of the fish for demonstration, rather than the original fish. I may, however, remind the reader that Mr. Page was a professional taxidermist, whose time was very filled. He chose, therefore, to adopt a method of recording this fish which presented less difficulty and expenditure of time than would be required to set the original specimen. If one questions his veracity, then this cast may be suspect as a 'doctored' exhibit. As I am not able to accept any such idea, and hope my reader will at least concede this point, the cast is acceptable as an absolute replica of the original where the arrangement and formation of the scales are concerned, which is the matter of immediate importance. Certain scales are defined by an outline. These tell the story which is the crux of Mr. Page's simple theory, i.e. the scales of every fish which is a true roach will give this count. It is this scale count which he has found to be inevitable and constant in every fish from which all evidence of hybridism was absent.

By the same token, when the scales of any fish which appeared to be a roach did not conform to this formula, other definite evidence of their hybrid nature was unfailing. This being the case, is not the present scale count of real assistance in recognizing a true specimen of the species roach. *Rutilus rutilus?*

This matter is, I think, clinched by the fact that Mr. Page has never been content to accept the scale count alone as perfect and unimpeachable evidence of the authenticity of any given fish. Nevertheless, let me repeat—he has *always* found it present in any fish which was devoid of any indications of hybridism.

Several attempts have been made to discredit or disprove Mr. Page's theory. Considerable comment was made in the Press by one authority who believed he had unearthed some existing data which would dispose of the claim that this theory is 'an ichthyological discovery' and wipe out the theory itself simultaneously. Neither object was attained. On the contrary, what he wrote was only second to the illustrations which accompanied his writing, in giving support to Mr. Page's scale counting test for roach.

Now let me quote what this writer said of the illustrations A and B on this page: 'Smitt, in his monumental work, *Scandinavian Fishes*, published in 1895, went thoroughly into this matter. I enclose two tracings from Vol. II, pages 807 and 809, from two process plate illustrations. Each of the fishes illustrated gives the 5–5–5 count, as

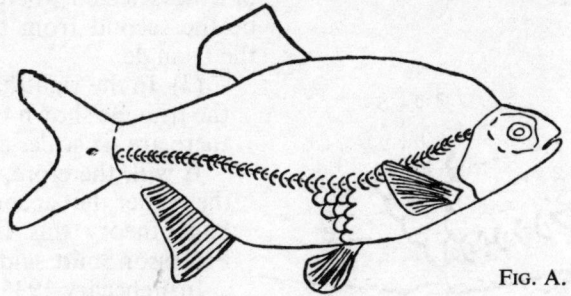

FIG. A.

Hybrid between white bream and rudd captured May 1830.

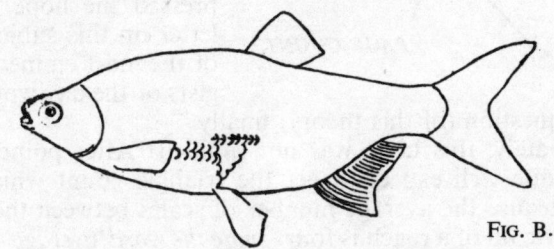

FIG. B.

Hybrid between white bream and roach captured May 4, 1872.
Reproduced by kind permission of R. L. Marston, Esq.

you will see; while the second test, i.e. the tip of the pectoral fin and vertical line from the beginning of the pelvic fin, in the one case is three and in the other is six. Unfortunately, Professor Smitt describes these as hybrids between the Silver (or White) Bream (*Blicca bjoerkna*) and the roach. . . .'

I am at a loss to know why this critic regarded Professor Smitt's dictum that both fish were hybrids as 'unfortunate.' In point of fact Professor Smitt's observations *completely coincide with the Page theory*.

Compare the two illustrations in Figure C and his (the critic's) mistake is apparent instantly, if he thought he had discovered a scale count in Professor Smitt's work, *Scandinavian Fishes*, which was identical with Mr. Page's data for true roach, but that the professor had actually used it to designate a *hybrid* white bream × roach.

FIG. C.

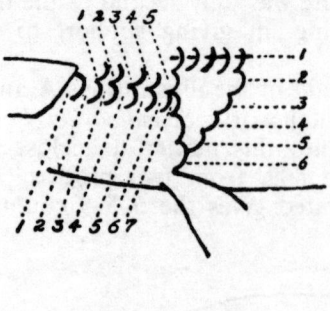

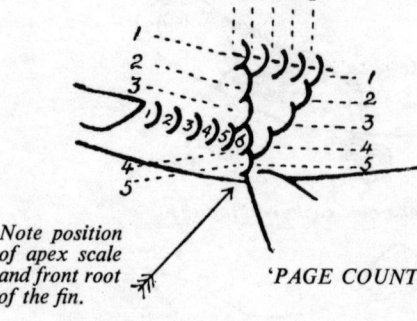

Note position
of apex scale
and front root
of the fin.

'PAGE COUNT'

The differences illustrated are so marked that brief details only are necessary.

(1) According to the critic's drawing the lateral count is either 5 or 7 and *not* six.

(2) The right-hand scale in his lateral count is the third or fourth up, according to the row of scales selected, whereas it should be the second from the apex of the triangle.

(3) In the right-hand side of the triangle shown by this critic there are six scales and *not* five.

It will, therefore, be clear to the reader that according to the Page theory this fish was as Professor Smitt said—*a hybrid.*

In February 1935, the editor of a well-known journal expressed the hope that a short letter on this subject from one of the most eminent ichthyologists of the day would 'clear up the whole question (of this theory) finally.'

Unfortunately, this hope was not fulfilled! After pointing out that one may quite well expect to get the triangle count which this data includes, because the average number of scales between the lateral line and the pelvic fin of a roach is four—*note the word 'average'*—this expert proceeded to an assurance that a museum specimen which weighed 2 lb. 8 oz. actually answers the Page test.

As I have shown already, it is quite possible for a hybrid (Fig. A, page 35), which has no relationship to roach, to answer the triangle count. Let it be clear, however, that the triangle cannot be separated from the lateral count of six scales between the tip of the pectoral fin and the second scale up, on the side of the triangle nearest the head.

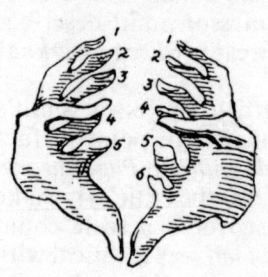

I am unable to understand why this eminent gentleman ignored the lateral count, which I illustrate again for the reader's convenience.

Yet another commentator asked: 'Is it not possible that by a certain age certain changes in relative scale positions may occur in this fish which have not been allowed for?'

Roach and chub pharyngeals

In reply to which suggestion I will quote

A. J. Rudd, F.Z.S. (one time Clerk to the Norfolk Fishery Board, now incorporated into the East Suffolk and Norfolk River Authority), in his book *Coarse Fishing*:

> Aristotle evidently recognised the fact that fish of the same species have the same number of scales, whether they be large or small; in other words, if a bream of a pound in weight has 50 scales along the lateral line, that bream at 10 lb. will have no more, the scales grow as the fish grows, not only in superficial area, but in thickness, and not increasing in number with the increased size of the fish. No other naturalist seems to have noticed this until 1696, when Anthony von Leuwenhock, by the aid of a crude form of microscope, found that the scales of a carp were formed by successive layers, each new layer being larger than that of the previous year. Like many people in advance of his time, he was jeered at for his pains.

The position taken up by the propounder of this theory is simple, i.e. any fish which is a true roach and therefore exhibits no trace of hybridism in any part of its anatomy will have the scale formation which is the basis of the theory. On the contrary, if it does not show this scale formation, other evidence of its mixed lineage will always be found.

Mr. Page has no wish to bolster up or maintain a shred of this theory one moment after it has been proved impossible by purely scientific deduction.

CHAPTER V

ROACH: ROACH TACKLE

ROACH are probably more sought by anglers than any other coarse species. Game fighters and cunning as they are, they appeal to the sportsman, while their wide distribution in British fresh waters had doubtless contributed materially to their special fascination for fishermen.

With the exception of Ireland, where the roach is found in the Blackwater and also in areas of Northern Ireland, and Devon, Cornwall and West Wales, where it is rare, roach are found in plenty throughout the country, and in Scotland as far as Loch Lomond.

Another advantage of roach from the angler's viewpoint is the fact that they thrive equally in still and running water. In this connection it is interesting to note that while in running water they show marked preference for swims with a clean shingle or gravel bottom, they are equally at home in ponds where the bottom is thick, slimy mud. While roach of running water fight more strongly, the pond fish appear to attain a greater size.

Roach are usually credited with very sharp vision, and almost intelligent discrimination where coarse and fine tackle are concerned. This is a most debatable point, but I am satisfied that the method of presenting the bait to a roach is of far greater importance than the fineness of the tackle used; this is a matter for future discussion, but it prompts an immediate question.

Do you know that the pupil of a roach's eye is not round?

If you wish your glass-case roach to be true to nature, have the eyes painted. While fish possibly make good use of their eyes, men also watch them and glean useful lessons. A most interesting detail is given by the late Dr. C. Tate Regan, the great ichthyologist. He says: 'I have often thrown a pellet of paste and seen one roach after another take it in and reject it, until one found it sufficiently to his liking to swallow it.'

Mr. Fennell found, while making similar experiments, that if the largest roach rejected the bait, none of the other fish in the shoal would touch it, and that when this happened the large roach would often swim away with the shoal following.

I suggest that in the case cited by Dr. Tate Regan, each successive fish washed the pellet of paste to some extent until it was acceptable, and that the series of previous rejections were due to some contamination which was distasteful to the fish. This goes to show how very important it is to use scrupulously clean baits when roach fishing, for there can be little doubt they are extremely dainty, especially if they are not feeding keenly.

Despite any comments regarding large specimens of the *Rutilus* family which have gone before, it is very proper that I should mention the official record rod-caught roach. A great fish, indeed, which fell to the wiles of Mr. W. Penney in 1938, at Lambeth reservoir in Middlesex. It turned the scale at 3 lb. 14 oz., and thus eclipsed the 3 lb. 10 oz. specimen taken by the late Mr. W. Cutting from Hornsea Mere, in Yorkshire, in 1917.

This record was equalled by A. Brown in August 1964 with a fish caught from a gravel pit at Tallington, near Stamford, Lincs.

Another interesting fish in this exclusive class was taken from the Test on a mayfly by Mrs. W. W. Fennell in 1929; it weighed 3 lb. 4 oz.

As far as I am aware, there are no records of roach taken with rod and line and weighing 3 lb. or more, prior to that caught in 1903 by C. O'Callaghan, at Shapwick near Blandford, on the Dorset Stour. Since that time comparatively few roach weighing 3 lb. and over have been reported, and one was a four-pounder! There was one 3 lb. capture recorded in 1972, the fish falling to maggot bait fished in Napton Reservoir in July.

Describing a fishing visit to Omagh (*Angling Times* 5.4.57) in County Tyrone, N. Ireland, Bernard Venables writes:

I shall never forget the Milk Pool on Fairy Water (tributary of the River Strule) . . . where a milk factory stands on the bank. The factory's effluent goes into Fairy Water and to feed on the milky particles in it there is a dense congregation of fish.

One Nat Holmes, his local guide on the occasion in question, explained that to fish this water no groundbait was necessary. So using two maggots on the hook, they having such a close resemblance to the particles he saw in the effluent, Venables hooked a fish before his float had travelled a foot.

Nat Holmes netted this, the first of 40 taken in an hour and a half, asking as he grassed it—'Don't you think it's like a roach?' Mr. Holmes had often noted the roach-like appearance of these fish from the Milk Pool and had sent specimens to a biologist for verification of species, only to receive the reply that their throat-teeth, or pharyngeals (see page 36) proved that the fish were rudd. So adding this scientific opinion to the then generally accepted dictum that the only true roach in Ireland were in the Blackwater away in the South, he accepted them as rudd.

Now let me turn to Venables' reply to the question 'Don't you think it's like a roach?' I quote:

I looked at it—I gaped at it. IT WAS A ROACH, A MOST BEAUTIFUL AND COMPLETELY INDISPUTABLE ROACH. All was right—the receding lower jaw, the fin positions, everything. And never, not even on the Kennet, had I seen a so perfect, so splendidly shaped and coloured roach.

But what of the four-pounder? Continuing, Venables, describing some of Mr. Holmes' catches of these roach, writes:

Two-pounders he takes casually. He catches them frequently—they come on almost any day. Three-pounders he has not found particularly uncommon and one day . . . two years ago (July 1955), he hooked a fish . . . did not see it for ten minutes. It bored powerfully—and fought with a heavy dogged fire. . . . I could see it as he described it, this huge fish with its brilliant red eyes. . . . I could see it as the finest roach that man ever caught.
And that, as it happens, is exactly what it was. THAT ROACH WEIGHED EXACTLY FOUR POUNDS! . . . Now where did this wonderful roach come from? Well, I know that too.
Nat told me that about fifty years ago, a few roach were put into the Lake at Baronscourt, the seat of the Duke of Abercorn, and this lake has a connection with the rivers of the Foyle system.
From there they have colonised widely through the system. It was only twenty years ago that they appeared in Fairy Water and the waters of that vicinity. So you see, though it was in Fairy Water that I discovered them, there are really many miles of this fabulous fishing—these roach have been taken twenty miles downstream, below Strabane, in the Mourne River.

Knowing Bernard Venables as a widely experienced fisherman and a careful observer, I must admit some astonishment on reading his unequivocal declaration that the 4 lb. fish to which his story relates was an indisputable roach.

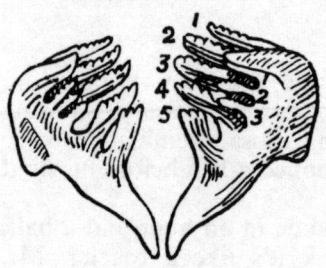

Rudd pharyngeals after Tate Regan after Fatio

Had not 'a scientist, one who made a study of fish,' said that these Fairy Water fish 'were rudd' and that 'their throat (pharyngeal) teeth proved they were'? And are not the throat teeth of roach and rudd very different both in form and number?

A cursory comparison of this illustration of the throat-teeth of a rudd and those of the roach illustrated on page 36 will supply the answer.

The late Dr. C. Tate Regan says:

The pharyngeal teeth (of roach and rudd) differ notably . . . both in structure and number. Those of the rudd . . . are strongly pectinated and are arranged in two series, five in the posterior and three in the anterior row.

I am loth to cast doubt on this 4 lb. roach, especially as it is sponsored by my friend Venables. Nevertheless, I find it very difficult to believe that any 'scientist' who 'makes a study of fish,' could make an error when comparing the throat-teeth of roach and rudd. My reader must decide therefore as to whether this great fish must be relegated to the realms of the leprechauns and 'little people' of Ireland.

The rarity of three-pounders is apparent from the foregoing, but let it not be thought that two-pounders are common—you can fish a lifetime without catching one.

References to roach (and other fishes) exhibiting black spots on the skin recur in the angling Press from time to time, raising the question as to whether this disease is dangerous or contagious. The facts are that 'Black Spot' is caused by a trematode worm. A fish-eating bird is the final host of the worm, the parasite coming to maturity within the bird, where it lays its eggs. These are subsequently excreted and are absorbed by a water snail in which they develop. A larval stage is then freed from the snail and continues to develop into a later larva known as the *Cercaria*, which penetrates the skin of fish. There it becomes enclosed in a cyst, and it is these cysts which appear as black spots. The cyst-imprisoned larva cannot develop further unless the fish is eaten by a suitable final host. There is, I believe, little danger to human beings from eating such fish, and all danger would be eliminated by removing the affected skin. As to the disease being transmitted from one fish to another, this is highly improbable, the bird and snail hosts being necessary to infection. 'Black Spot' disease, or Diplostomiasis, cannot be regarded as dangerous, because infected fish show little or no loss of condition or activity, and the incidence varies greatly, so that a stock which is heavily infested in one year, may be quite clear in the following year, as happened in the Avon in 1933 and 1934.

ROACH TACKLE

Now, how should the novice be equipped for roach fishing? Most would-be anglers know at least one 'old 'un' and I strongly advise that the necessary visit to the tackle shop be made in company with such a friend. Make it clear to him that your outfit shall not be more elaborate than efficiency dictates if you will; nevertheless, let every item of your kit be the best you can afford. I am prepared to stand by that advice—time is the test!

The rod is the first and most important item, particularly as it cannot be purchased without the reel, with which it must balance. These two essentials are the Darby and Joan of the gear, and if well chosen will last a lifetime.

Roach are caught by different styles of angling, and specialists in each use various types of rod and reel, but at the outset your friend will advise you to purchase a good all-round equipment.

When several rods have been produced, together with a selection of suitable reels, you come actively into the picture. The reels being fitted to the rods, handle each in turn, and select the one with which you feel most comfortable; your friend cannot help you in this, but your decision is vital to your subsequent pleasure. The matter of length is not so important as the resilience of your rod; it should be fairly stiff to give quickness in strike. A word of warning should however be added. If you are fortunate enough to be able to fish a water which holds really heavy fish, especially those of other species such as barbel and large chub, which you may hook while roach fishing; your rod should be more flexible. Otherwise you are likely to be 'broken up.' But this is a point regarding which either your 'old 'un' friend or any good tackle dealer will advise.

For boat fishing 8 to 10 ft. is ample, while rods of 14 ft., 16 ft., or even more, are favoured by many bank fishers. Your friend will guide you in this, though personally I am happy in most cases with a 10 ft. rod for both purposes. The all-in weight of a good rod should not exceed one ounce per foot of its length.

Yes, those glittering gadgets under the glass case are very interesting —'Devons,' 'Barspoons,' 'Archer Spinners,' 'Artificial Flies,' 'Watchets,' 'Clippers,' 'Rubber Frogs,' 'Eels,' and a hundred-and-one other whatnots—all these are as expensive as they are interesting. Turn from them quickly, they play no part in angling for you at present, and there are still several items you require—line, hooks and floats, etc. In the selection of these be guided by your friend, but a complete list of details will help those who do not know even one 'old stager.'

		£	p
Rod (two or three sections), cork grip, adjustable reel fittings, bridge rings, built cane or hollow glass about		9	00
Reel, 3½-in. narrow drum, centre-pin action, with optional check – – – – – – – about		5	00
Line, 50 yards of monofilament line of 4- or 6-lb. breaking strain – – – – – – – about			50
Hooks—6 No. 12 crystal bend – – – – –⎱ 6 No. 10 ,, ,, – – – – –⎰			50
Floats—1 Porcupine to carry 6 shots – – – –⎱ 1 cork on quill to carry 8 shots – – –⎰ 1 Ducker to carry 2 shots – – – –⎰			40
Shot, plummet and lead wire – – – – –			50
Landing net of ample size with a long handle about		4	00

This selection costs about £20. Your purchases may cost much more, but in the long run you will be glad if you do not attempt to buy more cheaply. The cost of the rod and reel can be doubled or halved, but the novice should buy as near the prices given as he is able to afford.

If he makes his first trip to the waterside with an 'old hand,' armed with the equipment I have advised, I can hear him say, 'Smith has a dozen knick-knacks in his kit of which I know nothing!' True, but, having the essentials, it is better to acquire 'knick-knacks' by experience. You will find yourself collecting rods (most of which will subsequently prove to be 'mistakes') and a hundred-and-one angler's gadgets quite soon enough. Another visit to the tackle shop is advisable, however. When you caught your first roach you found it difficult to retrieve the hook with your fingers, and Smith lent you his—

Disgorger.—Just a piece of metal with a cleft end, and it cost a few pence, but you would have been in a fix without it. Buy at least three and distribute them in the pockets of your fishing jacket. They are most elusive, and if you have only one it will certainly be missing when you want it. Those shots for the cast were a nuisance too; first, the lid of the tin flew off and the wretched things fell all over the bottom of the boat, but the real trouble was getting them on the line, and until Smith came to the rescue with his—

Pliers the business of attaching them seemed hopeless. A small pair of pliers for nipping the shot on is very useful and should not cost more than 25p. That snag you caught spoiled the point of your hook, but it seemed a pity to discard it. Smith's—

Watchmaker's file saved the situation—10p for a small file will save you many hooks.

That first day was beautiful and the sun was brilliant, but towards noon your eyes began to feel the strain of the glare on the water. Smith had a pair of—

Sun glasses—what a difference they make when the sun is bright! It was kind of him to lend them to you, or you might have ended the day with a nasty headache, all for the sake of 50p! At the price, you can afford to tread on a few pairs. I have done so many a time! By far the best are Polaroids. These have the optical property of only allowing light on one plane to reach the eyes. This cuts all glare out and makes these glasses ideal for anglers. You will pay more for these.

There are innumerable patterns of fishing bag and the prices vary. I advise the novice to buy as good a bag as he is able; it will last a lifetime. One or two cigarette or tobacco tins for baits, a good length of string, a penknife and a hand cloth complete the kit. As time goes on you will doubtless add to these details as your taste and experience dictate.

It is quite a common practice nowadays to tie an eyed or spade-end hook direct to a monofil cast; and many anglers who use monofil lines dispense with a cast entirely and tie the hook direct to the end of the reel-line. A simple and effective method is illustrated overleaf.

Now for hooks! Tackle-makers offer hooks of many kinds, some of them are illustrated over—left to right they are: 'Round bend,' 'Kendle sneck,' 'Barbless,' 'Spear point,' with side barb, 'Crystal' and

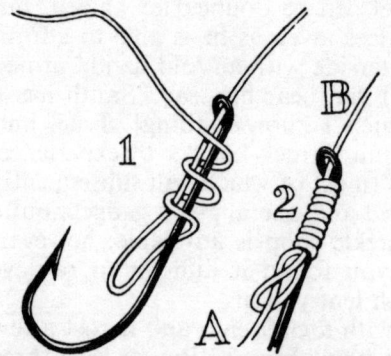

To attach an eyed (or spade-end) hook to nylon:

1. Pass a length of nylon downward through the eye, turn it back to form a loop and take two turns round the shank as shown—then

2. Whip the nylon down from the eye over these two turns, pass the end A through the loop and holding this in position draw taut by pulling on the main cast or line B.

a 'Marston worm hook.' There are scores of others. The hooks shown are in a scale designed by the late W. A. Hunter in the hope that makers would adopt a new and simpler standard for hook sizes. Many makers still appear to use their own scales, which causes endless confusion to anglers.

A vote might show that most anglers prefer the crystal hook— I do myself, but the great mystery is, why do so many of them use such small hooks? What benefit comes from the use of tiny hooks unless baits as small as 'bloodworms' are used when a small hook is a necessity? I have often heard anglers boast when showing a capture that they 'took it on a No. 18.' Their expression on these occasions indicates their own surprise. I have no hesitation in saying that the smaller the hook the less its hooking power, and the more fish will be lost in 'playing' or missed 'on the strike.'

The 'Hunter' hook scale *18 to 6 is an old numbering. 000 to 10 is Mr. Hunter's suggested scale.*

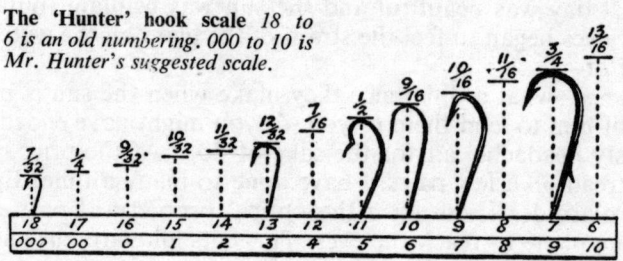

I am not advocating the use of butcher's hooks, but I do say, use the largest hook you can in proportion to the size of your bait and you will quickly reap the benefit. Fish are not so afraid of hooks as many imagine—on the contrary, they are often less fastidious in the matter than anglers themselves; but see to it that your hooks are needle sharp.

CHAPTER VI

ROACH BAITS: BAITING-UP AND GROUND-BAITING

THERE is a long list of baits for the capture of roach. None of the baits in question are, in my opinion, universal in their attractiveness, each varies in accordance with the nature of the water, the season of the year, and, I think, with local custom, for there is little doubt that roach become accustomed to certain baits in different waters and a change does not seem to be appreciated. An angler of my acquaintance who has fished all over the world once told me that no matter where he is, if in doubt as to a suitable bait he always tries bread. There has been much recommendation of breadcrust as a bait for roach, indeed, some writers suggest it as a panacea for roach angler's ills. This is far from true, but breadcrust properly prepared is one of the best roach baits in coloured water, especially in the winter. There are several methods of preparing this bait, the best of which is to cut strips from the bottom of an old square loaf, two thirds crumb and one third crust. Take the strips and lay them on a board, wrap them in a damp cloth and place another board over the whole. A good weight should then be placed on the top and left overnight or for a few hours. While this process toughens the strips of crust, which in turn makes the cubes cut from them adhere more firmly to the hook, it is not essential. Many experts make their cubes at the waterside after soaking the crust in the water where they are fishing; on the principle that this is better than domestic water, which while acceptable to humans may be chlorinated or otherwise medicated in such a way as to render it distasteful to fish. You may then either cut the strips into cubes or place them in a tin till you commence to fish and bite pieces off for hook-bait.

If you are not a smoker the biting method is better, because the bait will be somewhat irregular in shape, which perhaps gives it added attractiveness. Those who smoke should cut up their bread as the taint of tobacco is repellent to roach. The size of the cubes is governed by the size of the hook used, and it must be remembered when judging this that the bread swells in the water.

Flake.—At this point I must mention 'flake,' which, in either still water or suitably steady streams, is one of the most killing roach baits.

45

'Flake' is a cross between 'crust' and 'paste.' The angler simply tears off a piece of the soft crumb from the inside of a new loaf, pinches it on to a No. 10 or 12 hook, and *hey presto*, he has an excellent bait.

When in the water, this irregular squeeze of soft bread tends to break off at the edges and distribute small particles which probably act as an attraction to the larger piece on the hook.

Some anglers claim that the spongy bread gives off a kind of milky haze, which adds to its attraction for fish. This may be so, but I have never noticed it.

I was told by an eye-witness that a Japanese visitor had been obtaining phenomenal success with this bait in the Thames at Richmond, Surrey, by dipping each bait in gin. I shall make the experiment, you may prefer to drink the gin.

Paste—Another form of bread bait is paste, which, if not so attractive as either crust or flake, has the advantage of staying on the hook longer when fishing. The method of preparation is simple, but should be carried out with scrupulous care. Take a portion of the crumb only from a stale loaf and place it in a clean white cloth. Dip the cloth and bread in the water where you are fishing and work up the bread to a fine paste, handling the cloth only. The matter of having clean hands for this work is very essential. The paste when made should be just stiff enough to allow of easy hook penetration. I am fond of large baits, but the size of your paste hook-bait may vary with advantage, success may come from a big bait or a very small one—make experiments.

Some anglers colour their pastes and flavour them, but it is a matter of some doubt as to whether this has any appreciable effect.

Stewed wheat—Another allied bait is stewed wheat. This is much used in certain localities, and in these places is the most effective roach lure, particularly in late summer and autumn. There are several methods of preparing wheat for use, but the least troublesome is as follows: fill rather less than one-third of a vacuum flask with the wheat, then pour boiling water on to it within 2 in. of the full capacity of the vessel and leave it for 2 to 3 hours. The wheat will then be ready for the hook.

*Gentles or maggots—Gentles vary in quality according to their origin, whether from fish, flesh, or fowl. Claims as to the merits of these are made by many anglers, some preferring one kind, some another. I buy mine regardless of their pedigree, and only ask that they shall be as large as possible. The important matter is to keep them in good condition. This may be accomplished by placing them in either fine sand or bran, and keeping them cool to prevent them taking the chrysalis form. Sand or bran cleanses the gentles and imparts a very desirable liveliness to them. Sometimes sawdust is used, but this is

---

* It is an interesting fact that when a maggot pupates the whole of its internal structure liquefies and the cells rearrange themselves to form the new structure of the fly.

In this process the pointed end of the maggot which was its head, becomes the tail of the fly and what was the maggot's rear becomes the fly's head.

risky, as it may impart a flavour to the gentles which is disliked by roach. Many skilful anglers colour their gentles by placing them in damp bran to which one of the aniline dyes has been added. As they move about in this they take the colour of the dye used—red, green, yellow, etc. The advantage of this colouring is, to my mind, doubtful, but in the light of the high claims made for it by anglers of great experience, the reader may wish to make the experiment. When in chrysalis form gentles turn deep brown or even black. In this state they are occasionally acceptable to roach and other fish, but as a rule are better kept to mix with your ground bait.

Always remove the maggots from the usual sawdust or bran they are bought in. A useful thing is to put them in ordinary flour or custard powder. This makes them swell and when used to attract fish when thrown in by the handful the flour makes an attractive ground bait.

Some anglers make a vital mistake when they impale a gentle on their hook. The illustration makes the correct method quite clear, and no pains to attain this result will be wasted.

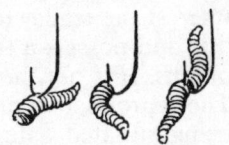

The gentle is free to wriggle, which it indeed does, thereby increasing its attractiveness. Sometimes a single gentle on a small hook, sometimes a bunch of four, five or more is the correct medicine; only a trial will tell the angler. In either event the method of hooking them is the same, each gentle being slid on to the hook

Methods of hooking gentles.

to make room for the next. Some anglers hook a single gentle nearer the head than the one in the illustration and slide it right down to the bend. This is doubtless good, but I prefer the method shown. It is a good plan in winter-time to keep your gentle box in your trousers pocket, as the cold air renders them dormant and inactive. The coldness of the water in winter has the same effect, and it is advisable therefore to renew your hook-bait more frequently than in summer.

Worms—'A fool at one end and a worm at the other,' is an oft-repeated gibe against anglers, but worms have accounted for many a good roach. In winter-time, and when the water is coloured, the tail of a 'lob,' a small red, or a marsh worm will be found very killing.

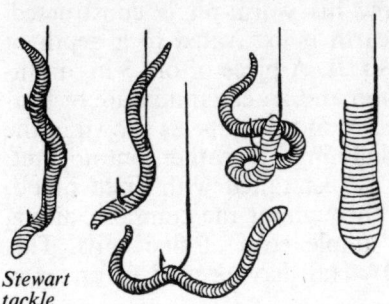

Stewart tackle

Some methods of hooking a worm.

The best method of keeping these baits in good condition is to place them in moss. This scours them and has a toughening effect. Small quantities of milk sprinkled on the moss will keep worms lively and well nourished for a long period. Care should be taken, however, not to allow the moss to become too moist or sodden. At the least sign of this it should be changed, as excessive moisture is detrimental to the preservation of worms. It is also important to take out any dead ones at once or the others will die. The illustration (p. 47) shows methods of hooking a worm. The 'Stewart' tackle is excellent, and worms appear to live longer when hooked by this means. It is quite unnecessary to attempt to hide the hooks—stick them right through the worm. Other simple methods of hooking a worm are by one puncture in the centre, or through the tail, leaving it otherwise quite free for natural movement.

Many anglers and some writers recommend 'maiden' lob worms as being particularly attractive to fish. By this it is presumed they mean a worm without a gelatinous band on it. Thus a fisherman might classify a worm which had just shed its cocoon as a 'maiden lob.' It is in fact unlikely that a worm will ever reach the size known as a 'lob' without having bred several times. It is therefore equally unlikely that the worms described as 'maiden' are actually so virginal as seems to be supposed. From this fact I deduce that 'maiden lobs' have no particular charm for fish, it being much more important to scour, toughen and liven the annelids as described above than to worry about their virginity. It may interest the reader to know that all British earthworms are hermaphrodite and possess a functional set of both male and female reproductive organs. It is not, however, possible for an earthworm to fertilize itself. The reproductive organs are fairly close to the head end, the male set being situated a few segments in front of the female. To breed the worms approach head to head so that the reproductive organs coincide in reverse. Sperms then pass from one to the other and are retained within the body. Later, eggs are shed into the gelatinous band which comes to encircle the body and some sperms are also enclosed, fertilization taking place there.

The gelatinous band becomes a cocoon which is passed over the worm's head and takes the fertilized eggs plus some albuminous nutriment with it. The ends of the cocoon are elastic and close when it is free of the worm, forming a closed bag.

Some anglers take considerable trouble and reap commensurate benefit from maintaining a worm-pit in a corner of the garden. I am indebted to Mr. G. T. Hall, a south country fisherman, for details of a method which he has found particularly successful. The accompanying illustration shows clearly how his worm-pit is constructed. Having selected a suitable spot, the earth is excavated to a depth of approximately 1 ft. 3 in., and some 3 sq. ft. A piece of old 3 in. drainpipe is set in the centre of the excavation and an equal mixture of leafmould and grass cuttings is then placed round the pipe as shown in the figure. This must be kept moist, especially in hot weather, but not wet.

An occasional can of water which is just tinted with dried blood, poured down the drain-pipe, spreads throughout the compost, aiding decomposition, and the result is an ample crop of fine baits. This method has stood the test of time, Mr. Hall having used it for many years with every satisfaction.

Caddis.—The most interesting of the less common roach baits is caddis grub, or stickbait. The latter description is doubtless derived from the appearance of some caddis cases, though the vast majority of the cases made by these animals are not in the least like a stick. To keep them alive put them in damp water-weed wrapped lightly in wet newspaper. Damp moss or rag is also good, but whichever you use see that the tin or other receptacle in which they are placed admits air.

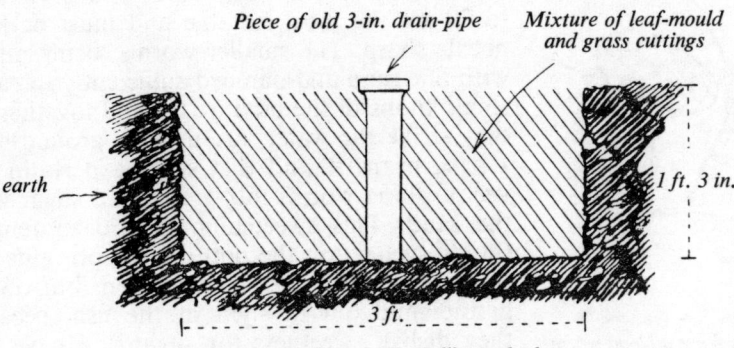

Worm-pit—Mr. G. T. Hall's method.

Do not place caddis in water. When removed from their case caddis have the appearance of splendid gentles, and are used in the same way.

Hook your caddis bait lightly through the tail. In the early season they are among the most deadly baits. Unless you know how to persuade caddis from their cases, this can present a real difficulty. Insert a pin gently into the narrow end of the case—that helps wonderfully in getting them to leave home. In some districts they are not easy to find, but a search in the shallows, under stones, and a careful watch on the bottom will disclose the odd-shaped cases of the caddis grub moving about in cumbersome fashion. It is said that a newly stripped cabbage stalk moored in the water where these larvae are known to be, will aid in drawing them together. The actual grubs vary somewhat in colour. The yellow ones make the most attractive baits. Some writers advise the services of a small boy to collect these baits. I may be singularly unfortunate, but I have never come in contact with a young caddis grub collector. However some aquarists sell them quite cheaply if you have difficulty in securing a supply.

Hardly less interesting as a creature or less effective as a bait is the Blood-worm *Chironomus*, which doubtless derives its name from its crimson colour. They are found in slow dirty streams, ditches and even water butts. There are several species, but only those which burrow in the mud and live deep have the red colouring which is due to haemoglobin, and has a direct bearing on their ability to absorb and retain sufficient oxygen from their unpropitious surroundings to support life.

Blood-worms are very delicate to handle; do not attempt to hold the larva with one hand and insert the hook with the other as when baiting with a gentle. Place the worm on the lobe of one finger, then pass the point of the hook through the segment nearest the head. They are extremely tender and it is a matter of some skill to acquire the knack of doing this without spoiling the tiny bait. Hooks Nos. 18 to 20 are the most suitable and must be kept needle sharp. The smaller worms, being mixed with fine sand and damped sufficiently to cause small knobs of the mixture to hold together till they strike the water, are used as ground-bait. I have heard it said that some experts in the use of blood-worms mix granulated sugar with the sand. This sweetening is said to remain (in still water) on the bottom and prevents the tiny larva in the ground-bait from burrowing in the mud out of sight of the fish, because they dislike sweetness (or sugar?). I have not tried this, but think it worthy of mention.

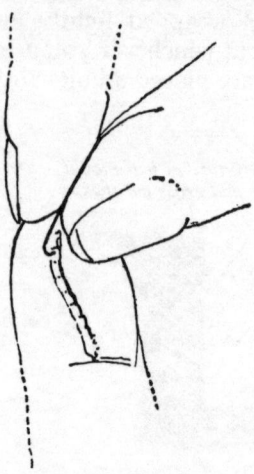

Hooking a blood-worm.

Wasp-grubs—Excellent summer baits for roach, wasp-grubs are very tender and difficult to hook without breaking them. To avoid this you may steam or gently bake them; this toughens the skin. If this is not possible, select the yellow ones, which will be found the least troublesome. Insert the point at the tail and thread the grub on to the hook. Looking through some old papers recently, I was reminded of an excellent tip for hooking a wasp-grub, sent to me many years ago by Mr. A. E. Bailey of Wheelock in Cheshire.

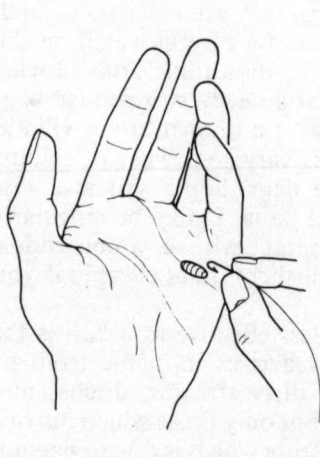

As he pointed out, many are burst by attempts to hold them between thumb and finger when inserting the hook.

The accompanying illustration of Mr. Bailey's method of overcoming this difficulty is, I hope, self-explanatory.

The grub is held in a crease in the palm and the hook *which has been honed to needle sharpness* can then be inserted with minimum risk of bursting the tender bait.

Live and dead flies and other insects of the waterside are sometimes killing.

That roach are at times predatory is beyond doubt. This occurs so seldom however that live-baiting could not be considered seriously as a means of capturing these fish.

To hook a tender wasp-grub.

Nevertheless, I believe that any

angler who had the courage to fish live minnow where large roach exist might be favourably surprised by the results, especially early in the season.

ROACH: BAITING-UP AND GROUND-BAITING

Baiting-up—This is the angler's description of the process of continued ground-baiting of a given spot over a period of days prior to fishing. This should be carried out at the same time each day and as near the hour at which you will commence your fishing as may be possible. *Baiting-up definitely collects fish at the place so treated and they will come to that place at the time of your baiting if this is done at a regular hour.*

At least twenty-four hours should pass without any bait being used immediately prior to fishing the swim. The ingredients used cannot be too clean, fresh and pure. They should be made up with scrupulous care, remember tobacco is anathema. Small quantities of the hook bait to be used should form part of the baiting mixture. Great care need not be taken to drop the bait in quietly, but its exact position should be most carefully noted, either by the use of a small buoy, when this is possible, or by land marks. These tactics are often highly successful.

Ground-baiting takes place while actual fishing is in progress, and its introduction is a matter for careful manipulation. The first point for consideration is how quietly this may be done, unlike the throwing in of the bait previously mentioned. *Clumsy administration of ground-bait when fishing will drive fish away as certainly as its skilful introduction will attract them.* The quantities of ground-bait used should, under normal conditions, be small, a good motto is 'little and often.' *The precise ingredients of some useful ground-baits will be discussed later, but it is a sound principle to make it much less feeding than that used when baiting-up.* Purity and cleanliness are essential.

The function of baiting-up is to collect large numbers of fish in a given place, while that of ground-baiting is to keep them there when you are fishing and to encourage them to feed. Someone who knew what he was talking about has said 'to fish for roach without ground-bait is as optimistic as to walk about without belt or braces.'

When the angler has thoroughly realized that ground-baits should attract without feeding, he has gone a long way toward success in its preparation. The nature of the water, still or running, weedy or clear, coloured or bright, and the hook-bait are the factors upon which your selection of ingredients should be based. In every instance it is advisable to add a very small quantity of the hook-bait to ground-bait, and it is better if this is of inferior quality.

Cloud-bait—There are many forms of cloud, some of which are most elaborate in their make-up. It is often hinted that successful roach anglers use secret and potent mixtures. This is not so. High claims are also made for certain commercial preparations, and while these are undoubtedly good, the simple home-made recipes are quite effective. One of the best clouds is prepared by drying a loaf in a 'slow' oven until it becomes crisp, care being taken not to burn or brown the crumb of the bread. The crust is cut off and the dried crumb crushed to a fine powder. To this is added castor sugar. The resultant mixture damped at the waterside and made into small balls is then ready for use. Some anglers also add either middlings, crushed hemp, oil of aniseed, or crushed biscuit. Silver sand is a useful addition when you desire cloud to sink quickly.

Bread—Soaked bread is another simple ground-bait for roach. It is prepared by soaking the crumb of stale bread in water and reducing the moist bread to a pulp in which there should be no lumps.

Bread and bran—This ground-bait is a direct development of the last-mentioned, and is prepared by adding bran to the pulped bread until it forms a stiff mixture. Other ingredients such as brewers' grains (the husks of barley) and cattle cake are sometimes added. This is one of the best baiting-up mixtures.

Hemp ground-bait—In addition to the use of the actual seed described later, bricks or cakes of 'hemp husk' (the residue after the seeds have been crushed to extract oil) mixed with dried blood are obtainable from the continent and when crushed constitute a good ground-bait when hemp is on the hook. A useful mixture may also be made by crushing hemp as finely as possible and mixing it with the cloud described previously.

Worm ground-bait—The worms used for ground-baiting should be of inferior quality and not so well scoured as those used on the hook. It is indeed better to chop them up and mix them with clay. This also is an excellent baiting-up mixture when eels or perch are not present. The foregoing constitute the chief and most useful ground-baits for roach.

But knowledge of them will be rendered abortive unless ground-baits are properly applied. There are two main points for consideration: how to get your ground-bait where you want it to be, i.e. in line with the track of or immediately below your hook-bait; and how to do it with the least possible noise or disturbance. I will therefore make some suggestions as to ways and means toward this end which are not in general use, but will be found of high value, particularly to the roach fisher. It is beyond doubt that the roach are very sensitive to vibration of any kind, and the indiscriminate casting-in of ground-bait will assuredly put them down. In still water or very slowly flowing streams, cloud is the ground-bait *par excellence*, imparting a fog of appetizing flavour without the slighest food value. Now to get to work quietly, squeeze a portion on the shots of your cast, swing it out gently over the swim and dip it quietly into the water. Then raise the point of your rod sharply (not too sharply); this will jerk the bait off the cast. By this means the splash which must result from throwing it in is avoided. The operation is a delicate one, as cloud is most anxious to be at work, and will fall from the shots on the least provocation. Practice will, however, accomplish wonders. In still water this is done immediately in front of the angler; in slow-flowing water the cloud is, of course, released at the head of the swim. It is well to remember that cloud does not lodge among weeds like heavier ground-baits, which, if this happens, causes fish to seek food where the hook-bait cannot be worked. I advise, however, the use of cloud in preference to a ground-bait of greater gravity whenever possible. The same method may be employed to place ground-bait on the bottom. When you feel the bait touch, raise your rod point as before. By this means you know exactly where it is. Any mixture which will adhere to your shots is suited to the method described. If for any reason you are unable to use it, and are compelled to throw in your bait, use very small quantities at frequent intervals for obvious reasons. In heavier or more streamy water more solid ground-baits are necessary, and must be weighted so that they sink to their appointed place quickly. If you are fishing from a boat, ground-bait balls may be placed on the blade of an oar and put gently into the water without disturbance. A splendid method of making certain where your ground-bait is without the slightest commotion is worthy of description. It is most useful when fishing in the Thames style from a boat or punt. Procure a large string-bag or net and attach a length of cord to it. Into the bottom of the net place sufficient stones to sink it vertically; fill the remaining space with your ground-bait, and all is ready. The net is then lowered to the bottom immediately in front of the angler, and the stream will wash the bait through the mesh and feed the swim consistently. If desired, a flood of ground-bait may be dispersed by giving the cord a twitch.

Ground-baiting with worms is often a difficult matter, especially in strong water. An excellent method is to fill a square, narrow-necked bottle with worms, and lower this into the swim by a cord. The worms will escape one or two at a time. You know where the ground-bait is, and make no disturbance in placing it there, the importance of which cannot be too much stressed.

CHAPTER VII

ROACH FISHING IN THE NOTTINGHAM STYLE

A GOOD working knowledge of the principal styles of roach angling will put the reader in a position to tackle these fish in any water. The most versatile method is that employed by the Nottingham school.

As the number of anglers increases steadily, fish get scarcer and more difficult to catch, and angling becomes more and more scientific. New devices designed to outwit roach are offered to the modern angler every day. None of these can, however, displace the necessity for a proper understanding of those methods which have established themselves as the direct result of years of experiment, experience and necessity. Varying water conditions demand and create different angling methods. The Trent has provided the Nottingham style.

An interesting legend relates that the name 'Trent' has its origin in the word 'Trente,' meaning 'thirty,' from the fact that thirty streams enter its course, thirty different fish inhabit its waters and thirty abbeys originally stood upon its banks. Be this as it may, the native anglers have learned their lesson from this wide and freshly flowing river, and have perfected the science of fishing fairly deep and fast water. Using a pliable rod which acts throughout its length, they 'long cast' and fish 'fine and far off.'

The Nottingham Cast is made by drawing one or two loops of line from between the rod rings, checking the reel with the finger. The rod is swung gently behind at an angle of 45°, then swept smoothly forward and upstream, the loop or loops of line which are held on the finger-tips of the free hand being released at the instant when the rod points in the direction of the cast. Some experts impart a gentle spin to the reel simultaneously with the release of the loops, whereby an extra three or four yards of line can be got out.

At the time when I wrote this brief description of a comparatively simple method of casting, I was aware of the most ingenious and very efficient cast which I then believed was the invention of F. W. K. Wallis, the celebrated Nottingham fisherman. I was not, however, and still am not able to master this cast, so refrained from attempting to describe it.

Nevertheless, I did not escape the omission unscathed, and received a kindly admonition from Alderman George E. Hodgkinson of Coventry, then President of the Coventry Angling Association and a member of the Severn Fishery Authority, in which he said:

I have had the pleasure of reading your *Angling Ways*, and no doubt you will welcome a criticism. Your description of the Nottingham style of casting I believe to be incorrect. My early fishing was undertaken in the river Trent at Beeston, and I have seen Nottingham experts in action at All-England Championship matches. Moreover, I have tried to get Coventry anglers to cultivate the Nottingham style, since the action is a pleasure to watch when proficiency is reached. . . . The correct method is described by 'Faddist'* in his *Roach Fishing*. Actually the baited hook is held loosely in the left hand—assuming a right-handed cast. The thumb of the left hand is hooked into the line near the reel in the *first* loop. As the rod is propelled sideways or forward, to make the cast, the bait is loosed from the hand, the thumb at the same time drawing the line from the reel. This method has many advantages. It enables a clean and long cast to be made between bushes on the river banks. It adds, moreover, to the speed of the angler in competitions, since as soon as the hook is baited after catching a fish, the first action in making the cast is completed, and no time is lost in getting the bait into the swim.

It is a method to be encouraged when facing a wind, because the shotted cast has the action of cutting under the wind. Or, to put it another way, the line and bait travel like the shot out of a gun. I don't claim to be an expert myself, but I feel certain that your illustration is rather misleading.

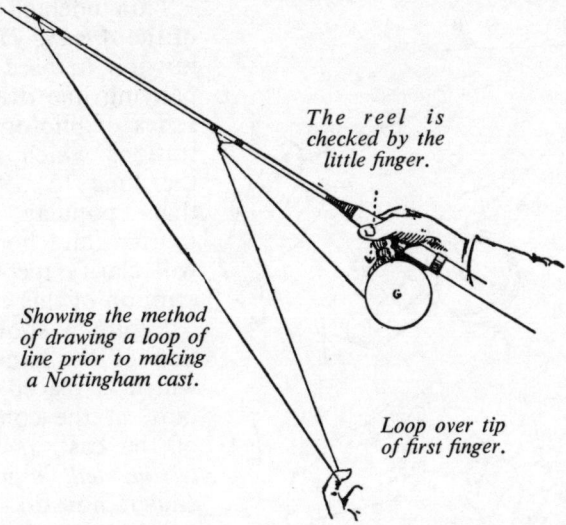

The reel is checked by the little finger.

Showing the method of drawing a loop of line prior to making a Nottingham cast.

Loop over tip of first finger.

I am grateful to my distinguished correspondent, but still feel unequal to the task of describing a cast which I am unable to put into practice. Furthermore, while this excellent if somewhat difficult cast has been mastered by some Nottingham anglers, I feel certain that the

* The late Edward Ensom.

vast majority of them still use that which I have described and illustrated or some modification of it. I have stood filled with envy while F. W. K. Wallis has demonstrated this cast, and while admitting its superiority freely, I cannot regard it as the Standard Nottingham cast.

It is I think opportune at this point to describe and illustrate an extremely simple and effective cast devised for use with a centre-pin reel, by that well known fisherman and caster Captain Terry B. Thomas, late of Milwards, Redditch.

For the many thousands who still prefer to use a centre-pin reel which gives direct control when playing a fish, Capt. Thomas' 'Slip Cast' is most useful, especially when it is necessary to cast a long line from a cramped position.

No special tackle or device is required and the only adjustment which may be necessary is the removal of the line-guard if your reel is fitted with one, to allow the line to spiral freely over the rim of the drum.

I am indebted to the editor of the *Angling Times* for permission to base the accompanying line drawings on a series of photographic illustrations which appeared in the June 15, 1956 issue of that popular fisherman's journal, and hope that they will clarify the written description of this cast.

Figure A shows the position of the hands and reel, which is placed low on the butt, at the commencement of the cast, *if you retrieve left-handed*, which so many anglers now do.

Note that the line is held lightly in the palm but firmly between the thumb and first finger of the left hand, *which is in line with the centre of the reel.*

The Terry Thomas 'Slip-Cast' with a centre-pin reel.

If, however, you wind in with your right hand, the reel must be uppermost on the rod butt while casting, as shown in Figure B. The procedure is otherwise the same.

Figure C shows the position of the hands at the moment when the tackle is released. *Left hand still near and in line with the centre of the reel.* The impetus of the swing of the cast draws the line over the edge of the reel drum (as in the case of a fixed-spool reel) through a loop made by the *thumb and second finger* of the left hand and through the rod rings as shown in Figure D. The effect of the line spiralling over the rim of the reel-drum in Figure D is exaggerated to make the mode of the lines release from the drum clear. Definitely defined spirals of line as shown will not actually be seen when making this cast, any more than they are when a fixed spool reel is used. This is however what actually happens, so fast that the eye cannot follow it. An overhead cast is recommended as being extremely accurate, but when circumstances demand a side swing is quite effective if not so accurate.

In this connection Captain Thomas stresses one point. I quote:

> The importance of keeping the left hand, which controls the line, opposite the centre of the reel all the time cannot be over-emphasised, because I find that there is an instinctive desire on the part of most anglers to move their left hand away from the reel as they cast.

You are therefore advised to watch your left hand when learning this cast.

When you are proficient in it, which will not be long, you will of course watch your float and check the running line as necessary with the left hand.

This cast is suggested for sparing use as an expedient when circumstances demand, rather than for habitual use, as it tends to create line kink; and you will find it better suited to braided than monofil lines.

Within reason, the fuller the reel-drum, the less will be the inertia offered to the line as it slips over the periphery of the reel. And remember that when making the 'Slip Cast,' force is neither necessary nor desirable. *Well-timed swing, release and follow-through are the keys to success.*

Having cast, as soon as the float has passed him on its way downstream, the Nottingham angler commences to pay out line from his reel with his hand, so smoothly that the float is not jerked. At the same time he holds his float in check gently in such a way as to cause the bait to precede it, which is most important. At the end of the swim, which may extend to twenty yards, he lifts quietly and recovers the line by tapping the rim of the reel drum with his fingers, then repeats his cast. The obvious advantage of covering so much water will be apparent.

The early apprenticeship of most anglers is usually devoted to a form of 'short swim' (little more than a rod length), which may well be termed 'swimming the stream.' It is at this stage when fishing a short line that a crop of bad habits is prone to develop especially with novices. For those who are on the threshold of their roach-angling career, and by way of reminder to some of the 'old hands,' I will mention the more salient points which are necessary to success when 'swimming the stream.' Every precaution should be taken to ensure as great a measure of invisibility as possible—a tuft of grass, a clump of rushes or a small bush offer ideal cover. The angler should sit as far from the bank as possible, and avoid making movements which will cause vibration in the earth, the effect of which will be felt immediately by any fish in the vicinity. Regard this advice as an axiom if you will, but how often is it put into practice? Having selected a swim offering the best possible cover, the tackle should be assembled well away from the point of fishing. This being done, the angler is faced with the necessity to take the depth down the whole length of the proposed swim. In a vast majority of cases a plummet is used for this purpose, but I much prefer, particularly in shallower swims, to ascertain the depth by trial in true Nottingham fashion. Make a guess first, and having adjusted your float, draw as much line from the reel as you can cast conveniently, and swing your float gently upstream, dropping the rod point immediately when the float and shots have swung to their extreme limit. This will cause the tackle to enter the water with the minimum of splash, which is highly important. If your float travels from the upstream limit of the swim to the downstream limit without any sign of obstruction, raise the float 2 or 3 in. and swim down again. If the hook drags, submerging the float, this indicates the necessity for going a little shallower. By this means a most delicate adjustment can be obtained with a minimum of disturbance. It is true that the operation takes more time than that of 'plumbing,' but most anglers will agree that five minutes spent in ascertaining the depth without disturbing the fish is more profitable than half an hour expended in fishing water from which the fish have been frightened by what is sometimes the clumsy use of that often unnecessary gadget, the plummet. Always swim the stream sitting down, and if the sun is shining, take up a position in which your shadow is not cast upon the water. If you are facing the sun do not wear light coloured clothing, the glare from which is as detrimental as a shadow.

The finest exponents of swimming the stream are possibly the old school of roach pole anglers, a mode of fishing which appears to be waning in and around London, where its best exponents have always been found. This may be due to the fact that the roach pole is a heavy and cumbersome affair when compared with Nottingham and Sheffield rods. They vary in length from 14 to 18 ft., and are gently tapered from the butt to the pole tip. Most of them are so constructed that the upper joints pack into the two lower lengths. The only portion of these poles in which there is any action is the top foot or eighteen inches. Some experts prefer a whalebone tip, others split cane or greenheart.

Roach poles are now available in hollow fibre-glass, the sections all collapsing back into the butt length. These poles, mostly from the

Continent, are not nearly as cumbersome as the old, traditional bamboo poles.

No reel is used in this type of fishing, the cast and hook link being attached to a short length of fine line known as topping, which in turn is tied to a ring at the tip of the rod. This method of fishing with a fixed line and cast is known as 'tight-lining,' and often calls for very considerable skill when playing a fish, it being impossible to give line as when a reel and running tackle are used. Some of the Lea experts use the finest possible tackle, and it is not uncommon for them to land a hefty chub when fishing for dace, or a barbel weighing 4 or 5 lb., when they had expected nothing larger than a ½ lb. roach. The pole tip is often no more than 2 ft. from the float, the angler following his float down-stream with the end of the pole immediately above it. At the slightest sign he raises the point gently and a fish is hooked. When a long roach pole is being used, it is sometimes difficult to bring a fish sufficiently near to net it; in this case the butt and sometimes the second joint are unshipped. Different types of float for swimming the stream with running tackle, or tight-lining with the roach pole, are shown in the illustration, and it is a safe rule to use the smallest float possible in accordance with conditions.

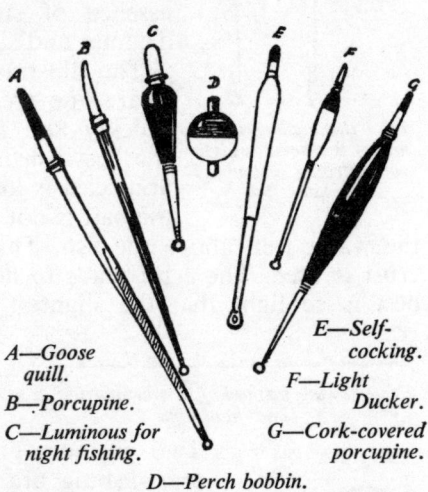

A—Goose quill.

B—Porcupine.

C—Luminous for night fishing.

D—Perch bobbin.

E—Self-cocking.

F—Light Ducker.

G—Cork-covered porcupine.

After finding the depth of the water by trial 'trots' down the swim, the angler turns his attention to ground-baiting. Visualising the complete length of his swim, and having ascertained its depth, he has to decide where he will pitch his ball of ground-bait to assure that it will be distributed over the track to be travelled by his float.

Only judgment born of experience can enable an angler to do this with certainty, but the factors which govern the position where the ground-bait should fall on the water remain constant when fishing a stream in the Nottingham style. The details for consideration are the speed and depth of the water, and the sinking density of the ground-bait.

Bread, bran and middlings mixed are a favourite ground-bait.

The art of Nottingham ground-baiting is very literally angling, for, if it is to be successful, the angler must be able to estimate accurately the angle at which a sinking object will descend in order to reach the river bed at a given spot. When ground-baiting in this style one must pitch the bait into the water.

Before passing to the more delicate Sheffield style, consideration of various points which are closely allied with Nottingham fishing is

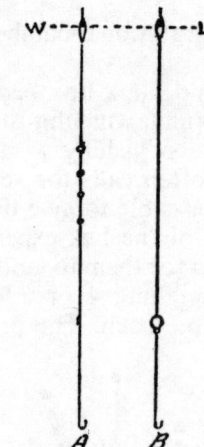

In A the loading is too high. B shows weight concentrated just above the hook-link.

merited. The question of presenting a bait is bound up closely with the mode of loading a cast. I use the word 'loading' in preference to the more usual 'shotting,' because shot are not always best by any means for adding the necessary weight to a cast. To fish as fine as possible is always good, but it is useless to rely on fine gear if it is wrongly 'loaded,' because the bait will not behave in a natural way, and will therefore arouse the suspicions—or is it the disgust?—of the fish. I am certain that a low centre of gravity is the essence of successful 'loading' for the Trent, Thames and similar waters.

The illustrations A and B make my meaning clear. The great thing is to get your bait down quickly and keep it there. Generally speaking, the best fish feed on or near the bottom, and if your cast is loaded 'high' (high centre of gravity) the bait is not controlled and may swing about in the water well above the fish. This is particularly true when breadcrust is used. The crust tends to float even when well soaked, and at best is so light that the slightest 'undertow' will raise it from the

C.

Showing method of 'Grain shotting' a 12-in. hook-link.

position in which it should be. Many anglers who have not tried the experiment may doubt the accuracy of my next statement. Two or more grain shots on the hook link when crust-fishing are an immense advantage. Contrary to the fetish that this shotting of the hook-link scares fish, I should never think of breadcrust-fishing in deepish heavy water without them, and my bags are sometimes big ones.

D.

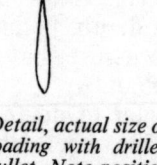

Detail, actual size of loading with drilled bullet. Note position just above lower loop of cast.

The illustrations C and D show a hook-link and cast end shotted in the way to which I refer, and I assure readers that the shot nearest to the hook is the most useful and not the most dangerous. Very many hook-links are too long—12 in. from loop to the bend of the hook is ample, assuming that the main loading is immediately above the loop when the cast is made up—illustration B, shows this. Loading in this way ensures the bait being where the angler wants it—that is the first point in the proper presentation of a bait.

The second is no less important. What angler has not heard a fellow sportsman say: 'I caught them all at the end of the swim?' This gives the clue to the second point in presenting a bait in the Nottingham style. Most anglers delay their float for a moment 'at the end of the swim'; this causes the cast weight and bait to swing upward from their original position because of the pressure of the stream, and it is when the bait appears to be leaving the bottom that fish so often take it. By delaying the float skilfully every yard or so down a swim, the bait will swing from the bottom, and the 'end of the swim' effect will be reproduced each time this is done. It is not the 'end of the swim' which attracts fish, but the swing of the bait—try it!

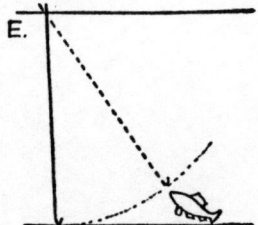

This upward swing is caused by delaying the float—it attracts fish.

I have stated categorically that low loading is the essence of success when fishing the Thames, Trent and similar waters; and in the main I adhere to that dictum. Nevertheless, I have learned that circumstances alter cases much as noses alter faces.

Fishing a stretch of the Hampshire Avon with a very expert local angler on one occasion, I shotted low to overcome the fast stream; but to my surprise my companion distributed BB shot at intervals up his cast. The lowest he placed about a foot from the hook, the next shot about 4 in. above it, the next 6 in. and so on up the cast.

It so happened that the water was interspersed with lanes of ribbon-weed, and it was not long before my gear was caught up in it. His tackle appeared to be almost immune!

A tactful inquiry elicited that he had found that by using a larger float than would be necessary for low shotting, and distributing the extra shot needed throughout the length of the cast, the passage of the tackle between the weeds was facilitated and that hangs-up were cut to a minimum.

Mention of shotting reminds me, that I have never been happy about, neither have I understood, the, to me, incongruous and in some instances quite abstruse system of identifying the various sizes of split-shot as used by anglers.

While it is true that the terms used derive from the descriptions adopted for the contents of shot-gun cartridges of various calibres, for which they may be quite appropriate for ought I know; I am still at a loss to understand why such terms as 'SSG' etc., should be applied to shot as used by anglers.

I'll wager that for every angler who asks for 'SSG shot' thousands request 'Swan Shot' where they require leads of this size.

Why not number them 1 to 8?

The present system is as archaic as military shot towers and serves only to confuse rather than simplify the purchase of these very necessary tackle items.

CHAPTER VIII

ROACH FISHING IN THE SHEFFIELD STYLE

FOR reasons which have never been disclosed, angling other than for salmon or trout has come to be known as 'coarse fishing.' Whenever I hear this reference to the art, I always think of the equipment of Sheffield experts which, far from being coarse, is the finest and lightest used in any type of fishing and would make the most gossamer trout tackle look like rope. I will describe the gear necessary for fishing in the finest Sheffield style and leave the reader to form his own estimate of the skill of these north country anglers who, armed with this cobweblike tackle, hook, play and land good specimen roach, chub, dace, and bream. On occasion hooks as small as the letter 'J' whipped to a foot or fifteen inches of fine nylon are used by the Sheffield men. To their one yard casts, which are a little coarser, they attach a 'half-moon' lead.

These 'half-moons' are easily applied by thumb and finger pressure, and are less likely to cut the fine cast than shot, which must be applied

TWICE ACTUAL SIZE

"HALF MOON" IN POSITION

with considerable force from pliers or teeth. The 'half-moon' cocks the tiny 'ducker,' a local name for dainty floats, which are often even smaller than the one illustrated on page 59. The 'ducker' is in turn attached to a threadlike line, size 000, with a breaking strain of little more than 1 lb.

Sheffield rods have their special characteristics. My Sheffield rod has two joints with a detachable cord grasp, and is 10 ft. in total length. The bottom joint is Spanish reed, the lightest and possibly the frailest material used in rod building. The top joint contains three materials, 14 in. of Spanish reed at the ferrule end into which is spliced one foot of whole bamboo which is in turn spliced to $2\frac{1}{2}$ ft. of split cane, the last 25 in. tapering very steeply. This gives the action shown by the curve in the illustration, and the rod is very 'quick striking.' The rings are of the 'Bridge' type throughout, which is essential when very fine lines are used, especially in wet weather when the line seems to have an uncanny affinity for the rod and makes casting very difficult. The traditional reel is a $3\frac{1}{2}$ in. narrow-spooled centre-pin, as for Nottingham fishing although the majority of anglers used fixed spool reels loaded with 1 lb. or 1½ lb. b.s. nylon. The reader will have realized that Sheffield angling in its finest form permits no 'skull hauling' or force when handling a fish. The 'Sheffield style' is fishing in its daintiest mode, when only consummate skill can defeat the efforts of the fish to make its escape. Handling this gossamer tackle makes the playing of the fish a real pleasure and, to balance the inconvenience of occasional 'breaks,' the angler is rewarded by frequent bites. It is a deadly method.

Necessity, the mother of invention, brought about the evolution of the Sheffield style of angling in canals, fen drains, sluggish water-courses, and still water. Quite often such waters are 'gin-bright,' shallow and weedy. These circumstances call for the finest possible tackle, an angler who takes advantage of every possible cover at the waterside, and a bait presented in the most natural way. The presentation of the bait is the secret of successful Sheffield angling and, in my opinion, is even more important than the invisibility of the tackle.

Let us watch a Sheffield expert at work. His tackle is assembled in the

Note sharp taper in the build of the top joint, and action from A to B only.

Sheffield 'ducker'

usual way, and it need only be noted that these preliminaries are carried out some distance from the swim in order that the fish, which are often visible under the conditions in question, shall not be disturbed or frightened. There is, however, one most important point in this tackling-up, namely, the 'shotting' of the cast. The Sheffield angler places his tiny half-moon lead as far from the hook as is practicable or, under ideal conditions, uses a self-cocking float and no lead at all. Thus he is certain that his bait will sink slowly and naturally.

The illustration (p. 64) shows this fundamental principle of Sheffield angling. The 'ducker,' 'half-moon,' cast and baited hook strike the water simultaneously—the 'half-moon' settles down at once and cocks the float, while the bait sinks practically as if unattached, the weight of the hook and fine gut being so slight as not to affect its descent. Is it to be wondered that the most wary fish are deceived as between the gentle on the tiny hook and those which are cast in around it as a freewill offering, particularly when the hook-bait is of finer quality than the gentles used as decoys? I will not call them ground-bait, for in this type of fishing the Sheffield angler does not use ground-bait in the true sense. Quite often, however, he uses what is known as 'fogdust,' which is cast in near his float and produces a cloud in the water. This has the double advantage of setting the fish on the alert for something more

solid and rendering the angler and the movements of his rod less visible
to them. The principle is that of a smoke screen, and the 'fogdust' has
no food value whatever. This being the case, a constant application of
knobs the size of a walnut need cause no fear of surfeiting the fish.
A simple and effective 'fog' may be made by powdering bread with
a rolling-pin after it has been slowly dried to biscuit consistency. To
avoid any possibility of domestic difference of opinion on this matter
it is advisable to purchase a rolling-pin specially for the work—quite
a good one may be had fairly cheaply. Of course the bread 'dust'
must be moistened before it is thrown in, sufficiently to cause it to cling
and sink, otherwise it will float away on the surface and serve no
purpose.

By the same rule that Sheffield anglers 'fish fine' they also 'fish
far off.' The question immediately arises: how do these anglers cast their

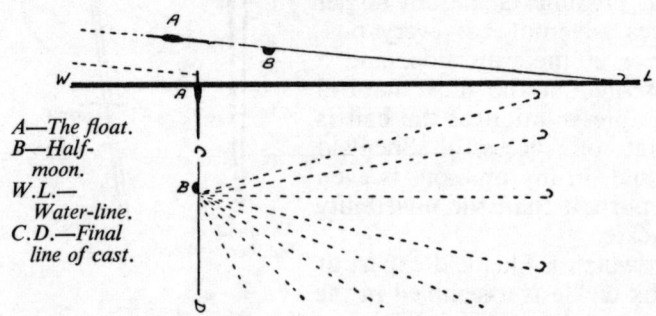

A—The float.
B—Half-
     moon.
W.L.—
     Water-line.
C.D.—Final
     line of cast.

tiny floats and sometimes unshotted casts distances of ten or more
yards with that ease which must be seen to be properly appreciated?

The initial stages of the Sheffield cast are similar to those practised
by the Nottingham school in that the reel is controlled by the finger
or thumb and a loop, or loops, of line are drawn from between the
rod rings. I am assuming here that a centre-pin reel is used. From this
point onward the Sheffield cast is quite different.

The diagram (p. 65) illustrates a side elevation of the movements of
the rod when casting in the Sheffield style. The dotted line A B shows
the first position of the rod, the line below the rod tip and the float and
cast being allowed to rest lightly on the water. The rod is then raised to
the position C D, which tightens the line prior to the act of casting.
From this position the rod is swept smartly backward to a point just
beyond the '12 o'clock line' shown in the diagram as 1 2—this lifts
the line and cast straight behind the angler as indicated. From here
and while the line and float are still well in the air, the rod is brought
smartly to the position 3 4, and, at the moment immediately prior to
the rod arriving in this position the loop or loops of line which have
been held on the finger-tips are released, permitting the line to shoot

The lower fish in this setting is the equal record roach taken by Bill Penney from Molesey Reservoir in 1938. This case of fish has been seen by thousands of anglers to various angling shows round the country. The top fish weighed 3 lb. 1 oz., with the lower fish, the record holder, having the magic figures of 3 lb. 14 oz.   *[Photograph: W. J. Howes]*

A hybrid roach × bream photographed by well-known angling photographer Bill Howes. How many readers can use the Page Theory to prove this fish a hybrid? The scale formation can clearly be seen.

Cast of 1¼ lb. true roach, the property of F. Page

Nine-inch hybrid taken in the Thames

forward in the desired direction. This cast is much in the manner of casting a fly and is very similar in that no force is either necessary or desirable and precise movement of the smoothest possible kind make for successful Sheffield casting. The best bait with which to practise is a gentle or small red worm, which will not be thrown off so easily as wheat, breadcrust and similar baits. An expert is able to cast with surprising accuracy and such skill that the most flimsy bait is projected to the water still adhering to the hook. Practice alone will make the novice master of this art, but it is worth considerable trouble to learn this dainty cast.

The depth is found by trial as in the Nottingham style. While the Nottingham angler expects his bites when the bait has sunk to its full extent, and that they will be indicated by the depression of the float

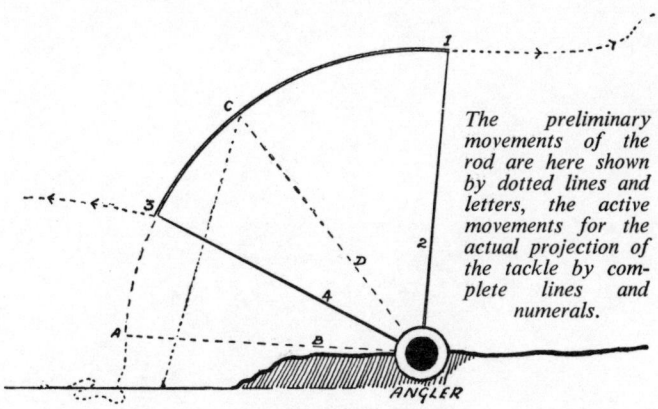

The preliminary movements of the rod are here shown by dotted lines and letters, the active movements for the actual projection of the tackle by complete lines and numerals.

below the surface of the water, Sheffield anglers are alert for a bite at any moment after the bait has struck the water, which may not be shown by the depression of the float. The slowly sinking bait of the Sheffield style will take fish at any depth.

How, then, does the angler detect a bite while the bait is still descending if the float is not drawn under the water, though it may be 'cocked' so fine that but an eighth of an inch is visible on the surface? The slightest tremor—a tiny ring round the float—it does not cock as early as it should—it hesitates for a moment on its leisurely way downstream—the merest move is sufficient cause for the Sheffield angler to strike. But I may hardly use the word strike in connection with this fishing. No! The Sheffield angler dare not 'strike,' he merely tightens his grip on the rod or raises it so delicately that, while the sharp hook penetrates the soft mouth of the fish, the fine nylon line will stand the strain. Many broken casts are the best teachers of the way to make contact with a fish in the finest Sheffield manner.

Strength of stream, wind and depth of the water to be fished may call for modification of the size of float and its loading, also the breaking strain of the cast and line to be used in this style—and, if big fish are encountered, it is foolish to adhere to the very finest tackle. Nevertheless, the essence of the Sheffield method is 'very fine,' 'very light,' 'very far off,' and a slowly sinking bait whenever possible.

CHAPTER IX

ROACH: HEMP FISHING; CATCHING ROACH WITH SILK-WEED

THAT 'hemping' is a controversial subject does not make it less interesting or necessary to a full discussion of ways and means of catching roach.

During the first world war a few of our Belgian friends came over here for a little peace and quietness, bringing with them their fishing rods and knowledge of 'hemp seed' as a lure for roach and dace. The value of this innovation has been much discussed, but the general opinion seems to be overwhelmingly in favour of the use of hemp by fishermen in the Thames and many other waters. I will therefore give the reader some details of tackle and devices which I have found killing when hemp seed is the bait. Its preparation for the hook is a matter of some importance. I soak one pint of seed in cold water overnight, then after adding a little water, simmer it until the seeds begin to split. Hemp should not be boiled until the white kernel protrudes. But a little common soda may be added to the water with advantage as this blackens the husks.

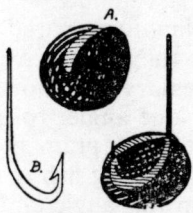

A—Note split in seed.
B—Note the flattened shank.

Flat shank is pressed into split in seed.

Doubt has been expressed as to whether it is the darker husk or a more attractive flavour produced by this treatment, which renders the seeds more attractive. It would indeed be difficult to say with certainty, but I favour the changed colour. A dark seed is probably more easily seen. There is, however, no doubt that seeds treated with soda are most attractive.

The best hooks for hemp fishing are flattened in the bend to fit into the split in the husk of the seed, and if it has been opened too wide by boiling, the seed will not remain on the hook; but if treated as I suggest, this difficulty will not arise.

I know the average hemp fisherman will have parted company with me already, but let me give a wrinkle which I have found most valuable in practice and have never seen used by a fellow-angler. Paint the shank of your hemp hooks white! This gives the appearance of a luscious white kernel coming from the seed, and I assure the reader this white shank dodge deceives both roach and dace when the plain shank will not.

Many anglers still shot their cast for this type of fishing. I do not hesitate to express the opinion that the procedure is wrong. Wire your casts for hemp fishing.

Immediately above the knot at the lower end of your cast squeeze a grain shot, now place a needle against the line and taking a piece of fine lead wire wrap it round the line and the needle. Having wrapped the lead wire withdraw the needle with a pair of pliers and affix another grain shot at the top of your lead coil. The shots at either end will prevent the coil from slipping down the line and fraying it. Many a time

Lead wire for cast on 'hemping'.

have I watched an exasperated angler miss bite after bite when hemp fishing. Why? Because the fish were going for the shots on his cast, mistaking them for the small hemp seeds. The method I describe makes it a certainty that every bite your float registers is a bite at your bait.

One more suggestion. Do this wiring at home. Don't wait till you are at the waterside, because neatness will pay you well. That tingling desire to be fishing, which grips every angler when he sees the water, does not help toward this desirable neatness. Further, it is so much simpler to measure the required length of lead to cock your favourite float at home, and it will mean you will be able to 'tackle-up' and start fishing ten minutes before the fellow who leaves everything to the last minute.

Having prepared a pint of large Dutch or Chilean hemp, let us offer it to the roach in exchange for a day's sport. I would stress the quantity necessary, for more than one pint of hemp is definitely too much for any one angler to use during a day's fishing. It has to be remembered that every grain of seed thrown into the water by way of attracting and holding fish in the 'swim' is a potential feed. Look at the question from this angle and couple with it the mathematical point of view and you are bound to agree. The angler who casts a thousand seeds into his 'swim' has one-tenth the chance of a fish selecting the particular seed on his hook when compared with the angler who only throws in one hundred seeds. In the ordinary way ground-bait is not feeding, but hemp thrown in as ground-bait is 'free feed,' pure and simple.

Apart from these considerations, there is another very important reason why an angler should use this bait as sparingly as possible. You will find that having got the fish 'on feed,' if you throw in a large quantity of hemp they will bite so sharply that it becomes almost impossible to strike sufficiently quickly to hook them. That comes about in this way. The hundreds of hemp seeds floating through your 'swim' cause a sort of excitement among the feeding fish, which dash hither and thither in their efforts to snatch passing food, and when in this state there is no doubt they bite much more rapidly, and thus give the angler less opportunity to come to terms with them.

The methods of an angling friend who is a wizard with a pint of hemp may be interesting. Many a time have I seen him count his catch by the score, prior to returning the fish to the water. At the outset he will cast as much hemp as covers his palm as far upstream as the depth of water and speed of the flow necessitate, to ensure the seeds passing down the 'swim' in close proximity to his hook-bait. Having chosen his 'swim' well, and fish being present, the drifting seeds arouse their curiosity, but they may not take them at once. It is a fallacy which dies hard with some hemp fishers, that unless they get a bit every other 'swim down' the fish are not feeding or are not present. My friend will fish steadily for twenty minutes or half an hour before throwing in a few more grains for encouragement, and this time only half the quantity. Then another biteless spell of fishing may be, and a third and even smaller peace-offering will be thrown in. Ere now well over an hour may have passed without a bite, but reward is near at hand. Reducing his 'free feed' to five or six seeds every few minutes, he gets his first bite and a nice roach finds its way into his keep net. This is the signal to stop throwing in more hemp—time and again the float will toddle down his 'swim' and time and again it dips and other fish join their friends. Suddenly or gradually the bites cease, and the process is reversed. The five or six seeds are again offered at short intervals, and so my friend will work backwards with his method of 'free feeding.' Almost invariably the fish will recommence to bite. There cannot, of course, be any rigid rules for the use of hemp, but I have described the average procedure of an angler who is a most successful and highly expert 'hemp fisherman.'

The more still the water the less hemp you use is an excellent maxim for those who hope to catch roach with this bait in lakes or slow-moving rivers. I have said a pint of seed is ample for a day's fishing in a river such as the Thames. For lake or slow-flowing river fishing, however, half this quantity or even less is plenty. You may have a demonstration of the main reason for this by allowing a little boiled hemp to stand about for a few days. The result is not pleasant, as the seed goes bad and sour. It putrefies in the same way when lying at the bottom of a lake and repels fish.

Hook-baits.—It is not necessary, and only at times even desirable, to use hemp on the hook when fishing with this bait. True, there are occasions when the seed itself is the only bait the fish will take, but often it is not so, and one or other of the following will be useful and have advantages: elderberries, small dried currants (not soaked), a black glass bead, a small piece of black insulation rubber cut from an electric wire, or a small piece of leather bootlace. Generally speaking, it is found that elder or currants when used on the hook have the effect of causing the feeding fish to hold on a little longer when they bite. This is a very obvious advantage. The glass bead stunt has one big disadvantage which must be weighed against the fact that the lure does not need renewing. The bead being hard often acts as a protection for the fish against the barb of the hook, and many are hooked and lost before they reach the net. The rubber tubing or piece of leather lace, while having the advantage of not requiring renewal during a day's fishing, is often ignored by roach, but it is always worth a trial.

Whether an actual seed or a coloured imitation of the seed is used on the hook, we are left wondering for what the fish mistake hemp seed. The rough and ready guess has usually been that it is mistaken for a young freshwater mussel.

More likely, however, is the suggestion that the so-called freshwater cockles offer the clue. It is possible that fish mistake hemp seed for the smaller specimens of the 'Orb-shell' cockles (*Sphaerium*), one species of which is found all over Britain. They have a cream or pale brown shell, and the fact that they climb up the stems of water plants lends colour to the idea that fish may pluck them from such places as easy prey.

Foot of cockle.   Shoot of seed.

Pea-shell cockle and hemp seed. Slightly enlarged.

The smaller 'Pea-shell' cockle (*Pisidium*) of which several species are very common in our waters, are also candidates for a place in this speculation. Indeed, the fact that their adult size and the colour of many of them is nearly approximate to that of a hemp seed makes it very probable, I think, that they are the molluscs for which fish mistake hemp.

Some of the smaller freshwater snails may also have some part in this deception, but I am satisfied that *Anodonta cygnea*, the freshwater mussel, is not guilty.

I am aware that all this scarcely falls into the category of coarse fishing; it will nevertheless be a matter of no little interest to many readers.

Rods for 'Hemping.'—I use a Sheffield rod with reel and running tackle. It is right in action when a fish is hooked, but sufficiently stiff to strike instantly from the point. If you are buying such a rod you may easily test it for this quality. Place the 'tip' 2 in. above any hard surface and dip the 'butt' sharply as if striking. If you are able to do this without the tip hitting the hard surface, that is a good rod for the work. Such tackle is light and pleasant to use. The 'good old roach pole'—a weapon varying from 12 to 18 ft. in length, and in my view weighing far too much to be comfortable, is preferred by many anglers and must therefore be mentioned. They are the favourites of some Thames and Lea fishermen, who are indeed experts. These poles are rigid and actionless except at the tip, and are therefore very quick in the strike. Every cobbler to his awl, of course, and a trial of the types of rod mentioned will convince you in one direction or the other; both are good, but the former is more comfortable.

Since I wrote *Angling Ways* I have made a special and very careful study of the objections raised against the use of hemp seed as a bait, and can assure my reader that the only valid fault found was to the effect that:

'It is a difficult bait for old anglers whose sight is failing.' This is presumably on account of the rapidity of the bites which usually result when this seed is used. I admit and regret the fault, but it does not preclude the successful use of other baits, despite ideas to the contrary. Did not north country teams vanquish London and south country anglers when they fished the hemp-ridden Thames with maggots in a not-very-far-off All-England Championship?

The reader would not wish me to occupy valuable space with a demolition of such absolute fallacies as:

'Hemp is a dope which drugs fish.'

'Hemp contains alcohol which produces hysteria in fish.'

'Hemp scours and purges fish which go to the shallows and die.'

'After feeding on hemp fish lie dormant for days and are easy prey for pike.'

'Hemp seed only catches small fish.'

'Hemp turns to weed on the bottom if not eaten by fish,' etc., etc., etc.

May I assure those who are interested that hemp is clean, handy, and as harmless as any other bait in regular use. It has many advantages over other baits and at the very worst only shares the disadvantages. Why such a clutter of ridiculous objections surrounds hemp I am at a loss to understand.

I hold no brief for any bait, but I am diametrically opposed to nonsense, and have based my opinion on a minute sifting of objections which have come to me from all parts of the country.

CATCHING ROACH WITH SILK-WEED

There are many types of aquatic vegetation, but the most attractive to roach is that known as 'Silk-Weed'—a fine fibrous growth having the appearance of green cotton wool, which is found on weir aprons, old piles and rocks in weirs. Roach are very partial to this bait, probably on account of the large quantity of insects and animalculae which live in it. If you are fishing from a boat or away from the source of your supply of weed, collect a quantity and put it in a suitable receptacle covering it with river water, otherwise it will rapidly lose its freshness and colour. If on the other hand you are fishing from a weir, it is far better to obtain each bait from the weir steps as you require it, taking the greatest care not to handle the weed more than is absolutely necessary. The best method of

Hook baited with weed. Note how the water splays it out.

A piece of weed twice or even three times this size may be used, but at times this is enough.

baiting is to drag the hook through the weed; a portion will adhere, and will not come off so quickly as one would think, when used in the strong water of the 'lashing.' Some anglers, however, prefer to wrap it neatly over the hook with the fingers—try both. No ground-bait is necessary for this type of fishing and the nearer you fish to the weir from which you take your weed the better your chance of success. The fish appear to hang about in the streamy water as it comes over, waiting for the fragments of weed which break away from the 'apron.' In a nutshell, to simulate such a broken fragment washing down-stream should be your object.

There is the usual difference of opinion as to the size and type of hook which should be used, but a No. 10, 11 or 12 round bend or Crystal will be found suitable. As to the depth at which you should set your float, this is entirely a matter for experiment and only general details can be given. Start well up, say 3 ft. deep, and work down. By this means you will find the fish, which are in this case feeding away from the bottom. Success is probably more the result of much practice and perseverance than in many other forms of angling. The art of working the bait, which is most important, only comes with experience. At times fish appear to prefer the rotten or brown weed, which should always be given a trial.

The Nottingham rod, reel and line mentioned earlier are first-rate tackle for weed fishing, but the business end of the gear needs special thought. To be ideal the float must be visible in the turbulent water of a weir pool and readily adjustable in respect of its weight-carrying capacity. The latter need arises from the fact that in a weir of any size there may be a dozen 'runs' each with varying characteristics which call for different shotting. This caused me some perplexity, but I think I have found a satisfactory solution. Let me deal first with the float.

The illustration above does away with the need for many words

Reel line.

4

Water ——————— Line

6 .... Split in cork

7

9

10

Assume that the quill carries four shot, the addition of one or other of the tapered corks will increase the buoyancy to 6, 7, 9 or 10 shot. Any desired adjustment can be accomplished in this way. Remember the corks must be split to enable their attachment or removal at will. No float cap is needed, the corks acting in this capacity. The sizes of the corks illustrated are of course hypothetical and demonstrate the principle only.

I use a 4 to 6 in. quill.

Plan of cork showing the split to admit the line.

Reel line or cast.

of explanation. All you need is a medium porcupine quill and a series of egg-shaped 'pilot floats' of various sizes. These are split after the fashion of a *Fishing Gazette* pike bung, so that they can be taken off or put on to the head of the quill at will without unshipping the gear. You will find probably that a little trouble is required to make the various pilots fit your float, but by cementing a hollow quill in some to reduce the bore, or filling out any which are too tight with a small rat-tail file, a very workmanlike result can be achieved. These pilot floats serve the double purpose of giving visibility on the surface of the water and varying the lead-carrying capacity of the float. I used the word lead here advisedly, because shots are not suitable for weighting the weed-fisher's cast.

This is a case where the Sheffielder's tiny half-moon leads which are pictured in Chapter VIII come into their own. They can be applied by thumb and finger pressure and removed by opening them with one's thumbnail or a blunt knife, which will not injure the fine cast. Thus by changing the cork tip of the porcupine and the number or position of the half-moons on the cast, absolute versatility is attained. This is a matter of great importance. I know that the vast majority of anglers fish weed with a standard and unvarying float and cast. It will, however, be seen that as almost every 'run' in a weir differs in depth and strength it is a great advantage to be able to adjust the business end to suit each as you come to fish it. I do not suggest that this refinement is an essential to a good day's weed fishing, for when the roach are 'on the weed' they will accept it from wellnigh any tackle. I am, however, satisfied that by careful and thoughtful manipulation of an adjustable rig, infinitely better results are obtained when the fish are 'not very anxious.' Sometimes to lower or heighten the leads on your cast, not to speak of adding or doing away with weight, will make a remarkable difference to results—try it. One word in conclusion: roach which are feeding on silk-weed in a streamy 'run' do so hurriedly. Where striking is concerned, you will do well to adopt the old motto, 'When in doubt, strike'—and do it smartly, or your fish will not be there.

CHAPTER X

SOME METHODS OF ROACH ANGLING

AS all the angling methods now described apply to the capture of roach, I propose to detail them in this chapter. It should be remembered, however, that they may be applied equally to the taking of other fish.

I have often thought that science and physics could have no part with the quiet beauty of nature, but for the roach angler this is not the case. No angler can have too great a knowledge of the many means at his disposal for turning the circumstances of the moment to his advantage. Some notes on the technique of roach angling in various styles, which are also used for the capture of many other freshwater fish, will help the angler to meet local conditions or emergencies.

One of the most neglected methods of fishing, yet probably the most effective means of taking large fish, is ledgering.

The somewhat strange name ledger which has been given to the tackle used in this mode of fishing, has, as might be expected, excited some curiosity. Speculations have been made as to its origin and meaning. Some authorities state categorically that the word ledger or leger (obsolete) is derived from the Latin *lego* (*legere*), to lay out.

This word *lego* has many meanings, but I have been unable to find any evidence of it meaning 'to lay out.' I must therefore reject this suggestion. It would seem to be far more likely that the word ledger comes from the English *liggen* or *leggen*, which are dialect forms of lie. To this day in some northern counties one hears the word used, i.e. 'liggen e bed'—lying in bed. A ledger lies on the bottom and, failing a better solution of this interesting point, I offer my readers this possible explanation of the origin of the term ledger.

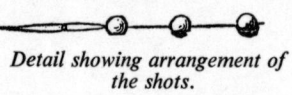

Detail showing arrangement of the shots.

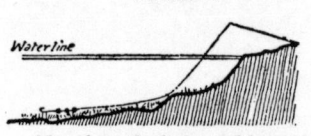

Note how the light tackle rests above a patch of fine weed.

There are various types of ledger tackle, and I will describe first that known as the 'shot ledger,' which is suitable only for fishing still waters, rivers where the flow is hardly perceptible or slacks in flood water.

The business end of this gear is illustrated.

The only manipulative difficulty which it presents is that of casting, and to enable the angler to project this light gear into a swim which may be 20 yards distant, a knob of 'cupping' or 'ground bait' is squeezed round the shot to provide the necessary weight. This also serves as a sprinkling of 'propaganda' when it strikes the water immediately above the place where the bait will come to rest. The texture of this 'cupping' should be such that it will break up and leave the shot as it reaches the water, allowing the bait to sink naturally. In summertime, when the bottom is covered with soft fine weed, it will lie on the top of this and remain visible to the fish, whereas if a heavier weight were used, or if the ground-bait were sufficiently firm to adhere to the shots, the bait might be drawn through the weeds and out of sight. Having made the cast, the line should not be pulled or tightened, as this movement might also draw the bait out of sight among the fine weeds on the bottom. This does not apply to the same extent when the weeds are down in winter, but in every case it is better to allow it to rest exactly where it sinks. With this light gear no 'telltale' is necessary, because when a feeding fish takes the bait the line shows a warning movement; raise the rod point promptly but gently and your fish will be hooked. This super light method of shot ledgering is killing not only for roach, but for bream, tench, perch and carp. When fishing for the latter, anglers will be well advised to use much stouter tackle than is necessary for any of the other fish named.

There is another method of 'ledger-fishing' which, while it may seem unduly heavy, is actually very light and is often employed with excellent results in deep, still water, the heavy runs of weir lashings and the strongly flowing streams where the bottom is firm and free from obstructions in which the bullet might become entangled.

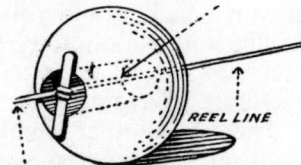

Note the very wide bore.

The cast and hook-link are attached to the line below the peg, the weight of the bullet being taken by the line.

The tackle illustrated is very similar to that employed in the ordinary 'bored-bullet' method, but the lead is considerably larger than usual and the boring much wider. It would seem at first that so large a lead would constitute a great resistance to a taking fish. On the contrary, however, the bullet is too heavy for a fish to lift and the result is a minimum possible resistance, namely, the weight of the line which will run freely through the wide boring as soon as the slightest pull is exerted upon it. The gear has the advantage that long casts may be made directly from the reel, and it is therefore particularly serviceable when the bank is rough and stubbly, but it should never be used in shallow water where the splash of the falling lead would alarm fish.

Water conditions permitting, that old favourite, the 'dough-bobbin tell-tale,' is a good means of detecting bites.

When the lead has landed on the bottom and the line is drawn taut between it and the rod, a foot of line is pulled from the reel and a pinch of paste or bank clay squeezed on as

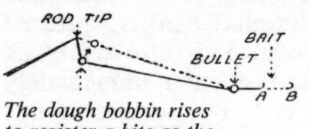

The dough bobbin rises to register a bite as the bait is drawn from A to B.

shown in the illustration. An upward jolt of this 'bobbin' signals a bite and should be answered by an immediate strike. If the water is too fast for this method of detecting bites, draw the line taut to the rod point and strike when the tip is depressed by a fish, or alternatively having drawn the line taut to the lead hold it between the thumb and finger and strike when a bite is felt (see Swing tip, page 86 *et seq.*). This method is very sensitive and is particularly effective when fishing at night. The rod and line must, of course, be rather heavier than those generally used on account of the weight of the bullet, which would strain a light rod when casting, and would break a fine line if any hitch occurred.

The normal 'bored shot ledger' is identical with that described, but the shot is much smaller and the boring much finer. There is always a risk that fish will lift these small weights and feeling the resistance drop the bait. Barbel, roach, chub and perch may be taken with this tackle, and, when the bottom is not too soft, bream, carp and tench. On a muddy bottom, lighter bullets are more serviceable, being less liable to become embedded in the mud. For fishing a strong cross stream which would roll a circular bullet out of position, a flat or 'coffin lead' is desirable. These flat leads are inclined to spin when the tackle is wound in, with a resultant kinking of the line, and should therefore be avoided whenever possible.

There is another simple form of floatless ledger tackle to which I must refer before passing to float ledgers. It is particularly useful where the bottom is rocky and full of obstructions between which the gear might become wedged, necessitating a break.

The illustration shows that a stone or pebble is used as a ledger

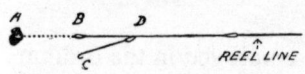

A—Stone or pebble attached by very thin line to loop in cast at B. C—The hook-link from a loop in the cast, D.

Fig. 1.

weight (rather than incur the expense of lead weights) which is attached by a thin piece of line of lower breaking strain than any other portion of the tackle. By this means, when the weight becomes wedged no important section of the gear is lost. There are other forms of ledger, but those with which I have dealt will suffice for most circumstances. Anglers of an experimental frame of mind will doubtless devise variations.

These lines were written more than twenty years ago, and have remained unaltered until now, in the hope that some genius would formulate new tackles of outstanding merit. That hope has been fulfilled *via* Richard Walker of Hitchin, a thoughtful, painstaking and successful angler.

This and other Walker devices, which are efficient and ingenious beyond praise that would not seem fulsome, will be mentioned later in their appropriate context.

I have great faith in the effectiveness of floatless ledgers, but must admit, in common with many anglers, I prefer to use tackle with a float, for there is something fascinating about watching a float ride at anchor to ledger gear.

Under certain conditions, float ledgering is no less effective than the floatless method, and it is particularly well adapted for fishing quiet waters when there is no wind. When these conditions prevail there can be no more dainty or deadly manner of taking roach, bream and tench.

The illustration shows the tackle used for shot-float ledgering. A sensitive and delicate gear composed of a tiny quill or ducker-float suspended above a 3 lb. bs cast to a 2½ lb. bs hook-link, with one shot pinched on about 1½ in. from the hook.

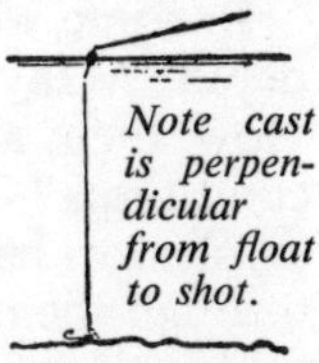

Note cast is perpendicular from float to shot.

Shot ledger tackle hook 1½ in. from shot.

Fig. 2.

It should be remembered that when fishing in this style, bites may be registered in three ways. The float may be drawn under the surface, but if a fish picks the bait up and rises, the float may be lifted or lie flat on the surface of the water.* Any of these signal the necessity for raising the rod point, which is quite sufficient to hook a fish; striking in the generally accepted way would certainly result in a break if the taking fish were a large one. When roach fishing with this tackle, I am satisfied that contact cannot be made too early, but experience alone tells an angler when to tighten.

If this method is used, plumbing the depth is a matter of great importance, and it should be carried out with extreme accuracy to ensure that, when the float-tip appears just above the surface of the water, the shot rests just on the bottom.

In latter years the more scientific angling fraternity has renamed this rig 'the lift method.' There is, however, little new about it save its name and the fact that the float is attached at the lower end only.

It was I think the well known tench specialists, the Taylor brothers who rechristened the method and developed a series of modifications for use with different baits and in varying conditions.

Tackle from rod top to the lead is almost in line.

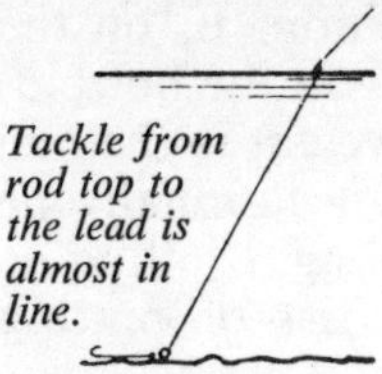

Normal float ledger tackle. Hook 12 to 18 in. from shot.

Fig. 3.

Further details appear in Chapter XVII.

For fishing in a slight stream, or if the surface is ruffled, another variation of the float-ledger will be found most useful. The illustration, Fig. 3, shows this tackle which varies only from that described previously in that a small-bored bullet kept in position by a grain-shot and a correspondingly larger float are used. The bullet is adjusted in this case a foot to 18 in. away from the hook. Bites are usually indicated by a sharp, decided depression of the float, the coming of which is very often heralded by slight

* See page 141.

trembling movements, and it is always a matter of difficulty to decide whether to strike immediately or to wait for a definite 'knock.'

I prefer to place my rod on a rest when float-ledgering, believing that when it is held in the hand imperceptible vibrations which pass from the rod to the tackle have a tendency to make fish wary. It must be remembered, however, that one hand must be kept in readiness to pick up the rod instantly or the fish will certainly be missed.

In some waters there are holes and depressions as much as 30 ft. in depth. Many anglers resist the idea of using floatless ledger tackle. How, then, are they to satisfy their desire to watch a float under these conditions? The reply is: use a slider float. The ideal slider is shaped as shown below, the rings being set away so that the line runs through them unobstructed. The float is gently curved. This method of fishing deep water with a float is not used to nearly such a great extent as one would expect. Slider-floats move up and down the line. When the tackle is out of the water the float rests on the shot just above the hook link, making casting possible. As the bait and shot strike the water, after the cast, they sink immediately, drawing the required length of line through the float-rings, the float remaining on the surface. In order that

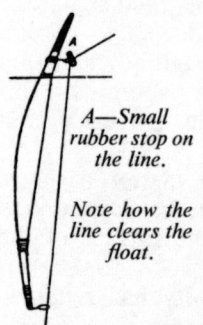

A—Small rubber stop on the line.

Note how the line clears the float.

only the required amount of line shall pass through the rings, a float-stop is fixed on the line, which must, of course, be sufficiently small to run freely through the rod-rings, yet too large to pass through the wire loop at the top of the float. Opinions vary as to the nature of the material used for these stops, but I prefer a small piece of rubber tubing; others use a small portion of hog's bristle, but if the rod-rings are of the large porcelain variety, either will be found eminently satisfactory. A 2 in. length of line tied firmly on the running line makes an excellent stop. The point on the line to which this stop should be fixed is decided by either trial or when possible plumbing the depth. If the angler elects to fish his bait just off the bottom, the shots of the cast must be balanced with the float as when float-fishing in the ordinary way, and little difficulty will be experienced in getting the bait to slide down into the fishing position. If, on the other hand, it is desired to float-fish with the bait dead on the bottom, the largest slider-float which will not raise the ledger weight is the one to use, otherwise it will be found that the float will occasionally be submerged with the remainder of the tackle, necessitating a jolting of the line to make it rise to the surface, with the obvious risk of 'putting the fish down.'

Fine, braided nylon, nylon monofil or braided terylene lines are all suitable for use with slider-floats.

This tackle is effective in deep water for the capture of roach, chub, bream, tench, perch, and barbel.

The illustration shows two methods of adjusting the tackle for

stret-pegging or laying-on. This method of
roach fishing is very deadly, and is often
used when results from swimming the stream
are not good. In both instances, the float is
raised so that the bait rests on the bottom.
In a high wind there is no more suitable
method of searching a swim. The tackle is
cast two or three yards downstream, and
the float is held. This has the effect of
causing the bait to wave gently on and off
the bottom in a most attractive manner. If there is
no response from the fish, allow the gear to roll down
a yard or two farther. This may be done close to the
bank, working as far as the angler desires, and then

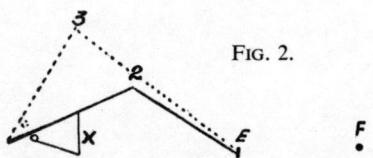

Shot and bait on bottom.

Bait only on bottom.

repeated at any distance from the shore which the length of the rod
permits. Bites are generally quite definite on stret-pegging tackle, but
this method also allows for a bite being indicated by the float rising,
rather than being depressed or lying flat on the surface of the water
when the fish take the bait and swim upward with it.

Not only roach, but dace, chub, bream, barbel and perch all find
stret-pegging to their liking.

The angler who wanders will find streams where the art of 'trotting'
or 'trenting' is necessary, either from the bank or some craft. The word

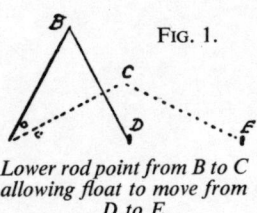

FIG. 1.

*Lower rod point from B to C
allowing float to move from
D to E.*

FIG. 2.

*Meanwhile draw loop of line X from
the reel. Release it and at the same time
raise rod point from 2 to 3. This draws
the line over end ring, after which proceed as in Fig. 1. The float progresses to
point F. Then repeat.*

'trotting' is applied to the process of swimming one's float tackle from
the point at which the angler sits to any desired distance downstream.
The reader will remember that this method was mentioned in dealing
with Nottingham fishing. It will therefore be seen that a 'trotter's'
swim may be any length. The simplest possible mode of 'trotting' is,
of course, direct from a freely-running, light-drummed centre-pin reel,
which will revolve without the angler's assistance in response to the
pull of the stream.

There is, however, another method available to those whose reels
are not sufficiently sensitive. 'Trotting' by hand without checking the
progress of the float is a highly skilful manipulation, a fact that will

be borne in on all anglers who attempt to hand-trot for the first time. They need not be discouraged, however, for once the principle is mastered it is simple. The illustration shows the manipulation, and the necessary movements as they would be seen by a spectator on the bank, watching an angler 'trot' from a boat set across stream, as in the Thames style. Controlling the reel by a gentle pressure of the thumb or finger on the rim, draw off about a rod length of line, and allow the float to travel forward from the boat by lowering the rod point slowly as the float moves away. According to the strength of the stream, this will take a greater or shorter time. As the float moves forward, draw off a further length of line with your free hand before the line between the rod point and the float is taut, and raise the rod gently to release it, as shown. Now dip the rod point again, following the float, and repeat these movements until the tackle has travelled as great a distance as circumstances or your wishes dictate. The great objective should be to feed out line and make all movements in such a way as to avoid any check or drag on the float.

CHAPTER XI

ROACH FISHING IN THE WIND

THERE is a popular idea that anglers relish fishing in a downpour of rain. While this is quite erroneous, many of them give ample cause for the belief by sallying forth on the wettest of days to pursue their hobby. There are few, however, who will face a really windy day. Not that they object to fresh air in motion, but because of its disastrous effects upon their operations. They dislike wind intensely. Many an angler has set out with calm conditions prevailing, only to find on

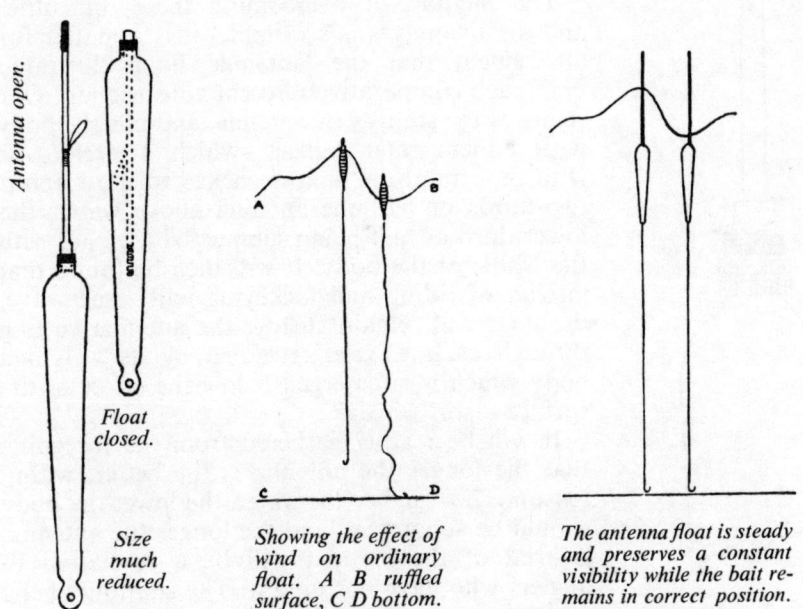

Antenna open.

Float closed.

Size much reduced.

Showing the effect of wind on ordinary float. A B ruffled surface, C D bottom.

The antenna float is steady and preserves a constant visibility while the bait remains in correct position.

arrival at the water-side that a fresh wind has sprung up and ruffled the water in such a way as to render float-fishing by normal methods almost impossible, and practically useless.

Monsieur Matout, a French angler, came to the rescue with a float which overcomes these difficulties. As with many another invention, improvements have been made on the original 'Matout' float, and I propose to discuss the use of the latest device of the kind, which is a British product.

The illustrations, page 81, show the 'Matout' float, collapsed for safety and in the interest of economy of space when in the tackle bag, and opened as for fishing. Some discussion of its use and functions can only prove of great benefit to all float anglers, and particularly those who seek the wily roach. Let me cite the detrimental effects of wind on the ordinary float.

The first and most obvious is the fact that visibility is rendered most difficult and often impossible. As the float rides the crests of wavelets, and disappears into the declivities, it becomes a matter of the greatest difficulty to detect those movements which indicate a bite. Furthermore, as it rides up and down on the disturbed surface the float lifts and drops the bait in the water in the most unnatural way, which undoubtedly causes fish to eye the morsel of food with that suspicion which anglers know from experience means at best a lean bag. See illustration, page 81.

The method of overcoming these difficulties and disadvantages is so simple, it is a matter for amazement that the 'antenna' float illustrated is of such comparatively recent construction. One removes the stopper or antenna, and fills the body with either water ballast—which I prefer—or with shot, until the float is cocked to show about two-thirds or half the antenna above water, the lower third or half being submerged together with the whole of the body. It will then be found that instead of riding and jockeying with each wave, the float will remain steady, the antenna cutting through each wavelet, steadied by its weighted body which is submerged below the effect of the surface disturbances.

It will be readily gathered from the foregoing that the longer the antenna is the better, within reason. The rougher the water, the lower the body should be submerged and the longer the antenna. A trial of the method will be a revelation to anglers who have not used it. The shotting of the cast, of course, affects the amount of ballast used.

I do not propose to go deeply into the physics governing the use of 'antenna' floats, but some additional details are necessary to assure a proper understanding of their use. Special attention to fitting an 'antenna' float to the line or cast is desirable, particularly

Loop for cast or line.

Red tip.

Float cap.

The body of these floats is transparent and markings of ballast points for various shottings can be made.

in respect of the loop on the antenna itself. These floats are fitted with a cap at the top, and a hole at the base in the ordinary way, but no provision is made for attachment of the line to the antenna, and it will be seen that, as the body of the float is always entirely submerged, the line or cast would also be submerged from the point where it leaves the float cap if no precaution is taken to prevent this. Every angler knows the result could only mean a completely sunken line which is

fatal to float-fishing. That was my first experience of the use of these floats, and I cast around for a method of overcoming the difficulty. I tried pinching a tiny piece of cork on to my line to keep it floating, and found the act of striking shook it off.

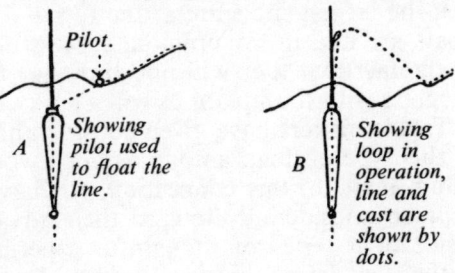

A Showing pilot used to float the line.

B Showing loop in operation, line and cast are shown by dots.

I then resorted to a small pilot float secured in position with a match (see illustration 'A'). This is practical and, I think, quite satisfactory; but I subsequently whipped a small loop on the antenna, as shown in Figure B, and prefer it to the former method. The whipping should be made rather more than half-way up the antenna, or slightly above that point which the angler means to regard as the water-line on the antenna when it is in action. The latter method is certainly the neater of the two, but it is an admittedly debatable point whether, in very rough water, the former is more practicable, as, of course, waves might easily submerge the loop and so set up a sinking of the line from its point of contact with the antenna. A great number of other types of solid antenna float are now available, any of which according to its shot carrying capacity is perfectly satisfactory. The type mentioned is, however, more versatile.

Note relation of loops to the water line.

FOR LAKES IDEAL

FOR RUNNING WATER

SLOW STREAM SHOTTING

A, B and C represent the approximate levels of the water ballast. Shotting is, of course, proportionate.

The reader will doubtless try both methods and adopt the one found preferable.

Now we come to the important matter of shotting the cast and apportioning water ballast to the float itself. This operation necessarily varies with conditions.

In still water the maximum of water ballast can be used in the float, with, say, one small shot

4 in. from the hook. The sensitiveness of tackle so arranged can only be appreciated by trial, but the method is only possible in water which has no stream. The nearest approach to this, and an excellent way of shotting the 'antenna' float when fishing slowly moving waters such as the Great Ouse, is shown in illustration B. Here it will be seen that less water ballast is used and the difference in weight made up by the application of graded split shot on the cast. It is of the greatest importance that the largest shots are at the top and the smallest at the base. These floats are not, in my opinion, successful in briskly flowing water, due to the fact that they will not draw line through the rings of a rod and progress with the stream as will a cork-covered porcupine, for example.

Tackle makers have given considerable attention to the construction of this type of float, among whom I would mention the makers of the 'Elfin' float. In this connection, I believe Dr. H. J. Denham has contributed considerably toward their advancement to perfection, as the result of a series of thoughtful experiments. Writing of these floats in the now defunct journal *Angling*, he says:

> These 'Elfin' floats have such great weight-carrying powers that one can try out all sorts of ideas with them. It is to be hoped that in a little while, when they are more generally used, it will be possible to standardise them both as regards shot-carrying capacity and sensitivity. One should, for instance, be able to have the same shotting on floats of different sensitivity, as well as different shotting on floats of the same response.

From this it would seem, that float-fishermen are well on the way to having some of that care put into the make-up of their 'tell-tales,' which is commonplace in the manufacture of artificial flies. The time is long overdue, for are not floats instruments of high importance to untold thousands of anglers? Speaking of some of his experiments regarding the under- and above-water colour of floats, the doctor makes some comments which are so pregnant with help to all float-fishermen that a further question is imperative. So many of us, the author included, have spent hours in thought and experiment in the hope of arriving at the least visible under-water colour for a float, that it comes as a jolt to find the doctor writing:

> Much more important than making a float less visible to the fish is the making of it more visible to the fisher.

How right he is! It is probably impossible to accomplish the former with any degree of success. As to the latter, let the doctor tell us through the pages of *Angling*:

> Think of the conditions in which the float has to be watched: in still water, in rippled water; in sunshine, brilliant or dull; in diffused light, midday or twilight; against a background of mirrored sky, or mirrored bank and trees; seen from above or far out and far away; a score or two possible conditions, half a dozen of which may occur between one end of the swim and the other. Small wonders that all the colours of the rainbow have crept into the tackle-maker's shop.

I have made a number of experiments in search of the most visible colour or combination of colours for the above-water portion of a float, and have arrived at four colours, one of which will meet almost any lighting condition. (*I am reminded that neither black nor white is a colour, but for the present purpose I hope I shall be forgiven for so describing them.*) They are orange, yellow, black and white. My orange is a truly violent hue, and the yellow, that advised by Dr. Denham, and described by him as 'the yellow of A.A. signs, spectrum yellow or cadmium yellow.' It remains only to outline the mode of applying these colours and the lighting conditions in which they are most applicable.

The 'Elfin' float here shown illustrates the method of applying the colours. It is fatal to split them up into small sections. A number of rings of equal size alternating up the antenna is ideal camouflage, which, of course, is absolutely opposed to the desired result. In this matter I am at one with the doctor. On the other hand, while he is satisfied that yellow with a black tip is the most visible combination for use against a dark background, reflected trees, etc., I am equally convinced that orange is better. I mention this because I believe our difference of opinion may have its origin in a fundamental difference between his sight and mine, which, if this is the case, enables me with some confidence to advise anglers to make personal experiments rather than accept with blind faith what is here written. Contrary to possible expectation, white is not good in these conditions, and black fails lamentably. By the way, it is important to remember that when I refer to yellow, black, etc., it is understood that this is the preponderating colour on the antenna of the float in question.

Black comes into its own against sky reflected on the water and in failing light. My own findings in this respect of the best combination for use in a mixed reflection are so much in tune with those of the doctor, that I will quote him yet again:

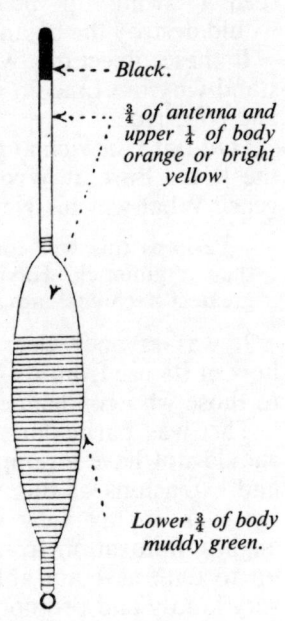

←- - - *Black.*

←- - - - *¾ of antenna and upper ¼ of body orange or bright yellow.*

Lower ¾ of body muddy green.

Against reflected leaves and twigs with the sky showing through—to my eyes the hardest of all conditions with which to cope—I found that yellow with a black top (in the proportion of 4:1 or 5:1) was a tremendous improvement on plain yellow or black; so, too, was the addition of a small sphere of cork, the size of a large pea, painted black, on the extreme tip (of the antenna).

In this connection I am personally equally happy with my orange, but there is so little in it that the difference is negligible. White is probably the least useful colour, but there are occasions when the water is highly coloured and the light of such quality that

white comes into its own. However, I hope I have succeeded in passing
on the idea in such a way as will make it a simple matter for any reader
to make his own trials and arrive at those combinations of colour which
are most visible to him, on the water and under the lighting conditions
in which he most frequently finds himself.

These antennae are not too easy to see and the effort is well worth
while, because the narrower the antenna the more difficult it is to see
unless it is properly coloured. But—and this is extremely important—
the narrower the antenna of your float the more sensitive it will be. The
factor which decides the sensitiveness of a float is its circumference at
the point where it leaves the water. It is assumed throughout the foregoing that the float is shotted so that the antenna only is above water.
You can't fish these floats successfully if you cannot see them, considerable effort is therefore warranted to find those colour combinations
which suit you best.

'SWING TIP'

In January 1959, the angling Press made quite a feature of a new
bite-detecting device for ledger fishing, called the 'swing tip'. According
to reports this invention of Mr. H. Clayton, the well-known Boston
(Lincs) tackle dealer, had met with instant acclaim from both Lincoln-
shire and Norfolk anglers; and as the fishermen of these counties
have a well-earned reputation for their skill, I determined to investigate
it and pass on the result of my findings to readers of *Angling Ways*.

As was inevitable the critics, many of whom I suspect had not even
seen a 'swing tip' before they inveighed against it, weighed in. It
would destroy the balance of any rod; it would hamper casting, etc., etc.

If these objections were indeed valid, I found it difficult to understand why the Lincoln and Norfolk fellows had found it so acceptable
and effective.

Had not Norwich angler Peter Collins collected 68 lb. of bream from
the River Bure at Wroxham when it was bank high with 'swing tip'
gear? What was his view of this new ledgering device? I quote:

> Perhaps this will convince people that the 'swing tip' is rather more
> than a gimmick. Having ledger fished for many years, I find this the
> greatest 'technical' advantage in ledgering ever.

It was at once clear that to acquire a 'swing tip' and the know-
how of its use from its inventor was preferable to paying any attention
to those who condemned the tackle out of hand.

This was particularly so, as at the time in question I knew that I
should not have an opportunity to test the device before the revisions
and extensions of this volume would go to press. That fact was not,
however, in my view a sufficient reason for omitting an important
angling innovation from the book which I am determined to keep as
up to date as I am able; and I sought Mr. Clayton's aid, which he
very kindly and promptly gave.

And here it is, a complete top joint made of fibre-glass to which the tough industrial nylon swing tip is permanently fixed. It is virtually a second top joint devised for use with any suitable rod when ledgering. The obvious advantages are that one is freed from the trouble of adjusting a new dough-bobbin, split-cork or silver paper bite indicator to the line after every bite and it is as sensitive as either of them. I know of course that some experts ignore all such visual bite detectors when ledgering, preferring to hold the line lightly and feel for their bites especially at night, and why not? But it is not everyone who wishes to be so concentrated and pinned to their tackle as is necessary when

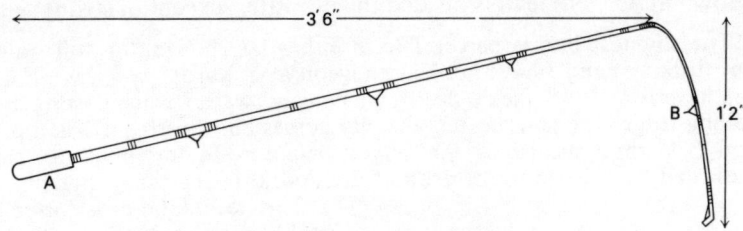

The Clayton 'Swing Tip'

A—This resin adaptor can be filed to fit any rod and should be kept greased.

B—The swing tip which is only $\frac{1}{16}$ in. at the upper end tapers up to $\frac{1}{8}$ in. at the tip and is very sensitive. It is made of very tough industrial nylon monofilament and will not be damaged by being pushed into a rod-bag.

detecting bites by feel in daylight. To feel for bites may be and probably is productive of a quicker reaction and strike but the difference in time saved would be difficult to measure. Rightly or wrongly, for me, fishing is a relaxation rather than a life or death job and here is a device which cuts out a lot of fiddling with dough-bobbins, etc. For match anglers, for whom time saving is all important, swing tips will I am sure play an important role by saving vital seconds when conditions call for them to ledger rather than float fish. It was in fact with this in mind that Mr. Clayton invented it.

At this point I should state that this equipment was first introduced for use in Midland and Eastern waters, but I can see no reason why its use should not be well nigh universal for ledgering. Its enthusiastic acceptance in the areas named lend colour to that view to say the least.

So much seems self-evident. Let us then see what Mr. Clayton has to say about his 'swing tip' and consider his 'say-so' with an open mind, free from the natural discount which can quite often be applied to an inventor's description of the excellencies of his own brain child. I quote:

The 'swing tip' was intended originally for my own use particularly when match-fishing. To satisfy my requirements in this connection, it had to be as sensitive as a float to the smallest fish and applicable to any combination of weather and water conditions.

After much experiment and ridicule from my friends, the present 'swing tip' which does fulfil these conditions was evolved. But I have not been able to keep it to myself.

Its main advantages are that it is ready instantly, once the initial balancing is correct, for continuous fishing without further attention; and by its use fish can be caught rapidly with a minimum of tackle manipulation.

This balancing is achieved quite simply by the addition of lead wire to the lower end of the tip behind the end ring if the stream is strong enough to lift it. All that is necessary is to add enough wire to hold the tip down at 45°. No lead is needed in still water, except in strong wind.

The slightest bite is perceptible in either fast flowing or still water at any distance; and I have hooked gudgeon at 50 yards.

I have found this tackle deadly in Fenland waters when casting a slow rolling ledger (or paternoster) directly across and upstream. The tip rises and falls rhythmically as the ledger weight rolls, but bites are clearly indicated by either a lift or drop of the tip out of the usual rhythm.

This technique calls for considerable practice, but it could not be achieved by the use of either a dough-bobbin or split-cork indicator.

The illustration makes this method clear, but don't be disappointed if your first efforts to use it present some tip balancing or other problems. There is little worth while which is come by easily in angling, or anything else for that matter. The points of importance are that the lead wire-balance of the swing tip must be right to give an angle of 45° against the prevailing stream. The Arlesey bomb (rolling weight) must be the lightest that will hold bottom in the existing water conditions. And you must learn to discriminate between bites and the movements of the tip which are caused by the stream.

1.

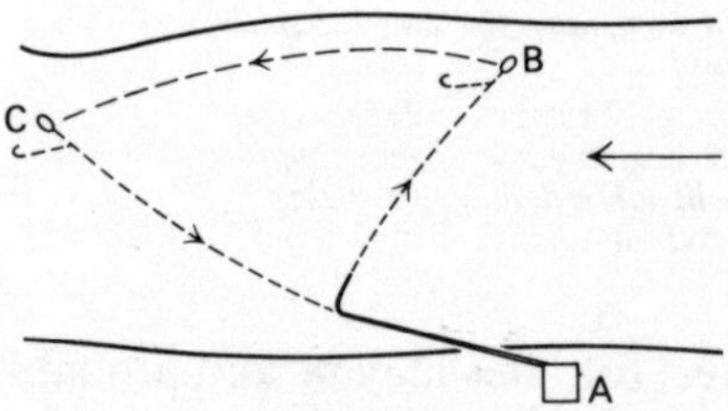

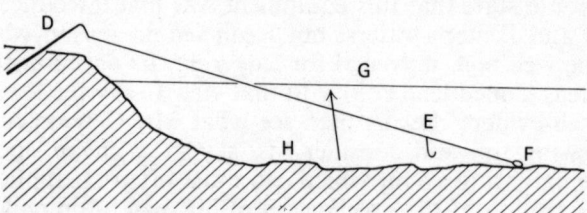

Rolling a ledger or paternoster with swing tip tackle

FIG. 1. *Shows a plan of the operation. A—The angler with rod facing downstream. B—The position of the Arlesey bomb (ledger weight) after the initial upstream cast. C—The tackle nearing the end of its roll downstream.*

2.

FIG. 2. *Is an elevation view from upstream. D—The rod facing downstream. E—The hook-length secured in position by either a rubber-tube or matchstick stop. F—The Arlesey bomb. G— The surface of the water. H—The river bed.*

All this will come quickly if you persevere.

In this connection there is one other point which is important. After much experiment that has given him an expert knowledge of the matter in question Mr. Clayton says:

> The distance at which the hook-length is fixed above the weight and the length of the hook-link is varied to suit prevailing conditions; and only general rules can be given as a guide to overcoming the problem which vary from day to day and in one water or another.
>
> As an example, when fishing the Great Ouse in fast much-coloured water, I set a 36 in. hook-link 30 in. up from the weight. By this arrangement the bait was kept clear of the foul bottom by the strength of the stream.
>
> On the other hand when fishing in still water I should use an 18 in. hook-link set 6 ft. up the line, to produce the same effect. But to fish the bait on the bottom in still water I set the hook-link only 8 in. up the line and vary its length according to the type of fish and the bait being used, i.e. for roach 1 ft.; for bream 18 in. except when fishing worm, when it sometimes pays to increase the length of the hook-link by 6 in.
>
> In a medium stream the hook-links should be increased to 2 ft. for roach and 1 yard for bream.
>
> When fishing a narrow river almost straight down stream I have found it necessary sometimes to increase the hook-link to 4 or 5 ft.
>
> Generally speaking, however, you can arrive at the correct length by starting with a 24 in. hook-link, then if bites are missed, shorten it, if fish are pricked and lost, lengthen it. If on the other hand you get numerous false bites you can assume that the fish are hitting the line and are not feeding on the bottom. In this case move the hook-link higher up the line to lift the bait off the bottom.

Well, there are the general principles of fishing this particular rig, which as Mr. Clayton rightly says are much simpler to put into operation than they are to describe. Frankly I am not able to make up my mind as to whether the foregoing rig and method should be called ledgering or paternostering. Perhaps a compromise will meet the case, i.e. when the bait is fished on the bottom it is ledgering and *vice versa*.

There is, however, no room for doubt where this second business end which Mr. Clayton recommends. It is a ledger tackle pure and simple.

He describes this rig as giving facilities for a

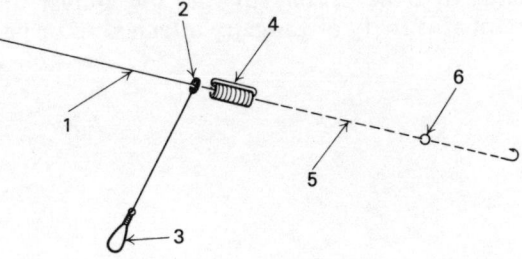

Fig. 3 A very versatile ledger tackle

1—The line. 2—A split-ring to which the Arlesey bomb (3) is attached. 4—The rubber-tube stop which is attached by passing the line through once then turning it back and through again to form a loop. This facilitates its movement up or down as desired. 5—A 12 to 16 in. hook-link to suit conditions. 6—A shot if necessary.

wide variety of bait presentation; and you may care to try it out if it is new to you. It would however seem that a 'swing tip' can be used with any type of ledger tackle in its capacity as a sensitive and troublefree bite indicator.

Before concluding this brief sketch of the 'swing tip' tackle, mention must be made of Mr. Clayton's reply to the criticism that the device hampers casting. He says:

> Casting is not impeded and the addition of lead wire for balancing in a stream has little effect, once the technique of casting with it is perfected.
>
> The balancing weight is never more than $\frac{2}{3}$ of the required ledger weight, the impetus of which when casting holds the tip and balancing wire more or less in line until the cast is complete.

Mr. Clayton's comment 'once the technique of casting is perfected' would appear to indicate that one may find it strange at first; but there is nothing unusual about that. If you are accustomed to using a Nottingham reel and change to a multiplier, growing pains will be experienced until you have accustomed yourself to the change. Those who use 'swing tips' have not to my knowledge made any complaints on this score; and it is I think reasonable to assume that any difficulty of this kind can be dismissed as negligible when compared with the advantages of this tackle.

I should mention that there is a type of temporary clip-on swing tip available for attachment to the top joint of a rod. It is perhaps to these that the critics who speak of a rod being put out of balance refer.

In those happy days when the tip end of a fishing rod was a simple matter of a top ring firmly affixed to the slender cane or fibreglass, the success or otherwise of the angler depended upon the sensitivity of his hand and eye. When the swing tip arrived it soon proved a great asset in many styles of fishing, the matchman especially finding it a boon towards his striving to hook more fish than his neighbour. Once the swing tip was established man's ingenuity soon got to work on the 'sling tip', the 'spring tip' and the 'quiver tip' all of which depend on extra sensitivity of gadgetry attached to or part of the rod tip.

CHAPTER XII

DACE: CATCHING DACE

C. TATE REGAN, the eminent ichthyologist, said 'The dace is closely related to the chub.' So closely is it, indeed, that the family likeness has led to these fishes being confounded and confused one with the other.

The reason for its old English name, Dart, is apparent to the angler who watches a shoal of dace move against a sharp stream in a series of quick dashes. They are sprightly and sporting fish which will fight every inch from the strike to the net. It is a pity they are so comparatively small. The largest dace of which I had heard when this volume was first written was taken by Mr. L. Cookson from the Ivel (Beds.) and weighed 1 lb. 8 oz.

A magnificent dace, weighing 1 lb. 8 oz. 5 dr., taken by Mr. R. W. Humphrey in 1932 from a tributary of the Hampshire Avon, stood for over 30 years as the recognised rod-caught record. The Record Committee however decided some years ago (see Chapter XVI) that various fish on their lists were not sufficiently proven. The 1 lb. 8 oz. 5 dr. dace was one of these offending fish. The record now stands at 1 lb. 4 oz. 4 dr., caught by Mr. J. L. Sasson from the Little Ouse at Thetford, Norfolk. This weight was equalled on June 16 1972 by Mr. L. Hall whose fish came from Andover Lake.

A dace weighing a pound is worthy of a glass case, but what they lack in size is amply made up in fight and willingness to feed. In Lancashire and Cheshire dace are called 'Graining.' This has given rise to the belief that graining and dace are separate species, a view held by some leading authorities. The late Dr. Tate Regan, however, wrote: 'I cannot see that the dace of Lancashire differ in any way from those of other parts of England.'

Their coloration is handsome—the back and the dorsal and caudal fins vary in different waters from green to a brown—the sides are a beautiful silvery white, and the under fins are usually pale pink. This is not universal, however, as in many specimens these fins are almost colourless. In the early season they are found on the swift gravelly shallows, but in the winter dace retire to deeper and quieter water. The natural foods of this species are flies, water insects, worms, crustacea, silk weed and other aquatic growths. These give a clue to the baits which will prove effective.

Whether dace are rod benders or not they are always a popular quarry. I have often thought that, weight for weight, there is no more game fish. The speed with which they take a bait has much to attract the angler, and the fisherman who can 'hit' four out of seven 'dace snatches' may pride himself on his skill and speed.

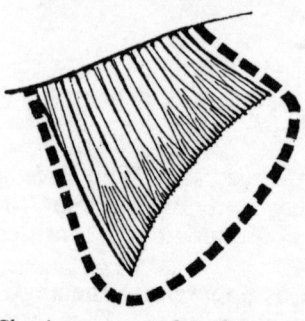

If one had a hundred yards of line for every controversy which had divided anglers as to whether a given fish was a dace or a small chub, the total would surely encircle the globe—but there is an infallible test. Examine the anal fin of the fish and there can be no doubt. That of the dace is curved inwards (concave) while the anal fin of a chub is always curved outwards (convex). The illustration makes this clear. The fin shown in detail is a dace fin, the dotted line represents the corresponding fin of a chub. There are, of course, many other differences between the two fish but none more definite and constant.

Showing concave edge of the anal fin of dace, the dark dotted line indicates the shape of the same fin in the chub which is convex.

The scales, head and mouth of dace are noticeably smaller than those of the chub, even in small specimens.

Dace are gregarious and move in large shoals—catch one and a score or a hundred may follow. Some consideration of one of the chief characteristics of these fish is important, however, if large catches are to be made. Dace ascend and descend in their movements through the stream. Sometimes they are to be taken right on the bottom, sometimes at the surface, and they will feed anywhere between these points. It has often been my experience to find that after a few fish on the bottom have been taken they will cease to give sport entirely. Raising the hook a few inches by dropping the float often finds them again. Dace must be followed in their upward and downward movements and continual changes of depth when sport flags will often be found beneficial. There are, nevertheless, occasions when even this appears to be fruitless. When this is the case, give the 'swim' a complete rest for a few minutes—it often has the desired effect. There is another strange characteristic of dace which is vital to the angler—they appear to have days when they are partial to a particular bait—perhaps gentles or may be bread cubes are the effective bait of the day. I strongly advise the dace fisher to have an assortment of bait, for where he takes fish with red worm on Monday he may find that only wheat will tempt them on Tuesday. In this connection, it is interesting to note that dace prefer the head to the tail of a lob worm—in my experience the reverse is the case with other fish.

London anglers are particularly fortunate in having excellent dace fishing near at hand. The tidal water of the Thames from Richmond to Teddington holds thousands, and both bank and boat anglers may expect good sport in this reach of London's river. Many large dace have been taken in streams within easy reach of London, and those in search of a whopper may meet with success in the Beane or Gade in Hertfordshire or that renowned tributary of the Thames, the Kennet. The Granta in Cambs., and the Suffolk Stour may be linked with the Hampshire Avon in their records of fine dace. Lea fishermen may be heartened to know that Walton's river has produced a brace of dace scaling 2 lb. $9\frac{1}{2}$ oz. There are plenty of dace—how and with what shall one capture them?

CATCHING DACE

To enjoy dace fishing thoroughly the angler must use the lightest tackle possible. The rod should be the daintiest of wands and the line and cast of gossamer slenderness. Complete lightness is not however possible. Dace prefer streamy runs, and the character of the water in which they are generally found demands a float and shotting which is comparatively heavy in order to get the bait down quickly and keep it in position against the stream. The best method of shotting a dace cast is debatable, but it is most usual to employ six or eight shot grouped fairly low, the bottom shot being 8 in. to a foot from the hook. As the result of considerable experiment I much prefer to use one small bored bullet suspended on the cast above a grain shot as shown in the illustration.

Bored shot eight inches from the hook.

Grain shot on the double section of the cast just above the loop supports bored shot.

Anglers will note that the bullet is 8 in. from the hook in the tackle I recommend, but, in very heavy water I do not hesitate to place my lead within 4 in. of the hook. I am well aware that this procedure may be regarded as a heresy, but being unwilling to accept angling rule of thumb I experimented and found that by this low shotting bites are registered much more sensitively and *the fish are not scared* in accordance with the impression generally held. This gear has several advantages, it is simple to assemble quickly, and it is only necessary to pinch one grain shot on the frail cast, above the loop as shown in the illustration, where the cast is doubled and whipped and is therefore less likely to be damaged. It will be seen at once that this minimizes the possibility of a break through the line being cut, which is always an imminent risk when a number of shots are applied to super-fine gut. One shot may also be applied above the bullet if desired to prevent fray, but there is some doubt as to which is the greater evil where fine line is concerned.

Now as to suitable hooks for dace fishing. Many experts recommend the smaller sizes, Nos. 14, 16 or even 18 in some cases. I never use a

hook smaller than No. 12, even for hemp fishing, and much prefer a
No. 9 when fishing bread crust and baits of similar kind. Careful
experiment has proved to me there is no virtue in the use of tiny hooks
for dace fishing. Dace 'take' the bait so quickly that the 'strike' must
be simultaneous with the slightest flicker of the float—this in itself is
a sufficient difficulty without adding impaired hooking power by
using small hooks. I assure those readers who have always used small
hooks that a trial of the larger ones I recommend will show a higher
average of fish hooked. The small hook prejudice dies hard I know,
but an experiment will satisfy the most sceptical angler that dace do
not recognize a hook when they see one, despite the fact that small
hook advocates claim it is virtuous for a hook to be invisible to the
fish.

Coming to terms with dace is pretty and at times fast and furious
sport. I have often known days when had I been quick enough to 'hit'
every fish that snatched at my bait, I should have caught hundreds
instead of the sixty or seventy which found their way into my keep-net.
Anglers whose interest flags or who wish fishing could be speeded up
should try a course with the dace—it is not a slow occupation for day-
dreamers. As to the methods which are applied to dace fishing, 'swimming the stream' with float tackle is by far the most popular, and for
catching large numbers of comparatively small fish, it is without doubt
the most effective. 'Stret-pegging' or 'laying-on' with float tackle,
float ledgering and ledgering are also good—but for taking a comparatively small number of 'big-uns' give me 'rolling the bank.'

Many anglers are familiar with the methods I have mentioned, but
comparatively few appear to understand 'rolling the bank.' A Thames
professional put me wise to the method years ago, and as all anglers
are out for the big fish, I will describe it because in my experience it
accounts for by far the best class of dace.

Select a swim with a gently sloping shingle bed in a streamy section
of the river. It need not be more than 2 ft deep, or even less in the
summer, and 4 or 5 ft. in the winter when the dace take to deeper
water. The best 'business end' for the tackle is a bored bullet and a
cork-covered porcupine float. I prefer to work from a boat, but it is
almost as simple to 'bank fish' in this style.

Now for the procedure. Drop gently downstream close to the bank
until you arrive at the head of your prosed swim and tie up the *stern*
of the boat or punt to the bank. This will throw the forward part about
a yard into the stream, and by fishing over the end of the boat the
angler is in an ideal position. Plumb carefully and set the float at from
3 to 6 in. in excess of the depth in accordance with the strength of
the stream; the stronger the flow the deeper you fish. Drop a ball of
bread and bran containing a small quantity of the hook-bait and a
pebble to sink it, immediately in front of you, and the stage is set.
Either a bunch of gentles, a small red worm or bread-crust (in the
quieter swims) will be found good baits. Lower your baited hook into

the stream and hold the float as when 'laying-on.' You will find the
stream will roll your float and bait gently toward and away from the
bank up and down the sloping bed of the river, as shown in the illustration. This movement gives rise to the term 'rolling the bank.' It is
immediately after one of these rolling movements that the fish appear
to bite. The bait and float have rolled, they remain steady for a moment,
then like a flash the float is gone—a simultaneous strike is necessary
or the dace will have gone also. By feeding out a little line at intervals
20 or 30 ft. of water may be fished, but I do not advise fishing at
any greater distance from the boat on account of the excessive speed
of the bites. It will be obvious that the greater the distance between
the angler and the bait, the greater the difficulty in contacting with a
fish. Fishing in this way one can drop downstream from swim to swim.

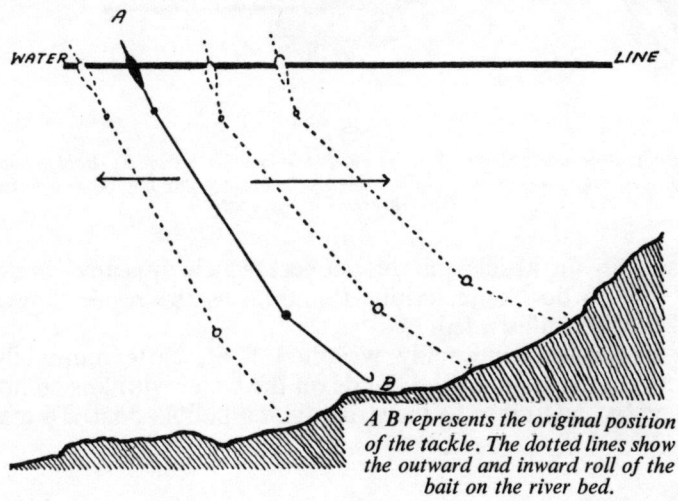

A B represents the original position
of the tackle. The dotted lines show
the outward and inward roll of the
bait on the river bed.

When conditions are favourable it will often happen that dropping
downstream one or two punt lengths finds the fish again when sport
has flagged in the original swim. One word of warning—don't strike
too hard, for every now and again you will catch a chub and a hard
strike against a heavy chub will spell victory for the fish. Excellent
alternative baits are meal-worms, paste, pearl-barley, caddis or wasp
grubs (in season) and the head or tail of a lob-worm when the water
is coloured after a flood.

Surface-fishing for dace
    There is a method of surface-fishing for dace with float-tackle which
must have a place here. As fished on the Suffolk Stour, a small bubble-
float (illustrated in a more appropriate context, page 227) half filled
with water is used to enable the angler to project a live bluebottle or
other insect, on an unshotted floating cast, to a spot upstream of a

shoal of dace, from which point this floating tackle and lure are allowed
to drift down over the shoal with satisfactory results.

As I have intimated earlier, to tell Richard Walker of an angling
method with which he is not familiar is liable to start something, and
that is just what happened on this occasion.

Having been told it by a friend, 'R.W.' tried the method as described
and concluded that a bubble-float had marked disadvantages, these

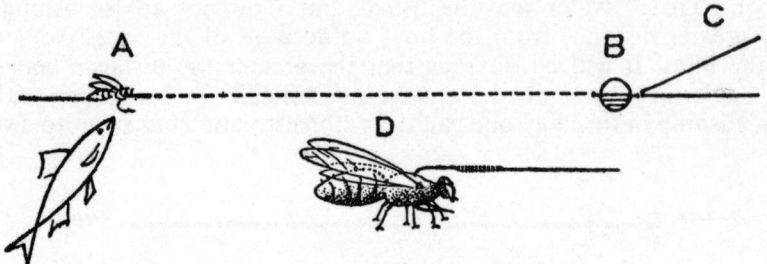

FIG. 1.

*The operative tackle floats. A—Live bluebottle or other insect. B—Bubble-float
half filled with water. C—Reel-line. D—Method of hooking the fly. The dotted
line represents a 2-ft. cast.*

as he said in an article on this subject which appeared in *Angling*,
caused him to do 'some serious thinking' as the result of which he
devised the float illustrated.

This streamlined internally weighted float, casts more efficiently
either into or across the wind, lands on the water with less commotion,
and offers less resistance to the strike than a bubble-float. To make this

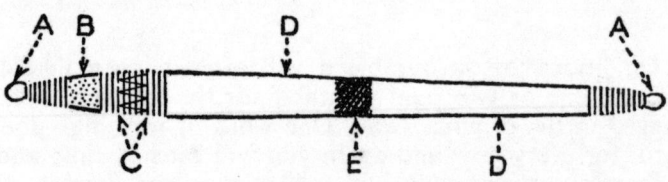

FIG. 2.

*Quill float. A—Nylon loops whipped to each end of the float. B—Tapered
balsa-wood plug at open end of the quill. C—Junction of plug with quill.
D—Quill body. E—Lead plug to give weight for casting.*

float he immersed a swan quill in hot water to soften it, then pushed
a lead plug into the quill, which when it had cooled and dried held the
lead firmly in position at the point of balance, which ensured that the
finished float would lie flat on the water when cast.

This accomplished, he plugged the open end of the quill with a

One of the early steps in the development of the modern fixed spool reel was the Illingworth. The late A. Holden Illingworth took out a patent for this reel on July 4, 1905, and it is remarkable that this instrument is still in perfect order after over 70 years. It can clearly be seen how the principle of the cotton reel was used, together with a simple bale arm, to allow gossamer line to flow off smoothly, as described in Chapter XXXVII.

Some years after the introduction of the Illingworth reel, the Helical Reel Co., of Birmingham, launched the Carswell Modified Illingworth. The transition from the 'cotton-reel' idea, already with a primitive bale arm mechanism, to the more recognisable, but still very narrow line spool can clearly be seen. From this and other early models the modern fixed spool reel evolved, usurping to a great extent the simpler centre-pin which, in the hands of the competent angler, is probably more satisfying to use and which for some angling methods is still the most efficient.

(a)

(b)

(c)

(d)

COARSE FISH SCALES

The carp family apart, most coarse fish species can be identified from their scale characteristics. Here we have (a) barbel, (b) perch, (c) roach and (d) tench scales, not pictured to their correct relative sizes. Given a selection of roach, chub, small carp and large dace scales it may be difficult to tell one species from another – they are all Cyprinoids, that is, members of the carp family and in consequence they show a similarity in scale shape and configuration. All fish scales, however, exhibit growth rate, which shows as groups of rings, laid down as the fish grows. Seasonal factors, spawning times, also have an effect on the ring formation and a fish's general health can also be assessed by the expert from a study of its scales.   [*Photographs: H. D. Torbett*] piece of balsa-wood, streamlined it and whipped a loop of nylon at each end as shown in Fig. 2.

As to the best tackle for this interesting method of taking *Leuciscus*, Mr. Walker advises a flexible 10 ft. split-cane rod, a small fixed-spool reel, 2 lb. b.s. nylon monofil line and a No. 12 crystal hook; the float being fixed by a piece of valve-rubber to the line (which is passed through both of the nylon loops) about 2 ft. from the hook.

Meanwhile, I am grateful to him for this description (which appeared in *Angling*) of his fishing technique when using this method.

Having found the fish, take up, if possible, a position that allows you to cast across and downstream, so that the gear will alight well above the dace. Just before the float alights, the line should be checked to cause the fly to fall below and beyond the float. Then a further check after the float hits the water will allow the fly to go well ahead of it, before they both start on their way towards the fish. It will be realised that a study of the current must be made to ensure that the right spot is chosen to start the swim-down, which is virtually trotting, as in float-fishing.

As the tackle glides downstream, keep just in touch with the float *without checking it*, This, though not difficult, is a somewhat delicate operation which demands one's whole attention. I have not found it necessary to strike very fast to hook even small dace when fishing in this way. They hold the natural fly much longer than they would hold an artificial, which, however, can be used if desired though it is not nearly so effective. Dead flies can also be used but they lack the attractive twizzle of the live ones. . . .

Only surface obstructions affect this tackle which passes over submerged weeds and extremely shallow water which it would be impossible to fish with ordinary float-tackle. Greasing the nylon very slightly above and below the float is a help. In conditions of very bright sunshine, however, it might be better to soap the nylon between the float and the fly, to avoid a shadow on the bottom and to tolerate the continual sinking of the fly with resignation.

I expected that, when retrieved the tackle, the fish would be alarmed; and, to avoid this, I let it swing round to my own bank before winding in. There were, however, several occasions when fish intercepted the bait while I was winding it in; and I concluded that the Ouse dace, at any rate, were not alarmed. The possibility of frightening larger and shyer dace by clumsy retrieving should, however, be borne in mind when good fish are a possibility.

I have no doubt that the same tactics, used with appropriately stronger tackle and larger insects such as grasshoppers, cock-chafers, moths, etc., would be effective if fished for large trout and chub.

In closing, perhaps I ought to say that bluebottles can be obained by the simple process of neglecting a tin of maggots sufficiently long; and flies obtained in this way have the advantage of being more tractable, at any rate in winter, than wild ones, which, by the way, can always be pacified by putting a few drops of carbon tetrachloride in their vicinity.

CHAPTER XIII

FLY-FISHING FOR COARSE FISH

HAVING set my hand not only to the revision of this book, but to its useful extension, I must mention one of the least usual but most artistic and sporting methods of taking certain coarse fishes. As the dace is probably the most ready riser to an artificial fly and as we have discussed its capture by other means, this is perhaps an opportune juncture at which to deal briefly with fly-fishing for those coarse fish which may be taken by this method.

As I have remarked fly-fishing is probably the least used mode of fishing for dace, chub, roach, rudd, grayling and perch (on the wet-fly), all of which respond admirably to these feathery lures. This may be due to the fact that most so-called coarse anglers are obsessed with an idea that casting a fly is a matter of great, almost insuperable difficulty. This is far from true, and in order to rid the reader's mind of what may be the principal obstacle in the way of his enjoyment of fly-fishing, I will quote an article which I wrote for the now defunct fisherman's journal *Angling* in 1936.

But let me first tell you what John Waller Hills had to say on this subject in his *A Summer on the Test*:

> What I want to impress on any reader who is not a dry-fly fisherman is that dry-fly fishing is much easier than it sounds. There is a conspiracy of anglers, started by Halford and carried on with increasing momentum by other writers, to make out that the art is so dreadfully obscure that none but the gifted should attempt it.
>
> The perplexed beginner, poring over the great masters, reads of the accuracy and delicacy required in casting; how the fly must fall exactly right at the first throw, how a single mistake is fatal, how he must be able to recognise at a glance each of the hundred and one insects on which trout feed, how, unless his fly is an exact copy, he had better stay at home, and in short, how he will never catch anything unless he acquires an abstruse and esoteric science of which certain austere practitioners are the sole depositories.
>
> He despairs of reaching this level and, perhaps, losing confidence, avoids Hampshire. He is completely misled. He believes what is really egregious nonsense. The sport has its difficulties, and they are not small; but in the first place anyone with ordinary ability can surmount them,

and in the second the price paid for failure is not nearly so great as writers would have us believe.

You can make heaps of mistakes and yet kill plenty of fish on a difficult river and a difficult day. . . .

You must cast delicately, and put your fly four inches this side or four inches that without a bungle; you must have on the right fly and it must float upright and without drag. But believe me, it is not nearly so hard as it sounds. Try it.

Here then, I repeat what I wrote, because I could not write anything different now. It contains, I hope, the essentials, which with practice will make you a proficient if not perfect caster.

Let me assume that as a beginner you have selected a suitable rod, reel and line, with the help of an experienced fly fisher, or guided by a good tackle dealer.

With this assumption I am content to say that if you are to have the greatest pleasure from, and comfort in their use, the rod, line and reel must be perfectly attuned and balanced one with the other. Now having set up your rod, fixed the reel and threaded the line through the rings, attach a 6 ft tapered nylon cast to the end of the line. To the end of it tie a small portion of orange-coloured knitting wool. You will find this very visible while practising and it will not catch up in obstacles or the seat of your trousers, as might a fly armed with a hook.

Everything is now ready for your first fly-casting lesson. The hours of unalloyed pleasure which await you when practice has made you perfect, can only be appreciated when they are experienced. This fact should supply the urge to persevere.

Don't attempt to make long casts at first. Strip off twenty or thirty feet of line and lay it out on the lawn in front of you. Now take up your position with rod in hand and lower the rod point as shown in Fig. 1. In this position you are ready to make the 'back cast'—raise your rod point slightly and pull in a little line with your left hand to take up any slack. Now 'snip' it smartly upward (see Fig. 2). This upward 'snip' of the rod is carried through to the vertical position and should be made firmly but not jerkily (see Fig. 3).

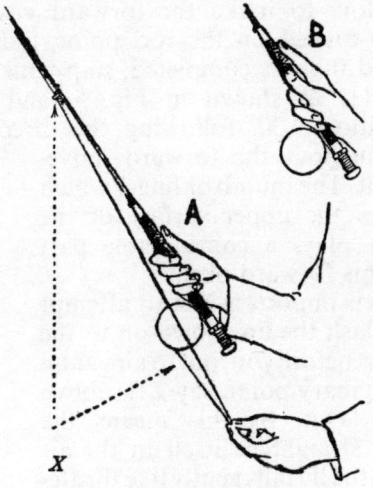

METHOD OF HOLDING THE ROD.
X—Loop of line between the first ring of the rod and the reel. B is an alternative grip to A, which is the more usual.

Fig. 1.

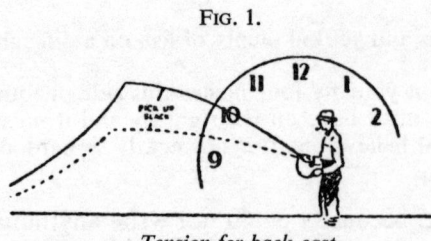

Tension for back cast.

In making this movement the beginner should remember that it is his object to get his line not so much behind him, as the words 'back cast' would intimate, but behind *and up*!

Now turn again to Fig. 3 and you will notice that having stopped the rod at the vertical or 12 o'clock, its own action and the weight of the line pulls on the rod point and bends it slightly backward to 12.30. This point in the act of casting is very critical. After flinging the line up and behind you by an upward twitch of the rod as shown in Fig. 2, you must pause till the line tugs almost imperceptibly at the rod tip. This pause is known as 'timing,' and is of vital importance. Like so many vitals it is difficult to master at first, but with practice it becomes automatic.

It will be clear that the longer the length of line you are casting, the greater the pause must be. If your timing is too fast and you commence to bring your rod forward too early, the end of the cast will crack like a whip lash. When you are using a fly and this happens, the fly is 'cracked' off. If on the other hand your timing is slow and you bring your rod forward late, the line falls and may catch up in undergrowth behind you. Furthermore, when the line has fallen in this way, it cannot be propelled forward as it should be. In 99 per cent of cases a beginner does not allow enough pause.

Now to make the forward cast. At that moment when the line has tugged on the rod point, indicating that its upward and backward flight is completed, snip your rod forward again from 12 o'clock to 11, as shown in Fig. 5, and allow it to sweep through to the position 9.30, following the direction of the line with the rod pit throughout the forward movement. The thumb or finger which is on the upper surface of the butt plays a considerable part in this forward push.

It is important not to attempt to slash the line down on to the grass before you, but to aim at an imaginary point, say 2 ft. above the lawn. By this means the line straightens itself in the air and the fly falls gently like thistledown. The benefit of this light landing of the fly will be found in actual fishing, and the effect of aiming above the horizontal

Fig. 2

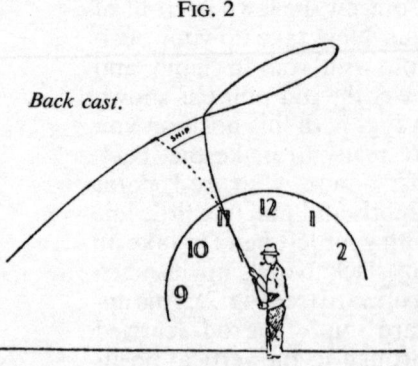

Back cast.

Aim back and up.

will be very marked when you make your first attempts on the water.

These are the elements of fly casting—raise the rod gently to take up the slack and slide the line off the surface of the water, then throw it back *and up.* Pause for the line to straighten behind you and whip it forward again well above the water.

All these movements are rhythmic and smooth but deliberate, and should be made as far as possible with the forearm and not by exaggerated movements of the upper arm and shoulder. Whatever you do,

FIG. 3.

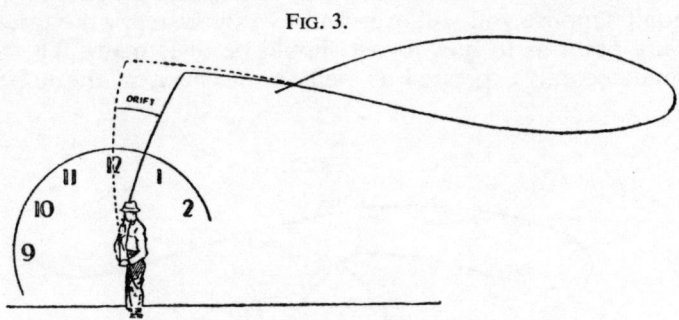

Pause until the line tugs at the tip of the rod.

don't force your movements; the rod will do the work if your timing is good and your movements are clean, smooth and free from effort.

There are just two final points which I should make. When you are fishing, always keep a short length of line between the thumb and finger of the left hand, as shown in the opening illustration. A fish may

FIG. 4.

Aim high.

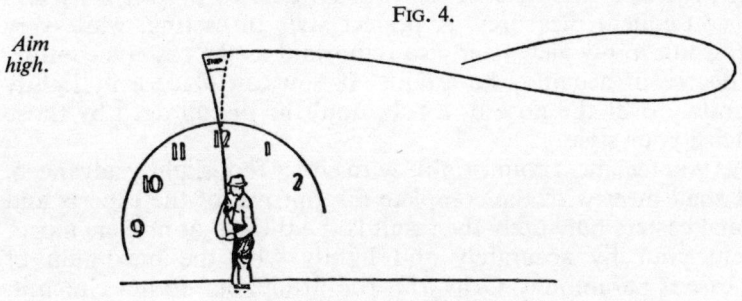

Commencement of the forward cast.

take your fly immediately it touches the water and you must have perfect control of the line. While casting, make your lifts strong and your returns easy. Don't whip the line off the water with a great 'slosh'; that is fatal, and it is a common failing with beginners. Draw the line off the water and when you have got it going then put some snap into the final stage of the lift.

To put out more line as required, 'shoot' a yard or so. This is accomplished by pulling off a yard or more of line from the reel with your left hand, hold it with your thumb and finger till your line has commenced to fly forward, then release it. The released line will shoot forward through the rod rings, lengthening your cast by its own length. Practice! Practice!! Practice!!! And get a professional caster or an old hand to coach you if you can. The most thrilling sport awaits when you have learned to cast a fly, not only with the noble salmon and trout, but with dace, chub, rudd, roach, and grayling.

I don't suppose you will ever find two fly casters who agree entirely on every point as to how a cast should be or is made. The foregoing are fundamentals expressed as well as one may, in the hope that by

FIG. 5.

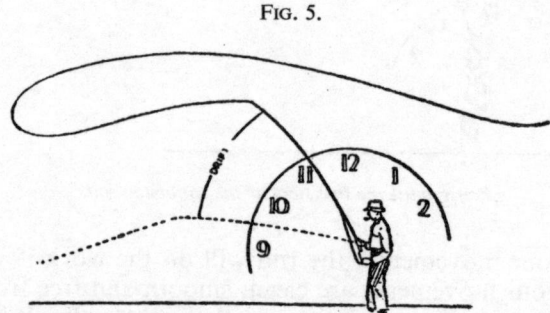

Follow the direction of the line with the rod tip.

following them the complete novice will be able to project a fly and reap the consequent pleasures. A perfect style in casting, while very desirable, is not in my view nearly so important as the caster's comfort and the degree of accuracy he attains. If you can place a fly lightly and accurately over the nose of a fish, don't be discouraged by those who criticize your style.

Stand as you feel most comfortable with either foot slightly advanced. I know I shall meet with the complete disapproval of the experts and professional casters but surely the result is the thing that matters most? To present your fly accurately and lightly with the maximum of personal ease is paramount. Grip your rod firmly, but do not clutch it, or you will soon have cramp in your hand and an aching wrist.

Speaking of the grip of a fly rod raises an interesting and, I think, an important point. In giving the foregoing instructions I adopted the most usual formula, namely, four fingers round the butt and the thumb on top. There is, however, the alternative method of grasping the rod with three fingers and the thumb as shown below, and placing the index finger on the top of the butt. Here again adopt the grip which suits you best. Mostly fly fishers use the first method but I feel sure there is much to be said for those who contend that the second is more delicate and tends to correspondingly delicate casting and striking. Some anglers cast with the thumb uppermost, and when the fly has landed, change to the index finger grip, to ensure a better (less snatchy) strike. Thus combining the two. We are told that the late and great G. S. Marryat, who was certainly one of the finest exponents of dry-fly fishing in his day, used this thumb and index finger above the butt method. These would appear to be the only feasible ways of gripping a fly-rod—adopt the one which is most comfortable and natural to you and to the devil with style. The end is greater than the means.

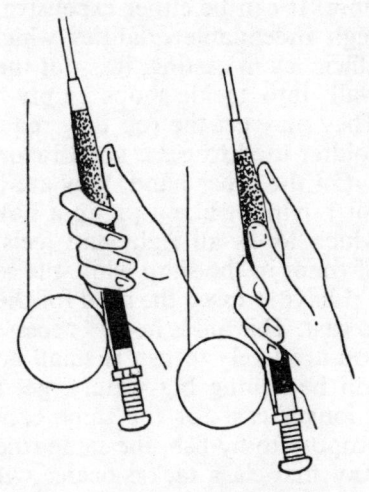

It is a matter of high importance to seek the guidance of an expert if you can. He will check faults which you would never notice, before they come to stay. It may all feel a little strange at first but you will find yourself casting automatically and without effort very quickly. Get rid of the idea that casting a fly is difficult and the battle is half won. There are of course other casts such as the Spey and steeple, etc., but these will develop when you have mastered the straightforward overhead, which I have tried to describe. You will meet others of greater experience who will put you right on what may be termed the fancy casts—and it is vastly more simple to teach at the waterside, than through the medium of cold print.

Remember the man who can fish a short line has more control over his cast—there is no virtue in projecting great lengths of line. Study to present your fly lightly, accurately and to get as near as possible to your fish. The urge to write on must give way to a repetition of my advice to secure the aid of an old hand. He will put you on the right track in a few minutes at the waterside, while further attempts to explain in writing may only foster an impression of difficulty. Casting a fly is not difficult—try. Fly fishing has a fascination which is its own reward. Before I turn to other matters one more word. Writers usually advise that the initial practice should take place on a lawn. I have in fact suggested this earlier. Nevertheless if you have suitable water available I think it better to practise on water from the word go. It is one thing to lift a line off a lawn but quite another to slide it off water, where suction plays an important part.

Believing that the casting bogey is probably the main obstacle to coarse fishermen taking up fly-fishing, I have dealt with this matter first, assuming that the beginner was equipped with the needful tackle.

Now, however, it is necessary to go into some detail regarding rods, reels and lines. Let us consider the rod first.

I feel safe in saying that in no phase of fishing are the attributes and qualities of the rod so important. It may be made of greenheart, whole cane and split bamboo, split cane, built cane, tubular-steel or glass fibre. It can be either expensive or cheap, but unless it has those well-nigh indefinable qualities which make for comfort in handling and efficiency in casting, it is not the rod for the job. Thousands of anglers walk into tackle-shops empty-handed and come out with a fly-rod. They may get the rod they require by this method about as often as a soldier used to get a good razor from the quartermaster's stores.

On the other hand, they are more likely to get the rod they deserve for buying it like a pig in a poke. It is not sufficient to have a fly-rod which looks all right and feels comfortable when switched a couple of times in the shop while the salesman sings the praises of his wares.

I have stressed the need for the aid of an expert when you are learning to cast. This aid is no less necessary when you buy a fly-rod. If the water you are likely to fish is small an 8 ft. 6 in. rod is long enough; if you will be fishing big waters, get a rod a foot longer—it will give you a longer cast for the same expenditure of energy. But wherever you propose to fly-fish, the same rule applies if you are to get the right rod. Any first-class tackle dealer will let you have a selection of rods on approval. Take them to the waterside or on your lawn if you prefer— fit the reel and line to each and try them out in actual practice. Only by this means can you be sure that the rod you buy is right for your physical and fishing requirements. A big man is often happier with a longer rod, and *vice versa*. You can only judge by actual test under outdoor conditions with the reel and line fitted. See that the rod will cast a short line with precision and a long line when called upon. See that the whole outfit balances and that the rod is not top heavy; there is nothing more tiring than an ill-balanced fly-rod. See that the total weight of the gear is the smallest possible commensurate with the work it is intended to do. Every ounce tells when you have been fishing an hour.

My own rod, a Farlow eight-footer, weighs 6 oz. and is a two-joint weapon of considerable power, yet pliant and comfortable in use. Even this is on the heavy side, and I have since found a veritable wand in the shape of an 8 ft. 'Scottie' (featherweight) by J. S. Sharpe of Aberdeen. This rod weighs only 4 oz., is shorn of all weight adding gadgets and is a delight to use. It is moreover impregnated with phenolic resin in such a way as to make it virtually impervious to the effects of moisture.

I am satisfied personally that providing a fly-rod has sufficient power with sweetness of action to do the work required, total lightness and precision of balance are the paramount considerations.

Strangely enough, two rods of exactly the same specification and weight may have quite different action. This drives home my contention that a fly-rod should be chosen at the waterside, *and not in a shop*. As I have intimated, it is most difficult to put on paper a recitation of the qualities of a good fly-rod, but they can be summed up in two words—personal comfort. If you are able to cast easily, accurately and lightly without any physical discomfort with a given fly-rod, that for you is a good rod, and you cannot take too much trouble to find it. Some experts hold that a three-jointed rod has a better action than a two-piece. There may be something in this, as there is no actionless ferrule in the centre of the former. In point of fact ferrules are never an aid to the sweet action of a fly-rod. Rods fitted with a spear in the butt are an advantage. One can push the spear into the river bank where the rod will stand, leaving you both hands free to make any adjustment you may wish—but rods with two tops are a snare of the devil. It is seldom that both tops are identical in action and quite frequent that the second top is trodden on and broken if it is taken on a fishing expedition, not to speak of it being a confounded nuisance to carry about. If you must have a rod with two tops, adopt the better top for use and leave the other at home. The reader will have noted the thumb-rest on the upper side of the butt of my rod. This is built up from plastic wood, and I find it a great benefit when casting. This gadget, however, is not everybody's medicine, and I think you will be well advised to forget it; it is really a tournament caster's toy. Some most excellent fly rods are manufactured from hollow glass, one of the most interesting properties of which is the fact that ferrules can be moulded from the very stuff of the rod itself. Here is a saving of weight and an aid to rod action never believed possible by the rod makers of bygone days.

I think the line is our next item. These lines for fly-fishing are quite different from those used in other forms of angling. It's like this: when you cast a spinner or float tackle with a level line, the weight of the lure or float, shot, and bait, as the case may be, carries the line out.

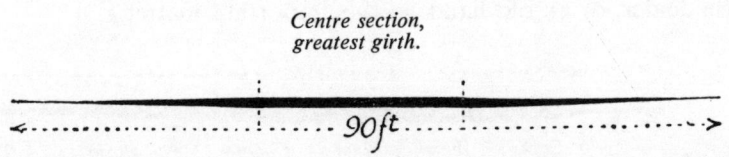

Centre section, greatest girth.

90 ft

The artificial fly, on the other hand, is a dainty and practically weightless little object, which could not be cast like a spinner or float. To overcome this difficulty the best and most economical fly-fishing lines are made with a double taper. Fine and light at the business end, they become thicker and consequently heavier as they run toward the centre section. The diagram above gives a rough impression of the idea.

You may be wondering how this overcomes the trouble to which I have referred. By giving the line taper and weight the process of casting is reversed. Instead of the lure carrying the line, the line carries the fly to its destination. It is unnecessary to go into detail, but, speaking broadly, the tapered fly-line is a flexible extension of the rod itself, and you cast the line, not the fly.

This very simple diagram will, I hope, give you an impression of my meaning. These lines are beautifully made and dressed with oil under pressure, which gives them a smooth, polished surface. When choosing a tapered line see that it is pliable and soft. Some of the cheaper ones are brittle and harsh to the touch and the outer skin flakes off them when they are used. It is the old story—buy the best, it will be the cheapest in the long run. Some are yellow, some green, others brown; the colour is, I think, immaterial. The reader will have gathered that the weight of the line is an all-important factor, and as

Line straightening out behind.

Line straightening out in front.

The rod, line and cast may be likened to a much elongated and very delicate whip-lash.

these lines are made in different weights and tapers, it is essential to see that your line is right for your rod. It will be obvious that to cast and lift a heavy line from the water with a light rod will put too great a strain on the rod and would in time break its back. On the other hand, it is well-nigh impossible to cast a light line with a powerful rod, because the line will not actuate the rod. Seek the guidance of a good tackle dealer, or an old hand on this important matter.

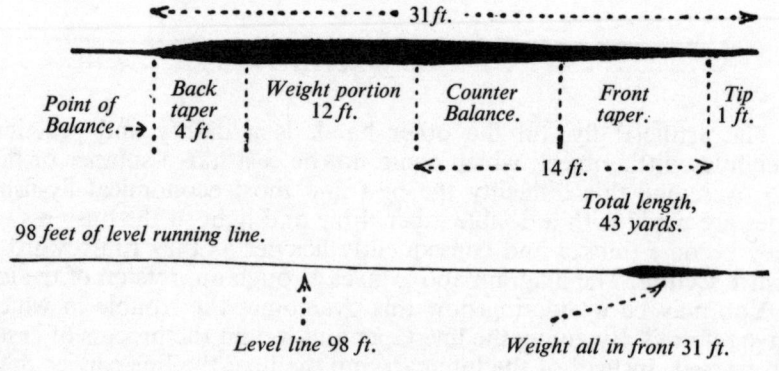

31 ft.

| Point of Balance. → | Back taper 4 ft. | Weight portion 12 ft. | Counter Balance. | Front taper. | Tip 1 ft. |

14 ft.

Total length, 43 yards.

98 feet of level running line.

Level line 98 ft.

Weight all in front 31 ft.

The rod and line must be absolutely in tune one with the other, or you will have trouble.

Before leaving the subject of lines I will mention the experiments of certain thoughtful anglers which have had a marked effect on the construction of fly-fishing lines. First of these was I believe, Mr. Herbert Greg, who in consort with the late P. D. Malloch of Perth, constructed lines for fly-fishing which, if they did nothing else, developed on common-sense lines the principle of giving line weight in the right place, with a view to its becoming a vehicle for casting a fly. This was as far back as 1902.*

Later the world-famous caster Marvin K. Hedge worked on similar principles.

There is little doubt that these gentlemen realised that, given an equally tapered line such as those in general use, the greater part of the weight of the line usually remains on the reel when fishing, and is therefore of no assistance to the caster. With this in mind they constructed lines the main weight of which is placed so far forward in the total length that it becomes operative as a casting agent almost immediately.

Whereas with the ordinary tapered line quite a length has to be got out before its weight is appreciably operative, the dimensions given with the foregoing diagram make the principle clear. I have one of these lines designed by Marvin Hedge and can testify that it makes casting easy, particularly against a wind. Nevertheless, I think it better that the beginner should learn to cast a normal double-tapered line. Having attained skill with it, he may care to experiment with the so-called 'balanced' lines.

A good line is essential to good and comfortable casting; it is equally certain that if it is to remain good it calls for great care.

No backing is necessary with a fly-line which is to be used exclusively for coarse fish. Do not, however, conclude that this indicates lack of fights to come. Chub can more than hold their own, as you will, I hope, find to your pleasure. And, finally, don't forget that your line is double

---

* In my capacity as editor of *Angling*, I received a letter in 1949, which throws more light on the probable origin of 'balanced lines'—it read:

SIR,—Referring to the subject of balanced lines mentioned in *Angling* No. 57, Vol. XI.

The construction of these lines was evolved and patented by that well-known angler and writer, H. Cholmondeley-Pennell in 1885. And Mr. Farlow, of the well-known London firm, made the first line to Mr. Pennell's instructions.

This line was designed on the same lines as those now used by Marvin K. Hedge, the American caster. I trust this information will be of interest.

Romiley.   A. G. HARTLEY.

This information is substantiated by the fact that Pennell mentions a line of this design in his *Modern Improvements in Fishing Tackle*, 1887, wherein he says:

p. 100.

I had some reel-lines manufactured a year ago. . . . The principle is to 'swell,' or double taper, the casting-line—like the thong of a whip—at a point so near the 'casting-end'; that the whole of the 'swelled part' shall usually be between the rod and the fly.

It would appear therefore that without doubt the laurels for this innovation should be awarded to H. Cholmondeley-Pennell. Incidentally Pennell called his 'balanced line' the 'Patent Whip-lash-line.'

tapered and both ends of it want to fish. To change it round and about
occasionally distributes wear evenly and is good for the line.

Whatever line you elect to use you must have a reel to carry it to
enable you to play a fish comfortably—and to aid in the balance of
your rod. If you secure a 3 or $3\frac{1}{2}$ in. narrow-drummed reel, which,
when fitted with line and fixed in its seating on the rod, equalizes the
weight above and below the point where you grip the rod, you establish
an ideal balance. But remember that a little more weight behind the
gripping hand is better than the reverse, for the simple reason that when
you have a length of line in operation this equalizes matters. Proper
balance reduces fatigue to a minimum, while every fraction of ill-placed
weight tells during a day's fishing. So does every ounce of total weight,
no matter how well balanced—go for the least total weight commensurate with retaining the power needed for your fishing; that way lies
comfortable fishing.

Buy a metal reel in any case, and one with a quiet check ratchet,
for obvious reasons. There are plenty of good reels available nowadays;
see that yours is a good one by a reputable maker, and you will not
regret it.

Of the items of tackle, casts and flies only remain for consideration.
As to the former, a two-yard cast tapering to 3 lb. b.s. is fine and long
enough to start with. If chub is your quarry, 4 lb. b.s. is a fine enough
termination. Longer casts aid in presenting the fly lightly, but they
make trouble for you if the wind is adverse—and it quite often is.

You can purchase line and tie your own casts if you are sufficiently
interested. Before attempting this, however, you should become familiar with the full blood knot, illustrated here.

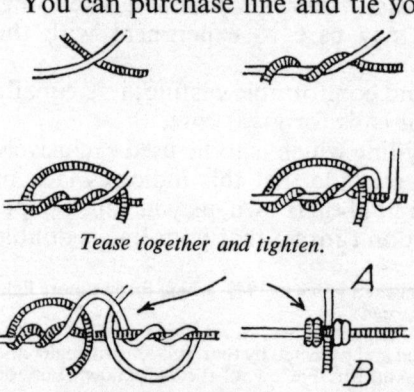

Tease together and tighten.

THE BLOOD KNOT.
Drawings after the late W. A. Hunter.

This knot, though somewhat elaborate, is, I think, the best for joining lengths of line and will satisfy your requirements. For my own part it is bad enough having to tie a fresh point (12 to 15 in. of fine line) to the end of a cast, not to speak of the tedium of sitting tying casts. I therefore buy mine ready tied. However, every man to his liking, and as this
book is intended to help in as many directions as possible, I give the
necessary details. The fact that even on winter evenings I can find
something better to do than attempt to defeat the somewhat high cost
of these necessities should not deter anyone. By the way, the two
ends A, B in the finished and tautened knot should be trimmed off with
a pair of fine scissors. As I have said in a previous chapter, tapered
nylon monofil casts are now available in one piece for those who prefer

them. The universal practice nowadays is to use tapered nylon casts, silk worm casts being rarely available. One other useful detail before we turn to the matter of flies, is the hitch for attaching the line to the cast. The illustration which follows makes this clear.

This hitch has the double advantage of being quite secure when it is drawn tight, while it is released instantly by a pull on the short end A.

And now about flies. Libraries have been written on flies for trout fishing, and thousands of anglers have found themselves floundering in a sea of choice. Fortunately, however, dace, roach, rudd, chub and grayling are not so particular about their choice of fly as many anglers appear to be. I can therefore simplify the matter of flies for these fishes with some degree of safety. To be orthodox, you should, of course, imitate the fly on the water at the time of fishing, and there can be no harm (save perhaps to your pocket) in so doing. I am, however, content to say that concentration on the proper presentation of a few flies will kill more fish than much fly changing and collecting. Here are a few useful ones:

Dace (hooks 00.0.1)   –   –   –   – Black Gnat
Wickham's Fancy
Coachman

Roach and Rudd (hooks 0.1)   –   – As for Dace

Chub (hooks 2.3)   –   –   –   – Zulu
Blue Bottle
Palmer (Red and Black)
Coachman

Grayling (hooks 0.1.2) –   –   –   – Orange Bumble
Steel Blue
Red Tag
Green Insect
Fog Black

You will find the Coachman useful in the late evening, and indeed at other times in the day—try it! It is also well to remember that as autumn turns into winter and hatches of natural fly become less frequent and thinner, grayling will accept one or other of the 'fancies' which do not resemble any living insect. Try a Wickham or Brunton's Fancy, or a Tup's Indispensable.

The esoteric meaning of the name of this fly is so interesting that it is worthy of record. This is the way of it.

Its creator, R. S. Austin, sent a sample of the fly to the late G. E. M. Skues together with details of the materials used in its construction.

Noting that the body of this fly was composed in the main of wool from the testicles of a ram, Mr. Skues suggested that as an indispensable part of a tup's anatomy provided a prominent part of the fly's make-up, Tup's Indispensable might be an appropriate name for the fly.

And so it was, and so it is. Odd how some names originate, isn't it?

Local information will help you a good deal in choice of fly, but should never be followed slavishly. In any case, you should be able to carry all the flies you are likely to need for dace, roach and rudd in a small celluloid box no larger than a pocket-watch. Those for chub and grayling can be accommodated in one or other of the fly-boxes which every dealer stocks. Buy a small one, friend; it may help to prevent you collecting useless patterns, if any such there be. At least where dace and rudd are concerned, I think I shall have a majority with me when I say that dry-fly fishing is the most interesting method. I may not, however, meet with so much approval when I say that (for me, at any rate) hackle flies such as the Black Spider and Pheasant Tail are all I require. I know many experts hold that winged flies alight on the water more lightly than hackle flies and that as imitations of the natural they are more realistic and therefore more killing. This might(?) be so with trout, but I am not impressed by either contention where the coarse fishes are concerned. What coarse blighters they must be; they don't appear to care two straws whether an artificial fly has wings or not! There is, however, one point on which I think nearly every angler is agreed, namely, that it is desirable that dry flies should float and sit as high as possible on the skin of the water.

I am not at all certain that even this point is quite so important to coarse fish as to fishermen, but as the angler should have his own way sometimes, here is a recipe which will ensure the desired result. Dissolve one unit of vaseline in four (by bulk) of petrol; this will call for a considerable shaking together. Place the resulting solution in an open-mouthed, screw-capped bottle of the kind in which halibut liver oil capsules are sold. This will enable you to immerse your fly completely and easily. Dip the fly in the mixture, make one or two 'false casts'* to dry off the spirit and the hackles will be coated with a thin film of vaseline which will float the fly perfectly without making an oily blob on the surface of the water. The latter consideration is important.

As to winged and hackle flies, I should make some simple explanation. All natural flies, of course, have wings. Without going into scientific details these wings are arranged as on opposite page.

Those flies of the family *Trichoptera*, of which the Caddis fly is an example, have wings which fold at a slight angle along the body, like the apex of a small triangle.

Flies of the family *Ephemeridae*—the March Brown is a well-known example—have their wings set upright and appear like tiny sailing boats as they glide downstream on the surface of the water.

In the family *Diptera*, of which the Black Gnat is an example, the

* Casting back and forth in the air, without allowing the line to settle on the water.

wings are positioned much like those of a house fly, while those of the *Perlidae* family have wings which overlap over the body and lie flat. The Stone fly is an example.

On account of these natural varieties man has produced scores, aye, hundreds of ingenious imitation flies, made with wool, feathers and the like, believing—or is it fearing?—that the discerning fish will have none but an exact replica of nature. This is a vast and hazardous subject which I intend to avoid, being content to comment that these coarse fish in which we are interested are not so fastidious and will take a fly that is merely a miniature chimney-sweep's brush or hackle fly, which has no wings at all. This being the case and as I find they cast so lightly and sit better on the water, I prefer hackle flies. In any case can a fish see the wings on a floating fly? I doubt it, and believe that their effect is on the angler only, which is in itself important. I know

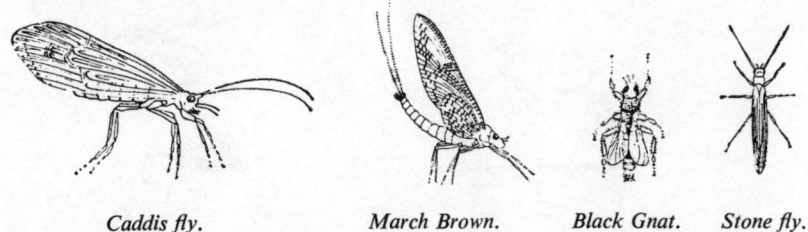

| Caddis fly. | March Brown. | Black Gnat. | Stone fly. |

I have omitted mention of scores of useful and killing patterns. Nevertheless, the reader will no doubt take fish on the flies I have mentioned (winged or otherwise) and will soon learn to collect flies and form his own opinion of their efficacy. This personal belief in the power of any given fly is important. Strangely enough, you are more likely to kill fish on a favourite fly than on any other. The reason is probably to be found in the fact that one fishes more carefully and assiduously with a proven favourite than with an unknown pattern. This fly business is probably the most complicated, controversial and angler-deceiving subject in the whole realm of fishing. I have a theory regarding floating flies which may be of interest if not comfort to any reader who has misgivings regarding the number of expensive artificials which it is *necessary* for him to buy and carry.

When a natural fly alights on the water its feet where they contact the surface skin must create what might be called a 'typical-food-pattern' from the fish's underwater point of view.

I believe that fish are naturally conditioned to this phenomenon, and that they associate it with the presence of floating natural food. I believe also that when the hackle points of a *lightly-dressed* high-floating dry-fly touch the water, they produce a similar effect. Is it then unreasonable to suppose that an artificial fly of the right size that is properly presented (lightly) will produce an effect so similar that fish will mistake it for the genuine article regardless of the above water appearance of the artificial?

The best of artificial flies are but poor imitations of their supposed natural counterparts and many of them which catch fish make no pretence to such a *raison d'être*. While trout fishermen may continue their unending arguments as between the 'one fly' and the 'exact imitation' (or purist) school which insists on the need for a host of flies to enable them to match the fly on the water at the time of fishing, those who ply the fly for coarse fish need have no scruples and can limit their expenditure in this direction to a minimum.

Having delivered myself of that idea, I will remind the novice of what to me is a comforting fact, namely, that bad presentation of a good fly is less productive than good presentation of a bad one—if

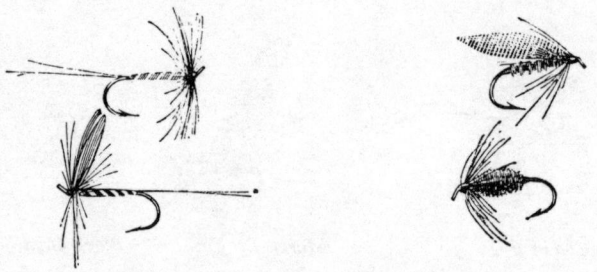

Hackle (above) and Winged Dry Flies.   Winged (above) and Hackle Wet Flies
There are innumerable varieties of both.

there are any bad flies! I have omitted to tell the reader that he can, should he so desire, learn to tie his own flies. I only once tied a fly and was neither enamoured of the process nor pleased with the result. The fact that it subsequently caught fish only heightened my belief that fish are less fastidious in the matter of flies than are many anglers, and I did not experience the special thrill which I was told to expect when I caught a fish on a fly of my own tying. However, the fact that I am satisfied with shop flies need only be a matter of indifference to my reader, who, if he is disposed to tie flies, can go further and fare much worse than studying the excellent treatise, *Fly-tying Principles and Practice*, by Major Gerald Burrard, D.S.O., and the *Fly Dresser's Guide*, in two volumes by John Veniard. However, that opens another avenue for argument so we pass on.

Having regard to dry flies, I should make the explanation that these flies are fished floating on the surface and are intended to simulate natural insects which may be floating on the skin of the water. That being so, when one is buying dry flies it is well to see that hackles (feather ruffle) are stiff and springy. Rigid hackles sit well up on the water and float well. You may find also that those flies which have

Also known traditionally as the dart, the dace is often seen only by the flash of its silvery flanks as it scurries away from the unwary footfall of the clumsy angler. Great sport can be had with fine fly fishing gear for the dace, which is a top feeder bobbling and ringing the surface in search of flies and other floating food. [*Photograph: W. J. Howes*]

The chub, *Squalius cephalus*. Note the strong 'shoulders' and large mouth of this doughty fighter. The fish shown here is a fine six-pounder from that big-fish river the Kennet. A sad note is struck when the caudal or tail fin is looked at closely. It has been badly worn and frayed. The damage was probably caused by periods of enforced confinement in too-small keepnets.

[*Photograph: W. J. Howes*]

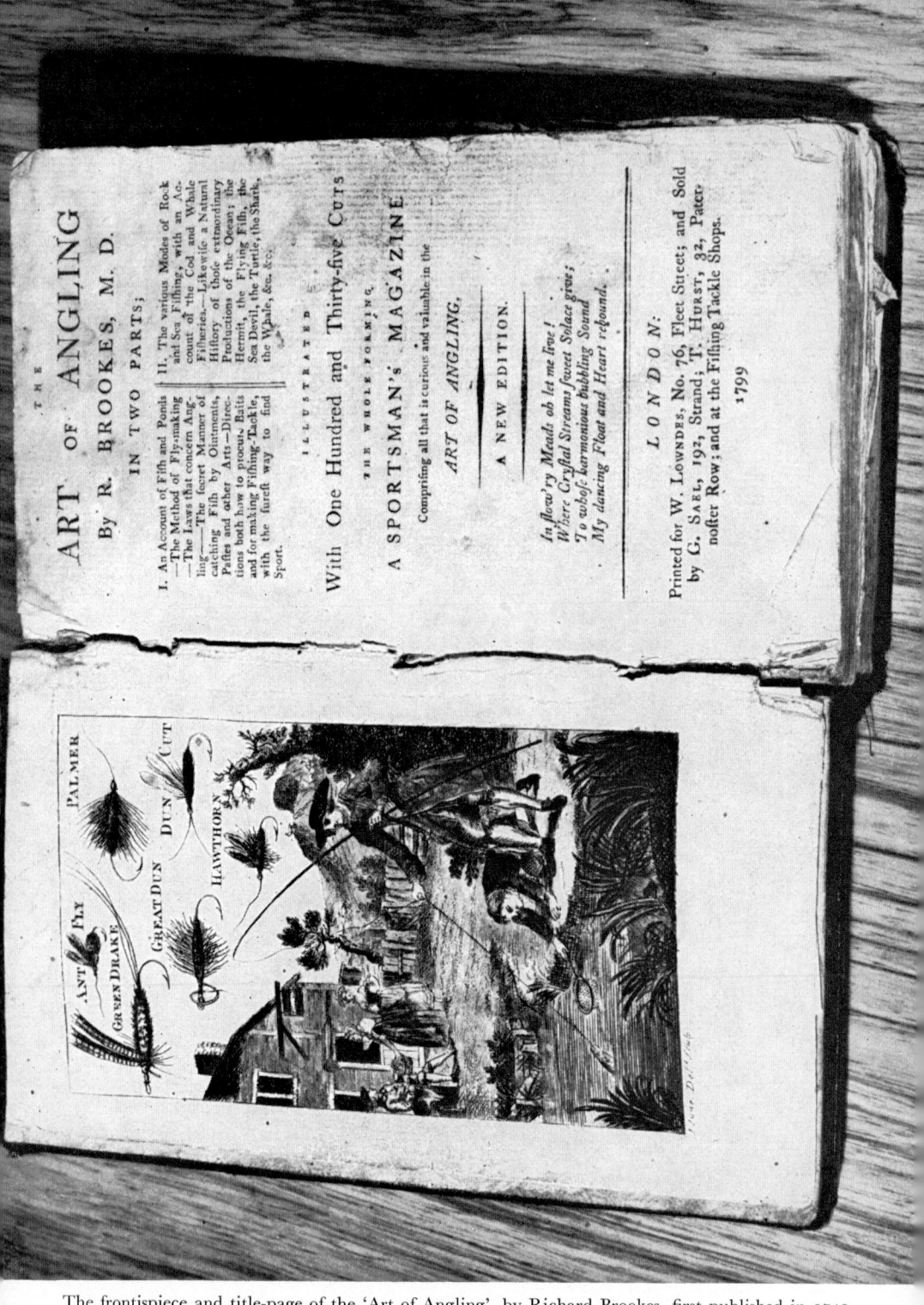

The frontispiece and title-page of the 'Art of Angling', by Richard Brookes, first published in 1740, its popularity was thereafter proven by the fact that it went through 14 editions. Midst a great deal of 'guestimation' on the part of its author about fish he had never seen, there are passages that show how chub and perch, and even trout and salmon, were caught plentifully in the Thames at Chelsea and Battersea, and how good the fishing was in the Thames tributaries such as the Wandle, now hardly more than an open sewer carrying no more than a pitiful trickle of polluted water. It proves that 200 years of industrial 'progress' have brought many of our fisheries to near extinction. It is now up to us to regain this by fighting pollution.

A fine specimen of the bronze or common bream, *Abramis brama*. This splendid fish, weighing over ten pounds, clearly shows the white tubercles on the head and shoulders, indicating the approach of the spawning season. *[Photograph: W. J. Howes]*

This photograph clearly shows the fine scale pattern of *Tinca tinca*, the tench. As in the previous photograph of the chub, the tail fin and ventral fins show wear and tear, probably due to small keepnets made from the cheaper – and harder – brands of nylon.

[Photograph: W. J. Howes]

The silvery and in some waters multitudinous bleak. Where it is abundant the bleak can be a godsend to match anglers and a curse to those seeking weightier quarry, unless it be perch or pike. For the livebait specialist the bleak can present an attractive, glittering sight for the lurking pike.

[*Photograph: W. J. Howes*]

The skin texture of the eel, *Anguilla anguilla*, is beautifully displayed here. Small eels can be the worst of nuisances to anglers seeking other, more sporting species, but this fish weighed 3 lb. 8 oz. and must have put up quite a struggle before being grassed.

[*Photograph: W. J. Howes*]

not too much hackle are more taking than an over-dressed fly in which the hackles are too thick and too long.

The reverse applies to wet flies, i.e. those which are fished under the surface and are presumably mistaken by the fish for nymphs or aquatic insects. It may not be altogether necessary, but I think it desirable to discuss these nymphs briefly. After her short breeding excursion in the air or among the reeds the female water-fly lays her eggs on the water and they sink to the bottom. Here they are concealed under the stones and among the weeds. Later a tiny grub emerges; this grows until the appointed time for it to emerge from the water to become a fly. These grubs are the nymphs to which I have referred.

To return, then, to these so-called flies, when a properly dressed (hackle) wet fly is submerged and worked by the stream and the angler, its *soft* hackles have a life-like movement which attracts fish. This movement would be much reduced if the hackles were stiff, as in the case of dry or surface flies. Incidentally, when you take a fish on either a dry or wet fly, the fly may look but a shadow of its former self. Don't worry; if it is a dry fly wash it, make a false cast or two to dry it, re-oil and continue to fish. Most authors mention, and some fly-fishermen use Amadou to dry their flies quickly. Amadou is a species of hard corky fungus which is beaten until it becomes soft and flexible. It then has the faculty of absorbing moisture instantly and is very useful as a fly drier, but is not an essential by any means. Amadou is a dry-fly fisher-

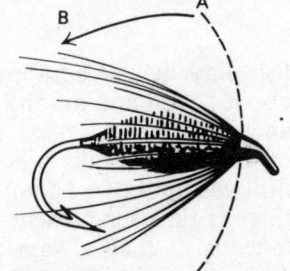

The action of the water oscillates the hackles between A and B.

man's refinement. If it is a wet fly wash off any slime to ensure the proper worling of the hackles and carry on. Dace, chub, etc., seem to like a well-chewed fly, and the same can be said of some trout. Strange?

As I shall have a few words to say later on wet fly-fishing for grayling it will be opportune here to give a short list of suitable wet flies for the capture of *Thymallus*.

Can I do better than quote T. E. Pritt's *Book of the Grayling* for two good wet-fly casts of three flies? Mr. F. M. Walbran advised: 'Tail fly, Red Tag; first dropper, Sea Swallow; second dropper, Waterhen, with body of peacock's quill, stripped and dyed yellow.' While Mr. Pritt himself said the following is 'a reliable cast any-where'; 'Tail fly, Crimson Tag; first dropper, Dark Needle; second dropper, Fog Black.'

These recommendations introduce yet another difference between dry and wet-fly fishing. When dry-fly fishing, only one fly tied to the tail of the cast is used. When fishing the wet fly two or more flies may be used on the same cast. Personally, I never use more than two flies, one at the tail and one 'dropper' about a yard up the cast. By the way, the term 'dropper' is given to any fly tied above the tail fly on the same cast. The reasons for my using only one 'dropper' are few, but, I think, good. First, if one uses a number of droppers, there is a tendency, particularly in a cross wind, for one or other of the dropper flies to get caught up in the top of the rod as they sweep forward from the back cast toward the water.... 'Bad casting,' says the expert; may be, say I, but there are far more bad than good exponents of the art of casting, and as I am no paragon, so I avoid trouble of this kind as far as possible. There is, however, a second reason for my using only one dropper, which is even more potent.

Let us consider the predicament of an angler who hooks a fish on, say, the third dropper in the vicinity of submerged weeds. As the

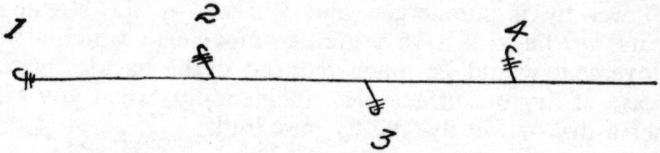

fish plays it will be apparent that the other three hooks are careering about round and among the weeds, with every possibility of one taking anchor in them—need I say more? How often, moreover, has one of the naked hooks become entangled in the mesh of the net when the fish was about to be landed—the result is disastrous. Then, of course, there is the ever-present likelihood of hooking two or more fish simul-taneously—they always want to go in opposite directions, and if one escapes it will almost certainly be the larger of the two. I may be gloomy on this point, but one 'dropper' is enough for me, and I only want to catch one fish at a time. The reader may well wonder what benefit one sees in even one dropper. Well, it does give the angler the opportunity to offer two different flies at the same time. There are occasions when the fish seem to show preference for one over the other. This is the signal to change the one which is least taking. In point of fact even this may be a fallacy, for I find that my fish almost invariably go for the tail fly. This is understandable enough when we remember that the tail fly is as a rule the first fly which comes to the fish's notice. Even if this is not so, it is not hanging out with a length of the main cast on either side of it. However, use as many droppers up to three as you feel inclined. There is nothing unsporting about a multiple cast; it brings its own limitations and disadvantages, as I have tried to show.

Before leaving this subject of wet flies I should say that, thanks mainly to the efforts of the late G. E. M. Skues, really excellent imita-tions of the various nymphs are now obtainable, and very killing they are. Mr. Skues experimented long and carefully, examining the stomach contents of hundreds of fish, emptying them into a white enamel bowl containing a little water, the better to study their form and colour. With consummate skill he then tied astonishingly natural imitations of these sub-aquatic insects, upon which fish sometimes feed avidly as they make their way to the surface of the water to become flies.* There are also many *ersatz* nymphs offered by tackle dealers. Wool, fur and feather concoctions the like of which is not to be found under, on or over the earth—and they catch fish! There I am again, running my head into a barrage from that very worthy and quite strong school of anglers who stickle for exactitude in imitation of

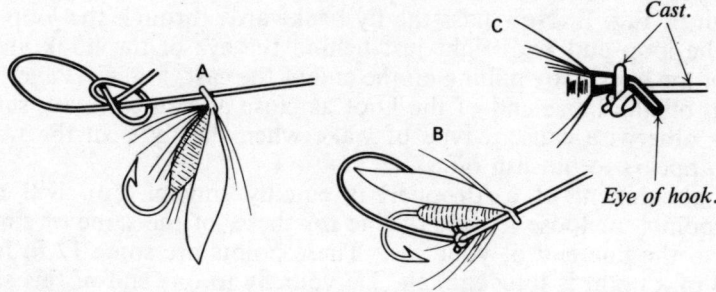

the natural insect. However, while it may not be diplomatic, it is I think, comparatively safe to state what one has found in practice. Yes, you may safely tie the nymphs to your cast in place of wet flies— a change, you will find, is often better than a rest. But a rest is good also—don't thrash the same water by the hour.

Take one of the large flies like a May-fly where comparison with the natural is both easy and odious, and you will see how crude most

* Writing to me on the 21st November, 1947, Mr. Skues said:

For grayling flies I have never known any more deadly than Landrail and Hare's Ear dressed thus:

Hook—No. 2 down eyed, round bend.
Tying silk—Hot orange.
Wing—Landrail—double
Hackle—body deep red cock.
Hackle—front—ditto.
Body—Hare's ear, dark.
Rib—Fine gold wire.
It is generally irresistible (also first-rate for trout).
Next to it I would put a hackle fly dressed thus:
Hook—No. 2 round bend.
Tying silk—Crimson.
Hackle (front only)—Dark blue hen.
Body—Peacock's herl dyed claret with the tying silk wound round it.
With this I have caught every grayling in a shoal of six, all pounders, on the Nadder.
For winging the Landrail and Hare's ear I straighten the Landrail primary feathers' plumage, cut or tear it from the quill—divide it—lay one half on the other, fold the doubled feather in the middle and tie it down on edge so that the wings split and the fly cocks. The front hackle is wound last. I have more than once had over two dozen of a shoal of Nadder grayling from one spot.

I am no fly-tyer and prefer to buy the handwork of professional tyers—but for those who are minded to produce their own flies, these two recipes should prove more than worth the trouble of tying flies which are so highly recommended by an authority of international repute.

of the feather reproductions of flies really are. Yet trout, not to speak of 'coarse' fish, will accept these feather makeshifts with wool bodies, etc., for the real thing—and this, mark you, at times when there is an abundance of the natural insects available. But I must go on to the more practical.

To attach the tail fly push the end of the cast through the eye of the fly and allow the fly to slide up the line a few inches, Fig. A. Making a running loop with the free end, open it enough to allow the fly to pass through it, Fig. B. Now pass the fly backwards through the loop and draw the loop and knot tight just behind the eye of the hook and in front of the hackle, by pulling on the end of the cast, Fig. C. (Page 115.)

Trim off the loose end of the knot as close as you can with safety. It may otherwise cause a type of wake when the fly is in the water, which appears to put fish off.

The attachment of a 'dropper' is equally simple. You will need some 'points' or loose lengths of line for these, of the same or similar gauge to the fine end of your cast. These points are some 12 in long, a third of a point is long enough. Tie your fly to one end of this short piece of line as described and illustrated p. 117, then tie the other

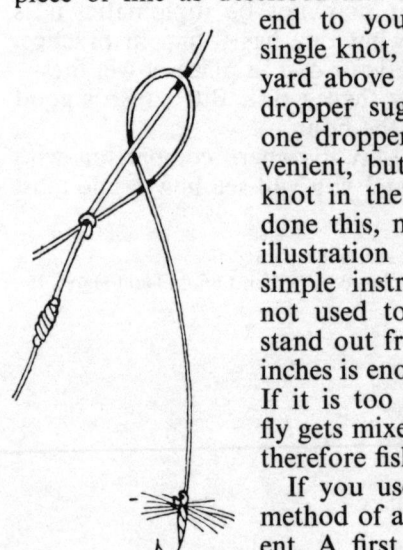

end to your cast with an ordinary overhand single knot, just above a knot in the cast, about a yard above the point fly, if you adopt my single dropper suggestion. Should you use more than one dropper, space them along the cast as convenient, but each must be immediately above a knot in the cast to keep it in position. Having done this, make a half-hitch as indicated in this illustration and draw it tight. Providing these simple instructions are followed and you have not used too long a piece of line, the fly will stand out from the main cast as it should. Three inches is enough for the projection of the dropper. If it is too long, you will find that the dropper fly gets mixed up with the main cast, and will not therefore fish properly.

If you use a one-piece tapered-nylon-cast, the method of attaching a dropper to it is very different. A first glance at the illustration on p. 117 may leave you with a feeling of despair; but look again and read the explanatory caption. It is really quite simple.

These casts being in one gently tapered piece, there is no anchorage for a dropper to be fixed in the way described above. To obviate this difficulty a loop is made in the cast itself at the desired point, to which the dropper can be hitched.

The loop illustrated and described p. 117 is known as the 'Blood Dropper Loop,' and is one of the strongest methods of making a dropper attachment in a one piece cast. Oh! and I should say in passing, that it is wise to make these loops at home, on a rainy night, at least until you can tie them with confidence at the riverside.

Wet flies, dry flies, winged flies and hackle flies, nymphs, knots, hitches and what not may be now be whirling round in your mind. Have no care, they will sort themselves out in no time. Few flies and simple knots is the motto.

You will require one or two other little gadgets which I had better mention now before making some short notes on actual fly-fishing. A pair of fine nail scissors for cutting line, a pin or needle, to clear the

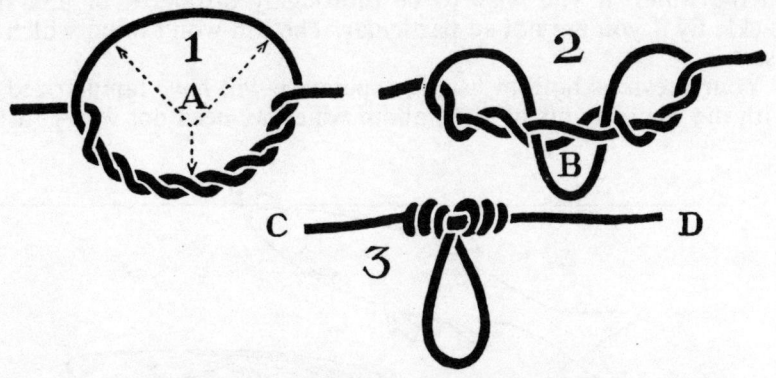

THE 'HARNESS DROPPER' OR 'BLOOD DROPPER' LOOP.

1. Loop the cast at the required point and make a series of consecutive overhand turns round the circle with the loose ends of the cast as illustrated. Some authorities say up to ten turns, i.e. five on each side, but six are enough.

2. Turn down the centre of the loop A and pass it between and through the centre of the coils as shown, leaving three coils on each side; being careful to use sufficient of the cast when making this loop-knot, to allow for considerable shortenings of the legs of the loop when working the coils close together.

3. Put a pencil through the loop B to keep it open while teasing the coils together, then draw taut on the two ends C and D.

eye of a fly which may have been closed by a speck of varnish and to help in untying knots when changing a fly, a disgorger, a cast damper, box for flies and a pair of tweezers to get the flies out with, a landing net, a pair of waders, a tin of line-floating grease and a creel or bag for your fish, and I think you have everything that will give you a good start. Just one word about the landing net. This should be of the collapsible kind, with a knuckle joint and a hook on the handle which will either clip on your belt or into a ring on your fishing bag while you are fishing—because you must have both hands free. At the same time it will be obvious that this necessary piece of equipment should be as neat and out of your way as possible while being instantly accessible. If you are right-handed, carry the net on your right and *vice versa*.

Dace.—We started out with the idea of fly-fishing for dace, roach, rudd, chub and grayling. Many and, I hope, useful deviations have intervened, but we can now return to these sprightly and free-rising fish, our casting learned and our equipment complete. The idea is to present a dry (i.e. floating) artificial fly to them in such a way as to deceive the fish into believing that our lure is a natural insect floating downstream for their special benefit.

Arrived at the waterside set up your rod without haste, taking care that the rod rings are perfectly aligned, or you will have trouble when casting. Thread the line, and attach a cast (slightly shorter than the length of the rod). Now tie on a dry fly in imitation of the 'natural' on the water, if you wish to be thoroughly orthodox, or any small hackle fly if you are not so particular. The fish won't mind which you use.

Your previous bottom fishing experience will have familiarized you with the whereabouts of dace, about which we need not worry further.

The fish rises and sucks in the fly, leaving a widening ring on the surface.

Let us assume that our trial trip takes place on a warm summer evening. We arrive at the water to find the surface dimpled with the rings of rising fish. Now, fish always face upstream, for the very sufficient reason that they cannot breathe if the water enters their gills from behind. This being so, keep behind, i.e. downstream, of the fish you aim to catch. Take every precaution to avoid showing yourself. All the cunning you have been accustomed to employ when bait-fishing, and some more will be needed if you are not to frighten the fish which are on the look-out for flies near the surface.

You are about to 'fish the rise,' that is, to cast to fish which you actually see rising.

This diagram shows what happens. The fish sees a fly floating toward it, rises to the surface, sucks in the fly, then descends either to wait for more or moves on in search of other flies. When a fish breaks the surface to take a fly it produces a ring known as a rise. If as in the present case the fish are rising to the natural fly, your difficulties are much reduced. Take up a position below the nearest rising fish and cast to it upstream and across. Your instructor will have shown you how to work your line out at the waterside by making a number of false casts, at the same time drawing line from the reel and feeding a little more out with each sweep of the rod back and forth—until you have sufficient line in the air to 'cover' (reach just beyond) the fish. Should there be no rise in progress you would cast similarly, but you would have to 'fish the water,' i.e. cast in likely places, in the hope that a fish might rise to take your offering.

Taking all possible cover cast up and across. Casting in the way illustrated, your line and cast will lie at an angle away from the fish, and is therefore less likely to be seen, while the fly if properly placed about a foot above the rising fish, will alight and glide quietly over it with every chance of being taken,

The take of a dace is as rapid on the surface as when it takes hemp seed fished in mid-water, and he is a good man who can hook one in five. Sometimes it is possible to see dace rising to your fly—then is

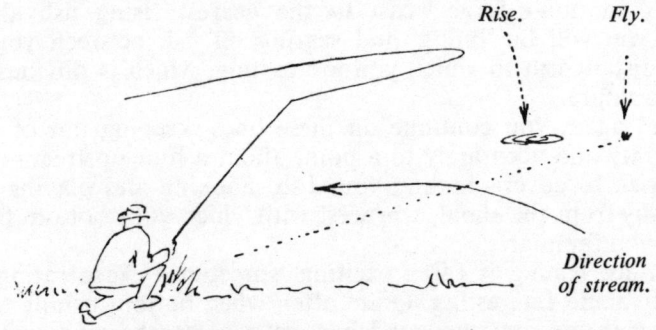

Taking all possible cover cast up and across.

the time to strike; it is wellnigh impossible to strike too quickly when fishing for *Leuciscus leuciscus.*

This fact tends to cause the angler to strike too violently in his effort to be quick. Study to avoid this. As the fly approaches the fish in its downstream journey, take in any slack line with the left hand and ensure a taut line. Alternatively, hold the line steady and raise the rod point slightly to produce the same effect.

There! The fish has taken your fly—flex your right wrist smartly, at the same time drawing on the line which is held between the thumb and finger of the left hand. This aids the process of striking, without producing the violent result which is sometimes the cause of a small fish hurtling up into the trees behind you, until you master this striking business. Instead of holding a loop of line in the left hand while the fly is actually fishing, some anglers tuck in under the fingers of the casting hand to ensure striking on a tight line. However, you will develop a technique of line control and need not worry unduly about it. You are already accustomed to handling fishing tackle, which is a great advantage. In any case, if you are in difficulty, your 'old hand' friend will show you what it is so difficult to describe.

Being below your fish when you struck, the effect is to draw the hook into its mouth, and it is securely hooked. Play it quickly away from the others or its antics will 'put them down.' I need hardly explain that phrase. Good! you have caught your first fish on an artificial fly—now repeat the process as often as you can. The fish are cruising upstream, rising as they go; follow them stealthily.

As I said earlier, get as near to your quarry as possible to avoid the disadvantages of long casting. You will, of course, find that proximity to the fish varies with conditions. If there is plenty of cover available your approach can be much nearer than if the banks are open. If you are wading the shallows for dace, wade very slowly and do not cast from directly behind a fish or the cast will fall right over or alongside it. This, which is known as 'lining' a fish, may deter even a hungry dace from taking the fly. Adopt the same diagonal cast as you would from the bank, your object being to show the fish the fly only. And don't forget, cast to the nearest rising fish always, otherwise you will be 'lining' and scaring off fish between you and the more distant fish to which you are casting, which is obviously an absurd procedure.

Ever and again you continue on these lines, keeping out of sight, casting lightly and accurately to a point about a foot upstream of the fish you wish to cover—finding your fish, hooking and playing them quickly away from the shoal, a process with which your bottom fishing. has made you familiar.

This surface fishing is often exciting, sometimes exasperating, but always active and interesting. Quite often when bottom fishing tactics are hopeless in the summer, good bags of dace can be made with the dry fly. Sometimes in deeper glides, more often in the faster shallows, you will find them, sometimes while wading, sometimes fishing from the bank or a boat, but always casting up and across. Remember that it is the fly in or on the water which catches fish. Don't waste time fiddling, changing the fly, etc. False cast frequently to keep the fly dry. You will soon get to the stage when you can feel whether your fly is going to land nicely; if you are in doubt, keep it in the air and re-cast; dud casting scares fish. It's all interesting and will hold you once you set out on this never-ending path of dry-fly fishing. There is nothing exclusive or mysterious about it—fly-fishing is for your enjoyment; try it. Don't get worried about the hundreds of superfluous flies which are available. Select two or three which you find effective and stick to them. Don't fall into the trap of trying to hurl vast lengths of line; work to control a short line perfectly and to efface yourself as far as possible. Always be prepared to try anything once and don't be disappointed when you miss fish after fish.

Roach and Rudd—Roach may be approached much in the same manner as dace, but are not such free risers to the artificial fly. Of all the fish which may be taken on the dry fly, roach are probably the least productive of sport. Nevertheless, should you find them rising, you are in for good fun. You will find shallow water more profitable than deeper swims; their rise is more leisurely than that of dace, but a prompt strike is necessary. Roach, like dace, are not fastidious in their choice of fly.

Rudd are free risers and large catches can be made on the dry fly in waters where they abound. I remember well a July evening at Slapton Lea when an angler, fishing the evening rise with a Coachman, covered the bottom of his boat with rudd of an average weight of one pound in the space of two hours. Why he killed these fish remains a mystery and a sorry memory to me, but the fact remains that his performance demonstrates the possibilities which these fish offer to the dry-fly fisher.

Chub—When Chevin is the dry-flyman's quarry I feel safe in saying that unobserved approach is the most telling factor. No matter how well you may present your fly or how accurately, if the fish see you your chances are nil. The prettiest and most successful fly-fishing for chub is in my view from the bows of a light canoe propelled slowly upstream by a friend. Your approach is quiet and you are enabled to cast under the overhanging branches of trees so beloved by these fish, not without difficulty, but with much less difficulty than is often the case if you approach them from the bank. Early morning and evening are the best times, especially the latter. They are good takers when in the mood, and take slowly. You must therefore forget the rapid strike needed for dace and allow the chub to close its big white lips over your fly before you strike, or you will miss every fish you rise. It is not essential, but a small length of washleather tied into the tail of your fly is sometimes an advantage. Alternatively you can hook a maggot on the bend of the hook with good results. Flies adorned with these washleather tail attachments are obtainable everywhere. Having risen your chub and hooked him, look out for squalls. The fish will plunge instantly, and believe me, move strongly to any underwater snag near hand. Pressure to prevent this is essential if you are to keep your fish. This being the case, you will be well advised not to fish finer than 4 lb. b.s. at the end of your cast. Strangely enough, light casting is not altogether an advantage when fishing for chub. To bang a fly down near them appears to arouse the fish's curiosity. They will even turn round and seize a fly which lands behind them—providing they have no inkling of the angler's presence. This is probably due to the fact that chub are accustomed to the plop of falling insects from the trees and bushes under which they lurk. I think the suggestion is quite feasible, don't you? You will not as a rule find chub actually rising, but 'fishing the water,' that is casting in likely places under overhanging branches and bushes, will prove effective.

Grayling—Those fishes of which I have written are in my view useful only as sport givers. Grayling, on the other hand, are first-rate food fish. Some people do not think so, but tastes vary, for do not some people prefer tinned to fresh salmon?

I have contented myself with treating dace, etc., as subjects for the dry fly only. Grayling can and should be caught as circumstance demands by both dry and wet fly methods. These notes will therefore deal with both forms of fishing. Grayling meet with not a little abuse from those who, for some reason beyond my dull wit, are unable to think in terms other than trout. Their disparagings need not however affect us. Enough to remember that having caught your grayling you have secured food which is deemed by many to excel that of trout flesh, and that the catching will provide endless interest and excitement. What more can an angler desire? There are fundamental differences between the approach of grayling with a dry fly and that applied to other fish to which I have referred.

In the case of dace, roach, etc., the fish you seek are near the surface on the look-out for floating food. This gives them a narrow surface

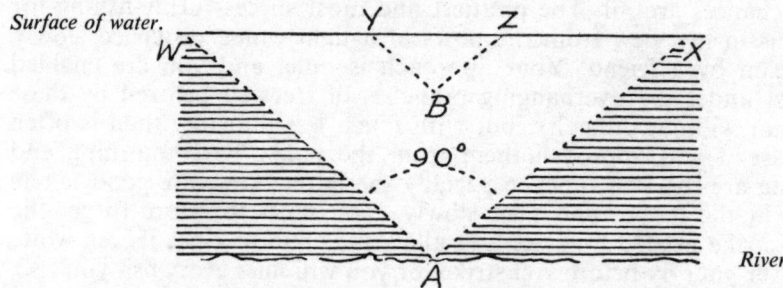

window. Grayling, however, lie on or near the bottom and accordingly have a much wider surface window. This chapter can only be regarded as some notes on a vast subject about which many volumes have been written, nevertheless a brief explanation of a fish's surface window is necessary to a proper understanding of both dry and wet fishing for *Thymallus*. Full and excellent data regarding this matter will be found in E. W. Harding's *The Flyfisher and the Trout's point of view*. For our present purpose this simple diagram will clarify the general principle involved.

Thus, if a fish lying at A has a surface vision of WX, a fish stationed at B will have the much restricted surface vision or 'window' YZ. I advised casting up and across for the other fishes, placing the fly about one foot ahead of the rising fish. For grayling it has been found much more effective to cast down and across allowing sufficient slack line to enable the fly to drift toward the rising fish without 'drag'—nasty word about which I shall have more to say at the end of this chapter— it indicates a condition of affairs which is fatal to success when fly-fishing, but we must not involve the present issue. I am grateful for this valuable and practical advice to cast down and across, to one of the best authorities on the subject, the late W. Carter Platts, author of that splendid work *Grayling Fishing*, who to confirm his own findings sought the opinion of another authority, the late Roger Woolley, author of *Modern Trout Fly Dressing*, which volume you may study with profit and interest should you elect to tie your own flies.

These men of unusual experience agree completely that as grayling lie low in the water, it is better to cast down and across stream to them. Mr. Carter Platts published Mr. Woolley's reply to his inquiry in the book to which I have referred. I quote an assuring extract as follows:

I *know* that I am right in fishing the dry fly for grayling downstream, and my knowledge is born, not of ingenious theories, but of actual and lengthy experience. At the same time, what I consider to be the chief reason for success of the method I so strongly advocate is that, fished in this way, the fly comes first to the notice of the fish, and is taken practically before the gut comes into view. For such keen-sighted fish as grayling this is, to me, an important point.

You and I can have no better advisers and I have found this advice well worthy of the passing on. Another marked difference when fishing the dry fly for *Thymallus* is the method of striking. As I have said these fish lie low in the water watching. On seeing an approaching fly, they dart to the surface, take it, and descend to their station at the bottom as rapidly as they rose. This procedure on the part of the fish calls for the slightest pause between the take and the strike, because if the hook is anchored as the fish heads downward, it will probably take hold in a firm portion of the mouth, with obvious advantage. In addition, as you are fishing downstream, your strike tends to snatch the fly away from the fish. If it is too quick you may strike before the fish has actually taken hold. This is a problem which can only be solved in practice; with experience your timing will become increasingly accurate. Strike your grayling firmly, you will lose less fish by so doing. I have more to say regarding this in the chapter on bottom fishing for grayling which follows later. One other point, do not fish a smaller hook than 00, a number 1 is even more likely to hook well, and hooks of good wide gape are advisable.

Having hooked a grayling, you will find that it fights in an unusual and characteristic way. The smaller fish quite frequently leap from the water. When this occurs one is continually advised to lower the rod point. This is presumably to avoid the disastrous possibility of the fish falling with its weight on the tight line. I do not subscribe to this theory, preferring to add a little pressure when a fish jumps, with the idea of keeping the fish's head facing in line with the cast, which I find an even surer way to prevent a break. Maybe my excitement gets the better of my ability to think of dipping my rod when the fish leaps and that I have so far been merely lucky. The reverse view to mine is so prevalent that there may be more in it than I have credited. Try both, then model your future procedure on the results you find. In any case for the comparatively small fish to which I refer, I am satisfied that a tight line is better, despite the fact that the cast for grayling should taper to 3 lb. b.s.

and is not therefore designed to withstand severe jerking or shock. The larger fish do not often leave the water, but will fight with that peculiar dogged stubbornness typical of grayling. They shake their heads, roll and tug like no other freshwater fish. Keep your rod point up and do not give line save to a really good fish; a hooked grayling should be brought to the net as quickly as possible. I am not recommending skull-hauling. What I wish rather to convey is the need for avoiding un-necessary disturbance, by allowing comparatively small fish to run about all over the water from which you hope to collect others. Be firm therefore without bullying the fish unduly. You can ply the dry fly for grayling with success quite late in the season after trout fishing has closed, and indeed to the close of the coarse fishing season, on suitably clement days. But—whenever you fish for *Thymallus* you will find them capricious, there is nothing certain about their willingness to take a fly. This is probably one of the charms of fishing for them. You may take few or no fish, you may kill a number in the first hour of your fishing, and none thereafter or *vice versa,* But one thing is certain, you will catch no fish unless your fly is on the water, so keep it fishing! This may appear to be an unnecessary injunction, but think of the causes for diversion—lighting one's pipe, changing one's fly, eating one's sandwiches, chatting with a passing angler, etc., etc., etc. Let me not encourage fanatical flogging of the water. Nevertheless it is surpris-ing what a big percentage of a fishing outing is frittered away by doing anything but fishing.

Try one of the flies I have recommended or a local favourite, they vary from river to river. This fly selection matter leaves me with one suggestion to make. Keep your ideas on flies as simple as you can, and your determination to present them well as rigid as you like.

It is a pleasant autumn day and we know the whereabouts of one or two shoals of grayling. Let us fish for them with the wet fly. Until now, our line, cast and fly have floated on the water and it has been possible to see the fish take the feather deception. Now the fly must sink below the surface and the angler must rely on touch to know when a fish has taken it. The cast must sink with the fly, but the line itself should still be greased and float. The reason for this needs little explanation. If the line sinks it is wellnigh impossible to strike effectively. I can assure the reader that he will find it difficult enough to hook fish when wet-fly fishing even when every precaution is taken to ensure that all aids to quick striking have been maintained. Soak the cast well and 'put up' a Crimson Tag, on the tail. Then tie a single dropper carrying a Dark Needle, about a yard up the cast, in the manner described earlier. Now you are ready to fish. The idea is to offer the grayling something which it will mistake for a sub-aquatic insect. It is a matter of import-ance to see that the hackles of your wet flies are soft and lie slightly back. This ensures their smooth passage through the water, without leaving a very tiny but alarming wake, such as would be made by a stiff and upright hackle or vertical perky wings. Remember also that you must tie the knot to your flies with every care to make them neat, removing any projecting end close to the knot. Clumsy knots and loose ends of line produce the same sort of wake as a wrongly shaped fly, while the lure hangs in the stream or is worked by the angler. Wet flies are never greased and rely much for their attractiveness on the life-like movement of the soft hackles under water. You will note one or two differences between your wet and dry flies. The eye of a wet fly is turned down and that of a dry fly is as a rule turned up. The down-turned eye of a wet fly doubtless acts as a miniature diving vane and is at the same time a passable representation of the head of a natural insect. The upturned eye of a dry fly enables the angler to tie his cast knot out of the way and to arrange the short end of the knot neatly among the upper hackles where it will have no ill effects. Then there is the semi-streamline of a wet fly either winged or hackled as against the upright sprightly setting of the wings and hackles of many dry flies. Use very few flies and you won't get muddled. But we must get back to the fishing.

I think it is generally agreed that to cast directly across stream or across and slightly down is better when fishing wet fly. It is certainly much simpler than fishing wet upstream, watching like a hawk for any halt in the downstream passage of the line—or straining to catch the flash of a turning fish to indicate an offer. Some there are who are clevèr enough for this and sufficiently energetic, but the writer seldom emulates them. It is undoubtedly a most killing method to fish the wet fly upstream on a short line; and where trout are the quarry, the effort entailed is merited. Having cast across you allow your flies to swing round in the stream until they hang immediately below you. Quite often you will find that the current will cause your floating line to belly downstream as the flies sweep along. This, if allowed to continue, will cause them to drag diagonally and unnaturally across the river, instead of swimming down naturally with the flow. To obviate this, switch your rod tip upstream, lifting the line off the water and reversing the belly in it, producing an up-stream belly. You will soon get accustomed to this 'line-mending' trick which is so necessary to success.

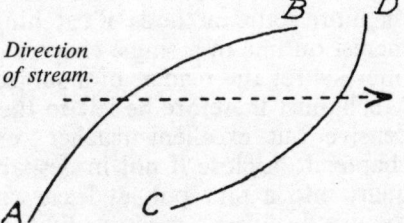

Direction of stream.

AB is the curve the line should take—not CD. Re-mend the line as necessary to ensure the natural downstream run of flies—they must not travel across the stream. You may see a fish turn just beneath the surface to take your lure—strike smartly when this happens. More often however you will feel a sharp pluck, almost a tug at the rod top, flex your wrist instantly and the fish may be yours. This striking of fish on wet fly fished downstream cannot be learned from a book, only practice can acquire it, and it is wellnigh impossible if you give way to throwing too long a line. Unlike the momentary pause when striking the dry fly—speed is the essence of the contract when you are fishing wet. If the flies cover their allotted span, i.e. if you 'fish out the cast' without a rise or take, work them slightly by raising and dipping your rod point an inch or two before you re-cast. This will cause the soft hackles to open and close in an attractive and lifelike manner. The trick sometimes deceives a fish which you would otherwise miss. Alternatively you can retrieve the line in a series of short jerks taking it in the left hand before casting again. This sometimes induces a take. If all these tactics fail, advance a yard or so and go through the same process, searching the water yard by yard until you find a taking fish. When possible it is a marked advantage to wade quietly down the centre of the stream, casting right and left alternatively, thus covering the whole water thoroughly. Some people call this 'chuck and chance it', others know the method as 'fishing the water.' Call it what you will it is good fun and produces fish, interest and exercise.

In my view it is more difficult to take fish on the wet than the dry fly, so much depends on instictive speed in making contact, without the aid of sight. Normally your wet flies will fish but a few inches below the surface. This depends much on the strength of the stream and the angle at which your line lies in relation to the current. If you are not successful with ordinary wet flies or nymphs, put in a leaded fly or two which will search the deeper water. In other words take your lures a little nearer to the quarry.

The foregoing it is hoped will set you on rightlines. As your ability and interest grow side by side, you will doubtless turn to the rich, vast and varied literature which has grown up round this intricate and sometimes bewildering subject. There is probably a larger library on fly fishing than that connected with any other sport. My own deficiencies and omissions may therefore be overcome quite easily by those of an inquiring turn of mind. Taking coarse fishes on the dry or wet fly is sport of unsurpassed interest and variety, and it is active as opposed to the more static methods of catching them. It is only possible to give the merest outline in a single chapter of a book, which has so many other interests for the reader, of a subject with so many facets as fly fishing. Much must therefore be left to the reader's common sense and the expensive but excellent teacher—experience. Let me then draw this chapter to a close if not in despair at my abortive attempt to cram a quart into a pint pot, at least with a final effort to mitigate one of the dry-fly fisher's greatest difficulties—Drag. 'Drag' which is fatal to success may be caused by one of three influences; the action of the stream or wind on the line and cast or by a sinking line. Its effect is to cause the fly to furrow across the water in a quite unnatural way. While one fish in five hundred will take a dragging fly, the others avoid it like the plague.

Let us then consider that most frequent and virulent cause of drag— the action of the stream on the line and cast. The proposition is to cover a fish rising where the dot appears in Fig. 1. It is lying in comparatively

quiet water, beyond the faster central flow of the stream. The cast is
made diagonally upstream. Now see
Fig. 2. No sooner have the line and
cast alighted than the fast water
takes charge of the line and bellies it
as shown, dragging the fly uncere-
moniously from A to B and away
goes the fish. The simple cure is of
course to go downstream, and cross
to the opposite bank where a straightforward cast would be possible, but
this must be ruled out. Your instructor may be one of those wizard
casters who can switch a sharply
curved hook cast to defeat this
trouble; if so you are fortunate and
he is a better man than I am. Being
unable to perform this feat I will
refrain from describing it, but it is
the ideal method. What then re-

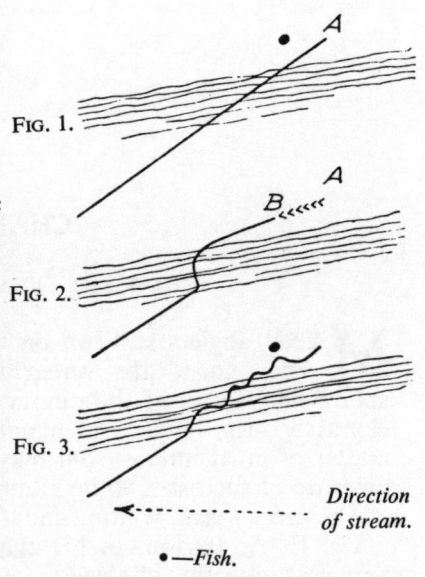

Direction of stream.

•—Fish.

mains? It is fairly simple. Do you remember when you were first learning to cast? How often the line, instead of landing neatly and arrow
straight, fell on the water in a snake-like wriggle. That was because as
you brought your rod forward to complete the cast, you hesitated for
a moment, halting the line and cast just before they came to rest on the
water, instead of following sweetly through. You have got out of that
now, but you must learn to do it at will, to help you to overcome this
arch difficulty. See Fig. 3. Work out a little more line than is needed
to cover the fish with a straight cast, then deliver it as usual until the
last moment—check the rod momentarily, then follow through and
quite a distance before the fly is dragged. There are many other
situations in which drag may be set up by the stream but the same
medicine is indicated. If even this is hopeless try to maneouvre into
a position from which you can place the fly almost into the fish's
mouth direct, so that it has no need to travel and may be taken before
it has time to drag. It works sometimes if you are accurate and lucky.
Drag caused by the wind on otherwise smoothly flowing water can be
checked by mending the line against the wind in the way indicated
earlier for wet-fly fishing. As to drag resulting from a sunken line, wind
in, dry and re-grease your line—that is the only cure.

CHAPTER XIV

CHUB THE 'FEARFULLEST OF FISH'

MANY anglers still fish on what I call the 'hit-or-miss' principle. They go to the waterside equipped with everything save a sound knowledge of the quarry they seek. Each species has peculiar characteristics, habits and haunts, knowledge of which is not only a matter of great interest, but may almost be called a necessity if a full measure of success is to be attained by the fisherman.

The great Izaak Walton said, 'A chub is the fearfullest of fishes.'

Dr. E. A. Barton, in his charming book *Running Waters* (Seeley Services), says this of chevin:

> In the sultry August days when all fishing is at its worst . . . then as a not unsporting substitute does the simple chub come into its own. Simple, did I say? Had the trout one-half the intelligence of the chub there would be fewer trout anglers and smaller bags. For the eyesight of the chub seems telescopic, and its lateral line appears to have greater sensitiveness to vibration than that of a trout . . . That the chub is impossible to eat is a side issue, and a matter of no moment when compared with the challenging competition of wits in its capture, and I have tasted chub no whit worse than some stock-bred trout.

With large scales shading from brown on the back to white beneath, chub are handsome fish built on powerful lines. Their shoulders and forepart are plump. The size of the scales and mouth, together with the fact that the anal fin is always convex, make it difficult to confuse a small chub with a large dace which has a much smaller mouth and scales and a concave anal fin. Yet there have been cases where prizes have been awarded for the capture of a large dace which, if properly identified, was a small chub.

The younger fish are gregarious, while the older and larger chub are often solitary. They prefer running water, but will live in lakes. Chub are predatory and vegetarian, but with age the predatory instinct increases.

They are most fascinating fish, a strange mixture of shy cunning and reckless gluttony. Their reputation for wariness is well deserved, yet they may at times be taken on the coarsest tackle. The shadow of a man or even his slender rod will cause chub to sink from sight into the depths as silently and surely as dew will disappear before the sun.

Even a footfall on the bank is sufficient to produce the same effect. No dart or scurry, they just sink from sight. Chub anglers must be stealthy and keen-eyed hunters as well as fishermen.

Gormandizers, yet they will often disdain the dainty offerings of the angler, subjecting the cravings of their hunger to their natural caution. Some who fish for salmon and trout regard chub as worthless brutes which, after making one determined dash for liberty, will cave in and wallow to the net in spiritless fashion. Such assertions I deny. A chub in good condition will give worthy battle to any angler who takes it on suitably fine tackle. Let detractors of the fighting qualities of chub angle one of four or five pounds weight on 3 or 4 lb b.s. line in heavy water thirty to forty yards from the boat, then they will revise their estimate of the prowess of these fish. While admitting the thieving propensities of chub, which will seize flies cast for the nobler kind, in their defence it must be said there is a world of misunderstanding in the 'game-fisher's' criticism of their fight.

Happily for the great army of 'coarse anglers,' chub are widely distributed in British waters south of the Forth, except in Cornwall, West Wales and Ireland. The origin of their name is obscure, but there is little doubt it is closely connected with the word chubby (round-faced or plump), and it is peculiar that in various languages the name of these fish has reference to the size or shape of the head.

A glance at the big fish records will leave the angler in no doubt as to the whereabouts of the élite chub. Over 50 per cent of the 'grandfathers' made their fatal mistake in the Hampshire Avon. The largest recorded chub from the river scaled 8 lb. 4 oz. But the fish that held the record until 1969, when the Record Committee declared the record open, was a grand 10 lb. 8 oz. chub, taken from the River Annan by Dr. J. A. Cameron in July 1955. The minimum qualifying weight for record claims was set at 7 lb. 8 oz. This criterion was missed by just 1 oz. by a specimen from the River Ure, at Ripon, Yorks, which when weighed by its captor, Stanley Pope, took the scales down to 7 lb. 7 oz. It happened in the first week of December 1972. Chub of three pounds are scarce, those of five pounds are rare, and any fish over that weight is well 'worth a case.' It is a long time since 1897 when Mr. Stanley Mead took a chub of 7 lb. 1 oz. from Father Thames, near Wargrave. But, while this is the only record Thames chub of which I know, there can be little doubt that London's river still contains specimens which would compare very favourably with Mr. Mead's fish, and I will admit a personal feeling that there is a chub somewhere in the Thames which would make that seven-pounder blush with shame. Other rivers worthy of special mention for their chub are the Sussex Rother from which D. Deeks took an $8\frac{1}{2}$ pounder in July 1951, the Great Ouse, Dorset Stour, Kennet, Wye and Severn. Where in these rivers may the angler expect to find chub?

Experience is prone to make me answer—in the most awkward and inaccessible places; that is not, however, strictly true, and may be amplified considerably. In the early weeks of the season chub are comparatively easy to find. They are on the streamy gravel shallows and at the tails of weir lashings, where they congregate to wash themselves and recuperate after their domestic operations of the closed season. At this time they are often ravenous but are seldom in good and mettlesome condition. Later they slip away to their regular haunts, from which they do not move to any marked extent throughout the season, unless they are driven to shelter by flood water and spates. They may be near and under clay banks, where withies grow in the water. Chub are found under overhanging willows or other trees, near walls and under bridges; in deep holes and along the edge of weed beds into which they will run for shelter. Camp sheathing and the roots of trees growing out of the water often give a home to chub. But some of the very best are not in the main river at all; they run up the streamy backwaters, particularly where the vegetation is wild and overgrown and the water is not disturbed by navigation. Chub will feed at any depth from the surface to the bottom. During the summer months they may often be seen, half a dozen together led by a big fellow, basking in the sun just below the surface of the water. This habit accounts probably for their marked preference for swims which are overhung by trees. There is little doubt that chub seek out these places and lie in wait for insects which fall in the water. It may also be that, as fish which habitually lie quite visible on the surface, they seek the protection trees and bushes afford against possible attack from the air.

Having studied the characteristics, habits and haunts of chub, the angler may turn to a consideration of the baits, tackle the methods suited to their capture. To list the few baits which are not acceptable to these fish would occupy less than to recite their full menu. However, for those who are not familiar with the chub diet I will give the principal items:

Small live gudgeon and minnows, gentles, wasp and caddis grubs, dock grubs, worms, bullocks' pith, cheese paste, cubes of banana, cherries (with the stones removed), macaroni, grasshoppers, flies and insects (natural or artificial) and small spinners. Surely no angler could desire a more generous selection for the adornment of his hook. Having arrived at the hook end of the tackle, I will commence there and work towards the angler. As chub delight in a large mouthful and possess ample mouths, large hooks are desirable. A range of suitable sizes is illustrated.

USEFUL CHUB HOOKS.
C—Thin wire side barb for grubs or gentles.
D—Spined shank for worms.

The nylon to these hooks should not be finer than 3 lb b.s. and generally speaking 4 lb. b.s. is amply fine. If the chub have no inkling of the angler's presence they do not appear to be fastidious in the matter of the girth of the line upon which the bait is suspended. It must also be remembered that they are almost always hooked within easy reach of obstructions, such as tree roots or lily lads, and unless the angler is able to stay that first rush for safety which chub generally make, a break is certain. The cast may be of the same gauge as the hook length or one degree stouter. The line should be of a slightly higher breaking strain than either cast or hook length to minimize the loss of tackle should an accident occur. A good Terylene line of 6 lb. b.s. should meet all needs. A whole cane rod with a spliced split-bamboo tip is fine although there are a number of excellent hollow fibreglass rods now on the market. The rod should be a little more powerful than that generally used for roach or dace fishing, but built on similar lines. Ten or twelve feet is a useful length. I prefer a $3\frac{1}{2}$ in. narrow-drummed Sheffield reel, which enables the angler to recover his line quickly, a matter of high importance when chub fishing, particularly when the fish runs towards the angler. There are numerous methods of 'bait fishing' for chub as averse from the use of artificial flies. The most effective where practicable is 'trotting'; but 'swimming the stream' as for roach, making long casts and operating at the greatest possible distance from the fish is good sport. The ledger and paternoster are also used occasionally when float fishing is not possible.

'Dapping,' or 'Dibbling,' as it is called in some parts of the country, is another method with a charm of its own—the procedure for this and 'trotting' are worthy of detailed description.

DAPPING AND TROTTING FOR CHUB

In the summer on rivers where trees, bushes and the general nature of the banking afford suitable cover, there is no more enthralling means of taking chub than 'dapping' or 'dibbling.' Unflagging interest and tingling excitement combine for the chub dapper's pleasure. The necessary gear is simple and must be assembled some distance from the nearest chub-hide. It consists of a fairly powerful rod, Nottingham reel, Terylene line of 6 lb. breaking strain, with a cast and hook length to match.

To cast, a small bored shot is attached, as shown in the illustration; no float is required. Having everything ready, the 'stalk' begins, for this is veritable fish hunting. The undergrowth and overhanging bushes at a point quite near offer excellent cover, but a clumsy approach will render this useless. It is often necessary to creep the last few feet, taking several minutes to cover a yard or so to the vantage point from which the angler is able to see his quarry without being seen. Every movement must be stealthy, the slightest unusual stir among the branches, a clumsy footfall or a dislodged stone rolling into the water will cause chub to sink from sight, nor to reappear maybe for hours, and only

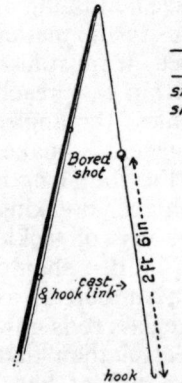

small rod rings
should be used /

Bored
shot

cast
& hook link

3ft 6in

hook

then very warily and with a sense of fear, which is a great disadvantage to the angler.

I cannot stress too much the absolute necessity for the most circumspect and trapper-like approach and the greatest care when proceeding to 'dap.' There they are! Four of them almost on the surface. How large they look! A little nearer the surface than the rest and slightly upstream is a big fellow having the appearance of a leader or the *paterfamilias*. Now to the actual fishing. Almost any of the baits I have mentioned may be used, but for compactness and easy carriage a little cheese paste is ideal for this experiment. Fortunately there is a small but fairly clear opening between the foliage behind which the angler is in hiding; through this he flicks a crumb or two of cheese. It strikes the water right among the waiting chub. One turns in a leisurely fashion, inspects the morsel as it begins to sink—and—it is gone! Now, keeping well out of sight, bait your hook with a generous knob of cheese and, having done so, wind the cast round the tip of your rod, with the baited hook at the end. This will enable you to thread the rod inch by inch through the twigs, a process which may well take minutes lest the fish be alarmed. When you have completed this difficult process, turn the rod very slowly to release the cast. The weight of the bait and small bullet will carry it down towards the water but do not move the rod, let line run off the reel, if this is necessary, to get the bait to the water. Then before the bait touches the surface, flip in another grain or two of cheese to make certain that the fish have not been alarmed by the projection of the rod. It is taken! Good! Now choose your fish and let your bait fall gently to the surface of the water—restrain your excitement! The big fellow has turned toward it, his leathery lips have closed over it. A smart tap has driven the hook home and with luck that fish is yours. The commotion of its struggles has frightened the others and you will have to move to another spot. But it was a great half-hour, and you are glad your gear was pretty strong.

Try dapping if you have not done so—it's well worth it. How each fish so caught is got out of the water is the angler's worry, and in my experience, a friend handy with a long-handled landing net is the best answer to the problem. The difficulties, however, add to the thrills. Moreover, as each spot presents its own problems, this type of fishing is full of variety.

Later in the season, when the weeds have died down, and long 'runs' without obstruction are fairly numerous, 'trotting' for chub is great sport. The fish may then be approached from distances of 40 to 50 yards. A fairly powerful 10 or 12 ft. rod and light-drummed Sheffield reel are good partners for the work. The rod should be fitted with bridge rings. A line of 6-lb. breaking strain, with cast and hook-link to match, complete the simple outfit with the exception of the float, which is deserving of special attention. After considerable experiment, I have found a 6½-in. cork-covered porcupine quill to be the best 'long trotting float.'

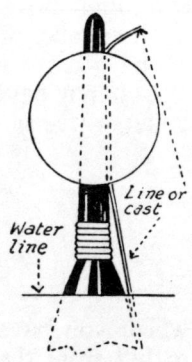

Float top.
Actual size.

To the tip of this I add a circular pilot which acts in the double capacity of float cap and observation point. This pilot gives the angler a dual visibility. For 20 or 30 yards he can see the small coloured circle of cork, which should be painted orange. As the trot is extended from that point to, say, 50 yards, a bite is detected by watching for the ring made on the surface of the water when the float is snatched downward by a chub. I have taken scores of fish by striking to the 'ring,' long after I was unable to see my float properly. If the stream is fairly fresh, the technique of 'trotting' is perfectly simple.

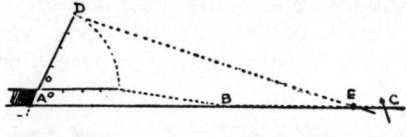

A, B, C shows position for trotting from reel.
D, E effect of vertical strike.

The rod is held practically horizontal with the water, when the stream will draw line direct from the reel which should be checked with the finger to keep the float slightly 'held' in order that the bait shall travel ahead of it.

If the stream is too slack to propel the reel, the procedure is a little more elaborate and requires some skill to 'trot' or give line to the moving float without causing it to halt in a jerky and unnatural way during its passage downstream. The method is described and illustrated in the section on roach. A boat or punt is essential for comfortable chub 'trotting.' Arriving some 40 yards above the 'hold,' the craft is moored to the

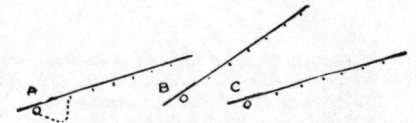

A—Pull some line from the reel just before it is required. B—Raise the rod point gently to take up this 'slack.' C—Lower the rod again at the same speed as the float is travelling, then repeat.

bank by the stern. This will swing the head of the boat out into the stream sufficiently to enable the angler to operate freely at a convenient distance from the bank and so far from the fish as to give him practical immunity from their suspicions. Bread and bran as ground-bait with a bunch of five or six gentles as hook-bait is 'good medicine.' The ground bait should be made up fairly soft and about the size of a cricket ball. One or two balls dropped in immediately in front of the angler and in line with the track of his swim will generally prove sufficient. If the fish do not respond in a few minutes, drop quietly downstream and repeat the process. You must almost certainly find them in this way. The bait should travel just off the bottom. If this method is carefully followed it will prove to be most killing. The continual movement necessary adds to the interest of 'trotting' two or three miles of water, and each new swim brings fresh hope of a good chub.

You may have toyed often with the idea of floating a couple of gentles under a tree or bush which was hanging low over the water, to chub

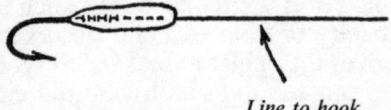

Line to hook.

which you have often seen lying near the surface waiting for tit-bits to fall from the foliage. The method of surface-fishing for dace described in Chapter XII supplies one answer to the problems involved. But there is another method of approaching fish placed in this way. The late Captain L. A. Parker, who devised it, has found it successful on the Hampshire Avon, and I am grateful to him for details of this way of fishing for chub which were otherwise virtually unget-at-able.

He found at the outset that the weight of any suitable hook was sufficient to sink the maggots which were impaled on it. To overcome

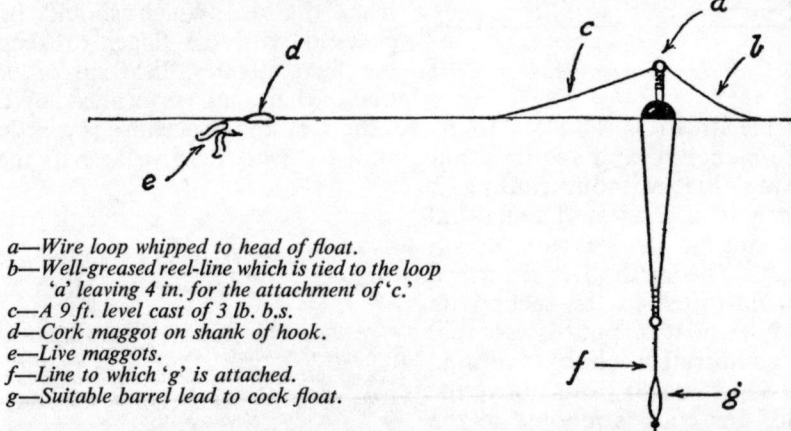

a—Wire loop whipped to head of float.
b—Well-greased reel-line which is tied to the loop
      'a' leaving 4 in. for the attachment of 'c.'
c—A 9 ft. level cast of 3 lb. b.s.
d—Cork maggot on shank of hook.
e—Live maggots.
f—Line to which 'g' is attached.
g—Suitable barrel lead to cock float.

this difficulty he bored a small piece of cork, slid it down the hook-line on to the shank of the hook, whittled it with a razor blade to roughly the size and shape of a maggot, then painted the cork to simulate the larvae on the hook, as illustrated above.

The rod, reel and line for this fishing and the general procedure are exactly the same as for long-trotting described earlier.

The large float and its balancing weight ensure that a moderate stream will draw line direct from a free-running revolving-drum reel; and this is therefore the method for anglers who like myself prefer these reels to the fixed-spool type. If the stream is very sluggish, line must of course be paid out by hand carefully to prevent jerk that would of course impart unnatural movement to the floating bait, which must precede the float downstream at the end of the fully extended cast at the same pace as the current. The line must be well greased to ensure a clean pick up from the water and a quick strike, but it is not essential to grease the whole of the cast.

Captain Parker used a level 9 ft. 3 lb. b.s. cast and commented that while one cannot see the maggots three yards ahead of the float, which by the way does not register bites; one sees the fish rise to take the floating bait and acts accordingly. But don't strike too quickly!

The illustration shows the rig he used. It is as practical as his method of sending down a few floating maggots in advance of those on the hook. To accomplish this he said:

> Put a spoonful of medicinal paraffin into your maggot tin and shake it gently, that will give the baits a light coat of grease sufficient to make them float.

This method is ideal for fishing certain types of water in the conditions described and in water which is too shallow for normal bottom fishing.

Floating dry bread-crust is by the way equally, if not more effective, as both bait and floating 'feed.'

CHAPTER XV

THERE ARE TWO BREAM: FLOAT FISHING FOR BREAM

I AM not an ichthyological authority, but experience has given me definite views on the subject of bronze and white or silver bream. The marked similarity between the young and immature fish of both species has raised discussion as to whether they are separate species. But there is no doubt, there are, in our waters, two species of bream, the common bronze (*Abramis brama*) and white or silver bream (*Blicca bjoerkna*).

The illustrations on this page and page 139 show both fish. They differ physically in many respects, but without going into minute

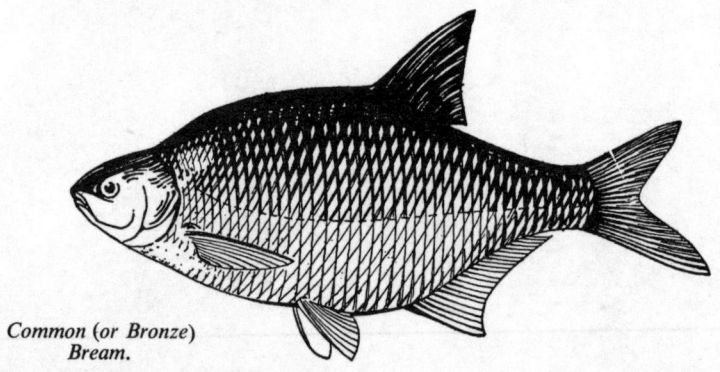

Common (or Bronze) Bream.

detail, some outstanding differences may be considered. Compare the position and relative size of the eyes. Even more convincing may be the fact that the number of scales along the lateral line of a bronze bream is fifty-one to sixty, while in the case of silver bream the number is forty-four to forty-eight.

Bronze bream are well distributed in the eastern and southern counties of England and in some parts of Ireland, elsewhere they are rare or unknown.

Silver bream, while very common on the Continent, may only be regarded as comparatively rare fish in the British Isles. Bronze bream vary considerably in shape and colour. Some are long and compressed, others deep and thick; while the colour varies from bronze and olive-green to dark brown. These colour variations are almost certainly due to environment. The body of the silver bream is always very compressed and the colour is constantly a delicate silver. It may be from these characteristics they have acquired the nicknames of 'Tinplates' and 'Breamflats.'

Both fish prefer lakes or sluggish watercourses, and their life history is very similar. When tiny they derive their food from minute matter in suspension in mid-water, but soon take to the shallows near the bank in search of food on the bottom. In the second year they forsake the shallow margins for the deeps, where they remain during the greater part of the day, returning to the shallows at night to feed. Their feeding habits remind me of another marked difference between these fish. The bronze variety almost invariably play and disport themselves on the surface prior to descending to feed, so much so that in some waters the bream fisher will not operate if the fish do not 'play'; and, indeed, I have often noticed that, when they do not, sport is bad and vice versa. On the other hand, I have never seen silver bream play in this manner. Bronze bream though poor fighters are weight for weight much more sporting than their silver relations, which are ethargic even on the finest tackle.

Bream are not, however, sought so much for their fighting qualities as for the fact that when they are feeding they offer the angler scope for great catches. Hundredweights may be taken at a sitting and this appeals to some. The days when anglers were proud to have their photographs taken, rod in hand, beside a heap of slain bream are happily far behind us, the sportsmen now return their fish to the water for their own and other anglers' pleasure.

A lubberly and sluggish fish which roots the mud with its strong snout in search of food, such is the bream. They move in large shoals, and this rooting habit is often their undoing when noticed by the knowing angler. A patch of water may be comparatively clear, then without warning it will become discoloured and clouded with the mud stirred up by a shoal of 'water-pigs.' Despite their lack of fight, when they are hooked, bream are a great favourite with many anglers, and, indeed, they provide fast and furious sport when 'on the feed.' Their dimensions are another attraction to the 'specimen' hunter. Dr. Tate Regan chronicles a whopper of 17 lb. from the Trent, but it is not clear that the fish in question was taken with rod and line. Disregarding this, however, there is a list of splendid fish caught by fair angling, calculated to inspire any angler to further effort. In July 1939, Mr. F. T. Bench captured a magnificent bream of 12 lb. 15 oz. in the Tring Reservoir. This eclipsed the previous record set up in 1933 by Mr. Pugh, who took a bream weighing 12 lb. 14 oz. from the same water. Another splendid bream taken at Tring in 1931 by Mr. A. J. Fisher, weighed 12 lb. 12½ oz. This water is not now producing very heavy specimens. Then, in October 1945, came news of the capture of a 13 lb. 8 oz. bronze bream from the Chiddingstone Castle lake in Kent, to the rod of Mr. E. G. Costin. Prior to the advent of these comparatively modern monsters, the record was held by Mr. A. Pike, who, in 1882, captured a bronze bream of 11¾ lb. from the Blackwater in Ireland.

I can imagine some anglers saying 'but I don't care for lake fishing, even for "grandfathers." ' Very well, here are some river bream records for those who prefer them. On 20th September, 1928, Mr. J. J. Perkins took a brace weighing respectively 10 lb. 13½ oz. and 9 lb. 14¼ oz. from the Thames at Eynsham. I have not seen the case in which they repose, but it must be nearly the size of a piano. Another for the river fishes is the 10 lb. 3½ oz. bream caught by Mr. Hilditch in the River Lea at Enfield in 1880. To these could be added many fine specimens from lake and river, but those mentioned will suffice to show that river or lake fishing for bream may produce the 'fish of a lifetime.'

In every case the records mentioned relate to 'bronze' bream, but their relatives, the 'white or 'silver' variety, should not be omitted. In February 1922, Mr. G. Burwash took a 4-pounder from the Thames at Egham, then in 1923 Mr. C. Rhind caught a 4½ lb. silver bream in Tortworth Lake.

At the end of July 1946, Mr. John Wiltshire, Secretary of the Airedale Hotel Angling Club, near Castleford, wrote me to say that Arthur Caulfield (aged 16), had caught a silver bream weighing 5 lb. 7 oz.

This fish was caught in the Derwent at Bubwith, near Selby, on the 25th July, 1946. On the 26th it was taken to the headquarters of the Leeds Amalgamated Angling Association to be weighed.

As Mr. Wiltshire rightly said—a silver bream of this weight would constitute a new British Record.

But!—How that word will creep in—if when it had been weighed at the Club, this fish had been taken straight to Leeds University, and a certificate of species obtained from a qualified biologist—all would have been well.

When a record is challenged, it is essential to establish the species and precise weight of the challenging fish beyond dispute.

The doubt which attaches to young Caulfield's bream, for lack of the scientific evidence to which I refer, prohibits its acceptance as a record specimen. Even in cases where the species of a fish is indisputable, it is always advisable to have the weight attested by two or three reliable witnesses. And the sooner the fish is weighed after capture, the more it will weigh. Accuracy and speed are paramount factors in these cases. The silver bream record is open at 2 lb. The bronze bream record (1972) is 12 lb. 14 oz. taken from the Suffolk Stour by Mr. G. Harper.

Full details of the official (and safest) way of establishing a record are given later (Chapter XVI).

This chapter would be incomplete without special mention of those prolific bream waters, the Norfolk Broads, the Fens of the Eastern Counties and the Great Ouse. It is remarkable, however, that neither of these notoriously good bream waters (where numbers are concerned) has produced any record bream. There are few or no bream in West Wales, Scotland north of Loch Lomond and the Firth of Forth or in Cornwall, Devon and Dorset.

Bream are essentially bottom feeders and water weed of various types, small shell fish, insect larvae and worms may be regarded as their staple foods. The list of bream baits in general use is comparatively

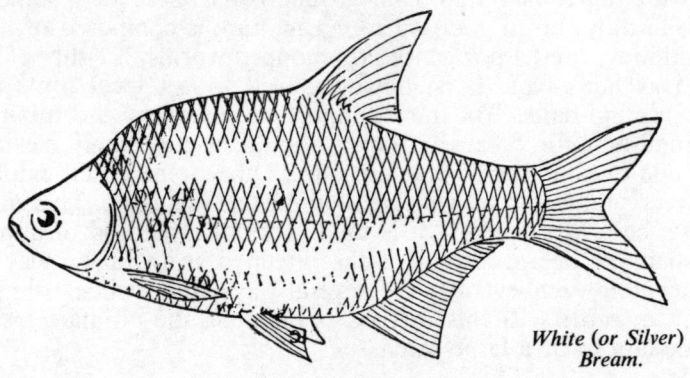

White (or Silver) Bream.

short, gentles, worms, bread paste and boiled wheat being the principal ones. Other good baits in some waters are breadcrust, bread flake, and stewed barley, and in season they will take wasp and caddis grubs. Bream have been known to take dead fish, as witness the following quotation from the *Angler's News* in which Mr. C. Crane of Streatham, London, reported:

> . . . a friend of mine ledgering with a dead bleak in the Thames at East Molesey on the 16th June (1945) caught two eels of about 1 lb. each. Shortly after a 2½ lb. bream took the bait on the same tackle and was hooked in the mouth.

While this is quite unusual, I have thought for quite a time now that many of the Cyprinoids become predacious after spawning; and it is quite likely that this fish having spawned was ravenous and developed this tendency. When bream fishing, however, I have found that ground-baiting is almost more important than the hook-bait.

I have in mind a certain 'bream pit' on the Great Ouse, where it is proverbial that the weight of the catch will be in direct ratio to the amount of ground-bait used. Time and again I have noticed this to be the case. This is probably a mere coincidence, but the strange fact remains. It does not seem possible to over ground-bait a deep bream hole. Nor do the fish appear to resent the commotion caused by hurling balls of bait half the size of a man's head into the water.

This may be due to the fact that their own surface splashings when 'playing' produce very similar sounds and a feeding shoal on the bottom may take the falling ground-bait for the sounds of exercises created by another shoal of bream on the surface. I do not, however, wish to give the impression that bream are unwary fish; they are often very shy and easily 'put down.' Clumsy movement or noise in a boat or on the bank is a danger signal to them and the good bream fisher is always a silent fisher, though cover and invisibility do not appear to be so important when 'breaming' as in other forms of angling unless, of course, the water is clear or shallow.

As to the ingredients of bream ground-baits, these vary somewhat with the locality, but a good all-round mixture is composed of bread, bran, middlings, and a few gentles or chopped worms, if either of these are used as hook-bait. It is, however, well to get local hints as to suitable ground-baits. The most important factor in the mixing of any ground-bait for bream is that it should be absolutely clean and sweet. Stale or sour ingredients are fatal. Other items often employed are brewers' grains and oil-cake as used for feeding cattle. This should, of course, be crushed before it is used. The ideal method of applying ground-bait for bream is to bait the intended swim fairly heavily at the same hour each evening for several days; then when fishing, to use small quantities. If this method is possible, the ultimate result is almost certain to be a large catch.

Float fishing for bream

It is not often that one may indulge and be really dogmatic about matters of angling. There is, however, one absolute certainty upon which a bream-fisher may rely—the bait must be on the bottom. This fact simplifies matters considerably and to a great extent limits procedure to two main methods, namely, 'float ledgering' and 'ledgering.' There are, of course, variations in the actual details of practising these methods. As bream are almost invariably found in sluggish rivers or still water, the use of a float while yet having the bait on the bottom presents no difficulty. Float fishing for bream is carried out with the same rod and reel as is used for roach fishing, but with slightly heavier line and hook-link. Suitable hooks are Crystals, numbers 7, 8 or 9. The precise size of the float and amount of shot used is governed entirely by the speed of the stream or the strength of the wind at the time of fishing. Assuming the angler is operating in a lake on a still evening, one shot and a tiny float are ideal.

To this shot a small knob of cupping or ground-bait may be squeezed which will aid in casting the light gear to the desired spot. It is a peculiarity of the bream that the bite is often registered by the float lying flat on the water prior to its gliding under as the fish moves away.

The illustration (p. 141) makes the reason for the phenomenon clear. The fish stands on its head to pick up the bait and, turning again on a level keel, lifts the shot. The angler should not, however, be in a hurry to strike when this flattening of the float is noticed, but should strike smartly immediately it shows signs of moving away. After this the fish should be played out of the swim as quickly as possible to avoid disturbing the shoal. In windy conditions or where there is a perceptive stream, more shot or a bored bullet and a larger or an antenna float are required, but the method is identical.

Another useful method of fishing a stream for bream close to the bank is known as 'stret-pegging.' The tackle is the same and the name is applied to the method.

Using a float to carry about four BB shots, set the tackle at approximately one foot above the depth of the water. Allow the bait to travel three or four yards downstream, then hold it. If unproductive in one part of the swim, the bait should, of course, be worked progressively downstream.

The reader may have noticed that in my description of float fishing for bream I make no mention

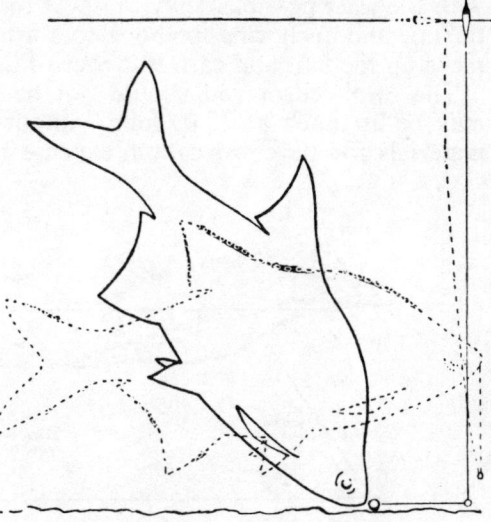

Diagram showing why bream lay a float flat.

of 'swimming the stream'; neither do I introduce 'slider floats' for use in deep water, where it is not possible to use a set float. These omissions are wilful, as I am not a believer in either method for bream fishing, though both are quite often employed. Under certain conditions there can be no harm in allowing a moving bait to trail the bottom for bream; but, even when this is possible, it is not so good as 'stret-pegging.' I also hold that when angling in very deep water for bream, 'ledgering' comes into its own, and is the most practical method. I have observed many anglers 'ledgering,' and have been struck by the needlessly powerful rods used by a very large number of fishermen for this type of angling. Any stiff piece of wood from a yard to four feet in length would appear to serve them as a 'ledger rod.' I well remember watching an angler, some years ago, operating with a truncheon-like rod which he assured me was made from solid TEAK! He invited me to watch him 'thump' them (the fish) with 'this' (the rod)! I watched hopefully, and all that happened was—he missed a number of good bites despite his violent 'strike' with that short and unyielding beanpole, or should I say pit-prop?

Fortunately for the bream the 'thumping' was too late every time.

Had it been successful the impact must have decapitated the luckless fish.

The whole principle and theory of ledger tackle and fishing was lost on that angler, and it is not appreciated by those who use these tiny lifeless rods for ledgering.

The illustration which follows will make matters clear, and I believe it will be agreed that the whole essence of the tackle used for ledger fishing is that the angler should be able to move the hook toward him with the least possible delay. A short rod is incapable of straightening the line and anchoring the hook to a fish, particularly when the bream picks up the bait and carries it toward the angler.

The ideal ledger rod should not be less than 7 ft. in length and may be as much as 10 ft. long without disadvantage. As to suitable materials for its construction, expense must play an important part,

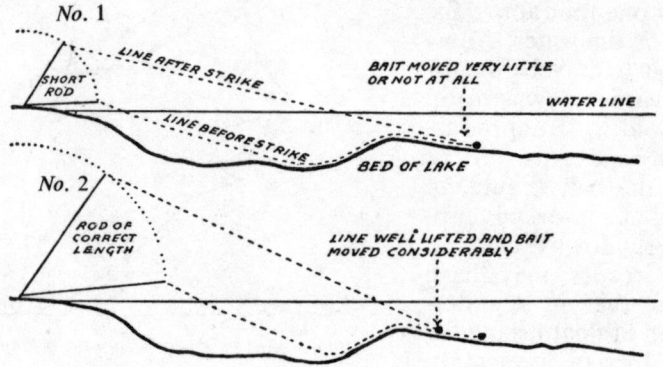

In the case of No. 1 the rod is scarcely long enough to lift the sag out of the line and efficient striking is almost impossible.

but a good all-round rod need not cost more than £7 or £8. At this price a serviceable hollow glass two-joint 8-ft. rod may be obtained. The size of the ring is, of course, governed by the length and power of the rod.

While rings of ample diameter are obviously an advantage, minimizing friction and giving freedom for the line when casting, it is a fallacy to fit unduly large rings for two reasons. In the first place, the larger the rings the more easily they appear to be broken; while the weight of large rings will cause the rod to take on a strained dip which spoils its appearance at once and its action subsequently.

Of the numerous 'business ends' suitable for bream ledgering, a bored bullet is the most popular and probably the most efficient.

The illustration shows the method of arranging this very simple tackle. There is, however, a matter of first-class importance attached to the use of this type of ledger which does not seem to receive the amount of consideration to which it is due. The size of the bullet—

should it be large or small? Most anglers will say as small as possible, but are they correct? The point at issue is, of course, 'lightness.' Every fisher will agree that the smaller the pre-strike resistance offered to a fish which

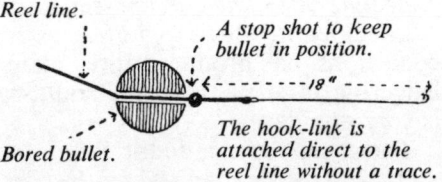

Reel line.

A stop shot to keep bullet in position.

Bored bullet.

The hook-link is attached direct to the reel line without a trace.

has taken the bait the better. The question, then, is—which offers the least resistance, a large and really heavy or a smaller and comparatively light bullet? After much thought and experiment I am inclined to favour the large bullet described and illustrated in the chapter on roach, p. 75. Let us first consider the pros and cons of the smaller lead.

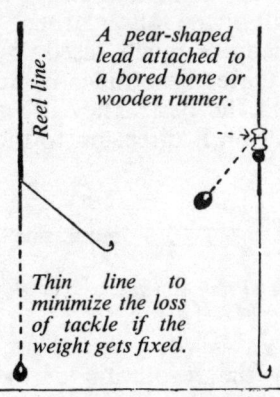

Reel line.

A pear-shaped lead attached to a bored bone or wooden runner.

Thin line to minimize the loss of tackle if the weight gets fixed.

If the weight sinks into the mud the sensitiveness of the tackle is not impaired.

If a fish is large and the hook within 18 in. of the weight which I advise, there is the possibility when the fish turns on a level keel, after taking the bait, that it will raise the bullet, in which case, feeling the resistance, it may reject the bait before the angler is able to strike. It often happens that, having detected a bite, a simultaneous strike proves ineffective. This is probably due to the cause I mention. On the other hand, if a large bullet is used and the bore considerably enlarged, to give the line free passage, the fish, having taken the bait, will not feel the resistance of the bullet at all, but will draw the line through its wide aperture and thus take the lightest possible pull. The line itself must be moved and its weight constitutes the minimum possible resistance. In any event, anglers may care to make the experiment with a bullet of, say, $\frac{3}{4}$ in. in diameter. The advantage in casting will be obvious. This method is not, of course, of any use on soft muddy bottom, but with firm conditions I believe it to be the most sensitive and least resisting. Soft mud calls for another procedure.

The illustrations show alternative methods of overcoming the effects of soft mud. The gear I have described is the simplest and while there are numerous variations, one or other will be found effective in any water.

One other item should, however, be mentioned. The 'coffin' lead is for use in water where the current would roll a circular bullet out of the desired position. These are used in exactly the same way as shown in the first illustration, but should be avoided whenever possible on account of the fact that their shape causes them to spin when being wound in, which imparts a most objectionable kink to the line.

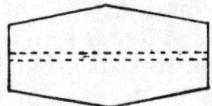

The 'coffin' lead.

Detecting bites when bream ledgering

Local habit, which to a great extent is the direct result of local water conditions, has produced three main methods of detecting a bite when ledgering for bream. In the south-eastern counties the dough bobbin is very popular.

There can be no doubt this is a sensitive and accurate indicator, and the strike is made when the piece of dough is raised by the pull of the fish. It has its disadvantages, however, the chief being the suddenness with which a slight 'take' is registered, causing the angler to strike excitedly and often too soon. Furthermore, a fish passing the line may cause a 'lift,' and a useless strike is the result of the false alarm.

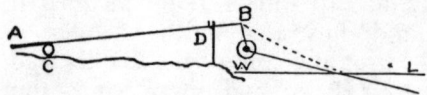

A B—The rod resting on the reel at C and a rod-rest at D. W.L. is the water-line. ⊙ shows position of dough bobbin. - - - - - shows the position of line when a bite is registered.

A method much used by Great Ouse fishermen is to my mind the best. They use a large sinker and tighten up on it direct on to the reel.

The bobbin is made of bread paste and should be as small as will preserve the angle in the line.

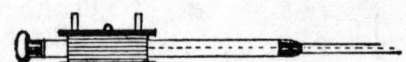

The rod is laid flat with the reel handles uppermost and free to revolve.

Any bite from bream is then registered by the revolution of the reel drum from which line is drawn direct by the fish. It is, of course, essential that the reel used in this way should be free running and offer the smallest possible resistance to a taking fish, but at the same time if it is fitted with an adjustable drag, this is an advantage and enables the angler to set the tension at just that pressure which will prevent the current or even the weight of the line itself from moving the reel. Bites are registered by this method in an unmistakable way. The reel drum commences to spin, the angler checks it with one hand, picks up his rod with the other and stops a running fish. There is no strike necessary and the method is pleasant to see and efficient in practice.

Another method of detecting bream bites when ledgering is to pull off from 18 in. to 3 ft. of line from the reel, the length of line in question being governed entirely by the angler's fancy as to how far he will allow a fish to run before he wishes to strike. When a bream bites, the loose line is seen disappearing through the rod rings. This is the signal not to strike, but merely to pick up the rod and stop a running fish, as in the case of the reel drum method. Either way is less open to false alarm than the dough bobbin, for while a passing fish touching the line will give a signal, this is not acted upon, as it is immediately apparent that the movement of the reel or coil of line, as the case may be, is not caused by a bite. In the case of the dough bobbin method, movement means an immediate strike, as for some reason the fish appear to drop the bait immediately after straightening the line and raising the bobbin. In the case of the two latter methods, the distance a fish will take the bait before dropping it is sometimes remarkable, and in my opinion the angler has a better chance to hook his fish.

CHAPTER XVI

THE BRITISH RECORD (ROD-CAUGHT) FISH COMMITTEE

YOU will have read, and will be reading numerous references in this book to record fish and, in the same context, the British Record (rod-caught) Fish Committee. This body, referred to in this Chapter as the 'Committee,' has at times held a love-hate relationship with the angling public. Nevertheless, we must have such a body to act as the archivist of the sport and in our efforts to bring this about we have discovered how difficult it is to please everyone in a sport which covers, contrary to what one would expect, a very wide range of interests and activities.

In previous editions of *Angling Ways*, the Committee has been mentioned many times, but its antecedents have never been outlined to any degree in an angling book. I have, then, taken this opportunity to give a brief outline of the formation of the Committee and its trials and tribulations since the early days.

Eric Marshall-Hardy was Editor of *Angling* from its launch in 1936 until September 1954. During his editorship many cases of wrong identification came to his notice when specimen fish claims were made and he came to realise the need for a centrally based authority to adjudicate all claims made for the establishment of rod-caught records. In 1950, the National Federation of Anglers accepted this responsibility and in 1951 set up a committee. There is little evidence of its activities.*

When *Angling Times* was founded in July 1953 it set up its own domestic panel of record judges, under the style of 'British Record Fish Committee'. Marshall-Hardy's comment at the time was: 'Frankly, I was not surprised when some of the judgments of this self-appointed tribunal failed to meet with unqualified approval'.

In 1957, four years later, a meeting was called by the *Angling Times*' proprietors. The meeting was to be held at Grosvenor House in London and the agenda consisted of one item, to discuss the numerous discrepancies in the existing unofficial list of record fish. These lists, published in *Angling Times*, the *Fishing Gazette* (now defunct) and its subsidiary 'Where to Fish', went some way to satisfy anglers' needs to be able to recognise the average fish from the specimen, and for all meritorious captures to be properly recorded. In order to maintain an acceptable

* There is a note of its formation in *Angling* June 1952.

list of such notable and record fish some method of systematic and qualified investigation of record claims was necessary, and it was essential that it be made by an acceptable and responsible authority.

The Grosvenor House meeting, organised as I have explained by *Angling Times* was chaired by Howard Marshall, then Editorial Director of that publication and well-known broadcasting personality, and the committee of invited members were asked to pledge the support of their various organisations or periodicals to maintain a British Record (rod-caught) List for future reference and the general good of angling. The new Committee consisted of the Chairman (Howard Marshall), Peter Tombleson (appointed Secretary and official Recorder, of *Angling Times*); Dr. J. W. Jones (ichthyologist, Liverpool University); Professor A. F. Magri MacMahon (ichthyologist, biologist and author); Major Brian Halliday (National Federation of Anglers); Leslie Hastilow (National Federation of Sea Anglers); F. E. Wiles (*Fishing Gazette*); R. C. Eaton (*The Field*), and Bernard Venables (*Trout and Salmon*).

From that date in 1957 the British Record (rod-caught) Fish Committee's list of accepted record fish became familiar to readers of the angling Press; they were published at intervals following the Committee's meetings. Up to 1967 the Committee had considered 90 claims for record fish, including 24 freshwater species and 66 for the saltwater kind. Of these claims, 46 of the sea fish were accepted as the official records, together with 11 freshwater fish: 33 claims were rejected for one reason or another.

The reasons why many record fish claims were unsuccessful were often the result of incorrect species identification: bass were claimed as mullet, carp as tench, chub as roach, chub as dace, common bream as silver bream, and—commonly—hybrids as true roach, dace and chub. In a number of cases, it is sad to report, scientifically trained opinion erred on fish species identification. There are on record two occasions when university departments, presumably having the backing of qualified authority and full resources, made wrong pronouncements of species. The London Zoo once invited the Secretary of the Committee to identify a fish claimed as an equal record dace: the fish proved to be a chub. The question poses itself—where were the Zoological Society's scientists?

In 1963, some tightening of the Rules of Procedure were made and the regulations concerning fish identification were strengthened to cover all eventualities, following the light of experience of the Committee. It had since its inception realised the importance of a close relationship between it and the official angling bodies such as the N.F.A. and the N.F.S.A. The presence of Major Halliday and Leslie Hastilow ensured this and at the same time made it possible for the Record List to bear a proper relationship with the list of specimen sizes published by those bodies and which were used as a basis for awards.

Some strange names began to appear in 1967: *Stizostedion vitreus* and *Stizostedion lucioperca*, being the Latin descriptions of the American

Walleye and the European Zander respectively. Anglers not familiar with the then current angling scene were surprised. It had been known for some years that the zander, or pike perch, was on the prowl in a number of waters, but who would have expected to find its close relation the walleye also occupying a place on the record list with 11 lb. 12 oz.? And who was responsible for introducing the American fish to our waters? Had it been obtained from a breeder who did not know the difference? The walleye was taken as long ago as 1934, coming from the River Delph at Witney, Oxfordshire. The record has held its place since it first appeared in the record list in 1967. The zander seems destined to attain greater weights, for the record zander was a 10 lb. 4 oz. fish from that matchman's water the Great Ouse Relief Channel, in 1968. Since then, that same water has yielded fish of 12 lb. 5 oz. and, in December 1971, the current (January 1972) record fish of 15 lb. 5 oz.

But for all its honest attempts to establish a continuing reputation for accuracy, the Committee became aware of a growing sense of dissatisfaction, even an uneasiness that there was not an equal balance of representation from all interested parties. The specimen groups, having inevitably organised themselves into a para-official body, would seem to have had a case for membership of the Committee. Other sections of the angling Press, apart from the *Angling Times*, too were nibbling away along the same lines.

Apart from the angling political front, some of the fish which had been listed from the beginning of the Committee's birth as the official records for their species and heaviest fish of their kind hooked and landed at the time of capture, began to be wondered at, to be probed and discussed to their inevitable detriment, mainly because the known and proven details of their captures were very often of a very sketchy nature. As far back as January 1967 the Committee had seriously considered the authenticity of the equal record roach of 3 lb. 14 oz., caught by Bill Brown at Stanford, Lincs, in 1964. This fish survived the investigation, for it still shares the top position among *Rutilus rutilus* alongside Bill Penney's fish, captured from a Molesey Reservoir way back in 1938. Many angling authorities continue to express their doubts, however, contending that this fish is a hybrid.

It may be that the Committee were themselves to blame, at least in part, for the rumblings in the Press and between anglers in private. Little information was published following their deliberations apart from the statement of acceptance or otherwise. But it is the small details, plus all that is known about the scientific investigation of the identification of species that is so important. These items and place of capture present facts and figures which, accompanied by the Committee's certificate of authenticity, allow thinking anglers to comment constructively on matters of such importance.

The angling Press is the only voice of the huge angling fraternity. Both radio and TV are almost totally disinterested in the sport as a social phenomenon. It is a sad fact that they do not consider angling newsworthy enough for time to be allocated to it, apart from short features, some of which seem designed to harm more than enhance the sport. The various angling journals, then, carried many letters of criticism; and in private and public well-known anglers voiced their opinions about records that were not and fish that were—or should have been. Among the listed fish under fire were the record pikes of England and Scotland (why two records?), and that great 10 lb. 8 oz. chub recorded as caught from the Scottish River Annan in 1955. No chub recorded before or since that date has come anywhere near this weight. From criticisms of this nature it became more and more obvious that something had to be done in order to continue as the nation's accepted, official body for the recognition of record rod-caught fish; worthy enough to continue to retain the confidence of the angler and the support of organised angling.

At the end of 1968 the responsibility for the management of the Committee passed from *Angling Times* to the National Anglers' Council. It was the proper and logical step, almost inevitable right from the founding of the N.A.C., and was universally applauded by all factions of the sport.

A further major step forward was taken when membership on the Committee was offered to a representative of *Angler's Mail*, the only other National weekly angling newspaper, which had been in existence since 1966. During my Editorship of *Angler's Mail* I had urged the Committee to offer membership to a wider section of the angling Press, and although my personal efforts had been fruitless I was gratified to see this being carried out. Membership was also offered to a representative from the National Society of Specimen Groups. The inclusion of a member of the N.S.S.G. gave recognition to a small but fantastically keen body of anglers, whose sum total of fishing know-how and expertise must be enormous.

So now the N.A.C. was running the show. The Committee was no longer what Eric Marshall-Hardy had described as a 'self-appointed tribunal,' but part of the one body solely representative of the whole of the sport of angling. This, in fact, is how the N.A.C. is described in Rule 1 in its Constitution. And we sat back to enjoy the fireworks as the new-look body began to see to its problems. But strangely enough nothing happened. There seemed at first to be no change in policy, apart from the fact that Press statements carried the N.A.C. badge.

In 1969, two years after the pike-perch and walleye came on the scene, another stranger made its appearance. It was the catfish, a species indigenous to the European Continent where it is known as the Wels, *Silurus glanis*. The record (January 1972) is 43 lb. 8 oz., and this ugly brute was caught from the Wilstone Reservoir, Tring, Herts, in 1970. This looks a fair size when compared with other fish on the record list, but the 44 lb. carp and the 64 lb. salmon are exceptions. Our freshwater fish are not really known for their weight but for their cunning in avoiding us. Will the wels flourish in our waters until it reaches sizes of incredible enormity, such as the recorded giant fish of 660 lb. taken from a Russian water? How long does it take for the wels to reach weights of this nature? That 660 lb. catfish was 80 years old.

In March 1969 the Committee announced in a Press statement that a new record list would be published, having as its basis all those fish which it had investigated and accepted since its inception in 1957. The Committee, under the Chairmanship of Major Halliday, added that to this list would be added a number of fish of which either the bodies or casts were available. The sea record fish list would be made up from lists compiled by the N.F.S.A., with two records left open for which qualifying minimum weights would be laid down. At this time the Committee (with Major Halliday as Chairman) consisted of Peter Tombleson (Secretary), Dr. J. W. Jones, R. W. Page (secretary of the N.F.S.A.), J. H. Piper, J. Thorndike, H. F. Wallis, D. Wilson, Brig. G. C. Wells, and Professor A. F. Magri MacMahon. Bob Page had replaced Leslie Hastilow, who died on April 8, 1970, after a long period of great ill health.

The announcement of the publication of the new record list raised an immediate hubbub, both by the general angling fraternity and by the higher echelons of piscatorial circles. A number of the old, familiar favourites, seemingly once in an impregnable position at the head of their species, were gone. The 1 lb. 8 oz. dace, that 10 lb. 8 oz. chub, the 7 lb. 2 oz. grayling (surely the most easily identifiable of freshwater fish), the sea trout, which, for British waters, seemed too good to be true—all these were no longer the kings (or queens) of their respective piscine castles. And, it was asked, inevitably 'How could all those be fish accepted as accredited records for years, if, as it now seems, the available evidence was so suspect?' The long held aura of infallibility and authority of the Committee looked shaky. The edifice had been rocked by its creators.

At times the result was bordering on the comic. A number of well-known anglers were heard to mutter that so far as they were concerned the old record list would stand. That monster chub was the biggest caught in Great Britain, no matter what the Committee said. The 1 lb. 8 oz. dace caught in 1932 from an Avon tributary, by R. W. Humphrey, *was* top dace even though the Committee had said the evidence was not conclusive to warrant the fish appearing on the list.

The record list itself, too, looked strange. The sea fish list seemed to be getting bigger and bigger; the freshwater list had been subject to considerable culling. It was noticeably shorter and at the foot was a terse heading: 'Species open for freshwater fish claims.' Beneath this were listed the chub, dace, grayling, gudgeon, pike, sea trout and silver bream—all once fabulous records which had been the ideal of young boys and old men, specimen hunters and matchmen, not forgetting the happy-go-lucky maggot drowner: that wandering angler who simply fishes for fish, but who in his wisdom is just as happy if he goes home with a dry keep-net: he fishes for pleasure as well as for fish.

For a while, too, there were three trout on the list, not counting the sea trout, which was one of the 'open' species, awaiting claimants, this one having a qualifying minimum weight of 20 lb. The three trout were the brown wildie, *Salmo trutta* (18 lb. 2 oz.); the rainbow trout, *S. gairdneri* (8 lb. 8 oz.), and another rainbow, a newcomer known as the 'cultivated variety' having a record weight of 10 lb. 4 oz., but with the same scientific description. The 'cultivated' variety, being hand-fed and reared in a protective environment, was supposed to grow larger, *ergo* it would have an advantage over the 'wild' rainbow and it would usually be caught in comparatively confined waters. This new approach to differentiate among fish of the same species caused all sorts of trouble. The letter columns of the angling Press boiled and bubbled merrily and the only people who were happy were the Letters Editors, whose job of finding the leading letter was made easy. Taking the 'cultivated' and the 'wild' concept a stage further, it seemed logical to say: 'Fine, we'll cultivate some roach, carp and so on, feed them up to record size, then release them in a suitable water and catch them. If it's all right for the rainbow trout, it's all right for the roach.' It was not, to say the least, a popular move to have two rainbow records. The rainbow trout is a rainbow trout whether cultivated, wild, or raised in the bathtub— and the same goes for all other species.

The message got through to the Committee, who on October 5, 1971, said: 'In the light of experience . . . when the decision was taken to have separate records for cultivated and natural fish, it was decided that it was not practical to have two lists. In future there will be one record for each species of fish,' So we are back with the well-authentic-ated 18 lb. 2 oz. brown trout and the rainbow, the record for which is now (January 1972) a fish of 10 lb. 4 oz., from Kings Lynn, Norfolk.

The story you have just read is a brief outline of the history of the British Record (rod-caught) Fish Committee. Fish records can be the most ephemeral of things, but we need them, and we like them. We also insist, as all thinking people should, that we must be free to criticise, and very often criticism based on a misunderstood or wrongly interpreted point can hurt and mystify those to whom it is addressed, who may be (and usually are) in possession of more detailed information. Let us not forget this, as we should not forget that the members of the Committee all offer their services, time and work, voluntarily. We are indebted to them for this service to angling, given because they believe angling should, like all other sports, have an acceptable record list.

One thing is of interest: the Rules of Procedure and method of investigating claims have been copied by many other angling bodies in this country as well as in Holland, Poland and the Channel Isles.

LEN CACUTT

NATIONAL ANGLERS' COUNCIL

RULES OF PROCEDURE OF THE BRITISH RECORD (ROD CAUGHT) FISH COMMITTEE

1. Claims must be made in writing to the Secretary stating
   (i) the species of fish and the weight
   (ii) the date and place of capture, and the tackle used, and
   (iii) the names and addresses of reliable witnesses both as to the capture by the claimant and the weight, who will be required to sign the forms supporting the claim.

   If no witnesses to the capture are available, the claimant must verify his claim by affidavit.

2. No claim will be accepted unless the Committee is satisfied as to species, method of capture and weight. The Committee reserve the right to reject any claim if not satisfied on any matter which the Committee may think in the circumstances to be material.

3. Identification of species.
   (a) To ensure correct identification, it is essential that claimants should retain the fish and immediately contact the Secretary of the Committee who will advise as to production of the fish for inspection on behalf of the Committee.
   (b) All carriage costs incurred in production of the fish for inspection by the Committee (if this is required) must be borne by the claimant.

4. Method of capture.
   (a) Fish caught at sea will be eligible for consideration as records if the boat used has set out from a port in England, Wales, Scotland, Northern Ireland, the Isle of Man or the Channel Isles and returns to the same port without having called at any port outside United Kingdom. Fish caught in the territorial waters of other countries will not be eligible.
   (b) Claims can only be accepted in respect of fish which are caught by fair angling with rod and line. Fair angling is defined by the fish taking the baited hook or lure into its mouth.

5. Weight.
   (a) The fish must be weighed as soon as possible on scales or steelyards which can be tested on behalf of the Committee.
   (b) The weight must be verified by two independent witnesses who should not be relations of the claimant or a member of his club or party.

6. Claims can be made for species not included in the Committee's Record Fish List.

7. The Committee will issue at least once a year its lists of British Record (rod-caught) Fish.

8. No fish caught out of season shall be accepted as a new record.

9. A fish for which a record is claimed must be normal and not obviously suffering from any disease by which the weight could be enhanced.

HOW TO PHOTOGRAPH YOUR FISH

When permission has been granted to submit photographs, these must:

(1) Be large and in focus.

(2) Show as many as possible of the specific characters of the fish. If these are not known consult *Know Your Fish* (Jones and Tombleson, Ernest Benn Ltd, London E.C.4, 60p) or any reliable book of fish identification. Remember: The fish should not be held by the head as this distorts the relative lengths of various parts of the body.
Fish should be photographed on a plain background with fins erect so that fin rays can be counted.
It may be necessary to photograph from several angles and also to photograph the teeth.
Some object of known size should be photographed alongside the fish if a measure is not available.

IF YOU CATCH A RECORD FISH

Medium-sized fish can be preserved for considerable periods by refrigeration (deep freeze) or immersion in formalin. If a fish is to be sent by post or rail it is best immersed in a solution of one tablespoon of formalin (40 per cent solution of formaldehyde) to a pint of water. For despatch, the fish should be wrapped in a cloth wrung out in the solution, placed in a plastic bag and wrapped in stout brown paper; please enclose the name and address of the sender and whether the fish should be returned.

The fish should be weighed as soon as possible after capture and before being placed in preserving liquids.

The claimant should contact the Committee Secretary by telephone, telegram or letter as soon as possible after the capture. Advice will then be given concerning preservation and identification.

WORLD RECORD FISH

World record marine game fishes are the concern of the International Game Fish Association, Holiday Inn Arcade, 3000 E. Las Olas Boulevard, Fort Lauderdale, Florida 33316, U.S.A. Species of fish included in the world records lists which are found off the British Isles are mako shark, porbeagle shark, thresher shark and blue shark. World record claims in respect of these fish should be made through the Shark Angling Club of Great Britain, Looe, Cornwall.

SHARK RECORDS

Shark records on the British list are for the heaviest fish of each species, irrespective of the strength of line used; for records of sharks caught on different breaking strains of line please refer to the records of the Shark Angling Club of Great Britain.

IRISH RECORD FISH

Claims for fish caught in Northern Ireland are dealt with by the British Record (rod-caught) Fish Committee.

Claims for fish caught in Eire should be made to the Irish Specimen Fish Committee, Balnagowan, Mobhi Boreen, Glasnevin, Dublin 9.

CHAPTER XVII

TINCA TINCA THE TENCH

THE name of this interesting fish comes from the French '*Tanche*,' which in turn was derived from the Latin '*Tinca*.'

There can be no mistake in identifying tench. The rounded shape of the fins and the powerful, almost straight tail are characteristic; the tiny scales and small orange-rimmed eyes, together with the general coloration of tench, are so distinctive that, once having seen these fish, the novice cannot be misled. The common or green tench varies in colour from yellowish-green to a deep greenish-black. There is another and much rarer species known as 'golden tench', the colour of these fish being brilliant orange on the back, shading down to lemon yellow.

A fine brace of golden tench taken by the writer can be seen in a coloration case at the British Museum (Natural History).

It is interesting to note that no hybrid with tench is known, and this golden variety is not the result of cross breeding, but of xanthochroism. In specimens exhibiting this peculiarity the black or brown pigment in the skin is entirely lacking, the orange and yellow only being developed. Carp, eels, trout and other fish are sometimes similarly affected, but the common goldfish is the most familiar example.

Tench are not fish which are commonly caught, and the question arises where shall we find them. They are distributed all over Europe and in the British Isles, especially in East Anglia and the Fens; and they are essentially inhabitants of still water, but may also be found in slow-flowing rivers like the Bedfordshire Ouse. They thrive in small weedy ponds where the bottom is thick mud. Many small ponds which had not been suspected of containing fish have ultimately produced fine tench.

The feeding habits of *Tinca tinca* are most uncertain, and the angler must not be disappointed if he fishes for days without a bite. On the other hand, go to a tench water when they are inclined to feed, and your float or ledger tackle will hardly have time to settle after the cast before a fish will be at the bait.

Tench bite in a peculiar way. The float will bob, bob, sometimes for minutes, then move along the surface slowly and dip. That is the time to strike. At times the fish will nibble and play with the bait, but will not take it seriously. I have found the advice of Bickerdyke profitable on these occasions, i.e. to draw the bait gently along the bottom a foot or so. This seems to have the effect of making the fish take it lest it shall be withdrawn entirely.

Tench are most tenacious of life and will live for long periods out of water. I well remember bringing a brace from Tring to London to be 'set up.' Opening the parcel before the taxidermist to show my prizes, I was amazed when one of the fish leapt from the table on to the floor.

During the summer months tench are sluggish, retiring fish; in the winter they dig themselves into the mud with their powerful fins and sleep. Seibold describes how some tench, having been so buried, were dredged up. They appeared to be dead, but being tapped gently with a stick, revived and made their way back to the water.

The reader may be assured that all sluggishness leaves a tench the moment it is hooked. They are good fighters, and you may not require your net the first time you see the hooked fish.

Apart from their fighting qualities which always appeal, tench grow to a good size.

For many years the record for rod-caught tench was held jointly at 7 lb. by a Mr. Stacey who took a fish of that weight from the Pottery Pits, near Weston-super-Mare in 1882; and the Rev. E. C. Alston, who, in 1933 caught one of the same weight from a mere near Thetford. Then in July 1948, claim to a new record was made by B. S. Dawson, of Worthing, in respect of a tench taken on the 10th of that month, from a gravel pit near Chichester, which was said to weigh 7 lb. 2 oz.

This fish was entered in the *Daily Mirror* angling contest and was sent by that paper to Messrs. J. Cooper & Sons, to be 'set up.' Having received the fish Messrs. Cooper wrote to the editor of the *Angler's News* (which has now ceased publication), as follows:

Angler's News—7th August, 1948.

THE RECORD TENCH

Sir,—With reference to the report in the *Angler's News* of 24th July, of the capture of a tench by Mr. B. S. Dawson, who claims it to be the record, if this is the same fish as reported by the *Daily Mirror*, which we have for mounting, I am afraid a mistake has been made in the weight.

The *Daily Mirror* reports it as 7 lb. 6 oz. You report it as 7 lb. 2 oz., and I made it 6 lb. 2½ oz. with newspaper, and in a frozen state. The weighing was witnessed by the 'D.M.' chauffeur and four friends of mine, and it was weighed on proper scales. I can only presume Mr. Dawson weighed it on a spring balance which had strained a pound.

Yours etc., J. COOPER & SONS.

The editor commented:

Perhaps Mr. Dawson will take this matter up, as we received from him the letter which appeared in our issue for 24th July, giving weight and names and addresses of witnesses of the weighing.—ED.

Mr. Dawson did in fact comply with this editorial request, and a considerable correspondence followed which space forbids me quoting. However, the outcome was that having sifted the facts, the editors of both the *Fishing Gazette*, the *Angler's News* and my good friend Bernard Venables, who was at the time angling correspondent of the *Daily Mirror*, accepted the originally recorded weight of this specimen, a decision with which I could have no complaint.

So it was that a dual record which had stood for sixty-six years was swept away, but it was not to reign long.

Came the evening of 1st August, 1950, and Mr. M. Foode, captain of the Highfields W.M.C.A.C. of Leicester, foregathered with his team, to fish a match against the South Leicester W.M.C.A.C. in the Leicester Canal, on the Aylestone side. Their opponents did not however put in appearance at the appropriate time, so the Highfield team decided to fish a sweepstake match amongst themselves.

Using a small portion of red worm, on a No. 16 hook tied to $1\frac{1}{2}$ lb. b.s. line, and a 3 lb. b.s. nylon line, Mr. Foode fished from 7.30 p.m. till just turned 9 o'clock.

Then it happened.

He made contact with the largest rod-caught tench on record. It weighed 8 lb. 8 oz.!

Some twenty people watched this skilful angler fight the great fish, which he subdued in as many minutes.

Once ashore, the water bailiff, the club secretary and ten witnesses, weighed the fish on automatic scales, at the shop of Mr. S. Chamberlain, of Leicester, and an official weight and species chit was issued to its captor.

Then—that tench was *returned to the water alive*! I can only say, what a pity.

At the time someone suggested that—alive—it would have been a wonderful draw at the aquarium of the Zoological Society of London. To which I add, that at its demise its stuffed carcass would have graced the British Museum of Natural History.

Some experts have doubts regarding the species of this fish and believe that it may have been confused with a leather carp.

On 22nd August, 1923, Messrs. Burn and Jackson made a tremendous catch of 172 tench weighing 602 lb.—an average of $3\frac{1}{2}$ lb. each. (Let us hope that these fish were not killed!) From this it will be seen that, despite their fastidiousness, tench will on occasion provide anglers with a 'red-letter day.'

Mr. Foode's record $8\frac{1}{2}$ pounder held sway until July 1959, then it looked like being beaten twice by giant tench from a water owned by a Wraysbury (Middx.) farmer.

The first, a magnificent 11 lb. specimen, was caught by 17-year-old Donald Laing of Moor Farm, Wraysbury, on ledgered bread-flake. And this was young Laing's first tench!

The following tracing of the outline of this fish taken from a Press picture, shows that it was an unprepossessing creature. Look at that belly! It is distended out of all proportion to say the least. Why and by what I wonder? In my view it is something more than middle-age-spread. It's my guess that the fish was either spawn-bound or diseased.

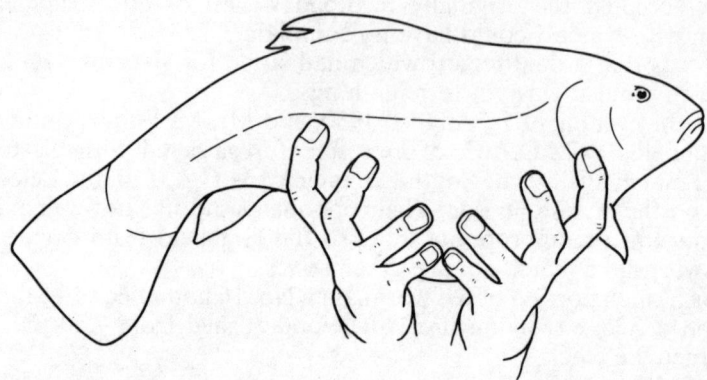

The second Wraysbury giant, also of the pot-bellied variety, was taken by Mr. Winston Dearsley and tipped the scale at 9 lb. 9¾ oz.

This fish was sent to the aquarium of the Zoological Society of London. One of the aquarium keepers with whom I discussed the distention of the fish, expressed the view that *it might* be due to an excess of hemp.

Late in 1959 the Zoological Authorities in London stated that the 9 lb. 9¾ oz. Wraysbury tench was suffering from some abnormal condition.

It died later in the Zoo Aquarium and the Rod-Caught Record Committee decided subsequently:

> That it could not accept as a new record a fish which was obviously abnormal although its rules of procedure did not cover this contingency.

Angling Times, 13 November, 1959.

Under the heading 'Tench record stands' said:

> The 9 lb. 9 oz. 12 dr. 'pretender' to the British record tench title . . . has died in the London Zoo Aquarium . . . And with it has gone any hope of a new record.

It also said:

> No decision on boy's 11-pounder.

In the light of the Record Committee's decision not to accept abnormal fish, however, it is difficult to see how any further consideration can be given to the 11 lb. fish which suffered the precise abnormality of the smaller tench taken from the same water.

On 12 July, 1963, Mr. J. Salisbury, of Chatteris, Cambs., took a healthy 9 lb. 1 oz. tench from Eggitt's Lake, Hemingford Grey, Hunts, which was subsequently attested as the new record for the species. Mr. Salisbury's bait was 'four red worms.' This record survived the record Fish purge, described in Chapter XVI, and still stands at August 1972.

Having discussed some large tench, a word about the smaller ones will not be amiss.

In a lecture given before a learned society the speaker stated:

> The food of tench is similar to that of roach and bream, but I have not had an opportunity of making an intensive study of these fish, owing to the extreme difficulty of catching any but large tench.
> *Small tench are never caught by an angler: I have never caught one weighing less than* $2\frac{1}{2}$ *lb.*

The italics are mine as I regard this statement as most interesting to say the least and I have reason to doubt its accuracy.

I have no doubt that it applied absolutely to the waters with which the speaker was familiar; and while agreeing that really small tench are comparatively rare, I think I should be right in saying that in some waters a $2\frac{1}{2}$ lb. tench would be regarded as a 'good'un.' I have caught tench weighing much less, but not what might be called a fry of the species. Never, by the way, is in my view a word to be avoided where matters of angling are concerned. As the late Professor Joad would have said: 'It all depends on what you mean by small.'

One other item of interest claims attention before I turn to angling procedure. It is more easy to distinguish the sex of tench than of any other fresh-water species—the shape of the ventral fins gives the clue. The illustration shows clearly the difference between the spoon-like fin of the male and the much flatter and less powerful fin of the female fish.

Powerful spoon-like ventral of male tench.

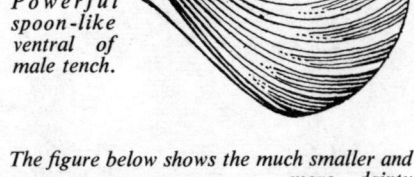

The figure below shows the much smaller and more dainty ventral of the hen fish.

It is seldom a disadvantage to prepare a swim before fishing, but the weedy and overgrown nature of the water in which tench delight often makes preparation essential. The angler's chief enemy is the fine weed growing below water in the mud. This, if allowed to remain, will completely hide the bait, with an obviously unsatisfactory result. This weed is too fine to cut, and the best way to clear it out of a swim is to drag a roll of barbed wire or a rake across the bottom where it is proposed to fish. In many instances water-lilies present difficulties. There are specially designed cutters for these, but some anglers join two scythe blades to make a most effective cutter. If the blades are dragged along the bottom they will cut the strong lily stems cleanly, and the cut portions which float can be removed from the water. This preparation may seem unduly elaborate to some, but the lack of it in some waters has more to do with 'blank days' than the capriciousness of the fish. If you can persuade a keeper (in private water, which usually offers the best tench fishing) to do this clearing, or can induce a friend to help you, so much the better. It is, of course, only necessary in very overgrown waters.

The tackle I use for tench angling is a 10- to 12-ft. rod, a 3½ in. narrow drummed Sheffield reel, and a Terylene line of 6 lb. breaking strain; 4 lb. b.s. casts with hook-links to match, are fine enough for day fishing, while 5 lb. line is not too thick at night. No. 8 or 9 Crystal hooks, or Marston worm hooks of the same size, are good. For water up to 6 ft. deep, the float should be the smallest possible, and if weather conditions permit, a 'self-cocker,' with not more than one or at most two shot on the cast is desirable. This allows the bait to sink in a leisurely and natural way, which is a matter of importance. The illustration shows another and much heavier tackle, which I have used with good effect in water from 10 to 14 ft. deep. It will be seen from this gear one bait lies on the bottom, while the other is suspended just above. It is my experience that the suspended bait takes more fish, but the one on the bottom seems to attract the larger specimens. In the case of golden tench, I found that to have a single bait 6 in. from the bottom was more effective than the arrangement shown, which was so successful with the green variety. Nevertheless, I should always try both methods if necessary, and do not believe that one is consistently more effective than the other.

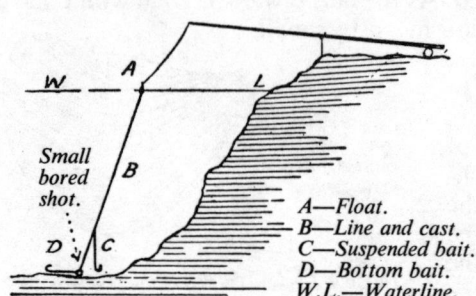

A—Float.
B—Line and cast.
C—Suspended bait.
D—Bottom bait.
W.L.—Waterline.

Showing an effective 'rig' for tench fishing.

I referred earlier (p. 140) to a well-tried and simple method of float-ledgering that has come to be known as 'the lift method,' the principle of which is illustrated on page 141. When the fish lifts the shot the float rises and lies flat on the water.

Some anglers maintain a series of 'lift rigs' to embrace various strengths of tackle, sizes and types of float, positioning of the shot and what not, to meet differing conditions of water, wind, etc. These 'rigs' vary very little in the main, but two of them if not invented certainly adopted by those expert tench anglers the Taylor brothers, are worthy of mention.

In his excellent book *Angling In Earnest* (MacGibbon & Kee, 1958) Fred Taylor illustrates and explains five 'lift method' tackles of which these are two.

What a rugged little fighter the gudgeon, *Gobio gobio*, is! Never weighing more than a few ounces (the rod caught record is 4 oz.) the gudgeon gives such a firm bite that the unfortunate angler usually expects a fish of considerably larger proportions.

[*Photograph: W. J. Howes*]

A sad picture this. The grayling (*Thymallus thymallus*) is one of the most attractive of our freshwater fishes, and fully deserves its name "lady of the stream". But not in this photograph, which is of a large specimen set in a poor background and not retaining any of the graceful lines one expects. Noticeable are the sadly distorted mouth and too-small eyes, which should be larger in proportion to the size of the head. The one good feature is the set of the distinctive and proud dorsal fin.

[*Photograph: W. J. Howes*]

Peter Thomas with Richard Walker's record 44 lb. carp.

The powerful, rugged conformation of the wild, or common carp (*Cyprinus carpio*) is well displayed in this photograph. The powerful tail fin, with its muscular "root", enables the carp to make extremely strong runs, very often bringing disaster to any terminal tackle not chosen wisely.

[Photograph: W. J. Howes]

Illustration A shows the tackle arranged to fish a grain of wheat *below the surface of the mud*. This may at first appear to be a crazy procedure. But is it? Who would deny that tench habitually root about in the mud in search of animalculae and that they often do so to the exclusion of more obvious food lying on the surface of the mud?

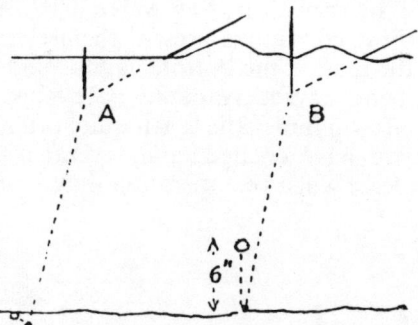

This, then, is the way of this submerged bait fishing. The bait understewed wheat which is small but if not over-cooked heavy enough to

Note line from base of float is held as taut as possible in readiness for quick bites.

sink into the mud. The hook a No. 16 to 4 lb. b.s. monofil with one heavy shot very near the hook. The area around the actual bait must be well sprinkled with loose grains of wheat. The bites are quick *verb sap*.

Mr. Taylor does not advise this method until or unless more orthodox methods have failed.

Illustration B which is self explanatory shows the 'lift' rig for use when fishing crust in rough conditions.

If possible, the depth should be known before fishing commences, as the use of a plummet is in my view an undesirable disturbance. Even if the depth is not known, it is better to find it by trial than to use a plummet.

Baits used for tench fishing are numerous, but of them all I prefer a lawn worm. These may be gathered on lawns at night by the light of an electric torch, but some skill is necessary to success. Seeing the worm lying half or three parts out of its hole, the angler should place a finger upon it, and then gently persuade the tail portion to leave home by a series of gentle jerks. Watch a blackbird extract a worm and you will see the perfect technique. Otherwise the worm will almost invariably retire into the ground with such speed that it will be lost. Bread paste, wasp grubs, gentles and brandling worms (used in a bunch) are all good baits at times and in different waters.

When possible, 'baiting-up,' carried out for three or four days prior to fishing, is a great advantage. But in any case ground-baiting for tench should be carried out with a sparing hand. Bread, bran and middlings make a good tench ground-bait, and it is important that a small quantity of the hook-bait should be mixed with it. Many anglers overlook this, and their bags are correspondingly light.

When to fish for tench is the final consideration. Most of the best fish have been taken either in the late evening or early morning. I prefer the time from sunrise to 8.30 on a warm summer morning. Those mornings when mist rises from the water, and there is hardly a breath of wind, are ideal for tench fishing.

In very clear, low water it is often impossible to take tench. When these conditions present themselves, it is an excellent device to stir up the mud at the bottom as thoroughly as possible with whatever instrument may be available. After this, throw in some ground-bait, and in a few minutes the tench quite often show a marked interest in the murk you have created, and several may be taken before the mud-clouds clear, when the operation may be repeated.

CHAPTER XVIII

THE EEL: A MYSTERIOUS FISH

I COULD hardly credit my hearing—a distinguished angler was expressing his dissatisfaction in a most forceful way because he had caught a 16 lb. pike! I agree with those who say he had small cause to complain, but he was fishing for a specimen eel, and his remarks were indicative of disappointment. There is no more mysterious fish in British freshwaters. Old Izaak thought that eels were produced 'either of dew or out of the corruption of the earth,' while David Cairncross wrote a book to prove that silver eels were the offspring of water-beetles.

We know now that eels migrate from the rivers in the autumn, and breed in the sea at depths of five hundred fathoms and more, but even today the fertilized egg of the eel is unknown. There is only one species of eel in British freshwater, but this species exhibits marked differences which have led many anglers to believe there are at least two kinds. The yellow eel is merely the fish in its everyday attire, while silver eels are the same fish in their wedding dress. Eels in their yellow state have much larger mouths and smaller eyes than when they become silver. The yellow eel is so voracious that it often develops a large ugly mouth, while the silver eel, which feeds very little, has a sharp snout and smaller mouth. On the other hand, the eye of the silver eel which is about to go to sea is developed to enable it to cope with conditions in the gloom of great depths.

Some anglers will not know that in its earliest form an eel is a flat fish. The illustration on the next page shows the young eel, or Leptocephalus—what a splendid name for the infant! It was the great Danish naturalist E. J. Schmidt who unravelled the mysteries of an eel from the time when these flat, almost transparent larvae are found at great depths in the sea to their ascent of our rivers as elvers. Adult eels travel thousands of miles, and it has been ascertained that in 93 days they are able to cover as much as 750 miles under water. This in itself is very wonderful, but what of their passage overland? This to me is the most extraordinary feature of the eel's life history. Dr. Tate Regan said that eels kept by him in an aquarium spent most of the day buried in the sand at the bottom, but that night after night they escaped and were found in the morning on the other side of the room apparently dead, but when returned to the water they swam about and were none the worse for their adventure.

It is easy to understand eels running into our rivers from the sea, but they are abundant in lakes and ponds which are absolutely land-locked, and are miles from the nearest river. How do they get there? It is held by ichthyologists that they travel overland to these isolated waters.

It is generally held that any such movement of eels is made by night, but my correspondent assures me that he witnessed this detour in broad daylight.

I am, however, able to find very few direct witnesses of the over-land migration of eels. This scarcity of witnesses is very remarkable and it would be a matter of the greatest interest if some further evidence of this *overland* movement of eels could be found. Has any reader of this

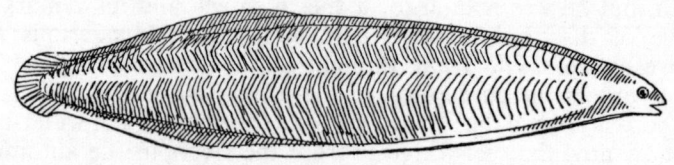

The Leptocephalus, or young eel.

book ever seen an eel or eels *crossing the open country*? There are ponds and lakes containing thousands of eels; is it possible that their migration to these waters, which must have been going on for centuries, has escaped even accidental observation?

Browsing through *Angling Times* (April 1962) I read with nostalgic interest an article by W. J. Wallis on Devon's famous Slapton Ley, in which he wrote:

> I think I am one of the few people who have witnessed the mass migra-tion of eels from the Ley over the road and shingle into the surf.

Having sought authentic evidence of this phenomenon for years, I lost no time in contacting Mr. Wallis, one-time angling correspondent of the *Western Morning News*, who supplied the following details:

> Just after dawn on a wild October day in 1921, I and two friends (C. J. Akhurst and S. Heydon, both since deceased) were walking towards Beesands along the coast road, which with the foreshore separates the Ley from the sea.
>
> As we neared Torcross at the southern end of the Ley we saw an eel crossing the road and two others leaving the lake. Standing at a discreet vantage point we watched for fully half an hour, meanwhile a score or more eels of varying sizes, some very large, crossed the road at considerable speed heading for the sea. I have not measured it but I estimated the over-land distance as some 500 yards from the Ley to the sea at high tide. This

migration may have been in progress before we arrived and it showed signs of slackening by the time we had to leave the fascinating sight to keep our appointment.

It was an experience I shall never forget. I stood spellbound by this amazing sight. Although I have met single eels travelling over fields towards the sea on several occasions, I have not seen anything like this either before or since.

Many anglers have never fished specially for eels, and have regarded them as unwelcome guests when they have annexed the bait intended for some other quarry. I have a vivid recollection of being 'smashed up' by a real whopper while tench fishing one evening. That eel gave me nearly an hour's play before it wallowed back from the rim of the net into the deeps, and the experience gave me a wholesome respect for the larger specimens at least. Freshwater eels have been recorded up to 30 lb. in weight—the one I lost could not have been much more than a third of that weight—so what may be expected from a really large specimen I can only leave to the imagination. The big fellows are worthy of the skill of any angler, but they are rare. As to the fry known as 'bootlaces,' their tails make exceedingly useful pike spinning baits.

An eel taken in 1922 by C. Mitchell at Bitterwell Lake, weighed 8 lb. 8 oz. It held the record until 1969, when Hunstrete Lake yielded an 8 lb. 10 oz. fish, caught by Mr. A. Dart. Two other noteworthy specimens come to mind. In October 1945, Norman Mackenzie (aged 16) caught a 7 lb. eel from one of the lochs of the Caledonian Canal at Fort Augustus.

'Vera Cruz' commenting on this fish said:

Eels, large or small, seldom find themselves in print so far as Scottish newspapers and sporting journals are concerned, but there has to be recorded the capture of a 'monster' eel. . . .

From such a comment, over the signature of an experienced angling writer, one may be sure that large eels do not favour anglers.

The second notable eel which has come to my notice weighed 6 lb. 5 oz. 4 dr. and was taken by C. Young, from Leasowes Pool, Halesowen, near Birmingham, on 25th September, 1946.

It was 3 ft. 6 in. long and $9\frac{3}{4}$ in. in girth. You may do better, I hope so. But kill every eel you catch is my advice.

It would appear that there is scope for a considerable improvement on the $8\frac{1}{2}$ lb. record.

According to Dr. Maurice Burton, D.Sc., F.R.S.A., F.L.S., F.Z.S., Deputy Keeper of Zoology at the British Museum, eels which are unable for any reason to make the breeding migration are known to attain a great size. He says:

There is, in fact, evidence that eels confined in cold water could grow to 15 ft. or more.

What an eel of this length would weigh, those of mathematical skill may care to compute using Mr. Young's fish as a yard stick. The necessary calculation is beyond me, but I'll hazard that quite exceptionally powerful tackle would be essential to its capture.

To catch big eels I favour a small dead fish as bait used on a ledger and threaded on a wire-served hook as shown in the illustration. A baiting needle is required to mount these baits, and if your expedition

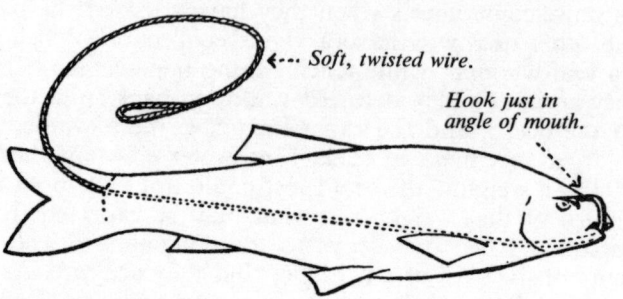

Showing method of mounting dead bait for eels.

is at night, which is by far the best time to take the 'big 'uns' it is well to have a supply of baits ready threaded, and to attach them to the line by the simple expedient of a link-swivel. To my mind it is important to secrete the hook as far as possible, for it is my experience that eels have an uncanny knack of dodging a hook. Time and again I have had an eel at my live bait when pike fishing, only to find that it had taken the tail portion of the bait immediately behind the dorsal hook of my 'snap tackle.'

There is no room for doubt that eels have an acute sense of smell, it is therefore an advantage to puncture or score your dead-bait with a sharp knife or stiletto to release its flavours. Some anglers smear with pilchard oil, even injecting the oil into the body cavity by means of a syringe. Ground-baiting with the entrails of either a chicken or rabbit is favoured by some, but it is a messy procedure.

As to the size of bait, I favour 3 in. fish. In this connection it is essential to give an eel plenty of time to pouch the bait before striking.

Some anglers are in a quandary as to whether eel baits, should be fresh or 'high'. I plump for fresh baits, believing that *Anguilla* is as resentful of putrefaction as I am. Right or wrong though I may be in this decision, no eel will ever induce me to handle stinking baits. It is up to you.

Warm summer nights are ideal for eel fishing, and it is a strange fact that, day or night, thundery weather causes them to feed ravenously. Large 'lobs' are excellent baits, and in some waters a big bunch of 'brandlings' is good.

Many eels are taken with the spear—a trident-like affair —but I have never speared eels, and cannot therefore do more than illustrate the 'business end' of the spear for the interest of those who may care to make a trial of this method.

Eels are such voracious destroyers of young fish and fish spawn that I strongly recommend they should never be returned when caught. A few eel-fishing contests among angling clubs might help to thin them out; in any case every eel killed would save thousands of other fish. Eels have only one advantage. When properly cooked they provide excellent food. Having read the above paragraph, the reader will no doubt share my trepidation at the decision of the Ministry of Agriculture and Fisheries in recent years to approve the turning of vast quantities of elvers into old Father Thames.

Head of eel spear.

In closing this short chapter I am reminded that I have at times encountered anglers fishing during the Statutory close season, who explained that they were 'after eels,' which they profess to believe are fair game throughout the year. That this is a dangerous misconception is evidenced by the opening lines of Section 35, Subsection 1 of the Salmon and Freshwater Fisheries Act, 1923, which reads:

> No person shall during the annual close season for freshwater fish, fish for eels by means of rod and line. . . .

Whether the enclosing dates for the fence period of freshwater fish other than trout are correctly placed is a matter which has often been disputed; but in the absence of any official change they are from the 15th March to the 15th day of June following, both dates inclusive.

CHAPTER XIX

BLEAK OR 'WHITLING DODGING'

'WHITLING dodging' is an old-time Trent-side expression indicating bleak fishing. Bleak are often neglected merely because they are small and deny the angler the joy of having his tackle 'smashed up.' Nevertheless, their usefulness and interesting characteristics merit the consideration of every all-round fisherman. Gregarious, they move about near the surface of the water in large shoals, and amongst their numbers are many 'glass-case' fish, any of which would gladden the heart of a 'specimen hunter.' In the 'nineties, Mr. H. Stubbins of Nottingham took a monster weighing 5¼ oz. at Radcliffe-on-Trent, and I am not aware that this record has been broken.

On the 22nd November, 1958, The British Record (Rod-Caught) Fish Committee issued the undernoted declaration:

'The following fish have been accepted as new British records:
BLEAK (*Alburnus alburnus*) of 3¼ oz. caught on the Thames near Kingston Bridge on September 27th by John Oliver (aged 12), etc., etc., etc.'

I can only presume that this body has not been able to substantiate Mr. Stubbins' 5¼ oz. fish to their satisfaction; and have accordingly revised this record in their lists. This 5¼ oz. bleak was first recorded by H. Coxon in *Coarse Fish Angling*, 1896.

As I have no cause to doubt the 5¼ oz. Stubbins' record, however, it will remain as an item of interest in this volume.

In March 1960 news came of the capture of a 4 oz. 2 dr. bleak by F. Brown of Nottingham, from the R. Trent at Long Higgin. It was witnessed as to weight and species by several anglers including The President of the Nottingham A.A. and the 1957 winner of the National Championship. This fish was not accepted by the Record Committee.

Fishing the Woking Water Company's reservoir at Walton, Surrey, on 14th August, 1933, D. Sizmur grassed a 3¾ oz. bleak to create, for a number of years, a new record. It beat the previous fish by half an ounce. The bait was maggot. The present record bleak (March 1973) is held by D. Pollard, who caught a fish of 3 oz. 15½ dr. from a pond at Staythorpe Power Station, near Newark, Notts., on 2nd August, 1971.

For my part, if I catch one of 4 oz. it will be hurried to the taxidermist.

Their brilliant silver scales render bleak a most attractive spinning lure for the elusive Thames trout, pike and perch. At the time of the year when other fish are often disinclined to feed, bleak are more obliging, and summer is the time to collect and grade them in sizes for spinning operations later on. The method of preserving them is simple yet so effective that they will keep perfectly for years.

Having selected the larger fish for pike and the smaller ones for trout and perch, they are washed and placed in glass jars of suitable size, the jars being fitted with airtight screw or lever tops. The bleak should be placed head foremost into these jars and care taken to keep them straight. It then only remains to cover them completely with formalin in the proportion of one tablespoonful of 40 per cent solution to a pint of water.

After being in formalin a day or so the fish may exude a murky discolouration. When this appears remove them from the liquor, which should be thrown away, and re-wash them thoroughly under a running tap. Then put them back into the jars and cover them with formalin as before. The addition of a little glycerine is said to keep the bait pliable but is not essential. After this second washing and renewal of the preservative, the baits will remain bright and keep indefinitely. It is not necessary to take a jar of baits with you when you go fishing. Simply take out the number you are likely to require (over-estimation is advised) and put them in an old baccy tin. When properly pickled they will keep for days and are very easily carried. Once out of the liquor there is a tendency for the baits to shrink, but I have not found this a disadvantage. Don't forget to wash the fish very thoroughly before putting them into the tin; this helps to rid them of the odour of formalin which is repellent to your quarry. Some anglers place their preserved baits in salt overnight after the final washing. Bleak are not good live baits, for, while they are most acceptable to large Thames trout when in their natural state, being 'surface swimmers,' they are extremely delicate and will soon die if taken from the water and harnessed to a live bait tackle.

It is interesting to note conversely, that many fish which live in the deeps and on the bottom have a comparatively low ratio of respiration, are much more tenacious of life, and will live for long periods out of water.

Years ago bleak were important to commerce in the production of synthetic pearls. The silver pigment or nacre was extracted from their scales and injected into thin hollow glass beads, giving them a pearly lustre. From four to six thousand bleak produced one pound of scales from which 4 oz. of pigment was obtained.

A most fascinating method of taking bleak is to cast one gentle on a Number 14 hook with a light fly rod. The line should be the finest procurable and no shot is necessary. For a float an eighth or quarter inch square of cork slotted on the cast one to three feet from the hook is ideal. With this apparatus a day's 'whitling dodging' is a most interesting diversion, and the fish caught may do great execution as spinning later on.

Moreover, a dish of bleak cooked in the manner of sprats is very appetizing.

On occasion in the summer you may see a bleak gyrating on the surface—round and round—without apparent reason. This is a 'mad bleak' and should, if possible, be caught and killed. Its distress is occasioned by an irritating parasite.

On summer evenings, in particular, you will quite often see roach and indeed many other of our freshwater fishes leaping out of the water. This may in some cases be an exhibition of *joie de vivre*. I think, however, that more often it is the result of the unwelcome attentions of *Argulus*, the fish-louse. Every angler has seen these little animals adhering to fish they caught. It is kindness to remove them, before returning the fish to the water.

CHAPTER XX

ANGLING FOR 'GOBIO' THE GUDGEON

THIS small fish defies the scorn of anglers despite its comparatively diminutive proportions. *Gobio* the gudgeon lives and feeds exclusively on the beds of rivers and lakes. These little fish are sombre in general colour and are irregularly speckled in such a way as to make them almost indistinguishable from their surroundings.

They are very similar to barbel in general appearance, but are easily distinguished from the fact that they have only two beards whereas barbel have four. There is little doubt that these beards, which are variously known as barbels or barbules, are highly sensitive feelers or nerve centres with which the fish feels objects on the bottom and is to some extent able by their use to detect and select food.

Gudgeon are often described as ubiquitous, but this is hardly accurate. While they are found generally throughout England, Wales and Ireland, they are absent from Cornwall, West Wales, the Lake District and Scotland. Large shoals of gudgeon are often to be seen on gravel or sandy beds near the water's edge, and it is a most fascinating pastime to catch them while actually observing their movements.

For their capture the very lightest tackle only is necessary. A Number 14 or 16 hook with a fragment of red worm or a gentle as bait will do incredible execution. No ground-bait is necessary, but a stirring or raking up of the bottom with a long-handled rake will be found most beneficial in bringing gudgeon together and keeping them 'on the feed' in one place.

It is useful to remember that if gudgeon are present they will feed almost at once—if they do not, the presence of a pike or a shoal of perch is probably the cause, and for this reason a paternoster should always be at hand to remove these not always unwelcome visitors. The advent of other than predatory fish will sometimes cause a lull in the sport. Attracted by the larvae, etc., which are raised by the raking operations, barbel will sometimes come into the swim and 'put down' the gudgeon. I assure readers that gudgeon fishing is far from tame. Hook a good barbel unexpectedly on your light tackle and all the thrills of a tight line will be yours before you land it. The bait on the bottom, frequent rakings, fine tackle and, if possible, a fine day, and gudgeon fishing is as fascinating as angling for any other fish that swims. The method of preserving them for spinning is as described on page 169 in the chapter on bleak.

Until 1955 the record for gudgeon was shared by three anglers, i.e., G. Cedric, who took a 4¼ oz. specimen at Datchet on the Thames, in August 1933, and W. R. Bostock, with a fish of the same weight from Hoggs Pond, Shipley, near Derby, in October 1935 and J. D. Lewin (or Lewtin), a Leicester schoolboy, who in 1950 caught a 4¼ oz. gudgeon from the River Soar in unusual circumstances.

I talked with this boy in London when he came up to receive a *Daily Mirror* prize, but foolishly did not record our conversation at the time. My recollection is, however, sufficiently clear to enable me to state he was fishing while he did his homework! And being without bait found a cigarette end which he attached to his hook and threw in. *The result was this 4¼ oz. gudgeon!*

My subsequent efforts to contact the lad with a view to putting this odd story in writing were unavailing, but the reader may be assured that in essence the foregoing is accurate. Wonders never cease for anglers.

Came the 29th June, 1955 and R. Summers, a pupil of the London County Council anglers' class, caught a gudgeon which weighed a fraction over 4¾ oz., while fishing a War Department lake at Woolwich, where the class has special facilities.

The fish was identified for species and weighed by Mr. Lewis A. Harris, then an L.C.C. instructor, and Chairman of the Central Association of London and Provincial Angling Clubs, and witnessed by a dozen anglers who were present at the time.

Two of the inexorable provisions under which the L.C.C. class is permitted to fish this lake are that all fish must be returned alive to the water; and cameras are strictly contraband under Defence Regulations in the area where the lake is situated. It is not therefore possible to make even a photographic record of any specimen taken.

At the time when this gudgeon was caught, Mr. Harris regarded it only as an exceptional specimen, believing that the record was held by a heavier fish, and it was not until 1956 when this error was realized, that he made a claim to establish Mr. Summers' specimen as the record for the species.

Now most of the record compiling authorities (none of which I believe are elected though they are generally accepted) have adopted a rule which demands that a record claimant must be able to produce the fish in question.

This as a protection against inaccurate identification of species by incompetent persons, is both necessary and admirable. It does not however in my view constitute a mandate to expunge indisputably authenticated claims merely because for reasons beyond control the fish in question cannot be produced.

And in my considered opinion its application in this instance would be an affront to the L.C.C. angling instructor who officiated and lodged a record claim on his pupil's behalf.

The precise weight of this fish was moreover measured on a scale, the accuracy of which was specially checked and was witnessed by so many people that it must be regarded as irrefutable.

These being the facts the 4¾ oz. fish caught by R. Summers must for me be set down as the record rod-caught gudgeon as at Feb. 1960. However, the Record Committee, as explained in an earlier chapter, decided to start from scratch so far as *Gobio* is concerned and announced a minimum qualifying weight of 3 oz. 8 dr. This was reached in October 1971, when a new record gudgeon, weighing 4 oz. was accepted. The fish was caught by M. Morris from Susworth Roach Ponds, Lincs.

In August 1972 the angling Press reported the capture of a 4 oz. 3 dr. gudgeon—3 dr. above the record—from the river Terne. There is no news of this fish being accepted by the Record Committee.

Small barbel and large gudgeon

In my experience really small barbel and really large gudgeon are more than scarce. It would be interesting, however, to compare a four-ounce specimen of both fish. I should be greatly surprised if a very large number of anglers did not mistake one for the other. Pardonable, indeed, for there are unfortunately far more gudgeon than barbel, and they have much in common in their general appearance. The placing of the fins, contour of the body and construction of the head, not to speak of their similarity (in many cases) in colour, would almost certainly cause the unwary to accept small barbel as gudgeon without a second thought. The illustrations, however, serve to show the main superficial difference at a glance The eye of a gudgeon is proportionately much larger than that of a barbel, while the former has two posterior barbels only, and the latter two posterior and two anterior.

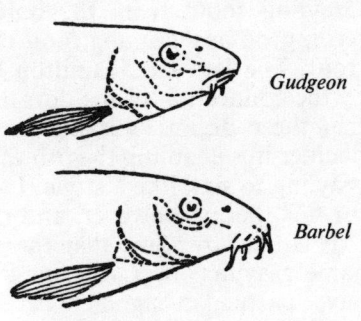

Gudgeon

Barbel

Head of gudgeon and barbel.

CHAPTER XXI

GRAYLING

GRAYLING are comparatively rare despite the fact that they abound in some localities. But this does not absolve any angler from acquiring some knowledge of these beautiful and sporting fish. A day with the grayling may come your way at any time. Be ready for it! The best grayling fishing is to be had in the winter months, and it is encouraging to remember that their flesh is fine eating.

In my opinion there is no more beautiful coarse fish. The colouring varies considerably in different waters. Purple, greenish gold and silver grey combine in the scales of a grayling to delight the angler's eye. The characteristically large dorsal fin is also richly coloured and marked. Grayling shoot from the bottom to the surface of the water when feeding on any floating food rather than remain near the surface like trout. The late Dr. Hamilton held that this movement was facilitated by the connection of the dorsal fin with the air bladder of the fish—and that these organs working in unison—when the fin is raised, the air bladder fills enabling the fish to rise rapidly, while the reverse causes the grayling to sink like a stone. I am not able to find any scientific support for this theory, however, and offer it merely as an item of interest.

It is held by some that the silvery grey of the sides give rise to the name grayling. Its Latin name (*Thymallus thymallus*) would appear to have particular significance and refers doubtless to the fact that grayling are said by some to have the scent of thyme when taken from the water. I have never been able to detect this perfume.

While dealing with the fish itself, I must make special mention of what has come to be a fetish, but is in my opinion a fallacy. Most writers will tell you that grayling are soft mouthed and that you should therefore 'strike' them gently less they should tear away. The fact is that the sides of a grayling's mouth are tender, but the interior and especially the roof of the mouth is firm and offers good anchorage for a sharp, well-tempered hook, which should be driven firmly home. It is true that large numbers of grayling are lost in the 'play,' the peculiar rolling tactics of their fight and the softness of the outer portion of the mouth being blamed. 'Hit' your grayling *a little* harder in future —it will pay you.

Grayling prefer swift running streams with clean rocky or shingle beds, and in waters of this type attain generous proportions.

From 1883 to July 1949, a 4 lb. 8 oz. grayling taken by Dr. T. Sanctuary from the Wylye at Bemerton, held pride of place as the largest rod-caught specimen recorded.

Then came a report that Mr. John Stewart, of Baitland Cottage, Airlie, by Kirriemuir, had caught a 7 lb. 2 oz. grayling with a brandling worm!

It appears that this monster had been observed for some time in the People's Pool on the River Melgum, a tributary of the Isla in Angus.

This astonishing news broke through the columns of *The Scottish Angler*, a quarterly periodical for anglers, edited by R. Crombie Saunders, who, writing to the editor of the *Fishing Gazette*, said:

> This fish was reported to me by Mr. B. G. Carnegie, of Messrs. J. A. Carnegie and Smith, solicitors, Kirriemuir, who is secretary of the local angling association. I have an affidavit signed by Mr. John Stewart, who caught the fish, Mr. Turner, who was with him, and Mr. Ramsay, who weighed it. Mr. Carnegie tells me that a photograph was taken of the grayling, which unfortunately did not come out properly. It is a great pity the fish was not preserved, but I imagine that its uniqueness was not recognised at the time, as grayling do not arouse much interest in these parts.
>
> I have not the relevant number of the *Fishing Gazette* at hand, but I remember that Mr. Alexander Wanless had a letter in it reporting an extremely large grayling he had seen in the River Isla itself around about the time this 7 lb. 2 oz. fish was caught.

The letter to which Mr. Saunders refers appeared in the *Fishing Gazette* (17th September, 1949) wherein the late Mr. Alexander Wanless reported having seen a grayling of exceptional size in the Earn at Millhills below Crieff.

Though dwarfed by this fish, I am constrained to mention one or two other notable specimens which are not likely to meet with much opposition, although the Record Committee have decided that the 7 lb-plus grayling did not meet with their approval. They have set a qualifying minimum weight of 4 lb.

On Boxing Day, 1905, Messrs. H. J. Mordaunt and M. Headlam caught three weighing just over 4 lb. each in the Oakley stream on the Test at Mottisfont; and in the autumn of 1931 the Bemerton water produced another fine fish of 3¾ lb. If you catch a two-pounder you have a good fish, but after this shattering of a sixty-six year old record, coupled with a report of other great grayling, from no less an authority than the late Alexander Wanless, the record may still be vulnerable.

A light roach rod built from hollow glass, fitted with stand-off rings, is the rod for grayling fishing. If the angler proposes to wade, it need not be of greater length than 10 ft., but for bank fishing a twelve or fourteen-foot rod has advantages. A 3½-in. or 4 in. Sheffield

reel with one hundred yards of fine Terylene line is suitable in conjunction with these rods.

The question of the reel is one of great importance. As we have seen
earlier it is possible to pay out line from a comparatively stiff reel
in such a way as to trot a bait downstream without drag or halt,
and the angler who acquires this art has mastered one of the most
useful manipulations of tackle in coarse fishing. Nevertheless, I think
most anglers will find that to trot direct from a light-drummed
freely-running reel is not only more simple but more efficient in the
long run. If a reel of this type is used, the stream will draw the line
from the drum and it is only necessary to control its revolutions with
the thumb or finger to prevent overrun. Furthermore, there is a
minimum delay in striking, it being impossible to have any slack line
between the float and the rod tip by this method. To strike, the controlling finger or thumb stops the reel immediately a bite is registered
and the rod point is raised smartly.

A one-yard nylon cast is quite long enough in most circumstances,
and this should be not finer than $2\frac{1}{2}$ lb. b.s. I prefer a 3 lb. cast with a

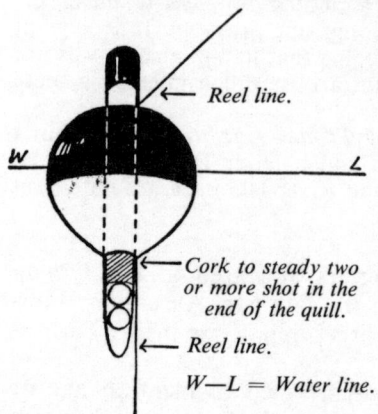

Reel line.

Cork to steady two
or more shot in the
end of the quill.

Reel line.

W—L = Water line.

hook-link one degree finer, as
generally used in bottom fishing. As to
hooks, a number 7, 8 or 9 round bend
will meet the case for worm fishing,
but when gentles are the bait a number
10 Model Perfect is better.

The final and certainly one of the
most important adjuncts is the float.
The illustration shows a typical
grayling float, actual size. Many
anglers use unshotted floats, but I
prefer the type shown for all-round
work. The shots aid in casting and
help to steady the float in the streamy
runs where the fish are often found.

Having so little under-water projection, these floats are ideal for use in
shallow water, and are not so liable to scare fish—this is a material
consideration. Shotted and unshotted floats have their devotees, and
I can only leave the final judgment to the reader.

The illustrations shows how these floats are made up from a cork
pilot float as used in pike fishing and a quill, the cork portion acting in
the double capacity of indicator and float cap. The above-water
colouring of grayling floats is a matter of some importance, for it must
be remembered that the type of water to be fished is often foam-flecked.
Many experts vote solidly for a bright red, but after much experiment
as to the visibility of the above-water colouring of floats of all kinds,
I prefer a bright orange. This colour is particularly good when the
angler is well above the water-line. When wading, however, the
angler's line of vision is much nearer the water level, it is a good plan

to use a quill which protrudes well above the cork, for obvious reasons. Some anglers use a small white feather wedged between the cork and the quill when the light is bad.

Shotting the cast for grayling is quite an important matter, and despite the fact that comparatively fast water has to be fished, heavy shotting is not advisable. Two or at most three medium shot are ample, unless the stream is very fast or coloured. The lowest shot should be about 12 in. from the hook—the second 3 or 4 in. higher, with the third 2 in. above that. Even this shotting is too heavy and too near the hook for fishing certain types of water. It must be remembered that grayling frequent the merest shallows on occasion, especially when the bottom is gravelly. There is also another interesting swim with which the angler must contend and indeed where his difficulties will often be compensated by the best fish.

The illustration will assist those who are not familiar with the method of fishing this type of water and will show clearly why the

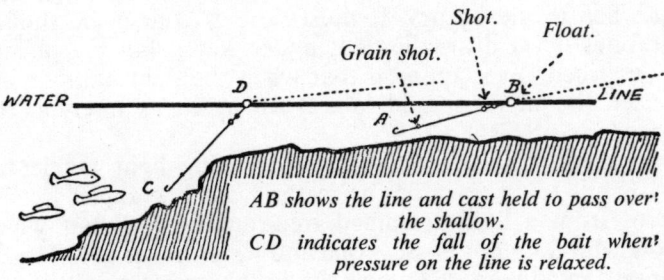

AB shows the line and cast held to pass over the shallow.
CD indicates the fall of the bait when pressure on the line is relaxed.

Fishing over a shallow to a hole, or dub.

shotting must be altered. It will be seen that one or two shots are placed 2 ft. or even more above the hook and one shot about a foot from the hook. By this means it is possible to 'lay-on' but at the same time feed out line so gently that the bait travels over the shallow at full stretch in front of the float until the edge of the hole where the 'big 'uns' are is reached. The angler then allows his float to travel a little faster and the lowest shot is just sufficient to carry the bait down to the fish.

In waters where the depth is 6 ft. or more, the more usual method of low shotting is advisable, especially in the quieter glides. In these cases a quill float is better than the typical grayling ducker. As to the depth at which to fish, it must be remembered that grayling will rise readily from the bottom to take a bait, and it may well pass a few inches above the river bed. Fish the water near you first, then farther away, to avoid frightening any fish which may be near, by playing one from more distant water past them. It is often well to bully a fish out of the swim for the same reason—do not allow a hooked grayling to wallow among its companions. Ten to fifteen minutes' fishing in one place is usually sufficient, after which time a move should be made. Many anglers contend that grayling 'take' in a peculiar way, but I think this is more due to the action of the water than the fish.

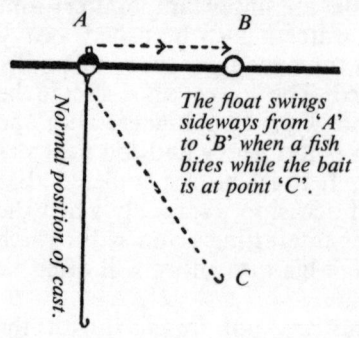

The float swings sideways from 'A' to 'B' when a fish bites while the bait is at point 'C'.

Normal position of cast.

The illustration shows how what may seem to be the peculiar bite of the fish is actually a matter of physics. Quite often the stream will swing the bait about under water out of line with the track of the float. It will be seen, therefore, that if a fish takes the bait when it has swung to the right or left, the float will tend to swing towards it as shown. This physical fact has, in my opinion, given rise to the belief that an act of the fish causes the float to move sometimes across the surface of the water instead of dipping when a bite occurs. It must not, of course, be thought that grayling bites never draw the float under water, but the phenomenon I have described is so common that when the float halts or moves to right or left the angler should take it for a bite as surely as though it had dipped, and STRIKE!

Having mentioned the difficulty of trotting light tackle from the bank by hand, I will describe the method. As one angler put it: 'Even I can trot from a light-drummed free-running reel, but what about the fellow who does not possess one and never hopes to?' The question is an important one, and I hope the following description will make it possible for the reader to trot by hand from any reel he may be compelled to use. Having taken up a suitable position on the bank, draw two or three yards of line from the reel, checking the rim with the finger or thumb, and cast upstream. As the tackle glides toward you, raise your rod point until the float is in front of you, then lower it gently till it is parallel with the water as the float passes on its way downstream. While this is happening your free hand must take another two or three feet of line off the reel so that *just before* the float has reached the spot where the line between it and the rod top is taut, you are able to 'pay out' a yard or so of the loose line you are holding'. This paying out is repeated as often as desired until the end of the swim is reached. The great point and difficulty lies in timing the release of the loose line so that the float is not jerked or stopped but glides smoothly and naturally. It is, of course, essential that thumb or finger control be used on the rim of the reel in order that it may be stopped instantly when it is necessary to strike and prevent over-run. The whole proceeding is more tricky than it would seem, but every angler should master the art of hand trotting—It is often of the highest value when fishing not only for grayling, but also for roach, dace, chub and other fish. The most suitable type of water for practice is a steady glide

—try a twenty-yard swim next time you go fishing with light tackle; practice is essential to success.

The illustrations show two types of 'Grasshopper'—a good artificial bait for grayling. These strangely named baits are presumably intended to appear like grubs of some kind. They are made by winding fine lead wire round the hook, to give the necessary weight to sink them, while their colouring is produced by wrapping coloured silk or wool over the wire. Yellow, green and scarlet are used, green predominating in the colour scheme. Fig. 2 shows a type which is made similarly, but instead of a hook being wrapped, any piece of bent wire will serve the purpose. Anglers who are fond of producing their own lures will revel in making

FIG. 1.   FIG. 2.

Fig. 1 shows a Grasshopper Bait with broad rings of green and yellow and thin ribs of black.
Fig. 2 shows another type in green, red and yellow.

these, which are very killing on some waters. They are cast into grayling holts and allowed to sink to the bottom, then worked back in a series of jerks to the surface, a kind of 'sink and draw.' Some experts recommend the attachment of a small cork to the line to act as an indicator when using this method, others deplore the idea—each angler must use his own judgment. One or two other considerations are of interest to the intending grayling fisher. Weather conditions do not appear to affect their feeding so quickly as in the case of many fish, and if the angler cares to brave the banks amid ice and snow, the fish will often oblige. Gilt tail worms are the best bait under these conditions, though gentles are often good. Coloured floodwater does not preclude grayling fishing. During floods they will often be found within a foot or two of the bank in any fairly steady water, regardless of the depth; and laying on with a bunch of gentles is then an effective method of taking *Thymallus*.

CHAPTER XXII

CUNNING CARP

IF success is to be achieved one cannot rush off to fish for carp without careful prior consideration, not only of the wily quarry but of what is probably the most specialised form of coarse angling. So much may be said of these powerful fighters, that they might well be termed the most interesting fish in British waters. Capricious to a degree, and almost humanly intelligent, carp have been much neglected by those who prefer to take a fish each minute, and scores of thousands of anglers have never essayed to catch one. I will admit that while carp fishing I have often been reminded of the opening words of a recipe for cooking them—'first catch your carp.' While it may at times prove a baffling business, carp angling is always fascinating; and I believe that much of the failure to take them comes from lack of proper angling tactics. Those who have failed should remember that carp are good feeders, and if the bait is suitably presented, lusty fish will almost certainly come to net.

Generally speaking, less appears to be known by anglers about this section of the vast carp family, of which over a thousand species have been recorded in Europe, Asia, North America and Africa alone, than of any other freshwater fish. Here, then, are some brief details of the main types found in British waters.

It is an interesting fact that carp are not indigenous to this country, but were introduced from abroad during the fourteenth or fifteenth century—first mention of them being made in 1496.

The natural food of carp appears to have little or no relation to the baits which are effective for their capture. Rooting in the mud at the bottom of lakes and some slow rivers, they take in quantities of mud, together with shrimps, aquatic insects, larvae, decaying vegetable matter, water plants and weeds, blood-worms, earth-worms, etc. From this one might conclude that worms were possibly the most natural and therefore the most effective of easily available bait, but this is not so, as will be seen later. One instance is in fact quoted by 'B.B.'* in his book *Confessions of a Carp Fisher*, i.e. the Old Copper Mine

* 'B.B.' is Denys Watkins-Pitchford.

180

water at Beechmere, where carp have never been known to take a lobworm.

Size always appeals to anglers and there are records of splendid carp to compensate for the difficulties of catching them.

The late Albert Buckley's 26 lb. carp from Mapperley reservoir held the record for twenty-one years. Then on October 3rd, 1951, Mr. R. D. Richards of Gloucester, took a 31 lb. 4 oz. specimen from the Bernithan Court water at Llangarren near Ross-on-Wye.

During his day's fishing (11 a.m. to 4.45 p.m.) he hooked six fish, three of which he lost, and the big fellow was the last of his captures. That the patron saint of fishermen was on his side, is evidenced by the fact that he took this fish with a roach rod, 6 lb. b.s. line and a No. 10 eyed-hook tied direct to the line which was loaded with a bored-bullet 2 ft. from the hook, and he did it in fifteen minutes! The bait was a knob of bread paste dipped in English honey.

I seem to recollect that Buckley's twenty-six pounder kept him busy for close on an hour, but he, if my memory serves me well, was using very fine roach tackle and fishing in deep open water.

With a 31 lb. 4 oz. carp in the bag one might be forgiven for believing that a record had been created which would stand for many a year to come, but that was not to be.

It was nearing 5 a.m. on September 15th 1952, by the brink of Redmire Pool in Herefordshire. Richard Walker and his friend Peter Thomas had travelled 130 miles to this venue, arriving at about 11.30 p.m. on the previous night and had fished through the night save for a short doze. Then!

'R.W.' heard a resounding splash at 4.33 a.m. and shortly after had a run, and what a run! Descriptions of just what happened between his contact with this fish and its appearance on the bank at 5.7 a.m. precisely, thanks to the practised intervention of Mr. Thomas with a specially built and ample net, appear in his book *Still Water Angling* (MacGibbon and Kee) and *Fisherman's Bedside Book* by B.B. (Eyre and Spottiswoode).

With typical foresight Walker had equipped himself with a sack in which he was able to retain this fish which scaled 44 lb. and he made arrangements for its subsequent transfer to the London Zoo aquarium.

That this is the largest freshwater fish taken in England to date is beyond doubt.

Writing of its dimensions Mr. Walker says:

I must confess that in the combination of excitement and a desire to get some sleep, we omitted to measure the fish.

However, by some crafty work with dividers, plus checks against the landing net, sack, etc., and comparison with photographs of the fish (taken by the same camera) the measurements of which were known. I estimated the length as 37 in. (to tip of tail) and the girth as 31 in.; and I should be surprised if these figures were more than half an inch out.

Mr. Percy Austin, the well-known Birmingham scale reader, states that the fish was fifteen years old, but that there was no sign of slowing down in its growth rate.

The fish lived contentedly in its large tank, where it was the object of admiration of all who visited the London Zoo's famous aquarium. In 1964, when the fish was considered to be some 28 years old, it began to lose weight, turning the scales at a mere 35 lb. 8 oz. After experimenting with various diets, the Zoo began to feed 'Clarissa' with dog biscuit, together with the normal fare considered suitable for cyprinids. To everyone's relief the fish began to regain some of the weight it had lost and by October 1966 its weight was back to 40 lb. 'The fish is in good spirits,' quoted a Zoo spokesman at the time. Early in 1972 the fish died, probably never having recovered enough weight to reach the 44 lb. at capture. Called 'Clarissa' by everyone except its captor, the fish has been set up by Fred Buller, well known angler and writer. It cost Fred £80 for the privilege, and the fish resides at his tackle shop in Edgware, London.

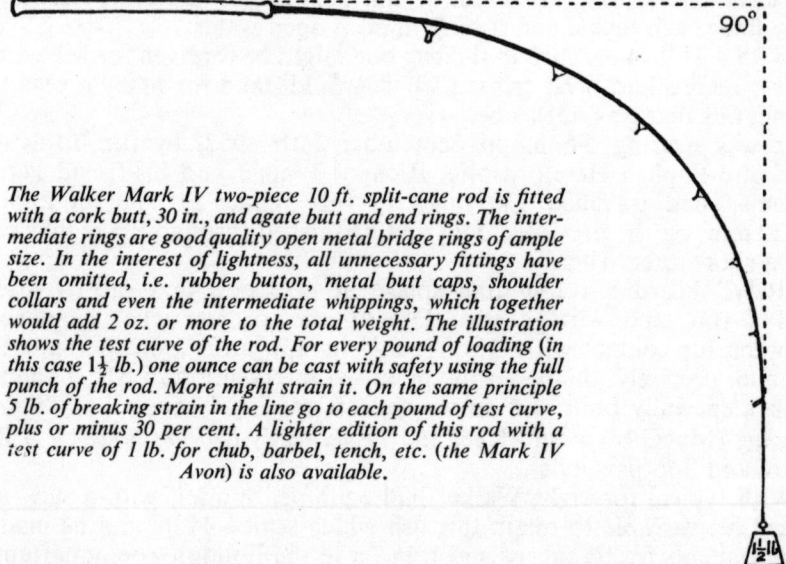

The Walker Mark IV two-piece 10 ft. split-cane rod is fitted with a cork butt, 30 in., and agate butt and end rings. The intermediate rings are good quality open metal bridge rings of ample size. In the interest of lightness, all unnecessary fittings have been omitted, i.e. rubber button, metal butt caps, shoulder collars and even the intermediate whippings, which together would add 2 oz. or more to the total weight. The illustration shows the test curve of the rod. For every pound of loading (in this case 1½ lb.) one ounce can be cast with safety using the full punch of the rod. More might strain it. On the same principle 5 lb. of breaking strain in the line go to each pound of test curve, plus or minus 30 per cent. A lighter edition of this rod with a test curve of 1 lb. for chub, barbel, tench, etc. (the Mark IV Avon) is also available.

Scientific opinion lends colour to the belief which Mr, Walker holds, that 'carp weighing 50 lb. certainly exist in Britain, and we shall probably see a fish of up to 60 lb. landed some day.' Commenting further on the subject Richard Walker says:

I know this sounds incredible, but I've been laughed to scorn so much over my views on the ultimate sizes of coarse fish, that I can take plenty more!

There are 12 lb. tench in two waters of which I know; and 7 lb. perch; 10 lb. chub; 20 lb. barbel and 15 lb. bream all exist in Britain. They only require catching, and as our knowledge grows, they'll be caught some day.

By now my reader must be itching to know with what and how the record carp was caught.

Quite exceptionally Mr. Walker used a split-cane rod of his own make. This 10 ft. two-joint weapon which weighs 10 oz. he calls Mark IV. It is designed for use with lines of from 6 to 12 lb. b.s. and will cast baits up to $1\frac{1}{2}$ oz. It is important to note also that it acts (bends) throughout its length right down through the cork butt. The resilience of a rod of this type makes casting effortless, defeats the shock of the sudden rushes of a fish, and therefore plays it more safely than a stiffer pattern, which would cause the fish to have to be played much more from the reel than the rod, if a break is to be avoided. A rod of this type and length is moreover much more effective in holding a fish out from undercut banking and inshore weeds than a shorter stiffer weapon would be.

The reel was a Mitchell fixed-spool carrying 100 yards of 12 lb. b.s. plaited nylon 'Green Butterfly' line, direct to the end of which a No. 2 Allcock's Model Perfect hook *which had been specially sharpened* was whipped.

No float, lead or knot was used, which is a matter of importance.

The only remaining equipment was a specially built triangular landing-net with 30 in. arms made of laminated bamboo from which a 4 ft. deep net is suspended; an electric bite-alarm and rod-rests. The need for a really ample landing-net is beyond dispute and it is not surprising that nets of this type are now available in a number of sizes and patterns. As to the use of the bite-alarms there has been much childish criticism from people who appear to draw a sharp line between visible and audible bite detectors! Their arguments are quite beyond my comprehension, and despite them these devices which are a godsend to night carp-fishers are also their own compliment to the ingenuity of their originator.

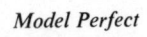

2/0

Model Perfect

So much for the equipment and I turn now to the method of fishing. In a nutshell it was just shotless and knotless ledgering, with a 'balanced' paste and bread-crust bait, about the size of a pheasant's egg.

This cleverly contrived method of baiting, which can be used for all bottom-feeding fish in either still or slow waters, was devised by Richard Walker and calls for some explanation.

I must make it clear at the outset that the essence of this method is to prepare a bait which sinks naturally and very slowly, so slowly in fact that it only just sinks.

To produce this effect a piece of breadcrust is attached to the hook which is, of course, buoyant. Paste is then added to just more than counterbalance the buoyancy of the crust. You will find it necessary to experiment with each bait at the outset, but with practice you will be able to achieve the ideal balance at the first attempt.

One of the advantages of this balanced bait will, I think, be immediately apparent, i.e. that sinking so slowly it will not sink into either a soft bottom, silk or flannel weed, and therefore remains visible. There is, however, another advantage which while less obvious is even

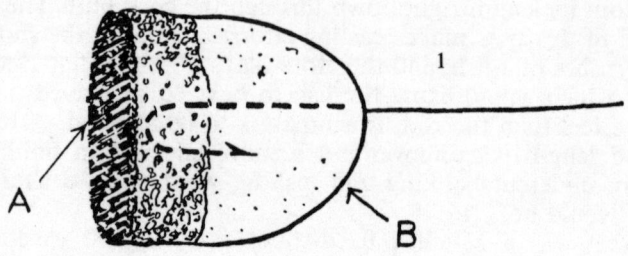

BALANCED CRUST AND PASTE BAIT.
*A—Crust which is buoyant. B—Paste built up below the crust to a
weight which will only just sink the whole bait very slowly.*

more important. These baits always come to rest crust side up with the line underneath, thus:

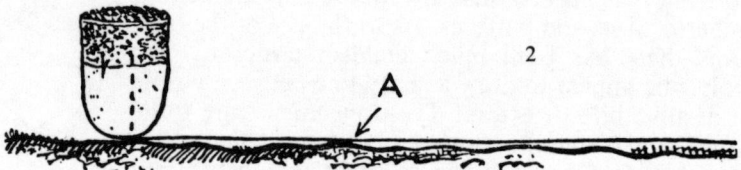

*The bait rests on the soft mud or fine weed, crust uppermost, with the line or cast
lying under it on the bottom.*

Ordinary baits such as potato, paste, etc., may lie like this:

And the lips of a fish are more than likely to come into contact with the line when closing on the bait, which in the case of both carp and tench may produce sufficient suspicion to cause the fish to reject it.

For the rest one need only mention that the ground-bait was mashed bread, pure and simple.

With regard to carp baits and ground-baits there is no mystery as some anglers appear to imagine, and secret potions and nostrums have no part in either. The cleaner and fresher one's ground-bait is the better, but it should be simple.

The well-known bread and bran mixture is good, so is a mixture of bread and boiled potato; and generous quantities of cloud ground-bait are effective at times when the fish are feeding freely.

Far more important than the actual ingredients, is to take every opportunity to bait up a pitch for some days before fishing. This accustoms the fish to the type of food which you wish them to take at the time of fishing. From this I infer that the ground-bait and hook-bait should be of similar nature. If, for example, you propose to use lob-worms on the hook, then worms should be the ground-bait.

Assuming the use of a mystery-free ground-bait one other matter of first-rate importance remains, i.e. that it must be placed accurately, its whereabouts known with certainty, and the hook-bait must be cast and fished where it lies.

My reader will see once again that need for meticulous care which characterizes every phase of carp fishing. One thought regarding hook-baits must be added, namely, that in different waters the fish exhibit preferences, in some cases to the extent that a bait which is paramount at A will be refused at B. This opens a field for thought and investigation in which the experts revel. And there is the oft repeated contingency that the carp in a water will take nothing for long periods, but that does not worry them either, they just keep trying. They are a wonderful breed indeed, these specialist carp fishers.

I have come to the conclusion that with one accord consistently successful carp fishers possess four all too often rare characteristics, i.e. inexhaustible patience, an analytical mind, an infinite capacity for taking pains with minutae which do not appear to occur to the average angler and common sense to a degree which is quite uncommon.

Robert Reynolds of Northampton, who performed the unique feat of capturing three carp in one night which weighed respectively 28¼ lb.; 27 lb. 13 oz.; and 24¾ lb., gave a simple but eloquent example of thought about and attention to detail in an article which appeared in the *Angling Times* (p. 5, 30th August, 1957). I quote:

> I baited up . . . with par-boiled potatoes regularly for some time before the season opened* . . . for days I fished with par-boiled potatoes but failed to get a knock.
> . . . Sitting down to a good hard think the penny suddenly dropped. The lake supported swans, geese and ducks which were fed continually with bread. . . .

No doubt you will have guessed. He turned from spuds to bread which as he observed:

> . . . The fish would obviously have come to recognise as a regular part of their diet.

---

* A well-boiled whole potato is preferable if the bottom is clean and firm; but when fishing over soft mud or fine weed a flat slice which will not sink out of view as the heavier bait almost certainly would, is the answer to this difficulty.

That conclusion plus the concomitant know-how was the secret of success.

A great reward awaits the careful student of carp and carp fishing. Luck plays little or no part in the matter.

The guiding principles governing success and the kit required for carp fishing may well be the first consideration of anglers who desire to outwit these knowing fish. Carp must be credited with keen sight, a terror of vibration, and an almost uncanny sense of taste and smell. I do not hesitate to say that unless these facts are thoroughly appreciated and acted upon by fishermen, few carp will come their way.

[In previous editions of *Angling Ways* a chapter appeared called 'A Carp Demonstration Piece.' In it Marshall-Hardy spent some time in describing what was, at the time of writing, a notable capture, namely the 18 lb. 8 oz. carp from Mapperly by John Norman. Now, I do not want in any way to detract proper recognition from Mr. Norman's angling prowess, but it is only fair to the anglers of 1972 to point out that since those days one has to have carp of over 30 lb. before they become notable. Suffice it to say that since Redmire became famous as the haunt of large carp in 1951 an 18 lb. fish is the norm, both in this and a number of other waters. As an illustration, it is interesting to note that in 1967 alone 47 carp over 20 lb., three over 30 lb. and two over 40 lb. were captured from Redmire, so small in actual extent but giant in stature in the eyes of the Jack Hilton-led syndicate which currently fishes it and carp anglers in general. In the first 6 months of 1972, no fewer than seven carp over 30 lb. were taken including three of 40 lb. and over.

The year 1972 was a pretty good year for carp anglers, and not only at Redmire, although Jack Hilton's 40 lb. 3 oz. mirror taken from just 12 in. of water beneath a blanket of branches was a remarkable angling feat as well as his best ever carp. Lastly, Chris Yates, a syndicate member thought he had wrested the carp record from Richard Walker when he netted a huge fish after a ten-minute struggle to keep it out of the Redmire weedbeds. Using a small scales hanging from a tree it seemed at first as if the fish would weigh the magic figure of 44 lb. 2 oz.—2 oz. over the record. But a second careful weighing read 43 lb. 12 oz., the second-best ever carp weight. Bait is reported to be caddis. That would be good enough for any mortal carp angler, but carp men are convinced that fish exist beyond the 50 lb. mark, and they will keep on, sitting out their long, patient vigils, listening to those fantastic sounds that feeding carp make and waiting for the fish that will put them into the record book. L.C.]

CHAPTER XXIII

MARGIN-FISHING FOR CARP

THE list of carp baits is quite extensive. In his most excellent mono-graph, *Still Water Angling*, which has no equal as a guide for would-be carp fishers, Richard Walker lists:

> ... various forms in which bread can be used (with or without honey), lobworms, boiled potatoes, redworms, gentles, slugs, snails, freshwater mussels, small fish, wasp grubs, boiled peas, beans and chestnuts, cheese, banana, macaroni, shrimps, prawns, cake, caterpillars, dock and other grubs, congealed blood. . . .

Then he makes a very significant and important comment:

> ... but the first three have probably accounted for more carp than all the rest together.

I should have been prepared to pin that remark on the bread baits alone, but that as it may be, there is no question that bread crust is a bait *par excellence* for margin-fishing.

Here again we are indebted to the modern school of carp-fishing experts for a new technique.

Watching as they always are, and collating the results of their observations, these men have noted that during warm nights and in the the early morning, some carp will cruise close to the bank in search of any food which has either drifted or fallen into the water near the side. They have marked also that almost anything edible does not come amiss to these food-hunting fish.

As one might expect, that fact called for the devising of a new fishing technique, to encompass their downfall, or should I say uplift? And so it was that the method that has come to be known as 'Margin-fishing' came into being.

To their disadvantage as a rule, anglers choose to fish downwind, but margin-fishers select a swim facing any wind that is driving tit-bits and so attracting the quarry towards them.

If the selected pitch has a natural screen of undergrowth this is ideal, if not an artificial cover of sapling branches or other herbage should be made. This is most important, because the fish come closer to the angler who is margin-fishing than on any other occasion.

This essential hide accomplished, fix a rod-rest so that when the rod is placed in it, the tip of the rod only just projects over the water. The business end of the gear is the acme of simplicity. A specially sharpened hook either whipped or knotted direct to the end of the line, carries a large piece of bread-crust crumb side down, with the hook point and shank at the upper or crust side.

Only the bait is allowed to rest on the water, and no line must touch the surface. Sufficient line must, however, be left between the rod point and the bait, to enable a fish to suck the bait down; and a coil of loose line between the bottom ring and the reel is laid on any suitable surface, i.e. paper, a groundsheet, etc.

Having arranged his gear as described the angler sits back out of sight and awaits events, which may well be as exciting as any which he is ever likely to encounter.

As might be expected a bait of this kind sometimes attracts the unwelcome attentions of small fish. The only cure is to raise the hook-crust off the water by pulling on the line and then to throw them a loose crust. Should this be necessary it has its compensations, in that at the approach of a carp the small fry decamp heralding possible pending action of a more desirable kind, when the hook-crust is, of course, returned to the water immediately.

Should the small fry be stubbornly persistent necessitating the prolonged raising of your bait, dip it occasionally to keep it moist despite their continued presence. The reason for this will be apparent. And before it slips my memory I should stress the necessity of staying put when margin-fishing and *keep still*. Fidgety and wandering margin-fishers catch few fish.

If and when your crust is taken by a carp release a little slack line allow the fish to turn down with the bait before you strike to avoid pulling it out of the fish's mouth. And make sure, doubly sure, that all your gear is in *perfect running order*, otherwise the first rush of the fish will be fatal.

This fishing is not quite so simple as it may sound but perseverance will bring its rewards, particularly if one remembers such details as, that other things being equal, carp show an inclination to move towards the westerly shore of a lake as the sun rises. How fraught with small but important things this carp fishing is, no wonder the new school of experts to which we owe so much is steeped in the minutiae of the craft.

There are, of course, circumstances when other methods than those described will take carp, such as floating bread-crust, drifting down-wind towards a carp holt, and on occasions laying on with light float tackle (providing that several feet of line or cast lie on the bottom) may be effective. I am, however, satisfied that either shotless and knotless ledgering or margin-fishing are the paramount methods.

I think it was the late Edward Marston, founder of the *Fishing Gazette*, who said:

Don't waste time carp fishing; life is too short.

If I have succeeded in creating the impression that catching large carp calls for a high degree of skill, sound and adequate tackle and dauntless perseverance, I am content that this is not an exaggeration.

Despite Mr. Marston's *dictum* and my own foreboding, should you be fascinated by the prospects offered by this very specialized branch of coarse fishing, don't start until you have read, marked, learned and inwardly digested Richard Walker's *Still Water Angling*. I can give no better advice and will turn now to some consideration of the less exacting task of catching the smaller Crucian member of the family.

CHAPTER XXIV

CRUCIAN CARP

CRUCIAN CARP seldom attain a weight of more than 4 lb. and are, I think, the most common of the species and the least difficult to capture.

Before the British Record (Rod-Caught) Fish Committee, controlled by the National Angler's Council, decided otherwise the record crucian (*Carassius carassius*) weighed 4 lb. 11 oz. This fish was taken by H. C. Hinton at Broadwater Lake, Godalming, on September 25, 1938. The fish once recognised as the 'record' was a crucian of 4 lb. 6 oz. 4 dr., caught by P. H. Oliver from a private lake in Surrey. However, a fish of 4 lb. 15 oz. 8 dr., caught from a Kent Lake in June 1972 by Mr. J. Johnstone was accepted as the record crucian as from November 1972.

Crucians are distinguishable from the larger species by the absence of barbels from the mouth and the higher dorsal fin.

These fish vary considerably in the length and depth of the body, some having the streamlined body of the common carp. These fish are sometimes called Prussian carp. There are also others almost bream-like in depth. And there is a confusing hybrid between the two in which very small barbels appear.

Being much smaller and less speedy in their runs than their larger *confrères* much lighter tackle can be used for their capture.

Marshall-Hardy's preference was for an 11 ft. Wallace 'Wizard' rod, with built cane centre and top joints, fitted with agate butt and end rings and 'Bell's Life' intermediates. The rod is light and delightfully flexible and its length is a very present help when the fish need holding out from weeds and other obstructions close to the bank. With a rod of this type and a narrow drummed 'Flickem' or an 'Aerial' reel carrying 100 yards of 4 lb. to 6 lb. b.s. Terylene line, you are adequately equipped. Should my reader take me to task for mentioning line of such comparatively high breaking strain for the capture of these, or for that matter even smaller species, I leave him or her with the thought that the underlying reason for this is purely economic. One is less likely to lose favourite floats and unexpectedly long lengths of line on occasions when snags are encountered, if using a line of this calibre. And I have yet to learn that crucian carp care a damn whether one uses a 1 lb. or 6 lb. line. Perhaps I've been lucky but there it is.

Whether one ledgers or lays-on with float tackle for these fish I find that a 4 or 5 ft. nylon monofil cast with a number 10 or 12 eyed hook tied direct to it, is ideal. This should of course be of, say, 2 to 4 lb. b.s., i.e. less than that of the line used, this for the sake of invisibility and also in the interests of economy.

In this connection I like my float to be attached to the line rather than than the cast and do not hesitate to adjust the length of the cast to ensure this.

As crucian carp seldom, if ever, feed on the surface, bottom-fishing in one or other of its forms is indicated. One of the most successful crucian carp anglers I ever knew fished a one shot ledger (shot 2 ft. from hook) close to the bank. Having distributed a generous offering of bread and bran ground-bait, he tore a piece of bread from the heart of a new loaf and squeezed or pinched it on to *a No. 8 hook*, leaving the rough edges to take care of themselves. This he lobbed rather than cast into the water where it sank slowly and left him waiting patiently rod in rest, interpreting the often very obscure movements of the line. Many a time I sat beside him and was I'm sure more surprised than the fish when he struck and his rod tip danced to the efforts of a crucian. It would appear that these fish have an almost uncanny knack of nibbling tiny pieces from a bait of this kind and whittling it down until to absorb the last fraction they must take the hook also.

In calm conditions the lightest possible float fishing is effective. A tooth-pick of a float carrying one shot (15 in. from the hook) is heavy enough, and the bait should rest just on the bottom. A pellet of paste, flake of bread-cube on a No. 12 hook is good medicine for this fishing. Some prefer maggots or a small red worm but give me one of the bread baits. If you adopt bread as a hook-bait, a powdered bread and sand cloud used on the little and often principle and thrown in around the float, makes a good attractor. With maggots or small red worms on the hook either squats (small maggots) or a few chopped worms used in the same manner should prove effective.

CHAPTER XXV

PERCH

THE external characteristics of perch (*Perca fluviatilis*) are so distinctive that it would not be possible to confuse them with any other species, save perhaps with ruffe (or pope) and the bullhead (or miller's thumb) which being of no interest to anglers should be killed when caught in order to conserve food supplies for more worthy fish.

Like perch, the latter have similar spinous dorsal fins followed by a soft fin; but, as will be seen from the accompanying illustration these fins are separate in perch and joined in ruffe and bullheads. Perch have often been described as our most beautiful coarse fish and a

1. PERCH.   2. RUFFE.   3. BULLHEAD, SHOWING THE DOUBLE DORSAL

normal specimen in good condition is indeed a pleasant sight. The upper part of the back varies in colour from dark olive green to dark bronze shading down to a metallic yellow and thence to the white belly from which are depended the orange pelvic and ventral fins; and the sides are slashed with dark vertical bars.

It is interesting to note that the depth of the colouring of perch varies under emotional stress such as fear or anger; and in some waters a slatey-blue type is found, the general colouring of which is anything but typical. Of such fish an expert of the Freshwater Biological Association says:

This photograph beautifully illustrates the characteristic build of large carp. The fish is a mirror carp, which when caught from Tiddenfoot Pits, near Leighton Buzzard, Bedfordshire, weighed 25 lb. The pattern of large irregularly spaced scales is peculiar to the mirror and leather carps; and the very size of the scales is the reason for the name 'mirror'.

[*Photograph: W. J. Howes*]

The one typical characteristic of the crucian carp is not visible in this picture. It is the tall dorsal fin of the crucian, *Carassius carassius*, which, together with a complete lack of barbules round the mouth, makes the crucian so unlike its close-related carp cousins. The fish here neared the crucian record; it turned the scales at 4 lb. 6½ oz.

[*Photograph: W. J. Howes*]

The pike, *Esox lucius*, really typifies the cold, calculating killer. The eyes are set to give binocular vision, rare in fishes; the jaws and receding teeth perfectly placed to grasp and swallow the prey; the stream-lined body with its battery of fins set near the tail to give great mobility; all these points add to the specifications of one of nature's perfect killing machines.

Belligerent, pugnacious, predatory: these three words summarise the perch, *Perca fluvialitis*. The hostile set of the spined dorsal cutting the surface and the explosive scattering of small-fish shoals are among the great sights of the river.

[*Photograph: W. J. Howes*]

Variation of colour in fishes is a common occurrence. It may be due
to some chemical or other feature of the water, in which case when
transplanted elsewhere the fish should become normal; or it may be some
genetical factor, when the colour would be maintained in any environment.

I think the latter is perhaps more likely, genetical mutants being the
cause of similar odd forms in other animals and plants.

When the leaves begin to fall, I always think of perch. I have noted
carefully over many seasons that with the falling leaf roach and dace
show a disinclination to feed. This is more pronounced as the period
of nature's dismantling progresses. There are, of course, those happy
exceptions when an angler may do well on an occasional outing, but
I am satisfied that in the main roach and dace fishing is less profitable
under these conditions than before and after the leaf-fall. What reason
can there be for this? Can it be that as the dead vegetable matter is
deposited on the bottom of rivers and lakes, its decay sets up a 'souring'
or partial pollution which is distasteful to these fish? Another possible

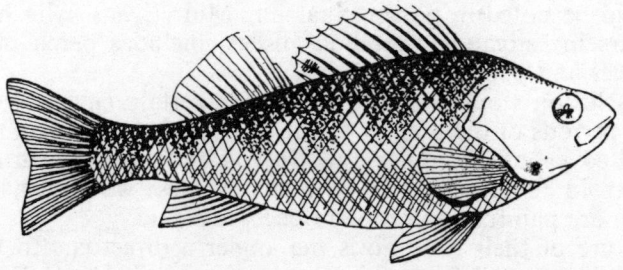

cause occurs to me, which, while I do not favour it, may prove interesting. The falling leaves perhaps take with them all kinds of insect life
which feed the fish, and for which they look at this period of the year
to the exclusion of other forms of food.

Basing my angling procedure on the foregoing, I abandon roach
and dace fishing at leaf-fall until the trees are bare and a good push of
water has flushed the rivers and rain has freshened the lakes. But
a'fishing one simply must go, and I find it an excellent opportunity to
seek new quarry. The fish least susceptible to the influences I have
mentioned are perch. Indeed, perch are a reckless species seeming to
care little for climatic or other conditions, save that they appear to
show a preference for a mild spell of weather following a frost. If you
can find perch you may be fairly certain of a catch. Some consideration
of their haunts and habits will be useful to the novice. These fish
shoal and, when one is caught, perseverance will generally reward
the angler. It is strange, but you will usually find that perch of a size
shoal together, and any idea that where there are small ones there will
be grandfathers is not founded on fact. Where are these fish? They have
a marked liking for sunken tree trunks and submerged roots, camp-
sheathing, holes under the banking, weirs, walls and bridge supports

and are often found in holes near weed beds. Perch prefer a gravelly or sandy bottom, but are also found over clay; I have had many good fish over a mud bottom when fishing for tench. As to water conditions, perch avoid sharply flowing shallows and take more to the deeper waters of medium flow in rivers, while in lakes and ponds they may be found almost anywhere. In some waters perch are remarkably parochial, keeping strictly to a given area. Find this spot and fish after fish will be your reward. Miss it by a yard and you may fish it for hours without result.

It is a fascinating occupation to rove for perch from place to place —spotting a likely haunt and fishing it a while, then moving on. Patience, that reputed quality of anglers, need not be too strongly taxed when fishing for them, for if perch are present and are at all inclined to feed they will oblige almost at once. They are determined biters too, and will literally hang themselves upon your hook when feeding. If, then, you find roach and dace disinclined when leaves are falling, try the perch.

It should be noted in passing that Dr. Muir Evans, who has spent many years investigating venomous fishes, includes perch in his list of probables and possibles.

His conclusion would seem to be that in certain environments and at certain periods of the year, both the spinous dorsal fin and the spike of the gill cover may be poisonous. In any event it is worth no small effort to avoid being punctured by either of these weapons as wounds from them are painful and prone to become septic.

The nature of their food gives the angler a direct cue to the baits which should be used for perch. Perch are cannibal, and I place the fry of their own species first in the list of excellent baits, particularly for the capture of the larger specimens. Let me stress the absurdity of removing the prickly dorsal fin before using them as baits. Many anglers clip it off with the idea that the spikes of the fin are a deterrent to the larger fish. This is definitely not so, and the small fry should be presented in their natural state.

Next in importance are live minnows and gudgeon, a plump minnow being particularly killing. Freshwater shrimps, worms, small frogs, gentles, wasp grubs and other insect larvae are all at times good baits for perch. I shall deal later with the methods of their presentation, but will say here that they prefer a moving bait.

Perch will seize almost any bright object which is moving through the water, a fact which brings us face to face with those interesting and sporting forms of angling known as 'spinning' and 'sink and draw.'

The illustration shows two killing artificials, and there are scores of others which are attractive to the 'Water Tiger.'

There is no good purpose served by fishing too fine for these fish and 2 lb. b.s. lines are undesirably fine for the work. It has to be remembered that perch are strong game fish that will fight every inch of the way to your net, and may weigh anything from a few ounces to several pounds.

From November 1936, to the beginning of 1950, a 5 lb. 4¾ oz. perch, taken from Stradsett Lake in Norfolk, by Mr. H. Green of King's Lynn, reigned as the rod-caught record for the species.

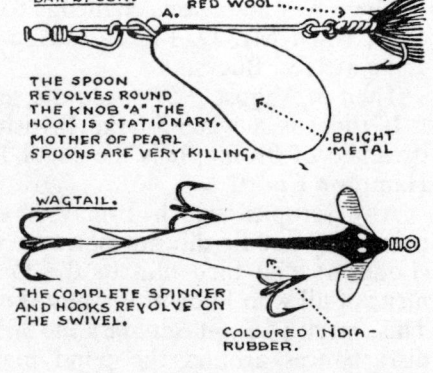

It is interesting to note that at the time of its capture Mr. Green was not aware that the fish was of record dimensions. He took it home, however, and after having its weight carefully checked—it was eaten!

Then early in January 1950, Mr. P. Clarke of Ipswich, fishing at Bures St. Mary, on the Suffolk Stour, caught a perch which he claimed weighed 6 lb. 0 oz. 14 dr.

The capture of this fish and its weighing were witnessed by Messrs. L. Tatton and R. S. Beckwith, both of Ipswich; who subsequently swore an affidavit to that effect at the request of Mr. Bernard Venables, at that time angling correspondent of the *Daily Mirror*, who travelled to Ipswich to investigate this claim to the establishment of a new record.

As the result of my investigations, it transpired that the fish was weighed at the waterside, on a spring-balance, graded in ¼ lb. up to 8 lb. and then was returned to the water.

I invited him to have his balance certified by the weights and measures authorities. This he did; and the Inspector's report read as follows:

The spring-balance brought into this office by Mr. Clarke, of 45 Vernon Street, Ipswich, was found to be reasonably correct at the gradations shown on the instrument. The maximum error does not exceed 2 oz.

S. W. J. Littlestone,
Inspector of Weights and Measures
for the County Borough of Ipswich.

It was later calculated that Mr. Clarke's spring-balance had a 1.56 per cent degree of error, i.e. 1 oz. 8 dr. up or down.

Taking this error into account therefore his perch may have weighed either 5 lb. 15 oz. 6 dr. or 6 lb. 2 oz. 6 dr.

At the lower figure it created a new British rod-caught record with a margin at 10 oz. 10 dr.

I have since wondered how it was possible to weigh this fish to the nearest dram on a scale graduated in quarter-pounds. But if the drams are eliminated Mr. Clarke's perch is still the master fish of the species to be taken on rod and line.

It is regrettable that this fish, which by the way was taken on a live 3½ in. roach, was not preserved. In this connection I should, I think, remind my reader, that any angler contending for a record in future may find it very difficult to establish his claim in the absence of the fish.

There was no serious challenge to Mr. Clarke's record till December 1953, when Mr. D. Florey took a 5 lb. 14½ oz. perch from Farlow's Lake at Iver, Bucks.

Then in August 1957 two quite remarkable perch stories broke.

If there is a water in the British Isles which I should never have dreamed of fishing, it is the small Diana Pond in Bushey Park, near Hampton Court.

Any scruples which I may have entertained regarding this un-promising puddle did not however worry Mr. E. V. Hodd of Tooting (London) who hied him to the Diana; where to the utter astonish-ment of all who know this water, he proceeded to catch a 5¾ lb. perch. This, mark you, on *Saturday* the 3rd of August 1957 which for general disturbances around the pond, may well have been ideal, children playing, dogs scampering, the lot!

But *Perca*, like so many fish, suffered during the 'purge' of records in 1969 (p. 150) and the current (Jan. 1973) rod-caught record is 4 lb. 12 oz. The fish was caught from Oulton Broad, Suffolk, by Mr. S. F. Baker in 1962. In June 1972 a perch of 5 lb. 1 oz. was recorded from Rochford, but was not submitted to the Record Committee.

In angling wonders never cease as witness the story of yet another August 1957 perch.

Hard on the heels of Mr. Hodd's capture, came well authenticated news that ten-year-old John Carroll of Castle Street, Birr, County Offaly, Eire, had caught a 6½ lb. perch. This fish engulfed a large lobworm which John had left dangling in the water while he helped a nearby friend to bait up.

On his return we are told he heaved this mighty fish on to the raft from which he was fishing and that was that, i.e. he had caught the largest properly authenticated perch ever taken in these islands. A not inconsiderable streak of luck would seem to have attended both these captures. This fact should not, however, be regarded as any kind of guarantee that catching *large* perch is an occupation for lucky people only.

Little John's wonder perch was not given record status because presumably the fish was taken outside the U.K.

You may catch one even larger, so why not be prepared? Do not, however, fish too coarsely! Four lb. b.s. line should serve you well, in spite of the fact that you will occasionally encounter a fair-sized or even a large pike when perch fishing with either live bait or spinner. If this is your fortune, you can only do your best against the odds.

Far less attention is paid to the capture of perch than they warrant. Hard fighting, beautiful in appearance and very edible when properly prepared for the table, one would almost excuse a 'pot hunter' for tackling them in earnest. Perch are, however, delicate fish, susceptible to disease from which in years past quantities have died, thus reducing the stock to an alarming extent. The same respect should therefore be given to their preservation as to that of other fish. Happily nowadays, perch appear to be on the increase, and may be found of good size and in commendable numbers in almost every river and lake. Among the waters where large specimens may be confidently sought are the Hampshire Avon, the Dorset Stour, the Broads, Irish rivers and loughs, Old Father Thames, Arlesey Lake and many gravel pits in the Home Counties. I contend however, that the very best perch are to be found in large lakes, and suggest that many reservoirs hold aldermanic specimens which would not only grace a glass case, but amaze even a taxidermist!

Despite the fact that perch will seize practically any small bright object which is moving through the water, and are therefore prey for the spinner, comparatively few anglers spin for them. But as spinning is undoubtedly a most skilful and pleasant method of taking perch, I will give it precedence over more prosaic methods of float fishing and paternostering. Later in this volume the reader will find some lines on the art of casting. May I, then, devote myself to a discussion of the tackle used, with a suggestion that the pleasures of a day's perch spinning are worthy of the trouble and prac-tice necessary to acquire this art? To the two useful mechanical baits illustrated earlier, let me add one of another class which is semi-mechanical, semi-natural.

Adjustable liphook to lengthen or shorten A—B for the bend in the tail.

One hook of triangle inserted to give bend.

This 'flight' enables the angler to present a small dead roach, dace, minnow or gudgeon in a way which gives it a lively and attractive movement when drawn through the water. The 2 ft. 6 in. to 3 ft. cast which may be of either fine Alasticum wire or nylon monofil, is fitted with two modern ball-bearing swivels, a plain single swivel at the upper and a link-swivel for easy change of lures at the business-end. With swivels of this type, line kink is practically impossible, they are really efficient. But to make sure doubly certain, squeeze a small half-moon lead on the line just above the swivel to which the line is attached; this will remain depended in the water as a kind of keel which causes the swivels to revolve.

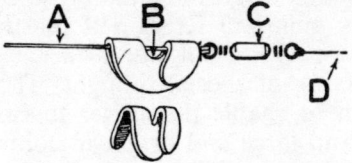

A—Reel-line with nip-on anti-kink lead just above swivel. B—Anti-kink attached by pressure of thumb and finger. C—Ball-bearing swivel. D—Cast.

The rod, reel and line should be balanced one with the other and as light as is practicable. A single-handed hollow or solid glass rod 6 ft. in length is ideal. The best reel is a multiplier with a very light drum, which will require the minimum weight to set it in motion when a cast is made. The lighter the line compatible with necessary strength the better. Armed with this gear the angler's proposition is to cast his spinning bait into likely spots and wind it back to him fairly briskly, keeping this bait travelling as nearly as possible from mid-water to the bottom. Practice alone will perfect the pretty and sporting art of perch spinning, and when it is mastered the angler will be rewarded by interest, exercise and fish!

Quite often perch seem unable to resist the glittering spinner when other devices fail.

Closely allied to spinning is 'sink and draw.' Cast out your bait and allow it to sink to the bottom, then raise your rod point in such a way as to lift the bait toward you about a yard, then allow it to sink again. This operation is repeated until you have recovered the bait, slack line being taken on the reel after each movement while the bait is resting on the bottom. The fish seize your lure as it is rising or sinking in its series of hops. There are other methods of sink and draw, but I prefer the one detailed, as it enables the angler to play his fish from the reel at any moment, avoiding hand manipulation of the line with its may disadvantages.

One last word—do not strike hard when spinning for perch; the chances are the fish will hook itself when it seizes your moving bait and to strike may tear the hooks away from its delicate mouth.

A few words on the homely and more commonly employed method of float fishing for perch are called for.

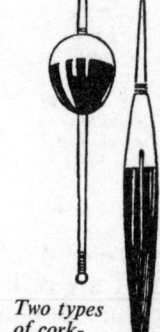

Two types of cork-covered quill float suitable for perch fishing. Half actual size.

A Nottingham rod from 9 to 11 ft. in length, fitted with bridge rings and a good 3½-in. narrow all-metal reel, are ideal tools. And despite the modern craze for the use of ultra-fine lines, of which I think match-fishermen are the fathers and mothers, a 4 or 6 lb. b.s. Terylene line is suitable. One can at least see lines of this calibre and is therefore able to mend bellies caused by wind and current as necessary. And in most instances the fish either don't see it or don't care about it when they do. In any case under certain conditions of water and light there is no such thing as an invisible line. But I am disgressing unduly on a subject which for me is almost a fetish and for the good of my neck I will not stick it out any farther.

Perch floats are deserving of special thought. They should be heavy enough to enable the angler to cast considerable distances, and large and bright in colour above the water-line to ensure visibility at a distance.

The most interesting and productive method of float fishing for perch is to rove from place to place fishing likely spots. If the fish are there, and feeding, you will not need to wait their pleasure long. To deceive the big fish your cast must not be too heavily or conspicuously weighted; carrying only sufficient lead to sink the bait, any extra weight necessary to cock the float should be added to the

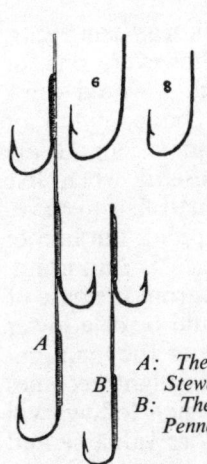

float itself. A simple and effective method is to wind lead wire round the base close up the ring through which the cast or line is passed. It is providential that the splash caused by casting does not seem to upset perch, indeed, it will often prove the reverse, and would seem to attract their attention. Throwing in a small portion of turf with its accompanying earth will at times act as an encouragement especially when a worm is the bait.

A 1½ yard 3 or 4 lb. b.s. cast is very satisfactory and

A: The three-hook
Stewart tackle.
B: The two-hook
Pennell tackle.

The 'Jardine' spiral lead is most convenient and is instantly attached or removed. The line lies in the grooves and is brought out through the end spirals.

Hooks—actual size

may be weighted most conveniently by the use of a spiral lead as shown in the illustration above. This should be placed about a foot or 15 in. above the bait.

There is no fear of cutting or nipping and thus weakening the line when these spirals are used and it can be moved higher or lower on the cast in a moment.

No. 6 or 8 blued steel crystal hooks are ideal when using live bait. If gentles or other larvae are used, slightly smaller hooks are preferable for ease in baiting, but the ample mouths of perch will easily accommodate the larger ones. The three-hook 'Stewart' or two-hook 'Pennel' flights are excellent for the presentation of a worm, but for some reason do not seem to be generally employed.

When float fishing for perch, commence with your bait in midwater and work to the bottom before trying a new 'swim.' Keep your bait on the move even in still water by occasionally raising your rod point, and do not stay longer in one place than results warrant.

The paternoster is a favourite tackle of many perch anglers. How this quaint device got its name is a question the reply to which is buried in obscurity. I prefer to believe that it is a relic of those days when merry monks fished for their Friday meal. It seems not unlikely that its form reminded these ecclesiastical sportsmen of the paternoster (Latin—'Our Father') beads on their rosaries. It will be noted from the accompanying illustration that a series of hooks are suspended from the cast. Personally, I do not use more than two hooks arranged as shown. Some anglers use three, and it is quite possible that those old-time fishers used even more the appearance of which gave rise to the interesting and strange name paternoster, which is now universally applied to this item of the fisher's equipment.

Precise dimensions for the arrangement of a paternoster are entirely a matter of personal taste, but for anglers who are not familiar with this

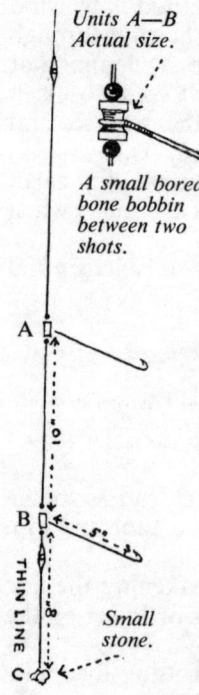

Units A—B
Actual size.

A small bored
bone bobbin
between two
shots.

A

B

THIN LINE

C

Small
stone.

I suggest those shown in the illustration as being gear, reasonably practical. There are, however, one or two details of importance to which I would draw special attention. First, the small bone, nylon or plastic bobbins upon which the hook lengths are whipped. These are particularly useful when live baits are used as they permit the small fish to move in a circular direction without wrapping the line of the hook-length round the cast which is important. Second, the short length of thin line from the base of the cast to the small stone. This should be of a lower breaking strain than either the line or the main gut cast. By using this device, if the end weight becomes fixed in any obstruction the break which follows will be in that length of line and the more valuable and important gear is saved. Third, the stone used as a weight has some advantage, in that it is more natural in appearance than the usual lead weight and if it is lost costs nothing to replace. The total length from the stone to the line need not exceed 4 ft., though many experts use longer casts. The casts and hook-lengths should be slightly heavier than those used when roach fishing.

A paternoster may be used either with or without a float. I prefer the floatless method of dropping the tackle into promising water and holding it taut between the top of the rod and the end weight. A bite is registered by a tug at the rod tip. The method of striking can only be determined by the conditions prevailing at the time. If the fish are feeding well, strike gently at once. But if they are at all shy, lower the rod point immediately a bite is felt and give the fish a few seconds in which to get hold of the bait properly without feeling any tension from the line, then strike gently.

I stress the gentleness necessary in striking because though a perch has a large mouth, its tissues are soft and easily torn. The significance of this is vital to the fisher, and he must handle his hooked fish with great care and delicacy if it is not to escape. To lose a perch (particularly a large one) in the swim may mean the closing of the angler's account with that shoal. It is possible that the 'pricked' perch, having escaped, dives back to the others and acts in such an agitated manner that they are frightened away. Or it may rush off, followed by the shoal, for perch are very inquisitive fish. One or more will often follow a hooked fish while it is being played. This may or may not explain the phenomenon that the losing of a fish almost invariably means the cessation of the catch for a considerable period if not absolutely.

When a float is used it is fixed so that it is visible when the end weight or stone is resting on the bottom and it must not be large enough to raise the stone. The fishing procedure is identical.

It will be obvious that this method is only suitable when the bottom is reasonably even.

No ground-bait is necessary when perch fishing, though a few gentles or chopped worms are sometimes helpful. I have not tried it, but am assured that to lower a fish globe containing minnows or gudgeon into a perch swim attracts and holds *Perca*. The procedure is simple. Fit a fine mesh wire cap to the globe, place a few live minnows into it and lower the deception into the water. Then fish near it. If the water you fish is near at hand this might be worth a trial, but I should not fancy carrying a glass fish-bowl as part of my equipment for a day's fishing far afield.

CHAPTER XXVI

FISHING DEEP WATER FOR PERCH

WHAT could be more appropriate here than to make reference to Richard Walker's ingenious and equally effective device for fishing really deep lakes for perch?

Arlesey Lake in Bedfordshire, which is perhaps the home of more really large perch than the next water of which one could think, was the birthplace of this idea.

Before explaining the tackle, however, I must stress that location of the fish is of primary importance. When the natural cover, from which large perch pounce on their prey in the summer, has died down they make for the deeps and lie behind irregularities on the bottom, from the cover of which they make their feeding dashes.

'R.W.'s' method of locating these lies is of that painstaking kind that is so typical of an expert carp-fisher's approach to his task. And it must be followed if consistent success is to be achieved.

First he makes a rough drawing of the landmarks on the bank

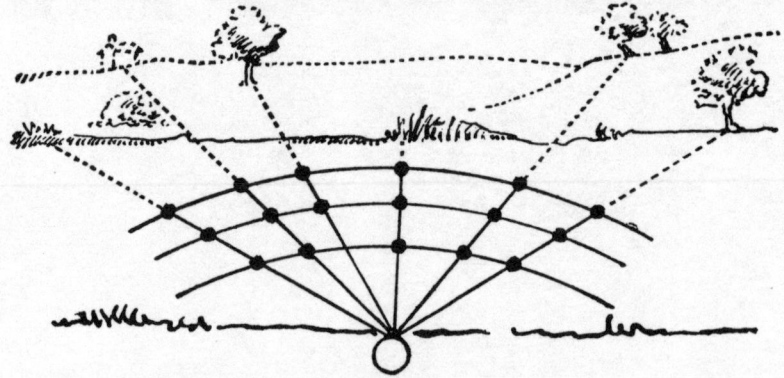

FIG. 1.
A rough drawing assists materially in determining the contour of the bed of the lake, a good knowledge of which is vital. The large circle represents the casting stance, the arcs, the casting distances which are marked on the drawing; and the black dots the depths, which are also marked. More or fewer casts may be made at will, but avoid the confusion which might result from over elaboration.
(After R. Walker.)

opposite to his casting stance. Having done this he then makes a series of casts fanwise towards these marks at varying distances from, say, 40 to 60 yards or more, estimating the depth of the water at each

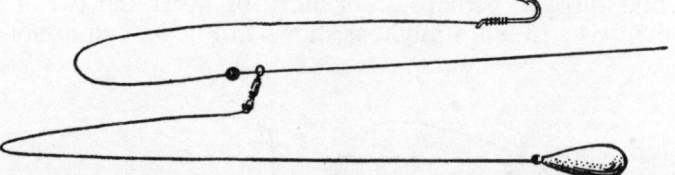

FIG. 2.
Running paternoster. The shot is placed 6 to 8 in. from the hook. The length of nylon between the swivel and the lead varies in accordance with the depth of water and the distance cast. The bait should hang 3 or 4 in. off the bottom.

point, by the time taken for his weight to touch bottom. These details he notes on his sketch carefully, then fishes the most likely marks with either a running swivelled paternoster (most useful at the nearest marks), or with a running ledger.

This brings us to the underlying reason for the construction of the now quite popular, but still often misunderstood 'Arlesey Bomb.'

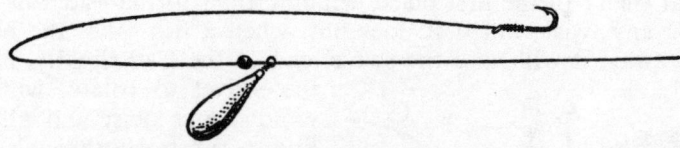

FIG. 3.
Arlesey bomb ledger tackle. The shot is placed not less than 2 ft. from the hook. In both this and the tackle shown in Fig. 2, a No. 4 or 6 eyed Model Perfect hook is tied direct to the reel-line.

In this Arlesey, and no doubt in many similar waters throughout the country, the large fish lie well out (in winter when most of them are taken) and long casting is necessary to reach them.

This being the case, a fixed-spool reel with a capacity for at least 100 yards of 6 lb. b.s. monofil line, and a 10 or 11 ft. split-cane rod of the Walker Mark IV type (mentioned in Chapter XXII) are necessary. A less powerful rod is useless for this type of fishing.

Now, if one uses the conventional leads for this long casting it is certain that in most cases, during its flight through the air, the comparatively light bait will drop behind the lead and twist round the line as shown.

Should a fish take a bait entangled in this way, it is bound to feel the resistance of the weight and will almost invariably drop it.

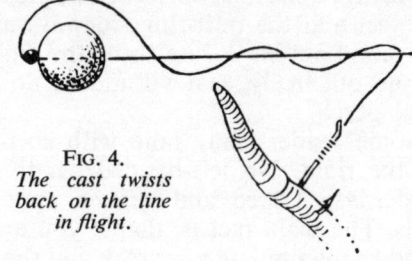

FIG. 4.
The cast twists back on the line in flight.

With a swivel-fitted lead (Arlesey bomb) this fatal risk is considerably minimised if not entirely eliminated.

Let us assume that the tackle lands on the water as shown in Fig. 5. As it sinks through perhaps 25 or 30 ft. of water the swivel tends to allow the twists to pull straight as shown in Fig. 6. You doubt it? Very

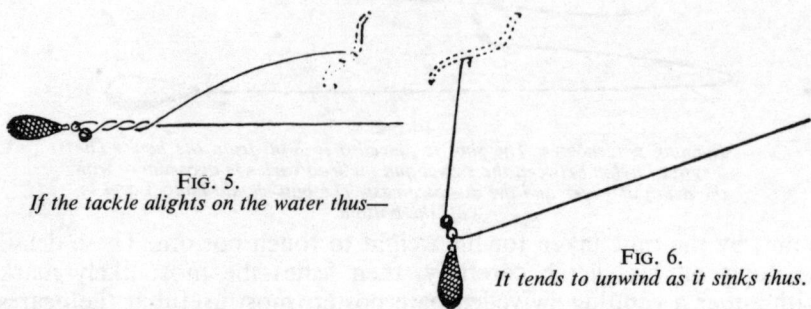

FIG. 5.
If the tackle alights on the water thus—

FIG. 6.
It tends to unwind as it sinks thus.

well, let us presume that you are right and that the tackle hits the bottom as shown in Fig. 7.

What then? In the first place, winding tight to the lead will help to remove any twist; but if it does not, when a fish takes the bait and moves away, it will raise the swivel end of the lead slightly, allowing the swivel to rotate, which will remove any twist and allow the line to run freely through its eye.

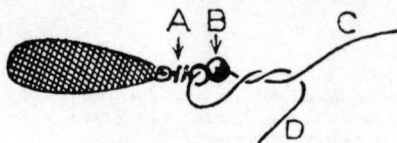

FIG. 7.
A—Swivel. B—Shot. C—To the bait.
D—The reel-line

It boils down to this. Any precaution against scaring a big fish by allowing it to feel the drag of a weight is worthwhile, and the efficiency of these leads has been demonstrated repeatedly in both still and running water both ledgering and paternostering.

Let us return then for a moment to the fishing. A No. 6 eyed Model Perfect hook is tied direct to the line and large lobworms are the baits generally used. The cast is made and the rod is placed in a rest of the type which leaves the line free to run without obstruction.

Having done this, open the line pick-up, draw a length of line between the reel and the butt-ring sideways and pass it round one edge of an old line-bobbin. A bite turns the empty spool over allowing the line to run out freely, as it will indeed do in response to the run of a really large perch.

Some readers may note with surprise that I show the reel-handle on the right. No left-handed winding for me! There has been much balderdash talked and written about the advantages of left-handed reels. The plain fact is, that if you are more at home using your right hand to manipulate your reel, and the left for controlling the rod, when playing a fish, right-handed equipment and methods are for you correct and *vice versa*.

Hundreds of anglers have been infected with this keck-handed bug to their mental and physical discomfort, by following the ridiculous left-handed wind fetish which has been plugged by so many angling scribes.

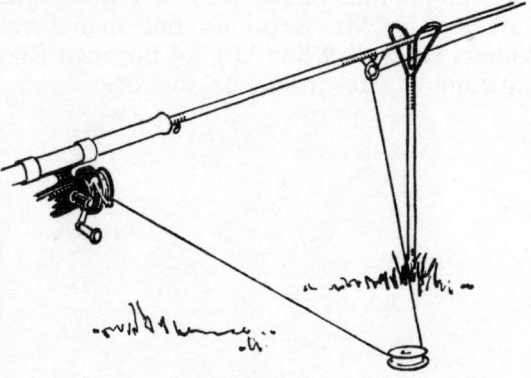

FIG. 8.

A good bite or run indicator. When a fish takes, the empty line-bobbin turns over and the line runs freely from the open spool.

As is the case always where one either ledgers or paternosters for deep-water perch, patience pending a bite is essential. Don't keep niggling and disturbing the gear to see if the bait is still on.

There are two other points of interest in connection with this deep-water fishing which should be mentioned. These perch are lying at from 25 to 30 ft. deep where the pressure is considerably greater than that in shallow water. If you catch a perch from really deep water and do not wish to retain it, release the fish immediately or it will swell rapidly and die. If, on the other hand, you intend to keep your specimen, kill it at once on capture to prevent the distress to which I refer.

The other important factor is the matter of striking. When fishing deep and far off as in this case, the strike is quite a major operation. It has to take up not only the sag but the elasticity of the line, which, with some 50 or 60 yards of line out in deep water is quite considerable and may well be measured in yards.* This being the case, the drill is: Allow several yards of line to run out, then strike firmly with a side swipe at the same time taking several steps backwards winding on the reel at the same time.

Arlesey experts take little notice of the weather or wind conditions when after these deep-water whoppers, but find that sunshine at midday is the most propitious time and condition for their capture.

It is appropriate here to mention another novel swivel-ledger-lead which appeared in 1959. Designed by S. J. Seymour, a keen and thoughtful angler, these shallow triangular pyramid shaped leads, fitted with a swivel, have the advantages that they enter the water with a minimum splash, their shape insures stability of position in a strong current, the position of the swivel lessens the possibility of the bait being entangled with the line when casting; and a

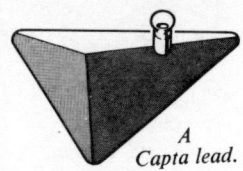

A Capta lead.

* Much of this difficulty can be eliminated by using Terylene line which has little or no stretch.

'Capta' lead of half the normal weight is adequate to meet any given water condition. 'Capta' leads are still available. They are no longer marketed by Mr. Seymour, but manufactured and distributed by William Hitchell & Son Ltd., of Borough Road, Birkenhead, Cheshire, and come in sizes from $\frac{1}{8}$ oz. to 1 oz.

CHAPTER XXVII

PIKE RECORDS: PIKE LORE

HAVING made a particular study of this branch of angling, I may be excused if, in the course of my writing, I express views which are individual or are not in keeping with ideas held generally. A frost overnight puts pike down, but the third day after a thaw is the day for big fish, said the late Jim Vincent, the famous Broads pike angler and he should know.

Don't worry about whether pike feed at night. Night is no time for pike fishing anyway. I have found that the best sport is to be obtained with pike during the months of January, February and those few remaining days of the season which come in the early part of March; for this reason I seldom put pike tackle together until the New Year. There is, however, no doubt that *Esox lucius* is to be taken by various methods throughout the season; a fact which was forced upon me when, having an unrivalled opportunity, I enjoyed excellent pike fishing in a Thames weir pool during July and August, over a period of three seasons. No doubt their well-oxygenated location assured the fine condition of these fish. I do not suggest that pike from still water would have been equally fit. But it is certain that the later you fish for pike the better is your chance of taking a heavy specimen on account of the amount of spawn which they contain later in the season. It is, by the way, illegal to kill a fish in spawn. This fact opens up a very important aspect of pike fishing, namely, the preservation of these fish. Few will refute the statement that if pike angling is not to deteriorate, the indiscriminate killing of the small fish of the species usually called 'Jack' or 'Johnnies' must cease.

Since the minimum length of pike was raised from 18 in. to 24 in., the fish population is steadily increasing. With this increase in the number of pike the angler is finding improved sport, and the balance of nature in our waters is finding its own level. While the 18 in. minimum was in force too many promising young pike were killed, instead of being put back to attain specimen proportions. In the Season 1932–33 I landed 215 pike, only one of which was not returned to the water alive. I mention this to clarify the urgent necessity for returning all pike which are not of glass-case standard, or are required for food.

Carefully cooked, a pike weighing about 7 or 8 lb. can be made very palatable. Try steaming it and serving cold with mayonnaise. I advocate a rigid minimum of 7 lb. in weight for any pike which must be killed. This would mean a minimum length of about 28 in. according to Mona's Scale. (p. 256). Reflect for a moment on the disastrous result if a number of anglers killed the amount of fish to which I have just referred. If my suggested minimum were established, pike fishing would improve immensely, and we should have more reports of specimens in the 20 and 30 pound range, which are still rare when compared with the total of pike caught.

It is interesting to note that while we have only one species of pike in the British Isles, there are five species in the waters of America, the largest of which *Muskellunge* (*Esox masquinong y*) attains a weight of 100 lb. The North American Indian words *mas Kinononge* mean ugly pike. Canada, too, would appear to be the home of not inconsiderable fish as witness the following report which appeared in the Nov.–Dec. 1947 issue of *Irish Angling:*

> Trolling homeward on the Moira River, Canada, one evening last autumn a fisherman hooked what appeared to be the father of all pike.
> Darkness fell and the fight continued, but at length the fish was brought near enough to the boat to enable the angler to attempt to lift it in-board— he had no gaff.
> The great pike gave a last plunge which broke the cast and was gone.
> Fishing the same water two days later in the hope that this fish would strike again he found his erstwhile antagonist floating dead among the weeds.
> The remains were 5 ft. 2 in. in length and despite the ravages of various carrion eaters they weighed 48 lb. Such a fish intact would weigh in the region of 60 lb. (*see page 256.*)

The one-time record pike for these islands, was taken in 1920 on Lough Conn in Ireland by Mr. John Garvin, and weighed 43 lb. On the same day Mr. Garvin caught a 30-pounder. This truly memorable exploit earned for him the £10 prize which had for years been offered by the late R. B. Marston for the capture of a 50 lb. pike. In July 1945, news broke of the capture of a 47 lb. 11 oz. Loch Lomond pike to the rod of T. Morgan which holds the Scottish rod-caught record. The English record pike was taken by Mr. C. Warwick from the Hampshire Avon, in 1944, and weighed 37 lb. 8 oz. It vomited several large roach before it was weighed!

That this magnificent specimen is the well-authenticated and accepted English record there should be no doubt, but the Record (Rod-caught) Fish Committee's purge of 1969 swept away both the English and Scottish records. Now the Record list awaits claimants and has as its qualifying weight a figure of 41 lb.

The nearest weight to approach the qualifying minimum in 1972 was a pike of 33 lb. 1 oz. This fish came from Green Lagoon and was caught by Mr. M. Bachini in March. In all, the year 1972 saw six pike over the 30 lb. mark.

Whatever the Record Committee may think, there are so many authenticated records of large pike captures that their reading puts beyond all doubt that one of them must constitute a record fish. But no, we have no record pike on our list. This being the case the reader will no doubt be most interested to read the following. When Mr. Warwick's once-record fish was accepted, the following passage appeared in the London *Evening News*:

> . . . I know nothing about angling, but I can use my eyes. In the Swan and Pyramid Hotel, High Road, North Finchley, which I visit on occasion, there is a pike in a glass case. This pike weighs 39 lb. 7 oz., is 49 in. long and 25 in. in girth. It is the property of Mr. Stanley Melhuish.
>
> This fish was caught by Mr. George Parrott, a wealthy Marble Arch silk merchant and racehorse owner, in the River Stour, on Lord Wimborne's Hampshire estate in March 1909; and was given to Mr. Melhuish's father who managed Mr. Parrott's sporting preserves.

I went hot-foot to see this splendid fish and was fortunate enough later to learn that my friend, that well-known angler T. W. Gomm, could give first-hand information regarding it. This is what he had to say:

> I do not think anybody is left who knew the circumstances as well as I do. The fish was caught on March 21st, 1909 (*There's the rub!*—My comment and italics, E. M-H.) Continuing, Mr. Gomm said: I had a postcard of that date from Henry Newlyn, an ex-Mayor of Bournemouth, reporting the capture; and on the 23rd of March 1909 I heard from G. I. Parrott, also a friend of mine, confirming the capture and weight at 39 lb.
>
> I saw Parrott at once, who said he caught the fish live-baiting in the big pool at the foot of Castle Hill, Dudsbury, near Longham; and he directed me to the shop of Milestone and Stainforth, the fishmongers in Swallow Passage, Oxford Circus.
>
> There was this immense and perfect fish, marked 39 lb. and I took it to a nearby butcher's shop and had it weighed again. It was as near as possible 39½ lb.
>
> I informed A. R. Matthews (late Editor *Angler's News*) at once and he went along the same day and inspected it.
>
> He also saw Parrott and obtained particulars of the capture, *but was requested not to give the matter any further publicity* (My italics, E. M-H). The Mundella Act did not apply to either the Stour or Avon (Hants) on which there was no statutory close time for coarse fish.
>
> I was very interested as, at that time, I held the lease of the lower reaches of the river which was probably the best coarse-fishing in the country, particularly for pike.

Although Mr. Gomm stated that at that time the Mundella Act did not apply to either the Stour or the Avon, a line must be drawn somewhere when the record status of a fish is under consideration.

The limit was exceeded on this occasion and, in my view, Mr. Parrott's great pike can be recorded only as such; and not as the English rod-caught record specimen.

Considerable correspondence regarding this fish appeared in the 8th and 15th May, 1959, issues of the *Angling Times*. As a direct result of this the 12th June issue carried a front page banner headline reading:

A RECORD ENGLISH PIKE
But it's 58 years old!

Going in with both feet the editor wrote:

It's happened again! Before the dust has had time to settle again on the 1909 records which divulged the secret of the 39 lb. 7 oz. mystery pike from the Stour in Hampshire, word has reached us from Hemsworth (Yorkshire) of an even mightier monster.

But this time there is no mystery attached to the tale. Every fact has been tabulated, the capture was witnessed. The vital statistics are:

WEIGHT: 42 lb. PLACE AND DATE OF CAPTURE: Wroxham Broad, Norfolk, 1901. CAPTOR: The late John Nudd of Norwich.

This magnificent specimen was presented by Gillie Tallowin of the New Inn, Horning, Norfolk, to the Hemsworth, Yorkshire, Blue Bell A.C. in the club-house of which it still holds a place of honour.

Having made a full investigation of the authenticity of this fish the editor declared:

The facts that *Angling Times* have been able to piece together are irrefutable.

According to the details supplied by living witnesses, this fish was taken on a live roach and took $1\frac{1}{2}$ hours to land. Quite apart from the fact that Mr. Nudd was elderly at the time of its capture, if he was using the hefty tackle that was customary in those days, this will give the reader some conception of the strength of this fish.

The ideal of most pike fishers is a 20-pounder which, alas, is all too often an unattainable objective. Pike are predatory, and nature has ordained that there are fewer of them than of the gregarious fishes. The fear which some anglers evince regarding the depredation of *Esox* are indeed misplaced. Pike are in fact nature's aquatic pruning-hooks, which help to maintain a proper balance in the piscine world, by devouring the injured and diseased, and thinning out redundant fish.

When trying out the various methods of capturing them, with which I shall deal in the chapters following, remember this, and resolve to place a high standard of size on any you kill.

The reader may have some misgivings as to the advisability of sparing pike, lest they shall deplete the stocks of other fish. Such fears are quite unfounded. As an example, I would quote Slapton Lea. In this great lake there are more pike than in any water of which I know, and very few of them are ever killed, yet there are literally millions of perch and rudd in the Lea, many of which are of considerable proportions.

Before passing to the interesting subject of pike gear, a line regarding the respective weights of male and female pike may be added. Among the fallacious tenets of many anglers is the idea that male fish do not grow to a greater weight than 10 lb. In March 1944, very reliable evidence came to my notice of a pike weighing 32 lb. taken by Mr. L. E. Perry, of Tetbury, Glos., at Symonds Yat on 26th February, which was a male fish. This is of course, an outstanding and quite exceptional weight for a male of the species, but it is not difficult to acquire evidence that male pike weighing more than 10 lb. are not infrequent. Nevertheless it is, of course, well known that lady *Esox* is as a rule the larger fish, but it is a mistake to assess the weight of male pike too low.

I know I should hurry on, but one other matter which may be of considerable importance to anglers claims attention here. Pike are the only freshwater fish which have a series of cavities along the under ridge of the lower jaw, known as mandipular pores. Being curious as to their function, I approached Dr. Winifred Frost, an eminent ichthyologist and a member of the Freshwater Biological Association, whom I knew to be making a special investigation of pike. She said:

> The lateral line has sensory pits, these communicating with sensory organs connecting with the nervous system. It has been found that these lateral line sense organs are sensitive to vibration of low frequency and thus the fish is made aware of slight vibrations in the water. The lateral line in many fish has branches to the head, and in the case of pike, the cavities to which you refer may be part of this system.

It would therefore appear that spinners which have a maximum vibratory factor should be among the most killing lures. This point is worthy of consideration, I think.

CHAPTER XXVIII

RODS AND OTHER GEAR FOR PIKE

HALF a century ago, and earlier, rods used for pike fishing were unwieldy weapons of great strength and terrific weight, made from ash or hickory, and later of greenheart. But in recent years pike rods have decreased in size and weight very considerably without losing necessary strength. The angler who means to live-bait and spin for pike should have two rods, each with the qualities peculiar to their particular task. I propose here to deal more especially with those suited to live-bait fishing. It has always been a subject for considerable debate as to whether pike rods should be long or short, and experts are never likely to be at one on this point. More important than any personal consideration as to weight and length is that the rod should be capable of casting a 6 or 7 oz. bait thirty yards, and at the critical moment it must be sufficiently powerful to drive the hook into the bony jaws of a pike. The importance of these points cannot be stressed too greatly. An angling friend once came to me explaining that at a certain fishing station he had no fewer than fourteen runs, from pike, none of which he landed, An examination of his gear showed conclusively that the rod was too 'soft.' Its action was such that it was impossible for him to drive home the hooks and establish a firm anchorage with his quarry. As to the advantages or otherwise of long or short rods, a comparison of the main points will be of interest, after which individual inclination must be the deciding factor when choosing a pike rod. Long rods will cast farther, short ones more accurately, there being no necessity to co-ordinate the action of both hands and arms when casting. A long rod will handle or steer a fish better, while a short rod exercises greater power over the fish. With a long rod the angler can reach over weeds and obstacles more easily, but the shorter weapons are less fatiguing and altogether more comfortable to use. My own live-baiting rod is of hollow glass. The cork-covered butt is 18 in. long and the reel fittings are adjustable to enable it to be placed at any convenient point. This is, of course purely a matter of personal convenience and the exact placing of the reel has no particular merit.

The rings are large and agate lined. This question of rings is one in which cost plays a considerable part. I maintain that agate lining is the best, but porcelain is little if any less efficient and much cheaper. That pike-rod rings should be the largest which the rod will properly carry is, however, beyond dispute. A rod of the kind I have described is ideal in my experience, but it is costly. Other cheaper and quite efficient rods are sold made from solid glass. Many very expert pike fishers use this type of rod exclusively with every satisfaction. Nevertheless, really cheap pike rods are never satisfactory and are a false economy in the long run.

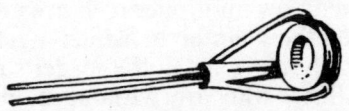

Typical top ring (porcelain), and below an excellent example of protected intermediate ring.

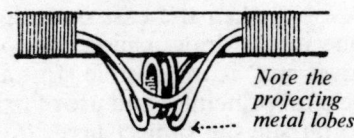

Note the projecting metal lobes.

The angler selecting a reel suitable for pike fishing is much in the same position as a hungry man into whose hands an obliging waiter has placed a menu containing scores of items—he is spoiled with choice. The number of reels with a claim upon the pike fisher is legion. This fact makes a selection more difficult, but I will give some details which will be of assistance to those in doubt. The number of them is no more remarkable than the cost of good reels, but while a good reel is always a sound and lasting investment, many must economise, and it is comforting to know that for live-bait fishing there is no great advantage as between the most costly and the moderately-priced models. My only warning is: avoid really cheap reels; they may be handsome in appearance, but they will inevitably develop faults, the effect of which will be apparent. Without doubt, the most useful pike reel is a Nottingham centre pin. They are made from various metals. The one I use is aluminium throughout with a diameter of 4 in. and a line capacity of from 100 to 150 yards (according to gauge). It is free from 'gadgets' of the automatic drag-and-brake type, which are quite unnecessary and very costly, but is fitted with a line guard and variable optional check. Many experts decry the use of guards. Nevertheless, I have no doubt they minimise the disastrous effects of 'over-runs' and prevent the line becoming entangled with the handles of the reel, which accidents sometimes happen in the best angling circles, so I prefer to have a guard. Some reels of the Nottingham type are made from vulcanite and various metals. These are good. While experts and those well practised in the art of casting are able to work with the reels already described, makers have designed other types which it must be admitted render casting from the reel less difficult, especially when the baits are small and comparatively light. It will be seen readily that the initial difficulty in casting is to give sufficient momentum to the drum to cause it to revolve fast and long enough to enable the bait to reach its distant objective. The lighter the drum, therefore, the more easily it may be set in motion. However, as a chapter dealing with these reels and their concomitant rods, method of use, etc., has been added to this volume, I need not dwell on them at this point. Even now multiplier reels are not so popular as they deserve, and I hope that the chapter to which I refer will aid in dispelling any prejudice which may exist in the reader's mind regarding them. Our friends in the U.S.A., who are without doubt great casters and anglers, use them almost universally.

The third and last type which I shall mention is undoubtedly the simplest with which to cast. It is the fixed spool reel. The drum does not revolve when the cast is made. The line is drawn off over its edge as one might draw a piece of cotton over the end of a bobbin, and an 'over-run' is impossible. In another chapter I attempt to describe the general principles and use of fixed-spool reels. It is therefore unnecessary to pursue the subject here. *If, then, the reader will regard what follows immediately as applying to the use of a Nottingham reel, confusion will be avoided.*

Passing from rods and reels to what I call the 'business end' of a pike-angler's gear, I must necessarily deal with that much-discussed question: Should one fish 'fine' for pike? Fishing fine is only a relative term. The size of the hooks and power of the rod control the gauge of the line. A powerful rod will break a light line and a too heavy line will strain a light rod. Harmony of rod, line and reel is more important than fineness. Aim at strength in its finest form, each item of the gear being in proportion to the others. Pike are susceptible to fine gear, but it must be strong. Any angler might have the good fortune to make contact with a pike of twenty or more pounds weight at a distance of from twenty-five to thirty yards, and unless his line will stand the strain of striking and hook firmly into the fish it is useless. Lines which were too thin for the rod have been the cause of many of those stories which anglers tell about being broken up by a whopper. Let the pike-angler make his motto 'fitness for purpose,' matching a light rod and line with small hooks, and increasing the all-round strength of his tackle wisely when fishing certain waters, for example, the Irish loughs, where very large fish may be expected.

I now use braided Terylene, which is finer than either silk or nylon, strength for strength and much more waterproof than either. It is, moreover, considerably more rigid, which has its advantages when driving hooks home at a distance. Line of this kind treated with any of the line-floating concoctions on the market will float exceedingly well during a whole day's fishing, and for float fishing or, as the pike angler more usually calls it, 'bunging,' this is most important. In days gone by unless the line was taken from the reel and dried immediately after use, whether silk or flax, it soon rotted and became worthless. All that is over now, Terylene being quite impervious to moisture.

The next item for consideration is the float or 'bung.' Here, again, we are face to face with popular superstition regarding fishing 'fine.' I am quite satisfied that mere size from a visibility point of view is immaterial. Many anglers insist on small bungs of raw cork, on the principle, presumably, that pike examine these details and refuse to have anything to do with large and brightly-painted bungs. My reply is that I have fished with every kind of bung, and have never been able to find that their size or colour had any effect on the fish.

The material characteristics of a good pike float are visibility to the angler and sleek shape. I find either a black top in poor light, or an orange top for all well-lit occasions by far the best colouring. With regard to shape, I give preference to those of long, narrow

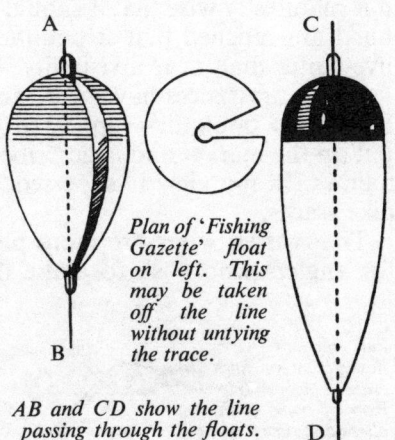

Plan of 'Fishing Gazette' float on left. This may be taken off the line without untying the trace.

AB and CD show the line passing through the floats.

dimensions, as illustrated above. They offer less resistance when the fish takes the bait and pulls the float under water, which is far more important than any consideration of the pike being frightened by their size of colour. In windy weather it will often be found a good device to fix a white feather to the top of the 'bung.' By this means it will be carried down wind and may be worked into otherwise inaccessible places with considerable profit. The use of pilot floats is a matter of personal choice. I always use two (not fixed), more to support the line near the bung after its immersion when the cast is made than as an indicator or pilot, which its name implies.

When discussing traces, or the under-water portion of a pike-angler's tackle, the question of 'fine' or 'coarse,' visible and strong, or invisible and not so strong, is most acute. The factor which weighs most with me in arriving at a decision is my firm belief that pike feed until they are replete, and during the feeding period visibility of the gear goes for little or nothing. Carp, roach, chub, indeed most other freshwater fish are shy; not so a feeding pike. That pike, in common with all other fish, shun man as a natural enemy cannot be doubted, but that they do not connect visible fishing tackle with any source of danger I am convinced. The pike angler who uses a trace, which is primarily strong and trustworthy, will secure more fish in the long run than he who through misguided seeking after invisibility sacrifices strength. A fine pike trace is a good trace only if it is strong.

There are numerous materials from which good traces may be made, and the science of metallurgy has provided immensely strong wire which is yet so fine that I am amazed when the most devoted disciples of fine pike fishing do not use it. I do not advocate tackle which would enable an angler to use his rod, reel and line as a windlass to wind in and bully any fish he may hook. What I recommend is well balanced gear of substantial strength in its slenderest form. If there is any doubt as to the desirability of the under-water tackle being visible it is manifestly wise that it should be as slender and invisible as possible, but I am satisfied that strong tackle is of greater accounts to the pike live-baiter than near invisibility.

Many substances have been, and are still, used for making up traces. Since this book first appeared, the alloy wire Alasticum has been put on the market and is described in the chapter on plug fishing which follows. In my view it supersedes any other material for making up pike traces.

The twisted wires are more pliable than those of single strand, but for anglers who wish to make their own traces, the single variety is much more convenient and will give longer service. As it is possible to make up traces for something like 75 per cent less than they can be bought, I will describe the method.

Put end of wire through swivel and cross evenly. Grip loop of wire with pliers and turn both ends equally three or four times. **A.**

B. *Now turn short end round the main wire.* *Cut off here.*

The double swivel is two as 'B' coupled.

Link spring swivel.

Bored 'Barleycorn' lead about half size.

Complete trace.

The required wire is sold on neat spools for which two lengths of approximately 18 in. should be cut. It is not necessary for the total length of a trace to exceed 3 ft. To one end of the first piece attach a single box swivel, to the other a double box swivel. The method of doing this is illustrated. The more efficient but much more expensive ball-bearing swivels are not necessary when live-baiting.

If a bored 'Barleycorn' lead is to be used on the trace, this must be slipped on the wire before the double swivel is attached. If 'Archer-Jardine' spiral leads are preferred, these may be attached at will to the finished trace. This is probably better, as the weight of a trace is governed by the size of the baits used and should only be enough to prevent the bait rising to the surface. When the 'Barleycorn' is once attached it is permanent. In either case, the weight should be placed immediately above the double swivel. Now attach the second wire to the other end of the double swivel and to the extreme end of the trace a link spring swivel should be served for easy attachment of the bait.

A trace made in this way is so inexpensive that the angler can afford to, and should, discard it immediately if it is kinked or develops any fault. The swivels may, of course, be used repeatedly and should be saved.

One word as to swivels. They are made in several ways from several metals. 'Blued' steel is the most reliable if kept oiled and free from rust. They should not be smaller than those illustrated, and should be individually tested for free working at the time of purchase.

In every phase of angling, hooks are of paramount importance. This is specially true of pike fishing. Yet a vast number of anglers appear to be satisfied with any piece of bent wire which is pointed and has a barb. Every portion of your gear may be of the finest and most reliable quality, and your personal skill beyond reproach, but a bad hook will nullify all this! There are two main causes for a hook being bad: it may be 'over tempered,' in which case it is so brittle that either the point will break off or the hook will snap at the bend, or 'under tempered,' and so soft that any reasonable pressure will bend it open. This is the greater evil of the two. It is quite useless to fish with an 'under-tempered' hook, when it bends the act of straightening it only makes it weaker than before. Most tackle dealers sell reliable hooks, but 'duds' will creep into the best tackle shops, and I advise severe test of every pike hook before it is used. There is no other means of being sure. Place the point of your hook into a piece of wood and give it a pull such as would occur when striking, keeping the shank as nearly in line with the pull as possible. If signs of under or over-tempering appear, discard the hook or be prepared for disappointment.

There are many hooking devices specially adapted for live-baiting for pike. Some are good, others indifferent and one is definitely bad. I refer to the abomination known as gorge-tackle. It is a thousand pities that this device is still obtainable, and even worse that there is any sale for the wretched things.* I am convinced, however, that any angler who uses gorge-tackle when live-baiting, does so in ignorance. My first impulse was to ignore this tackle, but after due consideration I think it better to deal with it fully, citing its inefficiency and disadvantages. I cannot perhaps do better than quote an article which I wrote in the October–December 1939, issue of *Angling*, an erstwhile *Country Life* publication.

On the 23rd May, 1939, an angler stood before a special bench of magistrates, charged with cruelty to a roach, in that he spitted it with a baiting-needle along its side and drew a wire (to which gorge-hooks were attached) through its flesh while it was yet alive.

I have no desire to reopen this matter to the detriment of the angler concerned. On the contrary, there is cause to sympathize with him, despite the fact that he was convicted. As a witness in the case, I am able to assure readers who feel strongly on this matter, that the defendant acted in complete ignorance of other methods, ways and means. Having but one year's experience he followed local practices, as you or I would have done. I am reliably informed that live gorge-baiting had been employed practically exclusively for many years in the water where he was initiated into the art of angling for pike.

* Gorge baiting and tackle has for some time been banned by River Authorities and is now considered to be an illegal form of angling. However, I leave the following passages concerning gorge baiting and tackle in this chapter, just as Marshall-Hardy wrote them, as a perfect illustration of the author's passionate concern for the upholding of fair methods and the least possible cruelty to fish.   L.C.

Happily this practice has now been forbidden by the owner of the water in question, and I hope the details which follow will cause any who read this book to turn their face steadfastly against this nefarious gorge-tackle method.

A point of interest to anglers, which could not be clear to any but those closely connected with the case, is the fact that the action was

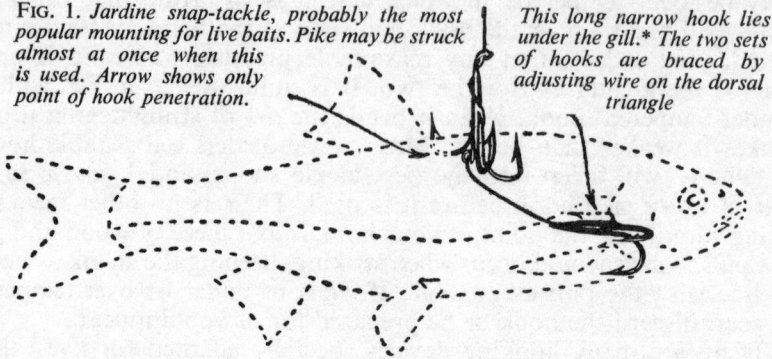

FIG. 1. *Jardine snap-tackle, probably the most popular mounting for live baits. Pike may be struck almost at once when this is used. Arrow shows only point of hook penetration.*

This long narrow hook lies under the gill.* The two sets of hooks are braced by adjusting wire on the dorsal triangle

not in itself an attack, neither was it the prelude to an assault by the R.S.P.C.A. on the practice of live-baiting by generally approved methods. Counsel for the Society made this amply clear when he invited me to give evidence as to alternative and better methods of attaching live baits.

FIG. 2.

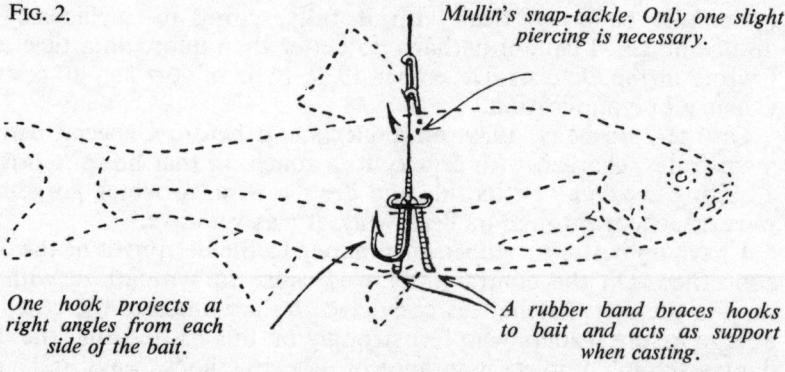

Mullin's snap-tackle. Only one slight piercing is necessary.

One hook projects at right angles from each side of the bait.

A rubber band braces hooks to bait and acts as support when casting.

Even so worthy a Society cannot 'have its cake and eat it,' and there is no doubt that those responsible for its conduct realize that such an attack would alienate thousands of its sympathizers, without adding one soul to its strength.

Leading writers have condemned gorge-baiting, among them are numbered the late Edward F. Spence, K.C.,* the late Alfred Jardine, the

* The late Edward F. Spence, K.C., had the gill-hooks of his snap-tackles made with a small ball end to avoid any discomfort which might be caused by the point and barb, both of which are unnecessary.

late John Bickerdyke, H. D. Turing and many others.

I could enumerate many expert expressions of opinion on this subject, but hope that the foregoing together with the accompanying diagrams of alternative methods, will carry conviction to readers. The designer and maker of the tackle shown in Figs. 2 and 3 are to be congratulated on its simplicity and effectiveness. The rubber sling under the belly of the fish is a good corrective against casting baits off. In 1945 some criticism of this snap was published in the angling Press, it being stated that the side hooks and bellyband were inclined to slip toward the tail of the bait. As a result of this, the late Mr. Mullins gave further thought to the snap and decided to add a small anchoring hook to each side-hook as shown here. I have not experienced the disadvantage to which critics referred, to any marked extent. The modified snap certainly eliminates any possibility of the side-hooks slipping aft, but it also adds two punctures to the bait which adds to the difficulty of mounting and is not so comfortable for the bait. I view this modification as a mixed blessing and hope that both types will continue to be available.

Now let me examine this question purely from a fisherman's point of view. Would any sane angler knowingly employ an inefficient method? The answer must be 'No!' Very well, then a look at the disadvantages of live gorge-baiting will prove useful.

Gorge tackle restricts the movement and therefore the attractiveness of the bait. It exhausts a bait more quickly than other methods of attachment. A pike hooked in its entrails, as is inevitable when gorge-bait is used, shows no fight, and every fish captured must be killed regardless of its size.

An unattractive bait produces few 'runs' if any. Does not the pike fisher desire the very maximum of runs? An exhausted bait is an unattractive bait and must be changed, with the consequent waste of good fishing time, and there is need for carrying more baits than would otherwise be necessary. Does any angler deny that only the bait which is in the water catches fish? Will any deny that one of the sore points in live-baiting is the need for

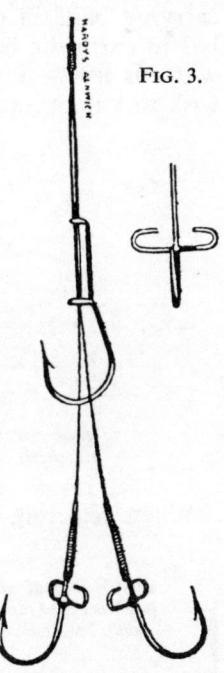

Fig. 3.

Mullin's snap tackle.

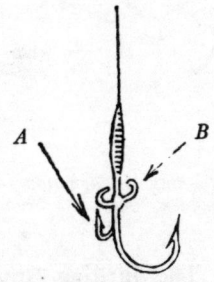

MODIFICATION OF MULLIN'S SNAP.

A—Small anchoring-hook which is intended for insertion in the root of the ventral fin. With this modification the rubber band is not essential but can be retained, as it is not possible to dispense with the cross bar B which holds the side hook at right angles to the bait.

carrying baits in cans heavily laden with water? The fewer baits one has to carry the better—surely! Does every angler enjoy a good scrap with his fish?—I need hardly ask. And finally, would any sportsman wish to kill an immature pike?

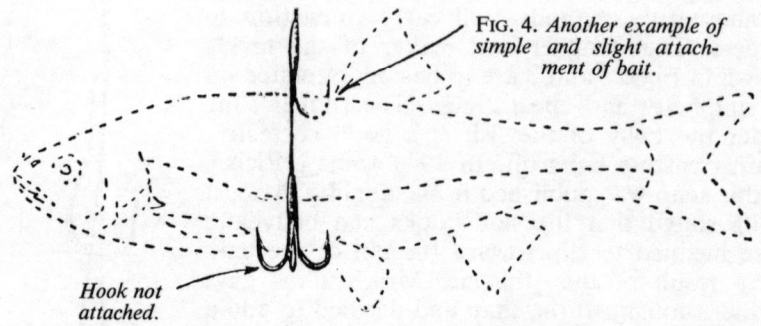

FIG. 4. *Another example of simple and slight attachment of bait.*

Hook not attached.

When selecting hooking devices for live-baiting you will be well advised to choose those which are made with hooks of square bend. That great authority, the late Mr. Pennell, made exhaustive tests which proved that hooks of square bend require a lighter pull to penetrate them beyond the barb than hooks of any other design. This question of penetration is highly important when fishing for a bony-mouthed quarry like pike.

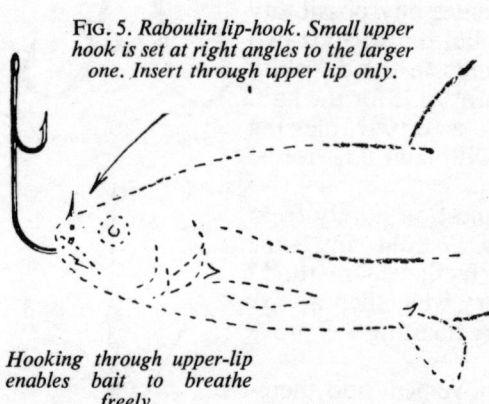

FIG. 5. *Raboulin lip-hook. Small upper hook is set at right angles to the larger one. Insert through upper lip only.*

Hooking through upper-lip enables bait to breathe freely.

The Jardine 'snap-tackle' illustrated in Fig. 1 is the most popular of the hooking devices I have mentioned. For baits of 6 or 7 in. it is excellent, so is the Mullins' snap shown in Fig. 2. When mounting a bait with the Jardine care must be taken not to restrict the free movement of the bait by bracing the wire between the dorsal and gill hooks too tightly. On the other hand if this wire is too loose the gill hooks will fall out of position. Practice is necessary to attain perfection in this rather tricky procedure. Trouble can be avoided when mounting the Mullins' snap, by putting the elastic band in place on the prongs provided, then slide the bait head first through the noose so formed and fix the dorsal hook last, just forward of the fin itself. If the latest model to which I have referred is used no slipping is possible. For use with baits a little smaller a single hook fixed just in front of the dorsal fin on the tackle shown in Fig. 4 is good. For still smaller baits I recommend the 'Raboulin' double lip hook (see Fig. 5). I do not advise hooks much smaller than those shown in Fig. 6 for live-baiting. The hooks depicted in the other figures are reduced for convenience of illustration and should not be taken as an absolute guide.

FIG. 6.

Small hooks mean thin wire and thin wire is weak wire. For the most part pike hooks when new are too long in the point and their barbs project too far. A watchmaker's file or a piece of carborundum will cure these bad defects, which hamper penetration.

It would be difficult to show that a live-bait, hooked by any of the devices recommended, suffered more than the inconvenience of captivity, only a small gristly portion of the bait being pierced by the anchoring hook in each case.

Mention of different sizes of bait may have whetted the reader's appetite for an expression of opinion regarding their merits. This is a very open question. Pike will sometimes attempt to swallow fish of their own or even greater size. Pike have been opened and found to contain the remains of fish weighing pounds, while an autopsy on other members of the *Esox* family has disclosed a belly full of minnows. I have authentic information regarding one pike which when opened was found to have been feeding on wasps. Now who would use a two-pound bait and who would use a wasp for the capture of pike? Yet had an angler been using either at the time when the fish I have just mentioned were in the vicinity, these strangely divergent baits might have proved successful.

Some anglers swear by large baits and others swear at them. Give me a 6 in. bait and I am happy. Larger baits strain a reasonably light rod in casting, and smaller baits do not in my view work so well. The answer can only be the omnibus one—sometimes large, sometimes small, with the pike the final arbiter every time.

With large baits in mind, there are Norfolk anglers who have used 4 lb. pike as live bait for the huge Broads pike. By this means, specimens up to 40 lb. have been taken.

In closing this chapter let me describe a most useful tackle devised by the late Captain L. A. Parker, of Fordingbridge, for live-baiting in fast water.

Any angler who fishes a fast river or from the apron of a weir will find it ideal. During his long experience of the briskly flowing Hampshire Avon, Captain Parker found that there were several marked disadvantages in using the Jardine snap, or any tackle where the main hooking of the bait was at or near the dorsal fin. This type of mount caused the bait to lie broadside to the stream, which is manifestly unnatural. Furthermore a bait lying at this angle in fast water will not live so long and cannot work so well as a bait which heads upstream.

He found in addition that any check on the downstream movement

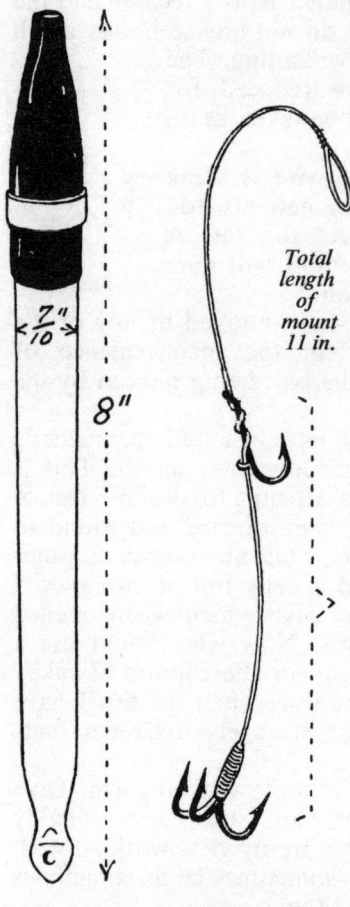

Total length of mount 11 in.

Hooks and wire painted red.

Capt. L. A. Parker's
Fast-water Tackle.

of the float caused a bait so hooked to rise to the surface; while to retrieve it meant dragging the bait broadside along the surface of the water, which quickly impaired its liveliness.

To overcome these disadvantages Captain Parker designed the simple snap illustrated here. To mount it he advises inserting the adjustable lip-hook through the lower lip of the bait, and out through the upper lip (i.e. both lips are pierced). Then one hook of the triangle is lightly hitched at the centre of the belly of the bait. It will be seen at once that a bait attached in this way is kept heading upstream, no matter how fast the water. Captain Parker suggests that the belly triangle acts as a keel and assists in preserving the natural swimming posture.

I am not, however, convinced that any fish needs such a keel. Despite all arguments to the contrary, I prefer to pass the lip-hook through the upper lip only; it being my considered opinion that this allows the bait to breathe more freely, at the same time eliminating all possibility of closing the mouth of the bait, which would of course hamper its respiration and reduce its efficiency, if it did not produce actual suffocation.

As to the triangle I insert it lightly at the first ray of the dorsal fin, which I am satisfied causes less inconvenience to the bait, which is in itself an important enough consideration. This is not a method of fishing where casting plays any part, and providing the lip-hook is carefully and firmly inserted in the upper lip there is no strain on the triangle which will remain in position and do its work whether it is fixed dorsally or ventrally. The reader has the pros and cons and will adopt the method he finds most satisfactory. In either case the bait will head upstream as desired whether it be allowed to drop slowly down-stream, is held in the stream, or is being recovered—and it will not rise in the water above the level of the lead on the trace.

For use with a large bait Captain Parker sometimes used a flight mounted with a second triangle, the triangles being in tandem. One triangle is, however, usually sufficient and I prefer the simpler tackle.

Had he only devised the fast-water snap Captain Parker would have earned the gratitude of anglers, but he went further and designed the fast-water float shown in the illustration. I regard this float as the best I have seen for any type of pike live-baiting. For use in fast water its advantages are obvious, but every argument which can be adduced in its favour for fast streams applies in any type of water.

Being slender these floats offer the minimum of resistance and do not create an undesirable 'boil'; even more important is the fact that they are far more sensitive and less resisting to either the bait or a taking fish than are the battleship-like contrivances one so often sees in use. These floats are made of celluloid in two sections. The above-water section is red and the under-water portion pale green. Being hollow it is a simple matter to weight them either to make the float self-cocking or as a counterbalance when it is necessary to use larger or smaller weight on the trace. The Parker float is excellent.

CHAPTER XXIX

STRIKING A PIKE AND OTHER MATTERS OF
IMPORTANCE

I HAVE seen many pike lost through faulty striking. If there are spectators when an angler gets a 'run' he will be inundated with kindly advice as to how and when he should strike his fish. 'Hit him!' 'No, let him run!' etc. The primary difficulty is to decide when to strike. If you are too early you will often draw the bait out of the pike's mouth, while to be too late means the fish will be so deeply hooked that the extraction of the hooks is fatal. Every sportsman deplores this circumstance, especially when the pike is small. Experience alone will enable an angler to make an art of striking pike. There are, however, certain guiding principles which should receive careful consideration. If a 'single lip-hook' or 'single triangle' is used, more time may be given before striking than when 'snap tackle' is employed. The size of the bait must also be taken into account and more time given for large than small baits, but in either case I am strongly in favour of striking early, and have found that the movements of the pike after taking the bait are the most reliable guide.

The 'bung' has disappeared but as yet there is no movement of the line. It is probable the pike has grabbed the bait and is holding it across its jaws—wait half a minute. The line begins to move away or falls slack, indicating that the fish is either going away from or coming towards the angler. Now is the time to take swift action. Reel your line in gently *until you feel your fish*—at that moment and not before—strike! This last injunction may be taken as a absolute rule for successful striking—*there must be no slack line*. And now how to deliver the *coup de grâce*. No invariable rule can be laid down, and with differing circumstances the angler's experience must of necessity play a most important part. Great pike anglers have held varying opinions as to the actual method of striking. That famous angler the late Mr. Pennel advised repeated striking. With this advice I am not in agreement, much preferring the method adopted by another angler of equal eminence and authority, the late Mr. Jardine. He said 'Don't strike, but give a long, steady pull and hold the pike hard for a few seconds to get the hook well home.' I use this method almost without exception, and have found it most satisfactory. As the line is reeled in to take up the slack, the rod is pointed toward the fish and downward to the surface of the water.

At the moment when the 'draw' is made, the rod point is swept sideways and backward parallel with the surface of the water, as shown in the diagram. Immediately contact has been established the rod point should be raised above and slightly behind the angler and the fish played with the rod point up. The words 'point up' really refer to the angular relation between rod and line, the rod itself need not be, and often is

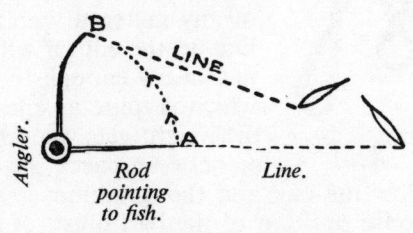

A to B shows the arc of the 'draw'. Note the rod in tension at B and changed direction of the fish.

not, perpendicular while playing a fish, but it should make a right angle with the line so far as possible, thus the full benefit of the rod's action is gained. When a fish is sufficiently strong to pull the rod top down, it should be 'given line,' and the rod thrown back again. If possible play your fish sitting down, especially if you are in a boat. This method has two great advantages. You will be less inclined to 'skull haul' your pike, and will play it more delicately and therefore

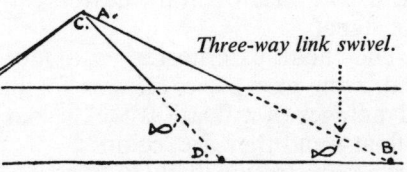

Showing effect of the length of the cast on the position of the bait. This variation is detrimental.

more safely. Even more important, you will be less visible and not so likely to frighten your fish, which has often meant a lost whopper.

'Bunging' is undoubtedly the most popular form of pike fishing, but I have often wondered why more anglers do not use the paternoster. There can be no doubt it is the only feasible method under certain conditions and that it is a most killing device is certain. For fishing very deep water, holes among weed beds, and against the wind or in water of uneven bottom the 'paternoster' has no equal. In deep water and weed holes the floatless gear is the best, but for general use it has a disadvantage worthy of note.

A glance at the diagram above shows that the distance cast materially affects the position of the bait in relation to the bottom, a matter of importance. In the case of AB, the bait is too low and might be hidden amongst weeds, while in CD it might be too high and out of range of the cruising fish. Having this in mind, I only use the method when circumstances permit the line to hang almost perpendicular from the rod point. See Fig. 1.

FIG. 1.

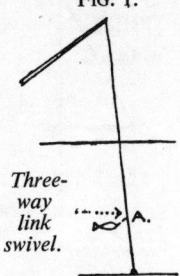

Three-way link swivel.

Three-way link swivel.

The construction of this form of paternoster is very simple and requires no trace. At the point A, Fig. 1, which is the end of the 'reel line,' fix a three-way swivel, as illustrated opposite.

To the bottom loop of this, tie from 18 in. to 2 ft. 6 in. of any material with a lower breaking strain than the line, to the end of which attach a stone or lead weight just heavy enough to anchor the bait. I prefer a stone which is quite as effective and cheaper than a lead. If the weight gets wedged in weed growth or between rocks the break will occur below the bait and the minimum loss will result. The precise position of the bait must, of course, vary with local conditions. If, for instance, the bottom is weedy it must be placed high enough to clear these weeds, but the dimensions given are a fair average. Alternatively, this tackle can be made up as shown in Fig. 2. A run is easily detected, and line should be given to the fish at once when the movement of the rod tip gives the signal.

The 'float paternoster' is a more elaborate device and is the gear *par excellence* for those who desire the advantages of a floatless tackle, but who like to watch a float—and they are legion.

The illustration (below) shows a tackle of my own construction, which could be obtained from any tackle shop or is quite simply to make up at home. With this gear the bait is held away from, and cannot entangle itself with the line as is frequently the case with the ordinary attachment. The great freedom for movement which it affords the bait is also an advantage.

The piece of line EF should be of low breaking strain as in the floatless gear. Its length gives the depth at which the bait is set in relation to the bottom and may vary from 2 ft. to 3 ft.

The weight of the stone or lead will be governed chiefly by the strength of the wind or flow of the stream, and must be sufficient to anchor the tackle securely. A most effective method of working this gear is to cast and after waiting a few minutes raise the rod point and draw the bait about a yard toward you, repeating the movement until it is drawn home. This searching of the water is very killing and runs will often occur just after the bait has been moved. It would seem that the pike will often lie and watch a bait without touching it while it is stationary, but when it is moved away the fish grabs.

FIG. 2.

Reel line.

18″ Fine Wire Trace

Hook to Fine Wire.

18″ Fine Line.

Stone.

Paternoster for pike.

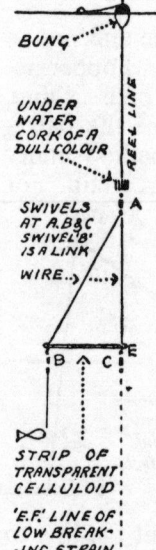

BUNG

UNDER WATER CORK OF A DULL COLOUR

REEL LINE

SWIVELS AT A.B&C SWIVEL 'B' IS A LINK

WIRE

A

B   C   E

STRIP OF TRANSPARENT CELLULOID

'E.F.' LINE OF LOW BREAK- -ING STRAIN

F

Hooks for paternostering are the same as those used for 'bunging.'

Those transparent plastic balls called 'bubble-floats,' which I believe came from the Continent and were at once hailed by some trout fishermen as godsends to enable them to insinuate a fly into places that their casting skill could not reach, were in my view little short of poaching devices in that capacity.

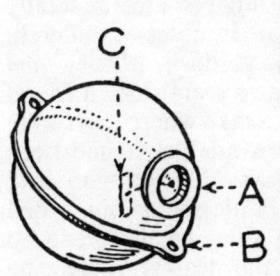

FIG. 1.

Transparent plastic 'bubble' float. A—Filling-cap. B— Bored lugs for attachment of line. C—Device to prevent loss of the cap.

Mr. O. M. Reed found better uses for them.

One of these was to use a bubble either partly filled, with a comparatively light lead, to enable the bait to tow this thus delicately balanced paternoster tackle with comparative ease; or empty with a larger weight when circumstances demand a stationary tackle.

He found this eminently satisfactory from the word go and took several fish including a 15 lb. 3 oz. specimen the first time he used it.

The accompanying diagram, Fig. 2, shows the make-up of the rig he used, and it is more than likely that the comparative invisibility of the gear may have contributed to its success.

My own experience goes to show that these bubbles are effective used in this way especially where very large pike are not expected.

In this connection I have more than a little misgiving. The weak point is where the line passes round the ball-like surface of the float.

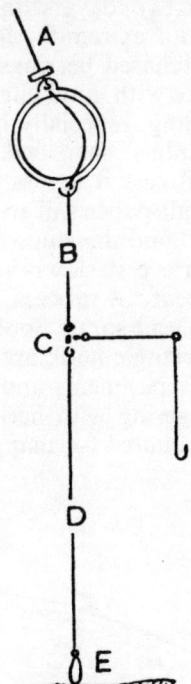

FIG. 2.

Bubble-float used with pike paternoster. A— Line threaded through lugs and wedged with a piece of matchstick hitched to the line. B— Twenty-four inches if for deep water. C—Three-way swivel carrying the paternoster boom and hook-link. D—Eighteen inches of low breaking strain line to stone or lead E.

What effect really severe strain might have on this must remain in doubt until it occurs. Nevertheless, I offer the warning in cases where a really large fish may be encountered.

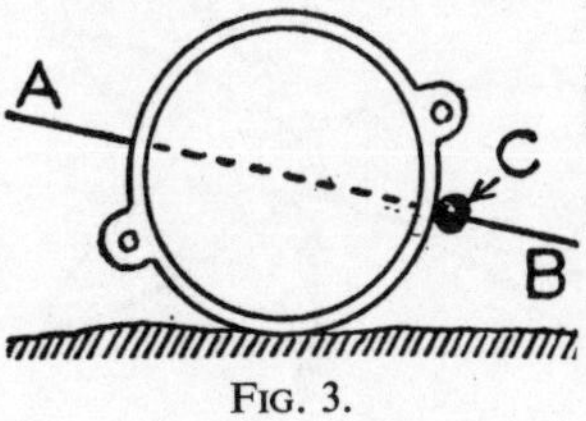

FIG. 3.

Bubble-float pierced for use as a ledger-weight. It is filled completely and becomes almost invisible. Having practically no weight in the water it will not sink into soft mud or fine weed; and offers little if any resistance to a taking fish. A—To the rod. B—To hook. C—Split shot stop.

Floats of this type are obtainable in various sizes and can be used in all circumstances with complete safety against perch.

They can also be converted for use as ledger

weights. I leave these thoughts with my reader and have no doubt that many will find experiments on the lines indicated are worthwhile.

A few details will round off the 'live-baiting' side of the sport. There is a considerable choice of baits, and anglers are, generally speaking, more conservative in this matter than is necessary. Perch, dace, roach, rudd, gudgeon, frogs, small carp, goldfish, pikelet, *and in Ireland, trout*, are all good baits. It is now many years since a friend of mine, having travelled a great distance to fish a lake where baits were usually prolific, arrived to find that none were available. It had been impossible to catch a bait of any kind for days, the boatman told him. He decided to break this sad record of baitlessness, but fished for two days without result. Being unable to spin, he was reduced to an extremity. Journeying some distance to the nearest village, he purchased herrings, and in desperation offered these dead fish to the pike with good effect. The dearth of live-baits need not mean a spoiled outing, especially in windy weather. Attach one of the corpses to the Mullins' snap tackle, p. 219, or the tackle shown on p. 220, Fig. 4, and cast it across wind. The float should be fitted with a feather or small paper sail to help the wind drift the bait across the water. You will find this quite effective. When the bait has drifted as far as possible retrieve it slowly (a run often occurs while this is being done), then repeat the process.

Dead sprats hooked in front of the dorsal fin with either a single or a triangle hook are often effective when fished in this manner.

Experiments and experiences over the years have gone to show that ledgering with herring is an even more effective technique which has accounted for many large specimens.

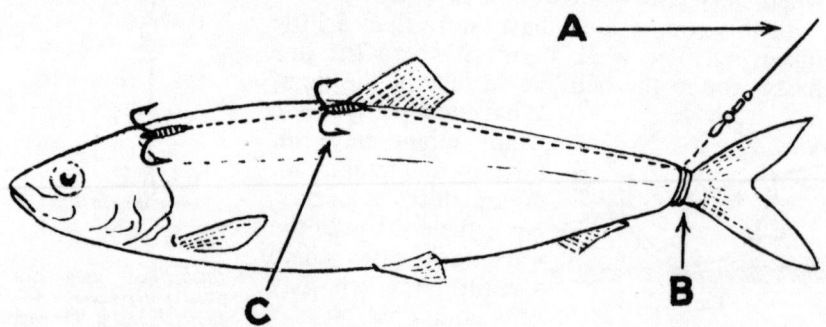

A. Wire castor reel line with link-swivel for attachment of tandem hook flight.
B. Hook flight tied securely to neck of caudal fin.
C. It is an advantage if this triangle is adjustable to suit baits of different sizes.

This illustration shows a simple method of hooking a herring for ledgering. There are of course many alternatives but within reason the less ironmongery these dead baits carry the better. Any extra weight, not absolutely necessary, adds to the strain on the rod when casting.

One word of warning is, I think, necessary. Don't be in a hurry to strike. Give line smoothly when the pike makes its first run. It most certainly will stop after some yards. Then as it moves off for the second time, take in all the slack until you feel the fish and strike firmly with a side swipe.

This method of fishing for pike does not seem to have become generally accepted on the Continent, where there are hundreds of waters holding very large pike. But, then, they do use—with success—spinning and fly fishing techniques for which species we still consider float fishing to be the only way to catch them.

My favourite live-bait is a perch for two excellent reasons. In the first place the problem of keeping baits alive when travelling to the fishing venue is generally a difficult one, as it is all too often impossible to replenish the water in which they are carried. Perch seem to be more tenacious of life than the other fish in the list of baits and are the most likely to survive a journey. Again, they are splendid workers, and will move about freely on 'bunging tackle' much longer than other fish. I cannot forbear to have another tilt at the ridiculous theory that their prickly dorsal fin should be removed before they are used. There is no doubt that pike are fond of perch, and as they have no means of removing the offending fin when they take perch naturally, there can be no advantage in the angler removing it. I have often pointed this out to fishermen only to see the operation repeated within five minutes—old angling prejudices die hard! The best bait cans are those with a perforated inner can; the water splashing through the holes of this is to some extent re-oxygenated, and the extra cost of this type is well worth the advantage. It is a great mistake to over-fill a bait can, better to land with six fresh lively baits than three live and nine dead ones.

It is necessary to have a 'gag' to keep the fish's mouth open while extracting the hooks. Pike gags can be bought very cheaply. They are usually fitted with a metal shield which prevents the spikes tearing one's fishing bag, which is a material consideration. When the gag is in use this shield slips back and is not a hindrance as might at first appear to be the case. A long wooden or metal disgorger is also essential. Some anglers use a gaff for landing their pike. An ample net is, however, preferable to avoid possible fatal injury to small fish. If a 'glass case' fish comes your way, that strangely named instrument, a priest, is handy to dispatch it, but as so many other instruments will do the work, it is not essential to buy one. Pike are most vulnerable immediately where the head joins the body, and a hard, smart rap with the priest at this point will kill the fish quickly. To prevent undue injury it is well to place a hand cloth over the point where you intend to strike the fish.

CHAPTER XXX

SPINNING FOR PIKE

SPINNING is admitted generally to be the most sporting and skilful means of capturing pike. But before approaching the many details necessary to a proper understanding of this art, consideration must be given to the broad principles of the method in relation to the fish itself. Some anglers believe that large pike will not 'run' at spinners. Let us see how this view braces up to the facts. In July 1920, Mr. John Garvin took his Irish record 53 lb. Lough Conn pike on a spoon (Mr. Clifford Warwick's 37½ lb. one-time English record pike fell to a live-bait.) In 1910 Major W. H. Booth captured a 37 lb. Wye pike on a Phantom Minnow. Another 30 lb. Wye fish fell to the Silver Devon of Mr. T. Seecombe Gray in 1905. In 1942 Mr. Jim Vincent stated in the *Fishing Gazette* that he had since the war 'caught twenty pike from 20 lb. to 29½ lb., all spinning.' The great John Bickerdyke asserted that the spinner will take pike of any dimensions equally with live-bait. Further, there can be no doubt the majority of the big Irish pike are caught on spinners trolled behind a boat. Some colour may be given to the idea that live-baiting accounts for larger fish than spinning from the fact that more anglers use live-baiting methods, and therefore more is heard of their captures. I believe the angler who spins will get more runs from pike of all sizes, than the live-bait fisherman, given normal and equal conditions. My own experience would extend this view to coloured and even deep water within reasonable limits. It is very seldom that pike will run to live-baits and refuse the spinner, while the reverse is the general rule. I have often put out a paternoster and a bung with live-baits from a boat, and employed the time while waiting for a run by spinning round the boat. Invariably the spinner has held its own against the combined efforts of the other two baits. If pike are feeding generally, they will take live-bait as readily as an artificial spinner; but when their mood is indifferent spinning lures seem to arouse their curiosity. I have been asked should spinners and hooks be large or small? No one would dispute the spaciousness of a pike's mouth, the interior of which is tough and bony. It is obvious that either large or small lures come within its scope. Sometimes one, sometimes the other is more effective,

but be your lure large or small, it must be armed with strong sharp
hooks. The size of the hooks is not an all-important matter. A well-
tempered small hook will hold the largest pike if it is in proportion to
the rest of the tackle. A better perception of this point will emerge
when the reader has studied the chapter on fixed-spool fishing which
follows. It will, however, be clear that if small hooks are used in conjunction with a heavy line and powerful rod, trouble is invited, particularly at the time of the strike. On the other hand, to use large
hooks with a light line and supple rod is simply ridiculous. Careful
tuning of the whole gear is absolutely necessary.

As is the case with most angling tackles, there is a diversity of expert
opinion regarding the material from which a pike-spinning trace should
be made, the number and nature of the swivels it should contain, and
and its length. In dealing with this subject I shall therefore adhere
closely to the materials and dimensions which I have found the best.
Ready-made traces are comparatively expensive, and I advise pike
anglers to make their own. How, then, is this to be done? Spools of
thin (single) steel or Alasticum wire are sold very cheaply, and either
is quite good for the purpose.
Cut from the spool a length of
wire approximately 20 in. long.
Fix a single ball-bearing swivel
at one end and a link-swivel at
the other for the easy attachment
of baits and lures. The method
of securing the wire to the swivels
is shown in the illustration.

*Take five or six equal
turns of both ends
producing twist A.
Now bend short end
at right-angles to
main wire, twist as
shown and cut off at
B.*

There are many types of swivel. *To make twist*
There is, however, one quality *grip wire loop*
essential in all swivels, namely, *firmly with*
that they should revolve freely. *pliers.*
To assure this each swivel should
be tested at the time of purchase. While they are more expensive, the
efficiency of modern ball-bearing swivels more than compensates for
this; and I strongly advise their use for all spinning.

For less exacting occasions such as live-baiting the
swivel here illustrated (Hardy Bros.) is very efficient.
Friction is reduced to a minimum through the fact that
only one bearing is used; the shape of the eyes, which are
central with this bearing, ensures that any attachment to
the swivel is also in line with the bearing, which eliminates
the possibility of binding and aids free revolution. They
are made in a number of sizes from a strong non-rusting

Enlargement metal.
showing the   It is necessary to counter the perversity of swivels. They
construction
of the Hardy are, of course, used to prevent twist and kinking in the
swivel. line and to facilitate the rotary movement of the bait.

If they always revolved as intended, one to each trace would be ample. In practice, however, it is found that the best of them sometimes object to work. A speck of grit or weed in the wrong place is sufficient to

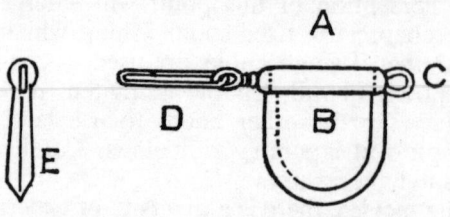

cause a stoppage, and a further precaution is necessary to be certain that at least one of them is operating when the bait is spinning. I refer to anti-kink leads. There are many devices for this purpose which are more or less expensive, and more or less effective, but the latest Hardy anti-kink lead is in my view the most efficient yet devised. I find this type less prone to get hung up between crevices in rocks or

A ball-bearing swivel A is incorporated with B which is either a lead or a transparent celluloid vane. The line is attached at C and the trace to the spring-link D. E shows the end elevation. The streamlining of the lead eliminates the wake of bubbles which follows some forms of anti-kink lead.

among weed for that matter, than any circular patterns, and line kink is virtually impossible when they are used. I also recommend a really ingenious little plastic device called the 'K'neverkink'. This anti-kink gadget is obtainable in a range of sizes to fit over swivels for both sea and freshwater fishing. Being plastic it does not corrode.

I doubt if there is a subject in the realms of angling more interesting, complicated and open to varying opinion than that of pike spinning lures. Having given the question special study, I am able, in the light of experimental experience, to unravel a good deal of the mass of conflicting evidence which confronts the would-be pike spinner, and to indicate sound lines upon which he may proceed. It is necessary to make a broad division between the two main types of spinner— 'mounted natural baits' and 'artificials.' Being a confirmed believer in 'natural baits,' I shall deal with this class first. One must procure a supply of dead roach, rudd, dace, perch, sprats or gudgeon; eel tails are also good 'medicine.' As to which are the best of these depends to a great extent on the mood of the pike, which will 'run' regardless on some days, refusing to be tempted at all on others. One thing, however, is definite—freshly caught baits are better than those which have been preserved. They do not break up so quickly under the strain of casting, and there is no possibility of their carrying any flavour of the preservative which might be objectionable to a pike following them through the water. There are occasions when pike, while refusing silvery baits, will accept a golden-hued lure. It is a simple matter to prepare such lures, by adding a pinch of powdered acriflavin to the preserving solution in each jar of baits. To overcome pikey prejudices against the flavour of such preservatives as formalin, some anglers immerse the baits in aniseed before use. I have not tried this, but am assured that it is effective.

Natural baits must, in turn, be subdivided—those which wobble in

a more or less slow irregular manner and those which have a fast
straight spinning action. It is improbable that there will ever be
complete agreement as to which is the more killing. My own leanings
are decidedly in favour of the 'wobblers,' and I will
mention two excellent types of hook mounting which
produce this attractive form of irregular revolution.

The mounting shown in Fig. A is known as the
Bromley-Pennell flight. To mount this tackle, insert
the single hook '1' in the root of the tail as shown.
Now bend the tail to the desired curve and secure the
bend by inserting the wire sprag '2,' and to complete
the mounting attach the adjustable lip hook '3' as
indicated. A fish measuring $4\frac{1}{2}$ to 5 in. not including
the caudal fin, is an ideal size for the purpose. The gear
has two advantages—the bait will revolve to right or
left in accordance with the direction of the tail bend,
which enables the angler to keep possible line twist
down to a minimum.

Fig. A

Furthermore, the speed of revolution is easily controlled, a gentle
tail bend giving a faster rotation than a more severe bend. Fig. B shows
another and much simpler mounting for 'wobbling baits.' The method
of attachment is by passing the main wire of the flight
(of the soft twisted kind) through the bait with a
baiting needle from the vent '4' out through the mouth
at '5.' The small composition or metal disc 'X' is
placed over the shank of the top triangle to prevent
it from becoming embedded in the bait as the result
of the force of casting. This tackle hooks well and its
attractive wobbling action is most killing. I have used
this simple flight with marked success and suggest its
trial. The precise dimensions of the tackle are entirely
dependent on the size of bait used, but the relative
positions of the hooks should be as shown in the
illustration, and if there is any difference in the size of
the triangles used, that near the tail should be the
smaller of the two.

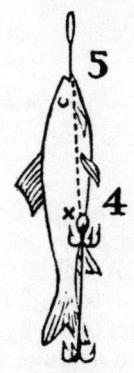

Fig. B

Experience and experiment have gone to show that
square bend hooks as shown in Fig. C have a very high
hooking and penetrating power, and I strongly recommend them for use with these flights. Fig. D (overleaf)
shows another useful type of hook which can be mounted
immediately without any whipping or soldering. This,
together with the fact that they may be moved up or down the wire or
other material used as required, make them ideal for the pike spinner
who has a *flair* for experiment and home-made gear. For mounting these
tackles I prefer soft twisted wire of the type generally used to make up
'snap tackles.' It will be found, however, that on occasion this wire

Fig. C

becomes badly bent when playing a fish. It is almost
impossible to remove the defect by bending it back, but a
serving of copper thread over the point where the kink
occurs will put things right. There are those who doubt
the advisability of giving the flight a clumsy appearance
by so doing—I assure readers I have adopted it scores
of times and have never experienced any disadvantage.

Fig. D   Following the 'wobbling tackles' just described, I
must mention one 'straight spinning' device for use with
natural baits before I turn to the 'artificials.' There is
probably none simpler or more typical than the 'Archer' flight.

To mount it the prong is inserted in the mouth of the bait, the flanges

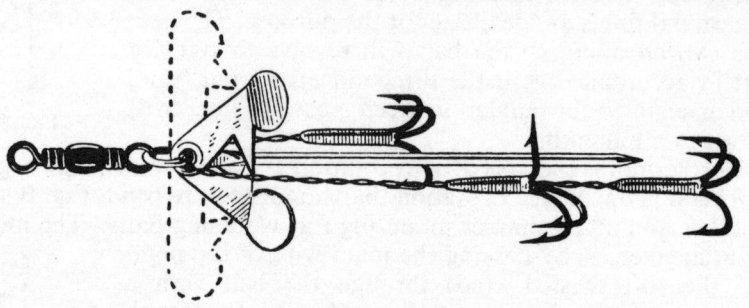

*The Archer spinner for use with dead natural baits. Dotted lines show flanges of
spinning fan in open position.*

of the fan are closed, and the barbed sprag is pushed into the bait to
keep the hooks close to it while the spinner is revolving.

Artificials! There are hundreds of them. But only a few have survived
the test of time and proved their worth; which I ought to state is
reckoned by the tackle makers at prices quite high enough to merit
the average angler's careful consideration of the ease with which they
are lost, a lesson quickly learned in the school of experience. Among
the most popular 'artificials' are those known as spoons—'Bar spoons,'
'Norwich spoons,' 'Collapsible spoons,' 'Punjabs,' and 'Kidney spoons,'
to mention but a few of them. Each has its own school of followers
ready to proclaim the merits of their favourite. The beginner need not
be worried as to his choice.

Let him try all of them—time and circumstance will make him an
enthusiast for one or the other. The truth is they will all catch fish,
and each angler praises the lure with which he is most successful. Despite
this there is one spoon for which I have a special regard, that I think
deserves special mention. I refer to the Horton Evans 'Vibro' illustrated
here. The shape of these spoons is ideal in that it cannot mask the
hooks when a fish takes. And for those who like me believe in the

value of vibration in a pike lure, these spoons have this quality well developed. Whether it is because of or in spite of this fact, I do not know, but they have the additional benefit of spinning freely at really low speeds, which is an indisputable excellence where *Esox* is concerned.

A sleek 'Punjab' of $3\frac{1}{2}$ to 4 in. a long narrow spoon with a 'run' provoking spin and splendid hooking qualities, is another of my favourites.

Before leaving the subject of spoons, I will pass on an idea for which I am indebted to Major Pery-Knox-Gore. The illustration below shows his simple but ingenious spoon, which can be made up by almost anyone. The addition of extra swivels and/or split rings in the hook carrier will give the desired length for any size of spoon, while a little sheet copper or brass provides the necessary material for fashioning the spoon itself. Experiments in colouring these lures may well pay good dividends, but the plain untreated metal will be found effective. To mount the spoon the link-swivel at the end of the trace is attached to the split ring at the head of the spoon. The trace swivel must be free-running as it is of course the operative swivel for the revolution of the spoon. The great advantages of this spoon are:

THE 'VIBRO' SPOON.
A—Lead incorporated on the bar. B— This spiral of strong spring-wire slides up to facilitate change of hooks as desired. C—Red plastic tail strips which cannot hold water and rust the hook like the traditional woollen tag.

1. It is a good hooker.

2. The hook can be changed instantly should it be broken or a larger or smaller one is desirable.

3. The chain of swivels and split rings on which the hook is suspended, being pliable, minimizes the risk of a hooked fish levering itself free while being played.

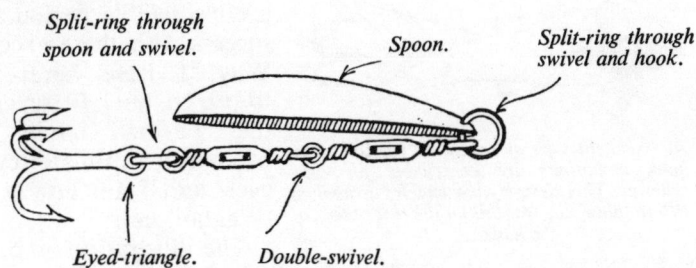

Split-ring through spoon and swivel.   Spoon.   Split-ring through swivel and hook.

Eyed-triangle.   Double-swivel.

4. Any portion of the device can be renewed at once as necessary. This applies especially to the split rings, which have a tendency to rust on the inner surface and become unreliable. On the same principle, a number of differently coloured spoons can be carried in a comparatively small space, being free from the hooks, and a change made as

desired. Such change is often effective, all that is necessary being to slide one spoon off the split ring and replace it with another.

Not a few efforts have been made to design a weed-dodging spinner. Most of these devices are not wholly effective and some of them should be shunned like the plague, because their weed avoiding mechanism acts as a protection for the fish, and renders them bad hookers.

Yet another useful spoon is the 'Anti-Kink' illustrated below. The head, which is lead, remains stationary and acts as an anti-kink, no

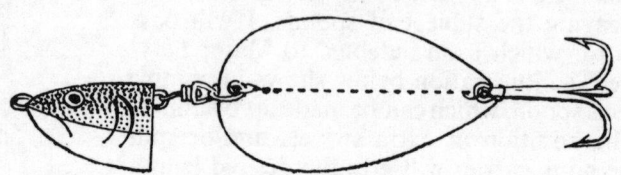

Hardy anti-kink spoon.

other lead on the trace being necessary. The spoon itself revolves. There are other lures of different design based on this principle, but the one shown is perhaps the most killing. It is a common experience that spoons which have become dull (oxidised) are more effective than those which are bright—I have often found it so.

There are many other spoons which arouse the interest of pike, but I must turn from these to a classic pike-spinning bait which is generally made of rubber or other soft material. If one is justified in assuming that a pike would hold a soft and therefore natural-feeling bait longer and more tenaciously than a hard and obviously unnatural mouthful, the undoubted popularity of these pike deceivers is not a matter for surprise.

Thousands of pike of all sizes have been taken on blue and silver or red and gold 'Wagtails.' For a considerable period I had little success with these excellent lures. Why, I have never been able to make out. Perseverance with the 'Farlow' model illustrated brought its ultimate reward, however, and I am now a confirmed 'Wagtail' user.

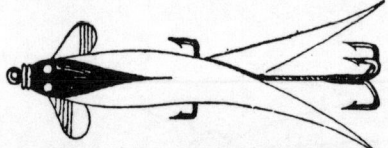

An excellent type of weighted 'wagtail.' The hook mountings are detachable for easy renewal. This design also enables a hooked fish to 'blow' the wagtail up the trace clear of the hooks.

The illustration on p. 237 shows the strangely named 'Vivif' rubber lure of modern Continental origin, the run-provoking action of which warrants its inclusion in any collection of pike artificial baits.

It does not spin but the depended tail which is attached to the thin pliable body causes it to wriggle in a most natural manner, even at slow speeds. The head of these lures is weighted sufficiently for it to be cast with either a fixed-spool or multiplier reel without the addition of further weight.

My only criticism of these lures is, that they are on the small side for use where really large pike are concerned. Not that large pike will not take a small lure. They sometimes do. But I believe that speaking generally the whoppers prefer a substantial bait.

'Vivif'—a modern eccentric rubber lure of lively action.

For this, which for lack of a better name I call heavy spinning, largish baits and ample hooks are preferable.

One can add to the lures discussed in this section a tremendous number of spinners and spoons from Scandinavia, the Continent and the U.S.

Whatever you do, don't make the fatal mistake of using a powerful rod and line in conjunction with hooks which are disproportionately small. Pike are not afraid of hooks. Work your lure attractively, giving it a varied and irregular course through the water, and work it slowly. This will bring you more fish than any given lure fished badly. Luck does not play nearly such an important part in spinning as many anglers seem to think. As with fly-fishing, so it is with spinning, presentation of the lure is nine-tenths of the secret of success. And keep your hooks needle sharp please!

CHAPTER XXXI

PIKE SPINNING:
A SIMPLE METHOD OF CASTING

HOW many anglers today would set out for a day's spinning equipped with a suitable rod and a Nottingham reel, that is, a free-running, revolving drum reel? The very fact that I feel it necessary to describe the basic make-up of a Nottingham reel surely suffices to illustrate the present trend. The great majority of anglers today have been brought up on the fixed spool reel to the near exclusion of yesterday's only reel, a simple, revolving drum. The fishing tackle manufacturers today offer us a wide range of fixed spool reels which have all been designed to match pretty well all rods of all actions. In fact, one fixed spool reel can, if accompanied by a set of spare spools loaded with

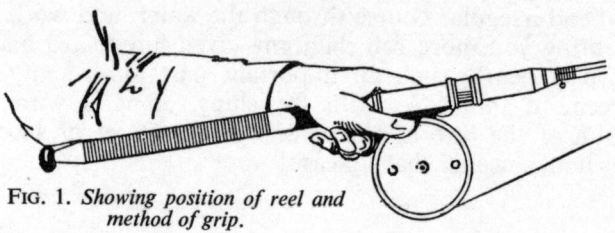

FIG. 1. *Showing position of reel and method of grip.*

varying breaking strain line, suffice for most angling methods. This section of *Angling Ways* introduces casting for pike with the Nottingham style reel. I recommend the newcomer to angling (and a fair proportion of anglers long in the tooth) to 'have a go' with such a reel as this. It is not easy to master, but once you have acquired the technique (like riding a bike or driving a car) there will come the time when you will be compelled to show off in front of all the anglers using the 'easy' one, the fixed spool reel. You will also be doing your part in perpetuating what I fear is a dying art, the ability to cast a light spinning lure accurately and to a fair distance while using (and controlling) a free-running drum.

Grip the rod in the left hand as shown in the illustration keeping the thumb on the rim of the reel (to prevent it revolving). Now take the 'check' off, leaving the drum free to revolve when the cast is made. Note how the butt rests under the forearm with the small rubber button just against the elbow. This comfortable grip allows you to exert considerable power when casting, the forearm being used as a lever.

When bottom-fishing your casting is much a matter of gentle swing and smooth follow-through; and to a marked extent this applies to casting a spinner from a free running revolving-drum reel.

Realise from the outset that force and jerk are enemies of good casting and your initial difficulties will be more than halved.

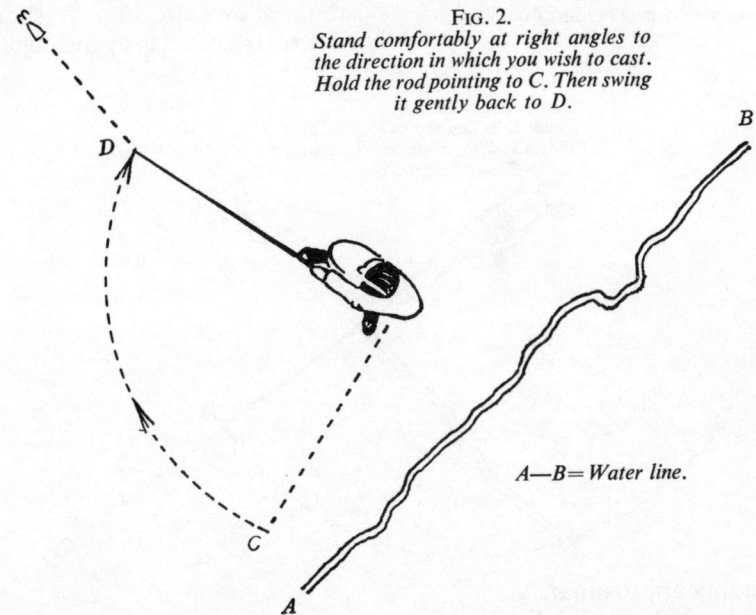

FIG. 2.
Stand comfortably at right angles to the direction in which you wish to cast. Hold the rod pointing to C. Then swing it gently back to D.

A—B= Water line.

To make the cast which I shall attempt to describe, your attention must be shared between the lure and the reel; and while a Nottingham reel which we shall use in this instance is an excellent servant, it is a devilish master. But have no fear, this cast is simple. So simple in fact, that with the aid of some diagrams and I hope clear instructions, I shall show how after an hour's practice on a lawn or in a field, you can cast a lure fifteen or twenty yards with accuracy and ease. This cast will not only enable you to take up the fascinating and productive art of spinning for pike and other predators, but it supplies the key to all other casts, double-handed, overhead, etc., etc.

Having set up your tackle with the reel in the position shown in Fig. 1, draw about 3 ft. 6 in. of line through the top ring of the rod

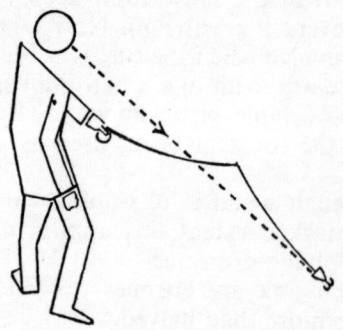

FIG. 3.
Keep your eye on the bait from start to finish of the cast.

and tie a stone or other suitable weight (about 2 oz.) to the end of the line, and you are ready to embark on a journey which will give you endless pleasure. Now look at Fig. 2, which shows the backward swing of the cast as seen from above, during which the reel is held still by the thumb. (Fig. 1.) To make this movement, take up a comfortable stance, for which no precise details can be given, because every angler's idea of comfort in this respect differs. The position shown in Fig. 2, should, however, strike a happy average, i.e.

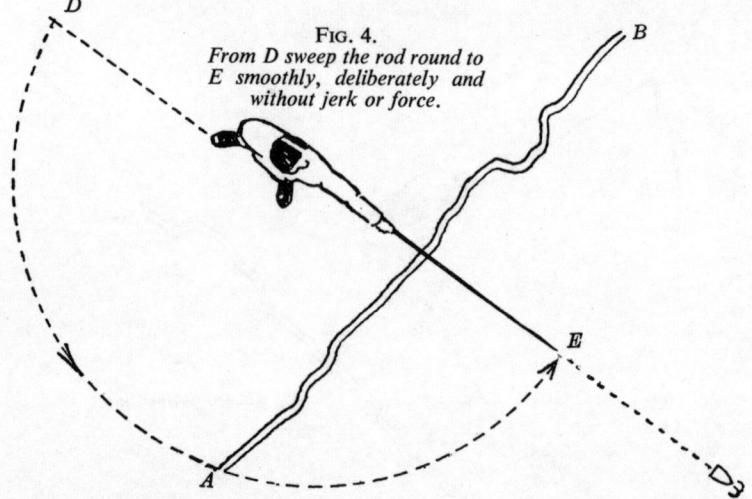

FIG. 4.
From D sweep the rod round to E smoothly, deliberately and without jerk or force.

standing approximately at a right-angle to the direction of the intended cast with the rod pointing straight in front of you to C. Now, keeping the feet in place, swing the body from the hips gently away from the direction of the cast, at the same time passing the casting arm (slightly bent) across the body thus gently sweeping the rod to the position D. Fig. 2.

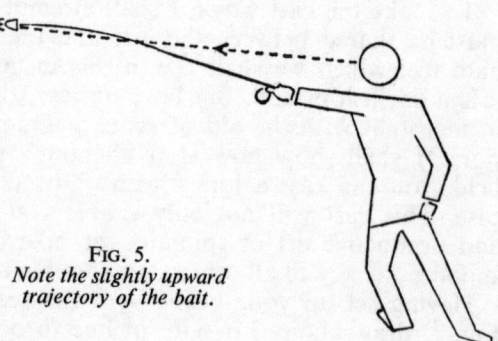

FIG. 5.
Note the slightly upward trajectory of the bait.

Figure 3 shows the final position of this movement as seen from behind the caster, the gentle impetus of which has caused the weight at the end of the line to swing outward. As it reaches the full extent of this outward swing that is the moment when the actual cast must commence.

Figure 4 illustrates the outward swing of the cast. The rod arm and body are swept smoothly round from D to E, i.e., in the direction of the cast, without jerk or force.

Figure 5 shows the same movement as seen from behind the caster. Note the upward trajectory of the cast and that the caster has his eye on the lure. This is important as we shall see.

Just before the rod reaches the full extent of this forward swing, the thumb which has until now held the reel-drum motionless, must be raised from the rim of the reel to allow it to revolve and give off line in response to the energy imparted by the flying bait.

I must give some warnings here. Don't try to cast a long way at first, or indeed ever. I have read some fantastic nonsense at different times of men casting from 50 to 70 yards while spinning. A 50-yard cast is not a fishing cast because at that distance the angler has little or no control over his bait, neither could he strike effectively should a fish take his lure so far away. Be satisfied with casts up to 30 yards; it's quite far enough for all practical purposes. Don't jerk or force the cast, but swing gently and smoothly. And don't forget to keep your eye on the bait. With a short, easy cast, little or no check on the reel is required, but the thumb must be in readiness to act as a brake just before the bait reaches the water, otherwise an 'over-run' or 'backlash' and a 'bird's-nest' may be the unhappy result. In the case of more powerful, and therefore longer casts, the reel should be checked almost at once, and varying pressure applied thereafter until the lure hits the water. 'Backlash' is the beginner's big difficulty, and practice alone will teach him how to control the revolutions of the reel and so prevent it. A better understanding of this difficult but all-important subject will be gained if I explain how 'backlash' is caused. When the rod is swung, the energy which is applied to the bait causes it to tug on the line, which in turn pulls on the drum of the reel and sets it in motion. The violence of the pull of the bait, and the speed at which the reel drum is thus caused to revolve, are in direct ratio to the force of the swing, and the greater the initial speed, the more care must be taken in applying a brake while the bait is passing through the air. When the bait commences its flight, the speed at which it is travelling is practically the same as that of the revolutions of the reel. As long as this is the case, all is well, and no braking is required. But when the bait has travelled a short distance, air pressure diminishes its speed materially, while the speed of the reel does not decrease nearly so quickly. This is the cause of the trouble. If the two speeds are not the same, the reel 'over-runs' or catches up the line and 'lashes it back' on to the drum, producing a miraculous tangle which is known as a 'bird's-nest.' It will therefore be clear that thumb control on the rim of the reel is to keep the speed of progression of the line and bait equal with that of the revolutions of the reel drum. This cast is for the light, single-handed rod I described earlier. By reversing the movements it may be made with the right-hand, the reel in this case being controlled by the index finger. Conquer the art of reel control and you can make any cast with little or no difficulty.

Having made the cast there are several matters of importance which claim the angler's attention. The bait has struck the water—what happens next? If the water is coloured, allow it to sink as near to the bottom as possible without it becoming entangled with weed. When the water is 'bright,' successful spinning is possible with the lure a little higher, but spin low and spin slowly is an excellent maxim.

A popular but uncomfortable way of holding the rod while spinning. The butt resting on the groin.

While the bait is sinking, many anglers busy themselves propping the butt of the rod in a precarious and uncomfortable position on their groin. One may become accustomed to this method of holding a rod while winding in the bait, but I have no hesitation in saying that the effort is not worth while. It is far more comfortable and efficient to tuck the butt under the arm as shown in the illustration below.

Angling conservatism dies hard, and I do not expect to gain approval for this method from anglers who are used to placing the butt on their groin *unless they try out my suggestion.* The great advantages apart from comfort, which is highly important, are that the angle at which the rod is held enables the angler to 'work his bait' more easily and to 'strike' more efficiently. 'Working the bait' denotes the lateral and vertical movements of the rod-point while winding in the lure, which cause it to move from side to side or up and down as it

Showing the method of holding the rod comfortably and efficiently when retrieving the bait. Note the angle of the rod.

is drawn through the water. These movements as supplements to the straight progression of the lure toward the angler often add materially to its attractiveness for pike, as results will prove on trial. These rod movements, which 'work the bait' as it journeys through the water from the farthermost point of the cast, are simple, and become almost automatic in practice. One other bait movement worth noting is often very killing. The lure is caused to rest on the bottom and then make a kind of hop by winding, say, three turns of the reel, then missing a turn. The effect is that of 'sink and draw'; try it when other methods fail.

There are occasions where one is working a natural bait 'sink and draw' when an immediate strike means a lost fish. If you are working your bait really slowly, which you should, a fish may take as the bait is sinking, rising, or actually while it rests on the bottom. Some delay is often advisable on these occasions. I have had a fish take my bait and run with it much as they run with a live-bait. When this happens I think it wise to let the fish end its run and commence to turn the bait before striking, or perhaps to delay striking till it moves off again after its first stop. If the pike runs toward you as it will, not infrequently, you must of course recover line as the fish advances and make every effort to maintain contact without in any way dragging and so alarming it.

As to the matter of 'striking' when the butt of the rod is perched on the groin with the rod point up, it is comparatively difficult to strike with the side sweep or draw which is so effective. On the other hand, with the butt under the arm, a lateral strike can be made strongly, instantly and easily, by gripping the rod firmly and swinging the body to the right or left.

The method of striking which I have found most effective is shown in the illustration. It will be seen that the effect is to draw the hooks into the jaws of the fish, at the same time hauling it a foot or so through the water, the force of which anchors one or other of the hooks securely. The illustration shows also that an approximate right-angle is made between the rod and the line when the strike is completed. This

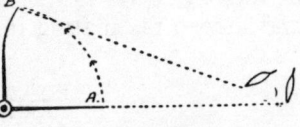

The Strike
The rod is swept from the direction of the fish to the right or left of the angler. A—B shows the arc of the strike.

angle should be preserved as far as possible when playing a fish, as by this means the full benefit of the rod's action is retained. When a pike pulls the rod down, it should be thrown back to the right-angle position at once, sufficient line being released from the reel (under check) to make this possible despite the pull of the fish. The moment to strike is indicated by a slight check on the line. Quite often a pike will take a spinning bait so gently that a novice would fail to recognise what had happened. Strike on the least stoppage is a good rule. The check should be put on the reel immediately after striking to minimise the risk of 'overrun' which may occur if the fish makes an unexpected rush. Nevertheless, when actually playing a pike the reel should be controlled (in the main) by the hand regardless of the check.

CHAPTER XXXII

PLUG-FISHING FOR PIKE: TROLLING FOR PIKE

FISHING for 'Muskies' and bass with plugs has been an established practice in America for years. British anglers did not, however, give the method appreciable recognition until after this book first appeared. Even now in 1973 we lag behind the American angler in the finer techniques of plug and lure fishing. This is even more so when sea fishing methods are under consideration, but this section of *Angling Ways* is not the place to elaborate. Plugs are so effective and indeed fascinating in use, that this chapter is added in the hope

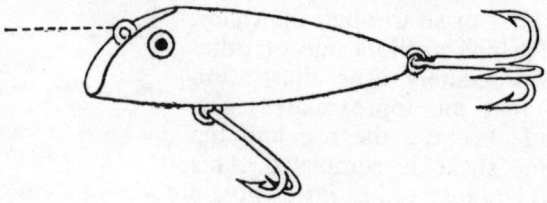

The 'Universal' (Floater).

that those who have not yet fished with them will glean a working knowledge of their use which will enrich their future angling experiences.

It is surprising how comparatively seldom one sees plugs in use even today. Broadly speaking, they can be divided into two classes—those which float and those which sink more or less slowly. The 'floaters' are the most important, interesting and useful. Let us, then, consider the mechanics of the simplest form of floating plug.

As will be seen from the illustration, the body in its simplest form is much like the stub of a cigar. The forward end is hollowed out in a sloping plane to produce a diving surface, when the plug is drawn through the water. The water presses against this surface, and the faster the plug is drawn along, the deeper it will dive, within limits. The full extent of this dive is governed by a number of factors, and is a matter of physics, into which it is unnecessary to delve. For all practical purposes it may be said that the limit of the dive of an average floating pike plug is from two to three feet. It is material to remember this, as floating plugs are essentially shallow and weedy water lures. I have heard of pike being taken on floating plugs fished in 20 ft. of water, and doubt not the accuracy of such statements. They are, however, the exception, and I prefer to adhere to the rule.

Only a fish cruising near the surface would rise to a plug in such deep water, and for the most part pike live near the bottom. One must, therefore, proceed on the assumption that the fish has to be attracted from its normal lie to a point near the surface to take a plug. This being so, it is apparent that comparatively shallow water, up to, say, five or six feet in depth, is the reasonable and ideal limit for fishing a 'floater.' In addition to the diving motion, which can be varied, the plug rising or falling within its range as the angler reels in slowly or fast, there is a wobbling or tailwagging motion. It will be seen, therefore, that the rise and fall, coupled with the lateral oscillation of a plug, produces a most attractive offering to any pike which may see it. The whole action might be likened to the gyrations of a sick or wounded fish, which is always regarded by anglers as a fascinating sight for *Esox*.

Now let me return for the space of a few lines to other features of this lure. It will be noted that a small loop is screwed into the head for the attachment of the trace. These trace-attachment devices are almost without exception too small and fiddling to enable an angler to attach the plug with an ordinary swivel. I have often wondered why this is. Some experts contend that the manufacturers mean plugs to be attached direct by twisting the wire of the trace into these tiny loops, because, they say, 'Plugs work better when no swivel is used.' I may be singularly unobservant, but having tried both I am not able to observe any difference. Give me the facile convenience of being able to attach or detach a plug at a moment's notice. To achieve this I resort to a safety-pin swivel, which can be immobilised with a strip of wire if desired. This, perhaps not so strong as the ordinary type, serves the purpose well enough. You will see also that the plug illustrated, p. 244, is fitted with a double hook amidships and a triangle at the stern. It is more usual for both hooks to be trebles.

'Cooper' safety pin.

H. E. Towner Coston, a plug fisherman of considerable experience, who has designed many plugs, says: 'I find two fine wire, quickly-detachable double hooks vastly superior to any others. . . . I have never liked the holding propensities of trebles on lively fish, but the double hook has the hooking propensities of a treble with the holding propensities of a single.' I feel sure Mr. Coston is right, yet, strangely enough, trebles are almost always used by makers of plugs.

The reaction of most anglers when they first see a plug is that the hooks are too large. I thought so, but have no doubt that the size of the hooks has a material bearing on the action and general set of a plug. Experience goes to show that they hook well and in practice are not too large. Nevertheless they might all be made with shorter barbs, and some of finer wire. This would aid penetration. An almost inexhaustible number of colour schemes is applied to the bodies of plugs. Some would appear to be more killing than others, but in my view the majority of the bizarre tintings are more likely to catch anglers than pike. This view has support from the fact that a plug of good action

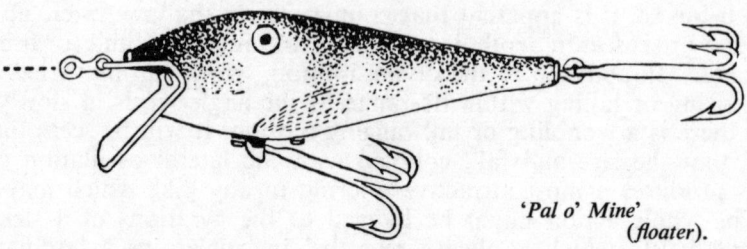

'Pal o' Mine'
(*floater*).

continues to catch fish after *Esox* and general wear have removed the paint. Outside a few proven examples, I doubt the value of much of the colour which is applied to plugs, and deplore the fact that quite often the application of a different colour calls for a different name, though the plugs may be of the same size, type and action. But who am I that I should throw a spanner into the easy-running wheels of plug collectors?

I have found that those colourings which most nearly approximate to nature are the most killing. For example the floater illustrated above

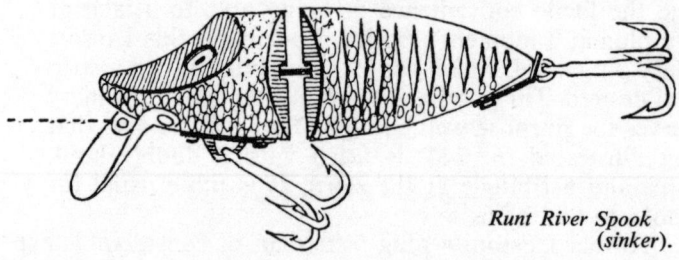

Runt River Spook
(*sinker*).

is painted to simulate a perch—what better? It kills! I have taken scores of pike on this and the larger hinged pattern which is finished in the same way.

Speaking of hinged plugs, I illustrate an interesting, slow sinking American example. The bodies of most plugs are made of wood but this is a hollow plastic construction finished to simulate a gudgeon or similar fish. The painting is so arranged that the body is translucent.

These hinged plugs have the same diving action as the one-piece models, but their wriggle is more elaborate. I prefer the action of a hinged plug and have killed more fish with them. This may be purely psychological on the principle that one fishes better and more carefully with a lure in which one believes. There is a great deal more in

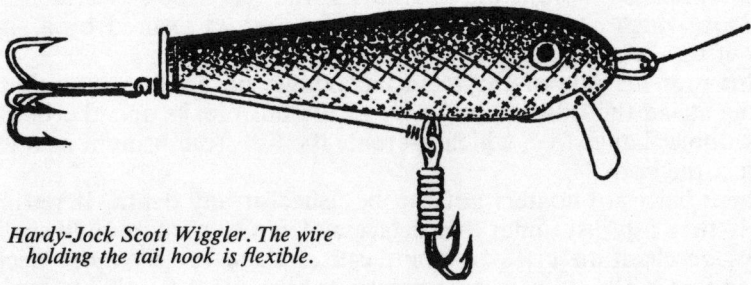

Hardy-Jock Scott Wiggler. The wire holding the tail hook is flexible.

this than meets the eye. Nevertheless, the amazingly lifelike effect of the independent oscillation of the head and tail of hinged plugs, must, I think, make a greater appeal to pike than the more stilted action of a one-piece plug.

There are scores of different plugs and I could enumerate them for

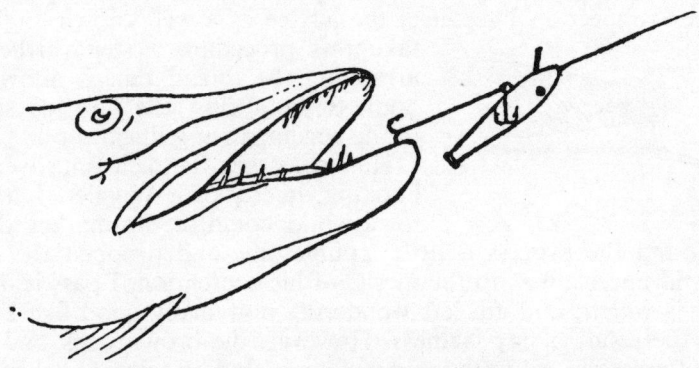

The body of the lure swings free preventing leverage.

pages. But as my present purpose is to deal with fundamentals, one other interesting example must suffice.

This simplified and improved Jock Scott Wiggler, the construction of which is the result of considerable experiment by a number of experts, has much to recommend it.

The streamlining of its very buoyant body is such that it eliminates that tell-tale streak of bubbles which follows some lures when drawn through the water and puts fish off.

The double hook beneath the belly being weighted with lead wire acts as a keel to keep the bait working horizontally and is positioned in such a way as to prevent it fishing head up, which is a common fault with many lures of this type.

As will be seen from the illustration the rear treble is attached to the loop which carries the double hooks, and is secured by a single turn of thin wire to the tail.

This presents one of the main advantages of the lure, namely that on the strike the thin holding wire at the tail breaks and the body of the wobbler hangs free, which prevents the fish from using it as a lever to eject the hook.

These baits are floaters but can be fished at any depth. If retrieved slowly they fish just under the surface and can be used in quite shallow water, acceleration up to a point causes them to fish more deeply. For fishing really deep it is necessary only to place a suitable lead on the trace some two or three feet above the lure. One other advantage should be mentioned, i.e. these lures do not rise to the surface even when retrieved rapidly or when fished in fast water.

The $3\frac{1}{2}$ in. model is the one for pike, but they are obtainable down to 1 in. for trout, chub, perch, etc.

I have found these lures to be both good hookers and holders, but am not enamoured with the idea of securing the tail triangle with wire; and much prefer to cut this away and replace it with nylon.

In this connection I recollect the advice of a well-known angler to 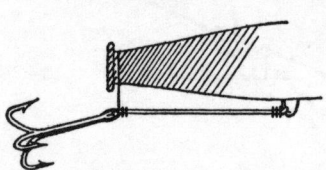 take this procedure a step further, so arranging the thread that it allows the hook to fall below the lure, as shown in the accompanying illustration.

He swore that it much improved the hooking quality of a Wiggler. I tried it for a while, could see no marked difference, found the process a little troublesome and dropped the plan. Being still uncertain as to the merits of his contention, I pass it on for what it is worth; and am left wondering how many good fish I have lost as the result of my laziness. However, the brown back and gold belly pattern owes me nothing in results (including salmon) fished with the tail hook in the orthodox position. You may care to try both, your opinion will then be as good as either mine or his.

I do not propose to deal with sinking plugs separately—for me a plug is essentially a floating lure, which serves the special function of fishing shallow water, and water where weed grows near the surface. Plugs which sink come in my view into the same category as spinning lures despite the fact that plugs do not spin. I quite frequently use plugs as ordinary spinners (both 'floaters' with a lead on the trace, and 'sinkers' without lead) with good effect. For the present purpose they are, however, regarded mainly as a means of fishing on or near the surface.

Now to the very important matter of reels for plug fishing. If you are the fortunate possessor of a small free running reel of the Aerial type and a light spinning rod, you can squeeze past without further expense.

The ideal instrument, and I use the word deliberately, is a really good multiplier.

Whatever multiplying reel you buy give it that care which they all demand if they are to retain their high pitch of efficiency. Take particular note of the manufacturer's instructions for oiling or greasing the reel. Printed details accompany each reel and it is only necessary to follow them to be sure of sweet and wear-free working. All moisture should be wiped from the outside of the reel before it is put away and grit of any kind avoided like the plague. A leather bag or the box in which it is bought is the best receptacle for a reel when not in use. If I have stressed seemingly elementary details in respect of the care of a good multiplier, I am unrepentant.

I should mention one item of self-protection when using these reels. As they are controlled when playing a fish by direct pressure of the thumb on the revolving line it is wise to wear a leather thumbstall (as shown) as protection against possible burns; they happen in a second and are very painful.

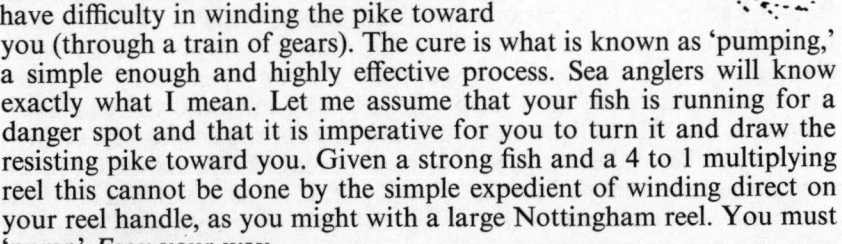

'Forewarned is forearmed' we are told, this then is the point at which those who have not used a multiplying reel should be told of a fishing peculiarity common to them all and marked in those with a high gear ratio. Having contacted a fish and commenced the fight, you will have difficulty in winding the pike toward you (through a train of gears). The cure is what is known as 'pumping,' a simple enough and highly effective process. Sea anglers will know exactly what I mean. Let me assume that your fish is running for a danger spot and that it is imperative for you to turn it and draw the resisting pike toward you. Given a strong fish and a 4 to 1 multiplying reel this cannot be done by the simple expedient of winding direct on your reel handle, as you might with a large Nottingham reel. You must 'pump' *Esox* your way.

Your rod point is up. Lower it, winding in as you do so, fast enough to keep a taut line all the time. Now hold the spool still and raise your rod point, drawing the fish toward you. That is 'pumping.' The process can be repeated as often as necessary and you will soon get used to this method of propelling a fish toward you. Control a running fish by pressure of the thumb direct on the line, and retrieve your quarry by 'pumping,' and all is well. Attempts to wind a fish in direct will end either in disaster to the line or strain of the rod and reel gears.

Side by side with the development multiplier reels a forest of rods has grown up, some of which are only 3 ft. long. Heaven forbid! I am

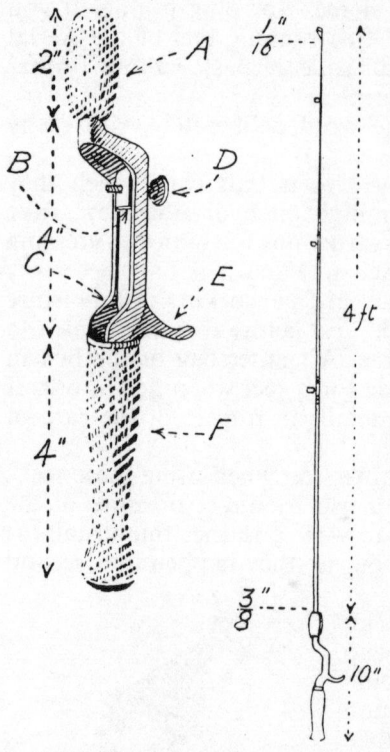

Heddon Life Pal. Butt 6 oz., rod shaft 2 oz.

sorry to be unduly unorthodox regarding rods for plug fishing and in fairness to these rapier-like implements, I will outline their benefits before naming the disadvantage which rules them out for me.

First, the details of their construction. A—Small upper grip either wood or cork. B—Clamp which holds the outer flange of the reel plate. C—Channel into which lower end of reel plate is fitted. D—Thumb screw for tightening B. E—Rest for first finger of the casting hand. F—Cork grip. The actual reel fittings vary considerably with different makes and prices. Now these rods are light, compact, strong, handy, and the best of them are beautifully made from tubular or solid steel which is almost unbreakable. This one weighs just 8 oz. For casting from cramped positions and in confined places, either overhead or by a lateral flick of the wrist, they are ideal. The fact that they are much used from light canoes in America has doubtless been responsible for their size and construction.

But—what to me is a paramount disadvantage remains. These single-handed rods impose a positively painful strain on one's wrist while playing a good fish. Even if one supports the rod by gripping the outer rim of the reel, or the small upper grip, it is an uncomfortable business playing a fish. These little steel rods are fine for those who like them—you may. When I desire the joys of casting plugs single-handed, I much prefer a rod of the type illustrated opposite. It is just a straight forward two-piece split-cane rod with a level cork grip. It weighs 6 oz. Being so light and having a double-handed butt, I am able to use it with either one or both hands to cast or play a fish. That is for me a consideration which outweighs other factors. But—and there is usually a but to be considered—should you wish to turn to ordinary spinning with heavier baits, or are likely to encounter heavy fish or fish of say 10 or 12 lb. in the fast waters of a weir, or should the water to be fished be very weedy, then something more powerful is indicated.

And now, what about lines for plug-fishing?

The braided Terylene line which I have come to regard as suitable for practically every occasion will serve you well. These lines have great strength for girth, they are supple, free from blemishes which tend to produce 'bird's-nests' and are the most highly waterproof lines obtainable.

Braided nylon are also excellent, but they are, I think, not so hard wearing, and they are both definitely more elastic, which is a disadvantage.

There are almost as many lines from which to choose as there are reels, rods, etc., but give me an 8 or 10 lb. b.s. Terylene line for spinning every time.

With regard to the colour of a line, I have used almost every shade from black to white and am not prepared to say that any particular colour shows an advantage when fishing. Actually I prefer white, believing that the dyeing process may have an injurious effect. This may be complete nonsense, but when in doubt play safe is a good angler's motto.

I was about to turn to the question of traces for plug fishing but a word of warning is necessary first. If for any reason you run line off a multiplier, take great care when winding it back, not to allow the end to slip through the automatic distributor. If you do this inadvertently you will find that it is virtually impossible to get the end of the line and the distributor in line again; that means that unless you take the whole line off the reel and put it on again from the beginning, your line will be binding against the distributor all the time, with obvious disadvantages. It is wise while there is still a yard of line hanging from the reel to tie a small pilot float on the end to prevent it slipping through the distributor on to the spool.

Diminutive traces are essential to facilitate casting if you are using a short rod. They need not be longer than one foot. A small split-ring for attachment to the line at one end and a safety-pin swivel at the other is all you need. As I indicated earlier, there is a school of thought which holds that swivels should not be used when fishing plugs, and that they should be attached direct to the trace and the trace in turn to the line. As plugs do not revolve the swivels will not rotate. How, then, can they be detrimental? The safety-pin swivel at the business end has the obvious benefit of making attachment and detachment of the plug easy. Try both, friend; you may form an opinion contrary to mine.

Of the available wire for making traces I know of none to equal 'Alasticum.' It does not rust or corrode. It will stretch 30 per cent of its length before breaking at the quoted strain and is not showy in the water. 'Alasticum' is pliable and easy to work by hand, no soldering being needed as with cable wires; and it is not weakened by kinking to nearly the same extent as more brittle single wires. If a single trace made of this wire is bent or distorted, take two ends and tug them sharply once or twice. The wire is straight again and as strong as ever. Another advantage is the entire absence of spring in this

$3'5\frac{1}{2}"$

$2'4\frac{1}{2}"$

$1'3\frac{1}{2}"$

Split cane rod by Carter.

wire, which rules out that irritating dance of the bait when suspended on some wires. So much for the essentials of the gear necessary for plug-fishing with modern tackle. I will assume that the reader has attained the necessary proficiency in the art of casting and pass to the how and where of this subject.

Where should the floating plug be fished and how should these lures be worked? As I have intimated, I am regarding plugs as surface-fishing lures, neglecting 'sinkers' which fall legitimately into the same category as deep spinners. During the summer months and on warm sunny winter days pike may be found in the shallows. I have in mind a stretch of slack water on the Thames which is from 18 in. to 3 ft. deep, where pike lie habitually. A 'floater' is ideal for fishing this type of water. Yet another of my haunts is a shallow lake where weeds grow in wide beds almost to the surface of the water. Here, again, to cast a plug between the weed beds and over them where they reach to within a few inches of the surface is very profitable.

'Floaters' should be tried when pike are seen rushing fry near the surface, and toward the end of the season when pike sometimes lie in shallow water, where they appear to enjoy the sunlight during the period prior to their spawning. In a nutshell, a floating plug is a very present help at times when the use of a sinking lure would be impossible. One could elaborate and theorize about the choice of a plug, its size, colour, action and what not, but as much of this would be tedious and probably unprofitable to the reader, I will forbear.

Nevertheless, there are one or two points worth mention. If the light is bad or the water coloured a showy bait is probably an advantage. On the other hand, a floating plug working over or near to a pike in well-lit, bright, shallow water must, I think, rely more on its action and size for provoking 'strikes' than on its colour. Will it not appear to the fish as a dark silhouette? As to the size of a plug or whether it should be a one-piece or jointed pattern is, I think, much a matter for trial. If you do not succeed with one try another, but do give each plug a real trial. Too frequent changing of baits is, I feel sure, a mistake. Nevertheless, pike are strange creatures and certainly do show preferences on the all-too-frequent occasions when they are not 'mad on.' Some red in the colour scheme of your pike plug is, I think, often right.

Now how should a floating plug be fished for pike? There are one or two methods. I usually commence by casting and winding the lure back steadily and direct. As to the speed of retrieving a plug, this need only be the slowest speed at which it acts fully, i.e. when it wriggles, dives, gyrates, wobbles or what not, as it is intended. If steady, direct winding is not productive, I resort to intermittent winding, which causes the plug to dive and rise alternately. There are occasions when this is more successful. More 'strikes' appear to result as the plug rises, though I have had frequent takes as the lure dived, just at the point where one was about to cease winding in. There can be no hard and fast rules where a moody fish like *Esox* is concerned.

Then, again it is sometimes profitable to wind in steadily and jerk the plug occasionally to right or left with the rod point as you wind. By this means the plug is made to dart to left or right and downward out of its normal path. To simulate a wounded or frightened fish is the whole purport of these manipulations of the rod and reel.

One thing the angler must remember. Quite often a pike will hook itself when it rushes at a plug. This is not, however, always the case by any means, and it always pays to strike smartly when a fish 'hits' your plug. This is first-rate fishing, in which as often as not the fisherman sees everything that happens. There is the plug wriggling its way through the water. Suddenly a pike flashes up from a weed bed and strikes the lure savagely. The whole take is visible and provides a thrill which is quite unknown to those who have not surface-fished for pike. For some reason best known to the fish, pike taken in this way usually fight with vivacity and sparkle, quite often leaping from the water and almost always thrashing the surface and shaking their head in a most dangerous manner.

I do not as a rule give a pike much line unless it is large and strong enough to compel me to yield. I think a held pike usually fights better than one which is allowed to cruise, and I like my fish to fight. But when pike adopt surface-thrashing and head-shaking tactics, I give line; it has a quietening effect. This may sound contradictory: first I hold to make the fish fight; then I advise giving line to quieten it. The answer is simple. There are two causes of losing a pike which I have found fatal on numerous occasions. One is allowing it to run under a boat, and the other holding a fish hard when it is shaking its head out of water.

Until I took up surface-plug fishing in the summer months I was bemused by the fetish that pike are essentially winter fish which are indolent and in poor fettle in the summer. What nonsense! During July and August of the 1942–43 season I must have taken over fifty pike from one Thames weir pool, and mettlesome fighters in fine condition they were. I say I took them. This may create a wrong impression; I actually killed only four, which were cooked, eaten and much enjoyed. One was served for luncheon at a famous hotel and there were no complaints. The others were returned to the river to provide sport some other day.

One may expect to find a creature, the movements of which are to a great extent governed by the dictates of its belly, in the vicinity of its food. It is so with pike. Near the mouth of carriers, in weed beds, and on sunny shallows where small fish congregate, there you may expect to find *Esox* in the summer. There is no doubt that pike like to have their larders handy, and they revel in sunlight, even to the extent of leaving deeper water, to lie on sunlit shallows on a sunny winter's day.

Floating plugs increase the scope of your pike-fishing to embrace otherwise unfishably shallow and weedy water. A substantial volume could be written on this fascinating subject, but I have said enough. Experiment and experience will extend what may be a new field of angling operations for you far more than any words of mine.

If you have not fished floating plugs for pike, I hope these lines will persuade you to do so. There is a wealth of interest, amusement and thrilling sport to be had by approaching this method of fishing with an open mind and a determination to learn by trial and error.

TROLLING FOR PIKE

We come now to the closely related subject of 'trolling' for pike. At the outset I want to establish a clear understanding of the difference between this quite skilled and interesting method of capturing these fish, and 'trailing,' which is a stupid and, to my mind, unsportsmanlike mode of taking pike. The Thames Fishery Bye-Laws say:

> *Trailing.*—No person on any vessel under way upon the Thames shall draw or cause or suffer to be drawn in the direction in which such vessel is proceeding any line with hook or bait attached thereto, whether such line be attached to a rod or otherwise.

This regulation is in itself a description of 'trailing' and its existence will be regarded by all anglers as a sufficient commentary on the method. No sportsman would wish to resort to such a foolproof procedure to catch his pike. On the other hand, 'trolling' not only requires skill and knowledge, but it is practically the only method of fishing certain types of weedy water. I recollect hearing 'trolling' described as fishing while strolling along the margin of a lake or river, and it will be seen that this is actually the case other than when a boat is used. The tackle for this type of fishing is simple. The rod should be fairly long to give the angler ample reach, and the line strong or many breakages will occur when the bait becomes entangled in weed, as it often does. It must be remembered also that when trolling among rushes the weed beds, strength of line is very necessary, as one is often compelled to play a fish which is entirely surrounded by weedy cover into which it is obviously undesirable to allow it to run. A spinning reel completes the equipment, with the exception of the bait mounting. The earliest mounting for trolling tackle was a gorge hook, a contrivance which I am glad to say is now illegal in many waters because its use necessitates the destruction of every fish 'run.' I have already expressed my views on this nefarious and unsportsmanlike tackle and need not therefore comment further.

The questions now are: How and when does one 'troll'? Visualise a reed-fringed lake in which there are openings amongst the reeds, or submerged patches of weed with similar clear spaces: these are the spots into which the angler drops his troll. Similarly, a weedy river with deep holes here and there presents the troller with opportunities. Long casting is neither necessary nor desirable, the bait being swung like a pendulum over the spot into which it is to be dropped. When the opening is just beyond reach of the rod, draw a yard or two of line from the reel, swing the bait as before, releasing the line and dipping the rod point as the lure swings over and toward the objective point of the cast. Having the weight in front, the bait will shoot downward into the water. It should be allowed to sink smoothly and unchecked nearly to the bottom, then stopped, raised a foot or more and allowed to sink again. To produce an attractive spin during the descent, some trollers cut off the fins on one side of the lure. This may be an advantage, but if a pike is resting in the hole, it is more than probable that it will resent the intrusion with its teeth, whereupon a slight check of the line, a tug or even a determined rush may be the signal to strike. Do not waste time on any given spot—two or three trials are ample, then stroll quietly to another place and try again. If a boat is used in trolling a river, it is better to work upstream when the current permits. Pike lie facing upstream, and the bait is therefore brought toward the fish as it is worked downstream to the angler. Trolling upstream as I suggest, the bait is moved in harmony with the lie of the weeds due to the flow of the river, and is therefore less likely to get wedged or fouled. To give his trolling lure a lively movement should be in the angler's aim; work it continually in holes up and down and, where the bottom is comparatively clear, keep moving it toward you in a marionette-like fashion, casting repeatedly and moving from place to place continually. Trolling is interesting—try it.

MONA'S PIKE SCALE

Mona's Scale.—Most anglers for pike have heard of Mona's Pike Scale, but from what I can make out comparatively few of them have seen this useful ready-reckoner. 'Mona' was the *nom de plume* of an old contributor to the *Fishing Gazette*, in which journal the scale was first published in September 1918, and I am grateful to the proprietors and the editor for permission kindly granted to reproduce it here.

There is no doubt that this scale, which is based on the assumption that a pike of 40 in. in length weighs 20 lb. has enjoyed a long period of credence and that if length only is taken into consideration it may well be reasonably correct.

Nevertheless there can be little room for doubt that the declaration of P. J. Bonfield, which appeared in *Angling*, is well founded, i.e.

> By now this hoary and fanciful scale should be described as an historical curiosity in Angling Works of Reference. . . . A formula combining length and girth measurements would be of more general application and accuracy.

If the pike you catch is appreciably over or under the weights here given in the following table for the length in question, you may assume fairly safely that your specimen has either partaken of an abnormal meal or is heavy in spawn, or that the missing girth factor accounts for the variation.

In.				lb.	In.				lb.
20	–	–	–	2·500	41	–	–	–	21·537
21	–	–	–	2·894	42	–	–	–	23·152
22	–	–	–	3·327	43	–	–	–	24·845
23	–	–	–	3·802	44	–	–	–	26·620
24	–	–	–	4·300	45	–	–	–	28·476
25	–	–	–	4·882	46	–	–	–	30·475
26	–	–	–	5·492	47	–	–	–	32·444
27	–	–	–	6·150	48	–	–	–	34·585
28	–	–	–	6·860	49	–	–	–	36·774
29	–	–	–	7·621	50	–	–	–	39·062
30	–	–	–	8·437	51	–	–	–	41·453
31	–	–	–	9·309	52	–	–	–	43·940
32	–	–	–	10·240	53	–	–	–	46·524
33	–	–	–	11·230	54	–	–	–	49·207
34	–	–	–	12·282	55	–	–	–	51·922
35	–	–	–	13·398	56	–	–	–	54·880
36	–	–	–	14·580	57	–	–	–	57·872
37	–	–	–	15·829	58	–	–	–	60·972
38	–	–	–	17·147	59	–	–	–	64·180
39	–	–	–	18·537	60	–	–	–	67·500
40	–	–	–	20·000					

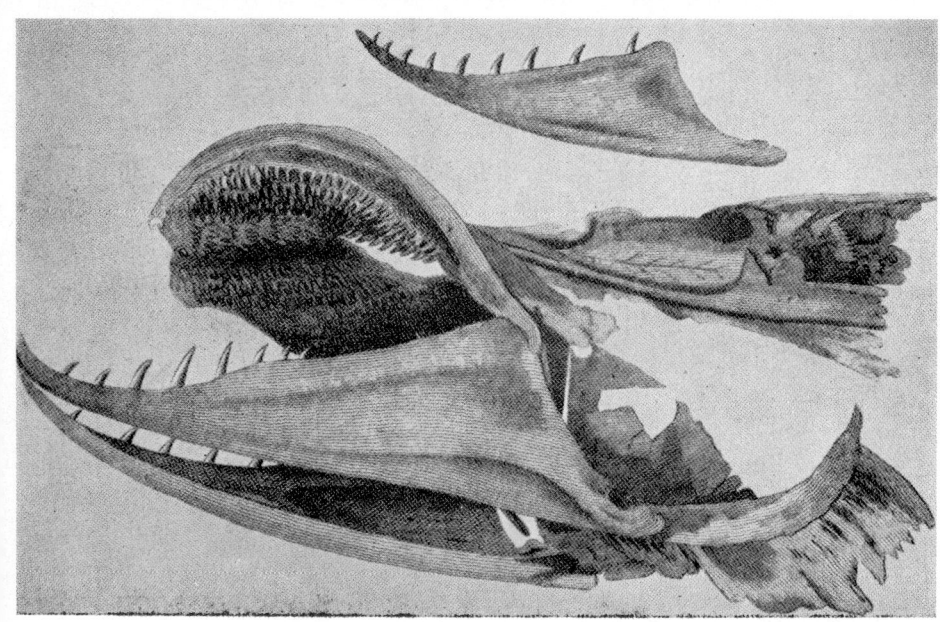

From an engraving of the skull of the reputed 72 lb. Kenmure Pike, which appeared in
The Sporting Magazine in 1798. Total length 13 inches.

The head of a predator, one of nature's most efficient underwater killers. There is an evil something
about the head and jaws of a pike, even a small one (this specimen weighed some 15 lb., just middling
good as *Esox* weights go), which emanates a deadly ferocity, surely equalled only in the fishes by the
feared barracuda, the tiger of the sea. Unlike the barracuda, which hunts in packs, the pike is a lone-
some killer, its body colouring of green, brown and silver mottling blending into the reeds from which
it makes lightning forays at unsuspecting prey.

[Photograph: W. J. Howes]

A lesson in how not to set up a fish. Note (below) how the mouth is totally underslung, pointing to its feeding habits. In the top photograph the fish has been set up with the mouth in an unnatural, pointed manner; the whole natural posture of the fish is distorted. The lower photograph shows the real barbel, a Kennet fish.

[*Photograph: W. J. Howes*]

[*Photograph: W. J. Howes*]

CHAPTER XXXIII

THAMES TROUTING

DURING the closed season for coarse fishing many anglers spend their time wishing for June 16th. Those who live within reach of Father Thames need have no care. This is what the Regulation says: '. . ., no person shall fish for, take, or attempt to take any freshwater fish in the Thames during the period from the 15th March up to the 15th June following (both inclusive). Provided that during the period from the 1st April to the 15th June following (both inclusive) any person may with a rod and line only, and by means of an artificial fly or spinning with artificial or preserved minnow, or with live bait taken in a minnow trap fish for, take or attempt to take trout.' The close season for trout in the Thames is from 14th October to the following 31st March, both dates inclusive.

Trout are undoubtedly present—trout worthy of the patience and skill of any angler. It will suffice to indicate the calibre of the trout in the Thames for me to say that no fish may be taken which is less than 14 in. in length. The words 'attempt to take,' which appear in the regulation quoted above, are full of meaning. Thames trout are as cunning as they are large, and luck plays little or no part in their capture. Trout are found all over the British Isles in suitable waters, and there is no family of fish exhibiting more variation in size and colouring, due to their environment, food, age or sex than this branch of the salmon family. Wherever they are found they exhibit a syhness which calls for high skill in the angler, and I am of the opinion that there is no trout more difficult to capture than those which are found in the Thames. They are caught principally in the turbulent waters of weirs and weir lashings, though they have their holts in the quieter reaches of the river, expecially in the early part of the season, around islands, on gravelly shallows where the water runs sharply, and beneath undercut banking a 'good 'un' may be located. The mouth of a carrier is sometimes the temporary home of a Thames trout later in the season. But my advice to those who are only able to devote a day here and there for a trouting expedition is to concentrate effort on the many wier pools from Hampton Court upstream. To do this, it will be necessary to take out a Thames Conservancy Weir permit, which costs one pound per annum, and provides anglers with facilities for fishing weirs which are named on the back of the permit itself. These are obtainable from the offices of the Thames Conservancy, Burdett House, 15 Buckingham Street, London, W.C.2.

The current rod-caught record for the brown trout is 18 lb. 2 oz. It beat a fine fish of 17 lb. 12 oz. caught from Loch Faskally by R. N. Campbell in 1961. The 18 lb. 2 oz. trout also came from north of the Border, and its captor, Kenneth Grant, fishing his local water Loch Garry, Inverness-shire, in the summer of 1965, took the record fish on a Finland Silver Minnow. Mr. Grant exercised considerable angling prowess in controlling his fish, for his tackle consisted of a light trout rod with 6.5 lb. line and cast. An examination of the fish showed it to be eleven years old.

Before March 1969 the record rod-caught trout in the British Isles weighed 39½ lb., and was caught by Mr. W. Muir in Loch Awe in 1866. While I do not suggest that the Thames holds any fish of that size, I should not be at all surprised to hear the capture of a 20 lb. Thames trout. Writing in the *Fishing Gazette* (October 1945) that prince of Thames trout fishermen A. Edward Hobbs, of Henley, said:

> In the course of my life I have made a great number of enquiries but have failed to obtain absolutely authentic information of the *killing*, by fair angling, of a Thames trout over 15 lb.
>
> The 16 lb. 15 oz. trout caught near Reading was undoubtedly a Kennet fish.
>
> I have seen in the Thames three trout, each of which I feel confident went over 15 lb., the largest of them about 29 lb., but never had an opportunity to kill either, not for want of trying.
>
> Trout of 5 lb. are not frequently caught, and a skilful angler will be doing *very* well if he can average two or three brace of such fish in a season.

My own search for the weight of the record Thames trout terminated in July 1959; when I came across the official list of Thames records as published by The Federation of Thames Angling Associations which quotes a 14 lb. 9 oz. fish as the best ever. Further enquiries elicited the information that this grand specimen was taken in 1870 from Chertsey weir pool by one O. J. Forbes. I am informed by the Federation Record Secretary, that this committee 'has gone to great lengths to get verification of all Thames records, and after five years of research and discussion have finalized their list.' They have been unable to find any evidence to deny this fish and 'have a mass of verbal evidence in its support.' This must then be accepted *until perhaps you catch an even larger one*.

It would appear from this that a 20-pounder is a forlorn hope, but one never knows. These Thames trout are grand fish—catch a 5-pounder in a strong weir lashing and you will have no room for doubt.

Readers will have noticed that the regulations governing Thames trout fishing permit the use of artificial flies, but this method of angling for them may be disregarded, because Thames trout are of the cannibal kind and do not rise to the fly, like the majority of their tribe, sufficiently to make fly-fishing worth while.

Spinning and live baiting are the killing methods. Those who long to experience the thrill of a tight line will not be disappointed if they make contact with trout in the Thames.

The type of rod used for Thames trouting depends very much on the venue to be fished; and whether one is live-baiting from a weir bridge or spinning from the apron. At weirs like Windsor, where the bridge is a long way from the apron fall, the rod should be as long as can be comfortably handled. Thames trout have a tendency to keep in after being hooked, rather than making a continuous effort to run away from the angler. An extra foot of rod and one's arm held aloft will sometimes induce a fish to run downstream because the angle of the line tends to lift the trout's nose, particularly if one stands close to the railings of the weir bridge. When opportunity offers, stand astride the first rail. You cannot be too near when a trout persists in remaining in the boil. They are wily and not above leaving your tackle tied up in one or other of the numerous obstructions which are often part of the geography of a weir. Thames trout do not care for these tactics, and usually sheer off as desired. As soon as a fish gets clear, it behoves the angler to get down from the bridge to the apron as quickly as possible —a very dangerous juncture in the struggle between fish and man, because the rod point must be kept well up on the way down and your eye on the line or float rather than where your feet are treading. Once on the apron below, the angler may fairly say: 'This fish is mine.'

A good Nottingham or Avon rod of from 12 to 13 ft., with a gentle action to the butt, is perhaps the best for live-baiting from either a weir bridge or elsewhere; but when spinning a light supple 8 or 9 ft. split-cane will meet most emergencies. It should, however, be remembered that whether the rod is short or long its action must be gentle and not too stiff, because the line and trace must be the finest possible, and unless the rod's action is tuned to their breaking strain, the result must be a smash. Nearly every angler has his preference for a certain type of reel, and modern reels are so beautifully made that comparisons are very difficult.

Any good $3\frac{1}{2}$ or 4-in. Nottingham reel or a multiplier is suitable, The main points are that it runs freely and has an adjustable check, because if the check is too fierce breakages may occur even when a supple rod is used. One hundred yards of Terylene line with a breaking strain of approximately 6 lb., with 30 or 40 yards of older line as backing, will be quite adequate.

The 'business end' of Thames trout spinning gear is so fine that it is nearly as difficult to see as to describe! The thinnest Alasticum wire of a gauge of about .007 in. is used for the trace, and 3 ft. of it deceives the sharpest-eyed trout.

This is served at the line end with a single and at the bait end with a link ball-bearing swivel, for the facile manipulation of baits. The anti-kink lead is placed on the line immediately above the upper swivel, where it is out of sight and acts efficiently.

One's leads should be of various sizes. Each pool has many runs with different 'tunes,' and constant changing of the leads is necessary to keep the bait at its proper depth. Half-moons are the most convenient. The proper depth at which to work a spinning bait for Thames trout depends on the time of the day, the temperature of the water, and general conditions. Suppose it's middle day, with a hot sun, the water well warmed, and the trout enjoying the fast flow. They rest, in such conditions, on the bottom, and will not leave that run for a surface fish. But let a small fish pass a trout where it lies. It will make a dart, take the bait, and return to its lie—or to the angler's landing-net as the case may be. A Thames trout, though it may be in want of food, would rather remain in a suitable run of water than go in search of small fry at midday. It is too lazy and can't be bothered. But as soon as the sun gets off the water and it is trout feeding time, things are different. For it is in the cool of the late evening that the Thames trout say good-bye to their runs for a few hours and don't mind chasing a bait.

Spinning then is entirely different. Let your bait spin 3 in. under the surface. Trout will actually take a bait that it is not touching the water; and will seize it as it skips the foam.

Five pound b.s. nylon is fine enough for hook flights, as it is not possible for gut as fine as the wire trace to stand the strain of spinning and playing the fish, and it is important that the gut to the hooks should not be longer than the bait itself. If you carry several flights varying by quarter inches, the correct one for any particular bait will easily be found. The bait itself hides the heavy nylon which becomes confused with the colouring of the little fish and is not noticed by the trout, but if a portion of it protrudes beyond the head of the lure, this may be noticed by a feeding trout, which will reject the angler's offering on this account.

Lip hook.

The illustration shows the flight. It must be explained that the curve of the 'Judge Brand' bait, is not obtained by the insertion of the triangle, which would tend to tear out when casting. A small wire running down the centre of the bait gives and maintains the desired bend which, of course, controls the speed of the spin. In harnessing the hook mount care must be taken to pass the lip hook through the lower lip, the loop at the head of the wire

The curve is not obtained by inserting the triangle.

(which is in the mouth of the bait) and the upper lip; this is important. It will be noted that the second triangle in the illustration is free. This is sometimes engaged just above the caudal fin of the bait. Either method may be equally effective and both should be tried.

These baits do not require expensive hook mountings, nor do they break up with casting nearly so quickly as the ordinary unwired type. I know of no more ingenious or simple device for the use of those who spin for Thames trout.

There are occasions when a 'live bait' appears to be more killing than a 'spinner.' Thames trout 'live-baiting' may be divided into two sections: 'Fishing open water' and 'weir fishing.' The open-water method favours those who live at the riverside, but is not beyond the reach of any angler. For this type of Thames trouting it is quite usual to make it worth some local waterman's while to 'spot' or mark the time and place where the best trout feed. By their regular feeding habits these fish become comparatively easy prey. The method is a simple one. A punt is fixed an hour or so before the known feeding time of the trout some 25 or 30 yards up stream from the feeding place where quite often bleak are playing. The trout comes to its self-appointed place, all the bleak hurry away with the exception of the one which, having been 'trotted' down to the trout's dining-room, is hindered in its efforts to escape by a fine three-yard cast and hook flight. The bait is taken, the hook anchored, and if you have a nice clear piece of water in which to play it (which is often the case) a minute a pound will bring your trout to net. Most of the best fish have I think, been caught in this way. True, the first few desperate runs of a fish taken under these conditions demand skill and careful handling, but it is simple by comparison with 'weir fishing,' where obstructions and heavy rushes of water aid the trout.

The underwater tackle used for 'open-water' trouting should, of course, be finer and the trace longer than that used in weirs; everything as invisible as possible with no swivels or other adjunct which might rouse the trout's suspicion. In weirs, however, the trace should be a little stouter, and need not be more than one yard long.

The gear for 'live-baiting' is similar to that for 'spinning' until you get to the float.

The trace and leads used for Thames trout live-baiting are as simple as their proper manipulation is difficult—until experience has taught its lessons.

Four feet of 3 or 4 lb. b.s. nylon monofil (according to prevailing fishing conditions) will provide an ideal cast, anything finer is not advised.

A ball-bearing link-swivel is served at the end of the reel-line for its easy attachment and *vice versa*.

At the business-end a flight as illustrated is looped to the cast (or the

Live-baiting flight, actual size.

flight and cast can be made in one piece); and a half-moon lead which should never be nearer than 2 ft. from the bait, is used to preserve its fishing position.

While this is a fair average, it is by no means universal. The size of lead and its position in relation to the bait is governed by the speed of the water and the size of the bait. For example a bleak or gudgeon used in strongly-flowing water would require a larger lead placed lower on the trace than a minnow fished in a comparatively quiet run. The lead must never be larger than is absolutely necessary to prevent the bait rising to the surface and lying on its side, as it will do when the weight is too light or too high up the trace. The necessary alterations which must take place while fishing a pool are facilitated by the use of half-moon leads of various sizes, which should be carried in an easily accessible pocket.

Thames trout are extremely suspicious and keen-sighted, and results will show how worth while these adjustments are. Keep your lead as small and as far from your bait as possible, is a good rule.

If a trout moves to a bait it will generally take it if the small fish is sufficiently free to make a short run away. But if the lead is too near, natural movement of the bait is hampered and the trout's suspicions are roused. But remember that during the trout's lazy hours about midday, when they are on the bottom, sufficient weight to take the bait down to them is essential.

Now for the 'ironmongery'. There are a number of hooking devices from which to choose for Thames trout live-baiting. The size of the bait influences the choice to a great extent. For use with a medium-sized bleak or gudgeon the flight illustrated is excellent, but the second triangle must be eliminated for smaller baits. With minnow or very small bleak and gudgeon a single hook passed through the upper lip only is sufficient.

Alternatively, a triangle with one hook passed through both lips of the bait in the extreme right or left corner of the mouth may be used.

No bait is better than a gudgeon about 3 in. long when the water is bright; if it is coloured, a bleak about the same size is preferable.

It will be found when live-baiting that as many fish are taken near the 'apron' as at the 'tail' of a weir. Nevertheless, those runs where the strong flow churns plenty of oxygen into the water are the best, because, in hot weather especially, Thames trout are almost as fond of oxygen as water. Despite this fact, they will run to a bait at any part of the pool after sunset, especially to a corner where capture of the prey seems most sure. Seeing bleak playing on the surface, the trout marks one fish and darts for it—a leap straight out of the water is the bleak's only chance of escape, for by the time it falls back one of the fastest of all swimmers has flashed past.

Any ample landing net of round, oval or V-shaped type is satisfactory when Thames trouting, providing the handle is long enough; but when fishing certain weirs, such as Marlow, two nets are necessary if you are alone, to avoid the danger of being compelled to coax a good fish through the heavy run of water from the 'lion's mouth.' In the shallow pools no net is necessary. Thames trout fight to the last, and having played a fish into a shallow it is a simple matter to 'grass it' by placing your finger and thumb behind its gills.

CHAPTER XXXIV

I KNOW of no more stubborn fighter than a barbel. Like an immense gudgeon, it gropes its way about the river bottom in search of food, even turning stones with its snout on occasion and always using its sensitive barbules or beards (from which its name is derived) to aid in the quest.

In the early season, especially when rivers are low, they appear to shoal in weir pools to cleanse after the breeding period, and are ravenous.

This presents opportunities for an unsporting method of taking these powerful fish known as 'snatching' and for the catching of large numbers of barbel by proper means. These temptations, I fear, overcome anglers occasionally, and at the outset of this chapter I want to appeal for the entire elimination of 'snatching' and the returning of all but fine specimen fish to the water. The barbel is the most valuable of our summer-time sport-givers in the Thames, Trent, Hampshire Avon, and the few other rivers where it thrives, and deserves the most careful preservation. In recent years, especially in the Hampshire Avon, barbel have been taken also in winter. This is a fact substantiated by the knowledgeable Head Bailiff at Christchurch, who has said that barbel are fished and fed (with ground-bait) throughout the season.

Speaking of barbel as food, I once made the experiment and contend that it is better to throw away the fish and eat the plate. For those who do not share my view I might mention the poisonous nature of the roe of these fish, which is sometimes absorbed by the lower part of the body. The great ichthyologist, the late C. Tate Regan, offers the advice that 'to be safe it is best to eat barbel in the late summer and autumn.'

Barbel 4 ft. in length and weighing in the region of 20 lb. are known in England, but the best rod-caught fish are not so aldermanic.

In 1888, Mr. T. Wheeler took a barbel at Molesey, River Thames, which weighed 14 lb. 6 oz. This fish was unequalled for many years until a fish of the same weight was caught by H. D. Tryon in the Hampshire Avon in 1934; and a third to the rod of F. W. K. Wallis in 1937.

In 1909 Mr. R. Jones, fishing the Thames at Radcot Bridge, caught a specimen which scaled 14 lb. 4 oz. That there are larger barbel than these, is demonstrated by the remarkable capture made by Mr. Roy Beddington in 1931. While salmon fishing in the Royalty water at Christchurch, he foul-hooked a barbel which weighed 16 lb. 4 oz. This happened during the coarse-fish close season and the fish was of course liberated. Though it cannot rank as a record, Mr. Beddington's barbel is the largest yet caught on rod and line.

The accepted record barbel is a fish weighing 13 lb. 12 oz. caught by Mr. J. Day from the Royalty Fishery, Hampshire in 1962. The Thames produced the best reported barbel for 1972. This fish weighed exactly 13 lb. and fell to luncheon meat fished by John Cadd late in October.

I believe both the Thames and Avon hold fish of 20-lb. calibre, and those anglers who essay to capture one will not be disappointed with the sport given by the smaller specimens they will encounter meanwhile.

The colouring of barbel varies, but generally speaking they are deep olive or bronze on the back, shading down to gold on the sides, while the belly is white. The eye has a golden iris.

The angler may at any time of the day or night hear the resounding splash of a leaping barbel as it falls back into the water. This habit, which discloses the whereabouts of barbel to an angler operating on strange waters, is due to an aquatic parasite, *Argulus*, which irritates the fish. But hook a 'good 'un' and there will be no leaping! It will roll, plunge and bore, giving the impression that it is standing on its head in an attempt to sever the tackle against a stone on the bottom. Their sudden turns will sometimes bring the angler's cast into perilous contact with the strong dorsal fin, and if there are any obstructions or snags in the vicinity, a barbel will run for them with the savage determination of a game fish. There are times also when barbel will sulk on the bottom, remaining immovable as though they were anchored there. This has often happened to me, and it is my practice to give such fish some line. Being relieved of the pressure of a tight line it will move away—and the fight may be resumed. The foregoing is not an overstatement of what must be expected, Indeed, I have in mind an authentic case of three skilled anglers who took it in turn to play a barbel in the Thames, the fight was so long and stern, and when they landed in the capture turned out to be a comparatively small fish which was foul-hooked in the dorsal fin. The inference that substantial tackle is necessary for barbel fishing will be clear to the reader but it should not be a fraction more powerful than will enable the angler to show a recalcitrant fish the way from a sunken tree root to the net when necessary.

Whether you float-fish or ledger for barbel there is no better reel than a $3\frac{1}{2}$-in. 'Aerial.' This balances well with the rod I have described, and gives the quick recovery which is so often necessary. It should carry not less than 100 yards of 6 to 8 lb. braided Terylene line, which will act equally well for either method.

When the bottom is level, the current not too fast, and the depth convenient, float-fishing, if not the more killing, is by far the most interesting method of angling for barbel. These fish are shy, capricious, and very strong. The essentials of the underwater gear are therefore the utmost invisibility combined with strength.

No. 1.

No. 2.

1 YARD

'*A*' *is a small bored shot supported on one grain shot.*
'*B*' *is one* '*BB*' *shot.*

A

B 1 FOOT

My favourite barbel float is a 6-in. cork-covered porcupine. These floats will carry sufficient weight for the water conditions in which float-fishing is practicable, and their shape offers a minimum resistance to the fish.

The method of weighting the cast varies considerably, but I have found that shown in the illustration very satisfactory. Barbel feed generally right on the bottom and the shot 6 in. from the hook is not noticed by them and aids materially in keeping the bait in position.

A 4 lb. b.s. cast to a 3 lb. b.s. hook-link is safe, but if the angler is skilful and the water conditions are favourable, one degree finer will be all to the good.

An interesting and noteworthy exception to these breaking strains is sometimes provided by the ultra skilful. Such a case was reported in 1947 when Mr. A. Price, Jnr., a Birmingham angler, while match-fishing in the Thames, landed a barbel weighing 5 lb. 2½ oz. on a No. 16 hook to 1½ lb. b.s. line. Mr. Price is credited with having duplicated this feat, which I assure my reader is considerable. Nevertheless, I am quite sure that he would not seek *Barbus barbus* with such fine tackle if he were out for this fish only. Aye, I will go further and say that if he did, his first such outing would probably modify his views on suitable tackle if the fish were feeding.

It must be remembered also that the fish might well have weighed 10 lb. and it is foolish to tempt providence.

The contents of a letter I received from Mr. E. Lewzey surprised me. He had been taking underwater photographs at the bottom of a 5 ft. deep pond, to ascertain the reaction of fish to the introduction of ground-bait. During his experiments he found that barbel often rose and fed on pieces of ground-bait in mid-water.

This goes to show how dangerous it is to be dogmatic in matters affecting angling. Nevertheless, barbel are in the main bottom-feeders, a fact which is emphasised by the shape and position of the mouth of these fish.

In passing he commented also that 'contrary to the general belief, barbel do well in still water.' We live and learn.

Terrifying stories of prolonged and expensive baiting-up with thousands of lobworms, hundredweights of bread and bran or clay and greaves, deter many anglers. But there are two sides to this question. Great takes have undoubtedly resulted from this pre-fishing preparation of a swim, so have ridiculously small captures been the result. More than once a thousand lobs have produced two undersized perch and a few small eels. I have found that fishing the same swim regularly using a few balls of ground bait while fishing is less expensive and gives good results.

Trotting from a boat is the most convenient way of float-fishing for barbel, the float being checked gently as the tackle glides down the swim to ensure the bait preceding the shots and cast.

Lobworms, gentles, knobs of bread paste and hemp or sometimes a single hemp seed are all good hook-baits.

For use with lobs I prefer the two-hook tackle designed by Major Ilderton. With gentles, or bread and hemp, a No. 7 or No. 8 crystal, and for the single grain of hemp a No. 12 flattened shank hook is small enough.

No. 3.

The requisite ground-baits are worms chopped, or of inferior quality, thrown in loose or made up in balls of bank clay. Balls of bread and bran mixed with a few gentles or hemp, to suit the hook-bait, while loose hemp seed or ground hemp and bank clay is used when a single seed is on the hook.

Major Ilderton's tackle.

Notwithstanding the foregoing, I know of one famous deep eddy where, to the best of my knowledge, the fishing technique is unique.

The equipment comprises a supple eleven- or twelve-foot rod with any suitable reel and line (up to 6 lb. b.s.); a 7 in. float as Fig. A, cocked as Fig. B. (p. 267).

The underwater tackle is an 8 ft. 3 lb. b.s. cast, shotted at widening intervals toward the lower end; the lowest shot being from 15 to 18 in. from the No. 14 fine-wire round-bend hook, which is mounted on a 15-in. 3 lb. b.s. hook-link. The bait is a single maggot.

Unorthodox though this equipment may seem for use in an eddy where double-figure barbel are not a matter for wonder and seven or eight pounders are almost a commonplace; it is not only highly successful, but would appear to be the only type of tackle with which the fish will have any truck at that particular spot.

This fact intrigued me for quite a while, particularly as it seemed to be fatal to alter the tackle even by as much as the use of a larger hook or two maggots in place of one on the No. 14.

Then I came upon what for me is satisfactory explanation.

At this venue maggots are the bait *de rigueur* and ground-baiting is by way of handsful of these larvae cast into the water loose.

This is, I think, the key to the situation. On entering the water the free maggots swirl, gyrate and pirouette downwards to the bottom where the fish have become accustomed to seeing and taking them individually or in open clusters; and are suspicious of a clump of gentles on a hook.

With regard to the finickiness of these barbel in respect of the size of the hook used, it may well be that the weight of a slightly larger hook would be sufficient to impair or hamper the natural swirling movement of a maggot impaled on it.

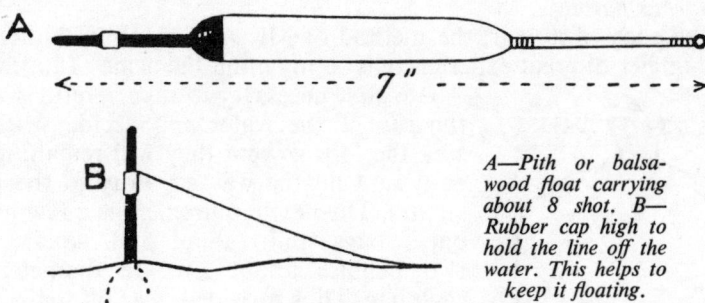

A—Pith or balsa-wood float carrying about 8 shot. B—Rubber cap high to hold the line off the water. This helps to keep it floating.

The unwillingness of these fish to respond to a bait presented on the heavier single bored-shot tackle illustrated on page 265 which is so effective in a fast run, is more easily explained. There are often quite a number of fish lying close together in this particular water, and a bored-shot placed low on the cast might bump against and alarm them, apart from the undesirable visual consideration. Moreover, the bottom is irregular, and any method of low centre of gravity shotting tends to cause hangs-up.

The willingness of the barbel in the open river to take more than one maggot from a larger hook, and ignore shot placed lower on the cast to keep the bait down in fast water, is probably due to the fact that the stream runs strongly in the main river. This makes it possible by holding back the float, to present the bait in advance of the rest of the tackle.

In addition to this, ground-bait is usually administered by way of balls of bread, bran, rusk, etc., mixed with a few maggots; which does not come to the fish in items of consistent size, as do the single maggots to which I referred earlier.

This is an excellent example of the need at times, to adopt different methods and tackle for the capture of fish of the same species, in different parts of the same river; and of the evolution of a technique based on local experience.

GROUND-BAITING FOR BARBEL

The angler's experience and judgment will govern his decision as to the desirability of costly baiting-up prior to barbel fishing. It is, however, certain that 'ground-baiting' just prior to and during fishing is necessary. Some experts contend that a barbel swim cannot be 'over-fed' with worms. This may be an exaggeration, but whether the swim is above or below a weir, or over some gravelly stretch of open river, good catches must not be expected without ground-bait. I would mention also that 'cross baiting' is wrong. One swim, one ground-bait is a good rule. As lobworms are a much-favoured hook-bait some notes on ground-baiting with them will help those who yet have to take their first *Barbus barbus*.

In the eddy of a weir, the method of Mr. A. E. Hobbs, who was a barbel angler of great experience, is to my mind the acme of ingenuity.

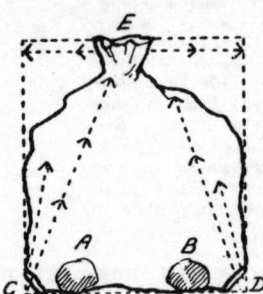

As the stones A B sink the bag and bait, the water enters holes C D forcing open the lightly screwed top E.

It is first necessary to take careful note of the run of the water and decide where to sink the lobs so that they will remain in the eddy and not be washed away to the main stream. The next requirement is a few brown paper bags (thin) about 5 in. square, and two pebbles about 2 in. in diameter for each bag. Thus provided, tear off the bottom corners of the bags, leaving holes of about 1 in. in diameter. Place a pebble near each hole and nearly fill the bag with lobs. Now screw the tops up slightly. When they are lowered quietly (not thrown) into the swim, the stones sink the bag and bait, the holes at the corners admit water, which forces the lightly screwed top open and the ground-bait is distributed about the swim. A boat is generally necessary to make this procedure possible, but if the angler is compelled to operate from the bank or is fishing an open-water swim, the old-fashioned clay ball comes into its own. Having secured some bank clay, make up a number of roughly-shaped clay basins about 5 in. in diameter, fill them with lobs and seal the tops with flat pads of clay, allowing a few of the worms to protrude, and your ground-bait is ready. Such generous use of lobs may cause the reader to wonder how they are obtained. Some professional fishermen and some tackle dealers will secure a supply from the Nottingham dealers on request, and, except in very hot weather, little difficulty is experienced in obtaining them.

It is hardly possible to fish too early or too late for barbel, and if the angler desires to 'bait up' a swim prior to fishing, this should be done, when possible, at the time of day at which he intends to start fishing.

I regret having to describe it as such, but it was a fishing accident that resulted in the landing of a once new British Record barbel. Spinning for salmon in the Hampshire Avon at Ibsley on Sunday, 6th March 1960, Mr. Charles Cassey, of Horndean, Hants, foul-hooked a 16 lb. 1 oz. monster in the right pectoral fin.

Paying tribute to the strength of this fish, Mr. Cassey, who had taken a 30 lb. salmon from the water a week previously, declared that this barbel fought harder and more fiercely than the salmon; so much so that he thought it was a 40 lb. salmon until he saw the fish.

[The British Record (Rod-Caught) Fish Committee rejected Mr. Cassey's fish because it was foul-hooked. 'Foul-hooking' as opposed to 'snatching' is invariably accidental. This being so, their decision, in Marshall-Hardy's view, was open to criticism. As he saw it this Committee's main function is to record and collect facts which in this instance were: that the fish was caught in season, by an angler fishing fairly, with rod and line. While he bowed to their superior judgement, this incident must be retained in *Angling Ways*, if only as an historical item, which should not be allowed to drop into Limbo.   L.C.]

CHAPTER XXXV

LEDGERING FOR BARBEL

I THINK more and more bigger barbel are caught with the ledger than by any other means.

Over a good shingle bottom which is free from obstructions between which the bullet might become wedged, I favour a bored shot hitched to the end of the line, as shown in Fig. 1. It will be noted that a

FIG. 1.

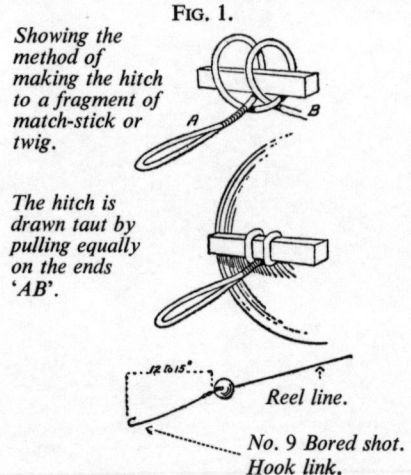

Showing the method of making the hitch to a fragment of match-stick or twig.

The hitch is drawn taut by pulling equally on the ends 'AB'.

Reel line.

No. 9 Bored shot.
Hook link.

loop is served for the easy attachment of the hook-link which is fixed direct to the line without the orthodox cast. I do not suggest that there is any disadvantage if a cast is placed between the line and the hook-link, but I have never been able to see any advantage in its use or detriment from its elimination.

When a swim is encumbered with boulders and other traps for a ledger weight, another tackle is necessary. Fig. 2 illustrates a good one. In place of the usual pear lead I use a stone or pebble of suitable shape for tying, which is natural in appearance, saves expense, and answers the purpose admirably. This should be attached by a piece of old line of lower breaking strain than the cast or reel line. It is also an advantage for the hook-link to be a degree finer. If either should become wedged or fast in an obstruction, the loss of time and tackle is thus minimized.

Barbel ledgering demands the fisherman's whole attention. It is useless to leave the rod to fish for itself. From the time when the ledger touches bottom to the moment of the bite, the angler must be on the *qui vive*. The rod should be held parallel over the water, with the line between the finger and thumb of the free hand. It is not the largest fish which bite most vigorously by any means, and this method of

270

detecting bites is very sensitive. Striking too hard is the cause of innumerable breaks when barbel fishing, especially if the fish snatch the bait, which is often the case in fast water. The strike should be made by raising the rod point quickly and firmly but not violently. If the line is held taut from the ledger weight to the rod point, the slightest movement is telegraphed along it, and the gentlest pluck from a fish calls for a strike.

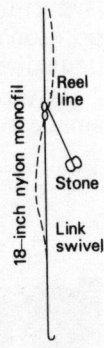

FIG. 2.

Early in the season one may use a large minnow or small gudgeon as bait, with good effect, but live baits are not of much use after the fish have recovered from spawning. Cheese paste, lobworms, a bunch of gentles or a prawn are good ledger baits. In the Thames particularly, and in other waters where hemp is used and barbel are present, a most effective bait is produced by making up bread paste with the juice in which hemp seed has been boiled, and kneading the seeds themselves into the paste which then has the appearance of currant pudding. Anglers using hemp for other fish quite often hook a barbel, and I can vouch from much personal experience that they display a marked liking for hemp seed paste, which places it high in position on the list of lures.

The tackle shown in Fig. 2 may be used with a float when water conditions permit, the distance between the float and the stone (weight) being about 18 in. greater than the depth of the water.

Opinions vary as to whether single or triangle hooks should be used when barbel fishing, but I prefer a single hook in all cases, and generally use rather larger hooks for ledger tackle than when float fishing. Nos. 5, 6 and 7 are all serviceable sizes: 3 lb. b.s. nylon dyed sorrel or weed green is quite fine enough for general purposes, and harmonises well with the shingle bottom or weeds in the swim.

One other item of importance remains for consideration, namely the size of the ledger bullet or weight of stone as the case may be. It is safe to say that this should be the smallest which will keep on the bottom, and the strength of the stream is therefore the deciding factor.

When the bottom is suitable, the Arlesey bomb ledger-tackle devised by Richard Walker and described in Chapter XXVI is also excellent.

Fishing a stream from the bank one can cast upstream and allow the gear to roll down with the current in an arc, thus covering a considerable area. And it is, of course, a first-class ledger for general use.

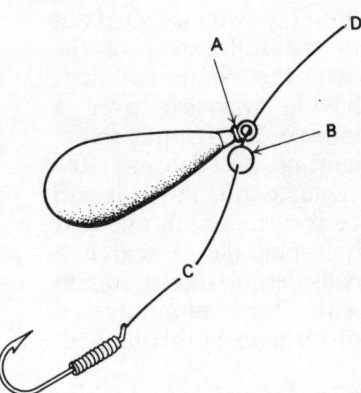

FIG. 3. *Rig for Arlesey bomb rolling ledger. A—Swivel. B—Stop-shot. C—2–3 feet of line to hook. D—Line to reel.*

The make-up of this simple tackle for rolling a bait downstream is shown in Fig. 3.

Using a fixed-spool reel and nylon monofil line, slide the eye of the bomb (swivel-fitted ledger weight) up the line 2 or 3 ft. and secure it in that position by nipping on a single shot below the eye. Now tie an eyed-hook direct to the line and the gear is complete, no trace being necessary.

At this point I must stress some most important factors. First, the smallest bomb which will just hold bottom in the prevailing stream is

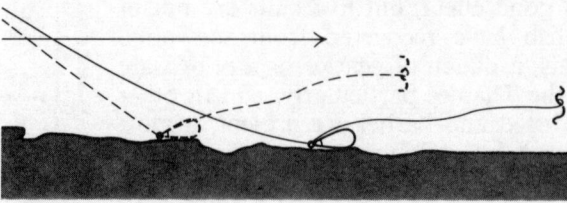

the one to use. A moment's thought will make the reason for this clear, i.e. unless the contour and nature of the bottom is suitable and the current is strong enough to move the bomb when the rod point is

FIG. 4. *On a suitable bottom where the current is brisk. The ledger will roll downstream each time the rod is raised. The arrow indicates the direction of the stream.*

raised, this rolling method is not practicable.

Given these essentials however this method of fishing is simple and admirably effective.

You cast slightly upstream and allow the bomb and bait to rest in that position for a while. The bait tends to trail downstream at an angle to the bomb, rising and falling attractively in direct ratio to the strength of the current. If no bite results after a fair pause, raise your rod point to

help the bomb to roll and the flow of the stream will move it downstream to a new fishing position. This is repeated at intervals until the swim is fished out to the full extent of the cast, the bomb and bait having travelled over a more or less fan-like track, halting to fish at the angler's will, thus: it will be seen that with one cast it is possible to search a considerable tract of stream with the minimum of disturbance by this method.

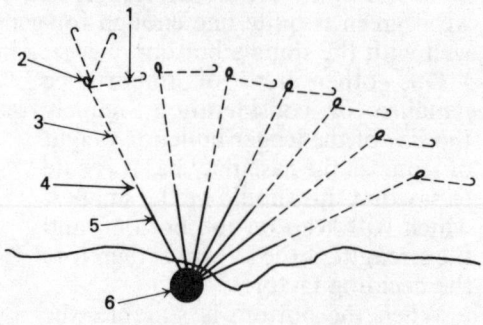

FIG. 5. 1. *Line from bomb to hook. This may swing over an arc as indicated, in accordance with the strength of the stream which also controls the total length of the roll. 2, Arlesey bomb. 3, Reel line. 4, Direction of current. 5, Rod. 6, The angler.*

Clay-balls and weed for barbel

Barbel are so worthy of the angler's attention that some consideration of one or two less used methods of fishing for them is merited. If the barbel are lying in very deep water near piles of other obstructions, or in a weir pool where the bottom is particularly irregular and filled with underwater obstructions, 'clay-balling' is effective.

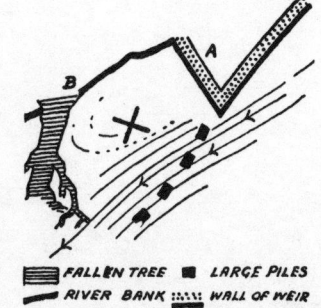

The illustration shows a 'clay-ball' swim which comes to my mind. It was about 20 ft. deep, and as the plan shows, offered the most serious type of obstruction to the angler, but it held good barbel For this fishing a more sturdy rod and tackle than those used for other methods are required to make it possible to hold the fish. when necessary. The 'clay-ball' is made up from bank clay, bran and middlings, with a small quantity of the hook-bait mixed in. I prefer to use bread instead of clay, however, believing that

FALLEN TREE   ■ LARGE PILES
RIVER BANK ∷∴∷ WALL OF WEIR

The deep eddy X could only be fished from A and B on shore or from a boat moored outside the piles.

the resultant mixture is more easily nosed off by the fish or washed away, leaving the cast and baited hook free and therefore more sensitive to bites.

The ball which should be just stiff enough to adhere until it reaches the bottom is welded round a string of BB shots at the end of the cast and the hook-link is then pulled round and slightly into it, leaving the actual bait protruding.

The tackle is then lowered to the bottom, and the angler waits developments.

The silk-weed which grows on the aprons and piles of weir pools is sometimes a fine bait for barbel, especially when the water is bright One would expect the fish to prefer the freshest green weed, but this is not always the case, and if green weed is rejected, that which is brown and faded will sometimes prove effective.

Float tackle is, to my mind, the most suitable for this fishing, but weed is sometimes fished without a float, the cast being weighted with one or two shots only, a method which, practically speaking, is very light ledgering.

When weed is used, don't handle it more than you can help. A hook dragged through a patch of weed will bait itself. Some anglers use a treble for this fishing; but my objection to the use of trebles dates from the day when a friend who had never caught barbel persuaded me to fish for them. I used a treble, hooked a fish, and thrust the rod into his hands that he might experience the thrill of its fight. To our mutual dismay it came in like a log. The reason was soon apparent— one hook of the treble had taken the upper and another the lower lip of the fish, which closed its mouth. Being thus prevented from breathing, by passing water through the mouth and over the gills, it could show no fight.

CHAPTER XXXVI

RUDD

IT is said that the name rudd is derived from the Anglo-Saxon *Rudu*, which means redness. The following words are an apt description of these handsome fish:

> The rudd: a kind of roach, all tinged with gold,
> Strong, broad and thick, most lovely to behold.

The author of these lines, whose name is unknown to me, extols the beauty of rudd without exaggeration and raises a point of interest and importance to anglers.

Despite the marked differences between roach and rudd, the two are often confused.

Apart from the difference of colouring, which is apparent to anyone when roach and rudd are compared side by side, and a host of technical differences, there are two salient marks which, if remembered, will always enable one to distinguish these fish.

The upper lip of the roach protrudes slightly over the lower, while in the rudd the reverse is the case.

In the roach the point at which the main ray of the dorsal fin meets the back is almost vertically above that at which the main ray of the ventral fin meets the belly. The dorsal fin of the rudd is set much farther back toward the caudal fin.

Rudd are much more localised in their distribution than roach, and thrive in the quiet waters of lakes, slow rivers, canals and drains. They are not found in Scotland, but abound in Ireland, where they are called roach.

Such waters as the Huntingdon Ouse, the Norfolk Broads, Slapton Lea and Irish loughs hold good rudd, and it is noteworthy that when water conditions suit rudd, they are generally found in great numbers. The big fellows, however, are elusive, and the means of taking them is a subject for future discussion. Having mentioned the magic words 'big fellows' some details of record rudd may inspire the reader to emulate their captors. Some record lists have it that in 1888 Mr. J. F. Green took a $4\frac{1}{4}$ lb. rudd at Blackheath. I think there is some doubt about this, however, At the time it was claimed as a record, but after the fish had been examined by C. Tate Regan (since deceased) and R. B. Marston it was considered to be a malformed and spawn-bound chub and the record was called off. In 1917 Mr. F. Beales took a splendid rudd of 3 lb. 8 oz. in the North Forty Foot Drain (Lincs.). In the same year Ruislip Reservoir distinguished itself by yielding a three-pounder to the rod of Mr. R. Wendover. But it was the Rev. E. C. Alston, who in June 1933, captured the rudd which set up and still holds the British record. This fish, which was caught in a lake near Thetford, weighed 4 lb. 8 oz.

Just 5 oz. below the record was a specimen rudd of 4 lb. 3 oz. 2 dr., caught at Low Bedford in July 1972 by Mr. R. Thomas.

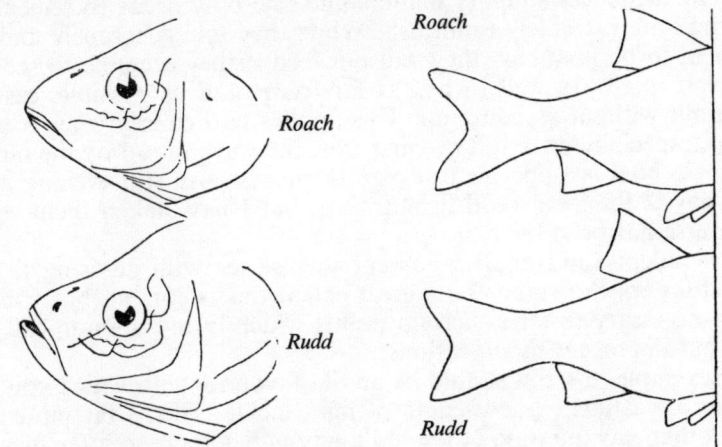

Roach

Roach

Rudd

Rudd

Twenty-four years after the capture of the record fish reports came to hand of an even larger rudd captured on the Shannon in Eire about half a mile below Athlone.

This fish, which took a lobworm, tipped the scales at 5 lb. 2 oz. and while it cannot be regarded as a British record for geographical reasons, it must rank as the largest rudd ever caught.

Some doubts as to whether it was not a rudd x bream hybrid were expressed in the English angling Press at the time (August 1957); but Mr. Don Dorking (Chelmsford, Essex) the captor, had the fish weighed by Messrs. Browne, tackle dealers of Athlone, and it was accepted as a true rudd by the Athlone Anglers' Association.

Your first rudd may disappoint you even though it's a 'good 'un.' Rudd are most deceptive, being the heaviest British freshwater fish when judged by length for weight.

Lake rudd may be found almost anywhere, with the reservation that the larger fish prefer water near lily pads or reed beds. River rudd often show a marked preference for certain localities only, and it is not uncommon for their haunts to be miles apart in a river.

The most likely haunts of the river fish are inaccessible bays of quiet water overhung by trees and thick with reeds or lily pads. In these places the rudd hide and present an angler with the pretty problem of how to get them out of their weedy fastness.

These fish disclose their whereabouts to the observant angler in a number of ways. Otherwise unaccountable movements of reeds or lily leaves as the fish nose their way among the submerged stems in search of the food which adheres to them are perhaps the best. At other times a sound like a snapping of the thumb and finger will indicate that they are rising to suck flies or other food which is floating on the surface. And there are occasions when the fish are cruising openly and may be seen with their dorsal fins rippling the surface of the water. Such circumstances simplify matters and one only needs to remember that rudd are extremely timid fish. While they bite generously and do not seem to be float shy, they will not feed if they are able to see the angler. It is always well to fish as far from rudd as possible, casting your limit without standing up. This applies particularly when a boat is used, especially on a still evening; for, the wave set up by the movement of a boat is sufficient to alarm them. A warm still evening after a hot day is the ideal rudd fishing time, but I have taken them when the reverse has been the case.

Many adept rudd anglers content themselves with advising tackle as used for roach fishing. To a great extent this is correct, but I think it very necessary to stress certain points which in my opinion call for slight but important modifications.

For example, the rod should be an old favourite with which you are capable of casting a good length of light tackle. This is far more important than any question of the rod's action. Rudd are so often located in difficult positions where accurate presentation of the bait is vital, that this factor becomes the paramount consideration when selecting the rod. The matter of accurate casting influences the selection of the line also. Rudd feed on or near the surface, generally speaking, and are very shy. It is essential therefore to be as far away from them as possible when casting. While the shyness of the fish calls for fine tackle the line should not be too light. It is not always possible to take advantage of any wind that may blow, and the slightest cross-line breeze will hamper seriously the angler whose line is too fine. With this fact in mind, I prefer Terylene line not less than 4 lb. breaking strain, i.e. some two pounds lighter than line used when trotting. The cast and hook-link may, however, be slightly heavier than are used for roach. Hook a good rudd and it will dive heavily for the weed or lily growths near which the best fish are often found. This must, of course, be checked or the fish will be lost. The amount of chance the angler can afford to take, therefore, depends on the type of rod he is using. With a fly rod of gentle action (which I prefer), a 1½ lb b.s. cast and hook-link would be as safe as one of 3 lb. b.s. gauge if a Sheffield rod of stiffer action is employed. Much also depends on the angler's skill, but I think that 3 lb. b.s. is fine enough, especially as it is always good policy to play the fish out of the swim as quickly as possible to avoid the risk of frightening the shoal.

Some experts prefer one and some another method of shotting the cast for rudd fishing. As I am in favour of a *Small* slowly and naturally sinking bait, I always use the *pilot float.* minimum of shot and the smallest possible float. The *Cocktail* one shown in the illustration is excellent. The stem is a *cherry stick.* cocktail cherry stick, to the bottom of which I whip a small metal loop, while the cap is simply a tiny bored pilot float. This will carry a pinch of lead wire just above the loop on the float itself, and one grain shot could be placed four inches from the hook. If the shot is farther up the cast, the gear is not so sensitive, and as it is so small the fish are not worried by it. You need have no qualms about it being so near the hook. This suggestion is not orthodox, I know, but I assure the reader it is practical. Richard Walker, as usual, came along with the following useful idea:

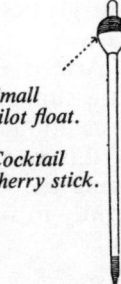

> Knowing your interest in useful gadgets you may wish to draw attention to my rudd float with coloured vanes at the top, which I now use for long-trotting as well as rudd fishing, as its visibility is enormously increased over that of an ordinary float, without its sensitivity being affected.
>
> I find that a good colour scheme is to have each vane black on one side and a daylight-fluorescent yellow on the other. The float can then be seen easily whether in shadow or in reflected light from the sky. In many swims the float moves from one condition to the other as it goes downstream, but either black or yellow is always visible.

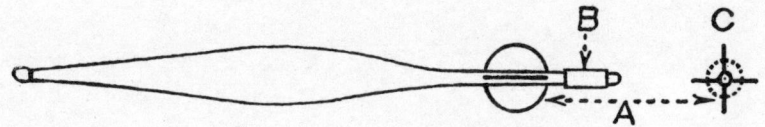

Richard Walker's Vaned Float.
A—Vanes. B—Rubber float cap. C—Plan view of float tip.

As I have stated earlier long casting is sometimes essential when rudd fishing; and it would seem that in addition to the enhanced visibility to which Mr. Walker refers, the vanes must exercise a stabilising effect on the flight of the float when casting, much like the vanes of a dart.

In calm conditions this is an obvious advantage, but in wind the vanes may cause drag which is, of course, detrimental. The vanes can, by the way, be made either of well varnished paper, light card or celluloid; and there would appear to be considerable scope for experiment with vanes of different shapes and sizes.

I shall be surprised if developments of this idea do not emerge.

Model Perfect hooks, size 10 or 12, are suitable. And the best baits are gentles or bread paste. Gentles are, of course, more simple to cast.

Armed with this equipment, the angler only needs to set his float at a suitably shallow depth and cast to the rudd. If the hair net lures I mentioned previously are used no other ground-bait is necessary. If this is not possible, a little dry bread thrown on the surface will bring the rudd round, and it is only necessary to cast the hook-bait lightly to where they are busily nosing the floating 'propaganda.'

CHAPTER XXXVII

COARSE FISH AND THE FIXED-SPOOL REEL

MR. L. R. HARDY, a director of the famous firm of tackle makers, introduced me to fixed-spool reels on 16th July, 1932, at a British Fly and Bait Casting Association Tournament.

During a lull in the proceedings he showed me one of his firm's 'Altex' reels. It may have been the original prototype, I do not remember, but I feel sure it was an early model.

To cut my story short, I borrowed, competed, and won an event with it.*

When Alfred Holden Illingworth, a Yorkshire woollen manufacturer, invented the first fixed-spool reel (patented on 4th July, 1905) he did this no doubt to enable him to cast very light lures using similarly light lines, for gossamer spinning on northern rivers and becks. And it is from this, I believe, that they came to be known as 'threadline-reels,' which I am satisfied to describe as a misnomer that has caused more misunderstanding of these reels than enough.

Nowadays, the world and his wife use them for every type of fishing, and many of them do not stint to clamp these reels, charged with gossamer lines, on to any old rod. That is wrong, but more of this anon, except to say at once that thousands of fish from salmon down, have as the result trailed yards of line behind them with benefit only to line and lure manufacturers.

The fundamental error which so many anglers make, is to believe that because these reels are equipped with a slipping clutch which can be adjusted to give line to a fish automatically, at a pressure less than the breaking strain of the line, that they can kill great fish with them using superfine lines. In snag and weed free open water with time to spare this may be true, but no more so than would be the case when using any other type of reel, the angler's skill being equal to the task The fact is, that while one may set the tension of the slipping clutch sufficiently high to strike against it, if the hook is small and sharp enough to penetrate the fish's mouth with less pressure than would break the line; when a fish is hooked the slipping clutch should be

* Marshall-Hardy cast a float 98 ft. 8 in. (see Biographical Note. L.C.)

relaxed immediately. And any pressure which is necessary while playing it must be exerted by the index finger on the rim of the spool which of course, revolves when a fish is taking line.

Another common fault is to continue to wind against a fish that is taking line (signalled on good models by a ticking device). This merely puts kinks into the line for every turn of the handle and has no effect on the fish whatsoever.

Then it is that preserving a taut line the finger pressure on the reel's spool to which I have referred is the only means of control available.

There can hardly be a phase of angling where absolute harmony between the test-curve of the rod, the breaking strain of the line and the weight of the lure is more essential, than when fishing with a fixed-spool reel. I dislike asking the reader to refer back, but I will ask him or her to recollect what was said on this subject in a foregoing carp chapter.

Frankly, from spinning to ledgering with a fixed-spool reel, one's fishing methods are the same as when using a centre-pin revolving type; and as I see it, the only advantages these reels offer are perhaps increased accuracy and certainly distance when casting really light baits. There is practically only one occasion when any manual control is needed while casting, i.e. when the lure is overshooting the mark. It is then only necessary to apply that useful index finger to the rim of the spool to check the line as it runs over the lip. And when a fish is beaten and ready to be grassed it must be remembered that it is not possible to wind it toward you against the train of gears with which these reels are fitted. It must be pumped in.

This is a simple process (which applies to all geared reels) which if not so versatile and exhilarating as playing a fish on a revolving-drum reel is soon mastered.

Keeping a tight line which one must always do, the rod is dipped to the horizontal position, the angler winding in line as the rod is depressed. Then, when it is parallel with the water, finger pressure is exerted on the spool and the rod point is raised to the vertical (without winding) which of course draws the fish towards you; and the process is repeated as necessary.

At the crucial moment of landing your fish with a fixed-spool reel (if the quarry's dimensions warrant) care must be taken against those last minute plunges and unexpected final runs which so often spell disaster if neglected.

At this point the bale arm which revolves when the reel takes line back on to the spool, should be prevented from moving by finger manipulation, thus virtually locking the reel, while the fish is drawn over the net. Any effort from a properly subdued fish should at this stage be controlled by dipping the rod point if necessary.

Simplifying the difference between playing a fish with either a fixed-spool or a revolving centre-pin to the nth degree, it boils down to this.

In the first instance one controls a fish by pressure on the revolving spool and in the second by similar pressure on either the rim of the revolving drum of the reel, or in the case of multipliers on the line.

It will be seen, therefore, that (all the circumstances being taken into consideration, strength of fish, weeds, currents, etc.) the relationship between rod and line must in both cases be so close that any idea that ultra-fine lines can be used safely with a fixed-spool reel in contradistinction to those required when a centre-pin revolving type of reel is used, is to say the least fallacious.

Having, I hope, established these fundamental principles I will proceed to a discussion of the mechanics of a fixed-spool reel.

The Mechanics of a fixed spool reel

There is no doubt that a thorough knowledge of the mechanism and performance of your fixed-spool reel is essential to its successful use.

As is generally the case the best of these reels are the most expensive and my advice must therefore be to buy the best you can afford. If you know what to expect of a reel, good or bad, you can then take advantage of the former and avoid the latter. So to our consideration of the '300.'

The spool or drum of all reels of this type remains stationary when casting, with its axis facing the tip of the rod; and when the weight of the lure exerts its force the line is drawn over the rim of the spool in a series of loops, much after the manner of drawing a coil of string off the end of one's finger. It will be seen from this that the energy needed to set a revolving 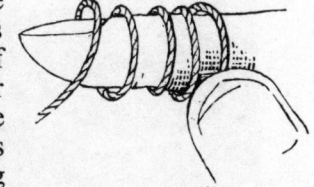 drum in motion is eliminated. This facilitates longer casting with lures and lines of the same weight than would be possible with the average revolving-drum reel. I would, however, interpolate here, that the difference in this respect between the performance of a fixed-spool reel and a multiplier with a super-light drum is not considerable; and for this and other reasons which I will not argue here, some experts prefer the latter for all-round purposes.

There is, however, no room for doubt that used as originally intended, to cast very light lures with superfine lines when waters are low and gin clear, these reels are paramount. But their use has been much extended since that time, and fixed-spool reels of various sizes are now available even for use with heavy lines and weights in sea-fishing.

Now let us look at the Garcia-Mitchell '300.' Figure 1 (p. 282) shows the reel in the closed position, the pick-up arm, or bail, is down, preventing line from running off. It is important here to note that when the bail arm is opened the line must be held by the index finger of the casting hand in order to prevent it slipping over the rim of the spool, due to the weight of the lure or terminal tackle. And it must be held in this way until the moment when the lure is released to its destination in the water.

Let us assume that you are spinning and that the lure has struck the water, what then?

First check any tendency for loose coils of line to leave the spool after the cast is complete, by placing your index finger against the rim of the spool. Then after a suitable pause to allow the bait to sink to the desired depth, remove your finger and commence to wind in in the usual way.

FIG. 1.

The Garcia-Mitchell 300. A—The pick-up, or bail arm, in the closed position. B—The tungsten-carbide line guide which picks up and distributes the line on the spool when winding in. C—Lip of the spool, which moves to and fro as line is taken on, thus distributing the line evenly. D—The tension adjustment, with push-button release for easy change of spool.

As the reel handle begins to turn it releases the pick-up or bail arm which springs back automatically into position shown. This picks up and as it revolves guides the line into the line-guide.

As you continue to wind in, the line is wound back on to the spool C in the same direction as it lay before the cast was made. This tends to untwist any kink which was put into the line as it flew over the lip of the spool when you cast.

Now, if the line were wound straight back and the spool remained stationary, it would either pile up unevenly or the strands might bite one between the other making further casting difficult or impossible.

To eliminate this, the spool moves in and out as you wind, distributing the line evenly in such a way as to prevent it becoming hitched up in its own coils.

The tension adjustment D, while useful to hold the line when you are moving from place to place is, as we have seen previously, of minor importance when playing a fish, a fact which frankly eluded me for quite a while during my initial fixed-spool forays. And it is still a stumbling block to many users of these reels.

In the '300' it is operated by turning the tension adjustment D on the face of the spool clockwise. But when a good fish is hooked it should be turned back at once to a very low tension and any necessary pressure while playing a fish applied on the rim of the spool (which revolves when line is being taken) with the index finger; then unless your quarry is running into danger (from your point of view) the less pressure you exert, within reason, the sooner it will exhaust itself.

Many a lusty salmon has been killed on this principle, namely to allow the fish to rush about under comparatively light, but to it aggravating pressure, until it is tired out by its own exertions.

I have referred throughout to these reels as fixed-spool rather than threadline for the good reason given earlier. It should however, be remembered from the outset, that the spool of these reels is fixed only when casting. Apart from its reciprocal movement when retrieving line, it revolves as we have seen in response to a pull on the line, which sets up a warning sound to indicate that line is being taken.

This signal is obviously of considerable importance when playing a fish. And so long as this continues the reel handle *must be held still*.

Winding in when a fish is running is *prima facie* evidence of the novice.

The '300' is designed to enable the angler to change from a spool holding one breaking strain to another very quickly. The tension adjustment has a push-button, which when depressed allows the spool to come away from the reel. When the other spool is placed in position the tension is still right and does not need adjustment.

Speaking of these spools I am reminded to say that whatever line is used, they should be filled to the lip. This facilitates casting. Monofil lines may show a tendency to spring off the spool when not in use, but a turn of tape will prevent this satisfactorily. Braided Terylene lines which do not present this difficulty will not cast so far, but it is seldom that one needs to cast to the fullest extent of the reels (and the angler's) ability, and the difference is in any case negligible. Should it be desirable to grease a line used with a fixed-spool reel select a thin (not tacky) line flotant and apply it sparingly. Any tendency for the line to stick especially in the finer gauges is fatal to efficient casting; and over-greased lines collect grit which is an enemy to all fishing tackle and to fine lines in particular.

To ensure rapid line recovery as necessary, reels of this type are geared in a ratio of approximately three to one, and all the gears are enclosed, and there is just one lubrication point. I need hardly emphasise the desirability of keeping these reels well, but not over-oiled and scrupulously clean.

One of my complaints against many fixed spool reels was that they did not cater for those anglers who prefer to use a left-hand wind. Nowadays most fixed spool reels, including the '300,' can be bought with left- or right-hand wind.

If I have omitted any important point in my attempt to describe the essential know-hows of a fixed-spool reel I am indeed sorry. But the task is not a simple one and as each manufacturer gives careful details regarding the mechanism if not of the subsequent use of his particular pattern, between the two I hope all gaps will be filled.

Mention of manufacturers encourages me to stress that there are literally dozens of fixed-spool reels on the market not a few of which are first-class engineers' jobs. I would like to stress that I have no interest, either direct or indirect, in any item of tackle mentioned in this book.

More years ago than I care to remember, when fixed-spool reels were in their infancy, I predicted that they would have their little day then fizzle out.

How wrong I was!

I quite overlooked the fact that they eliminate the often long and always assiduous practise necessary to master the art of casting with a revolving-drum reel; and that they render line projection well nigh foolproof.

However, had I considered these quite important facts, I doubt that I should have contemplated the seemingly irresistible appeal that fixed-spool reels have made. Be this as it may. I still believe that revolving-drum reels provide better control when playing a fish, especially in weedy and snag-strewn waters and I act accordingly.

All this discussion of mechanics, physics and what have you, makes me wonder if our sport is not becoming too scientific, too mechanised, too serious and too commercialised, to merit the sobriquet 'Contemplative Man's Recreation.' I hope not!

CHAPTER XXXVIII

A SIMPLE REFERENCE FOR BAITS AND LURES

MENTION is made elsewhere in these pages of suitable baits for the various coarse fish. I feel, however, that a readily accessible list arranged alphabetically will be useful. Some I shall almost certainly overlook, while others there are in plenty of which I have no knowledge. The baits here listed will, however, encompass the undoing of the fishes for which they are prescribed and are I hope sufficiently numerous to satisfy most readers. Alphabetically then, the baits for barbel must be our first care.

BARBEL—*Barbus barbus*

BACON BEEF	Boiled or raw, should be fatty. Particularly useful near a houseboat or other craft from which plate scraps may be emptied.
CADDIS GRUBS	Stripped of their cases.
HEMP PASTE	This can be made from either ground hemp mixed with bread or by pressing hemp seed into the paste after it is made. Make the paste from the water in which the hemp is boiled. This bait is very killing in all waters where hemp is regularly used.
LOBWORMS	These should be well scoured in moss. A good bait.
MUSSELS (FRESHWATER)	Sometimes killing.
MUTTON	Raw and fatty. Good on occasion near houseboats.
SAUSAGES	Good when cooked.
SHRIMPS	Boiled (pink) or fresh (brown).
SILKWEED	This is often effective in weir lashings.

Ground-baits may be made up with either bank clay containing inferior samples of the hook-bait, or bread, bran and middlings instead of clay. The latter is certainly preferable where hemp paste is used on the hook.

BLEAK—*Alburnus alburnus*

BREAD CRUST ⎫		
BREAD PASTE ⎭	– –	Very small pieces.
MAGGOTS	– – –	Small.
WORMS	– – –	Small pieces only.

No ground-bait is required.

BREAM—*Abramis brama* (bronze).
              Blicca bjoerkna (silver or white).

The baits for these fishes are the same.

BREAD FLAKE   –   –   Produced by pinching a piece of new bread on to the hook, leaving the edges of the bait rough. This is excellent in some waters.

BREAD PASTE   –   –   This may be used plain or coloured, but should be made up with the water where you fish. The value of colouring and flavouring is very doubtful. Nevertheless if you wipe some of the slime off a fish you have caught on to the paste on the hook this appears to add to its attractiveness.

Mona, to whom I refer more fully in the section which deals with roach baits, devised a bait for bream composed of custard powder and flour worked together with weak tea. Of this unusual mixture Mr. Ernest J. Barrow, writing in the *Fishing Gazette* of 3rd February, 1945, said: 'This I found exceptionally 'killing' on the Broads.' He does not, however, give a date or month for its use (see Macaroni under CHUB, p. 290).

CADDIS GRUBS   –   –   Stripped of their cases.

GENTLES (MAGGOTS)   –   Not very good.

OIL CAKE PASTE   –   –   This is made up with crushed cattle cake.

WHEAT (OR BARLEY)   –   This should be creed. If placed in a thermos flask of boiling water overnight the bait will be ready for use. Very useful in certain localities.

Many of the baits prescribed for roach will take bream, but the best of all baits for these fish are:

WORMS   –   –   –   Lobs which should be well scoured (bream prefer the tail). Brandlings of which two or three may be used together and the same applies to small red worms.

Ground-bait should be generously administered. Bread, bran and middlings make as useful a mixture as you can wish whatever hook-bait you may be using. If using wheat or barley these may be thrown in loose, but are better enclosed in a ball of the first-mentioned mixture.

CARP—*Cyprinus carpio.*

BREAD PASTE – –	Dipped in honey or golden syrup, the paste made up with the water where you fish.
	Pastes for carp may also be made with beer, sugar or cheese flavouring, but either of the former are preferable. Francis Francis advised the use of brandy, but had no knowledge of present prices.
BEANS – – – –	Either small broad beans or haricot beans, boiled till tender, are sometimes acceptable.
CADDIS GRUBS – –	Stripped of their cases.
CHERRIES – –	These should be stoned and are improved by dipping in golden syrup.
GREEN PEAS – – –	Sometimes useful.
POTATO – – –	Par-boiled, the addition of a little sugar to the water may be an advantage.
SPONGE CAKE PASTE –	Made as with bread. A little bread may be added if required to get a right consistency.
WASP GRUBS – –	These must be steamed or gently baked to toughen. Dipping in honey is an advantage.
WORMS – – –	Either lobs, small red worms or brandlings. These should be well scoured to toughen and make them lively.

Bread, bran and middlings with a little (inferior) hook-bait is a good general carp ground-bait. If potato is on the hook mix in some mashed potato. Some anglers think it well worth while to mix their ground-bait with beer—others prefer to drink it. If worms are used a few inferior quality (but not dead or stale) should be cast in round the hook-bait Pre-ground-baiting, when possible, is a great advantage.

CHUB—*Leuciscus cephalus.*

BANANA – – –	Cut into cubes.
BULLOCK'S PITH – –	This pith which is probably the best of all winter baits for chub is derived from the spinal cord of the animal. Cut the outer skin from it with a sharp knife or pair of scissors, then wash it thoroughly until it is perfectly clean and it is ready for use. Scalding or boiling pith softens it and makes it difficult to keep on the hook. Difficult to obtain.

The ground-bait *par excellence* for use with pith should be mentioned

at once. I refer to the brains of a bullock, or sheep. Wash them carefully then scald and cut up small. These small pieces of brain should
be thrown in sparingly.

CHEESE PASTE   –   –   Milk may be used as a moistening agent
with advantage. Mix day-old bread
with an equal part of strong cheese.
Cheese may also be used alone in rough
irregular shaped knobs, if it is not too
hard. Some cream cheeses are very
effective used in this way.

CHERRIES   –   –   –   These should be stoned. Use in season.

Most writers mention the Dock, or Docken grub as a bait for one
or other of the coarse fishes. This animal is the larva or caterpillar of
the Ghost Moth. I have always refrained from using Dock grubs
because I dislike handling the creatures. This need not, however, deter
those who are not averse to a certain amount of hard work to acquire
their baits and have no such scruples. These larvae are perfectly harmless
and my prejudice is purely personal. It is as well to remember, nevertheless, that there are one or two British caterpillars the hairs of which
have a similar effect to those of the stinging nettle.

The almost universal mention of Dock grubs as an effective bait is
strong evidence of their efficacy. They may be found practically throughout the year at the roots of the Dock plant, Burdock, Hop, White
Deadnettle, Daffodil, Marsh Thistle, Horehound and Stinging Nettle,
and are said to feed for two years, which may account for the length
and corpulence of some specimens (up to 2 in. long). It will be seen
from the foregoing that if Dock plants are not accessible you have plenty
of other food-plants from which to choose.

As Sidney Spencer suggests in his good book *Clear-water Trout
'Fishing with Worm*, you will have the best chance of unearthing these
caterpillars if you fork up those plants which show signs of being
'sickly, with brown or withered leaves. This is quite often a sign that the
plant has been attacked by the larvae. Don't attempt to pull on the
plant itself in an effort to uproot it. The grubs seem somehow to
disappear when warned in this way.

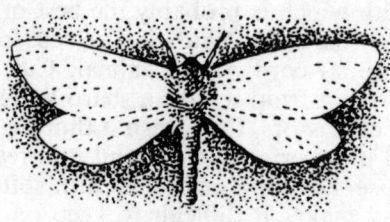

FIG. 1.
*Male Ghost Moth (Hepialus humuli)
after R. South.*

The caterpillar to which
Mr. Spencer referred was the
larva of the Frosted Orange
Moth, but his advice may be
applied equally to that of the
Ghost Moth, i.e. the 'Dock
grub.' Fig. 1.

The Frosted Orange larvae
can be found from April to
September at the roots of Agri-
mony, Dock, Burdock, Elder,

If ever a fish looked like a hybrid between perch and pike it is the zander, or pike-perch. But while belonging to the perch-type fish, such as the perch, ruffe, and so on, the pike-perch is a separate species. In our waters there are, according to most authorities, two species, one *Stizostedion lucioperca* (the European pike-perch, or zander); the other *S. vitreum* (the American pike-perch or walleye).

[Photograph: W. J. Howes]

Fish are as susceptible as human beings to illness and disease. Many of the bone diseases and viral infections known to us are found in fish. They also suffer from the attacks of parasites which exist in large numbers in water, using fish as major or secondary hosts. This Avon chub, killed and opened on the river bank, was found to be infested by one of the most evil parasites, *Pomphorhynchus laevis*, a thorny headed worm. There are large numbers of the creature to be seen attached to the gut and stomach of the chub, having got there by first infesting a freshwater shrimp or insect larva which in turn was eaten by the fish. Should any angler catch a fish obviously suffering from a serious disease or parasitic infestation, which cannot be removed, it is humane to kill the fish quickly and efficiently.

[Photograph: Peter Wheat]

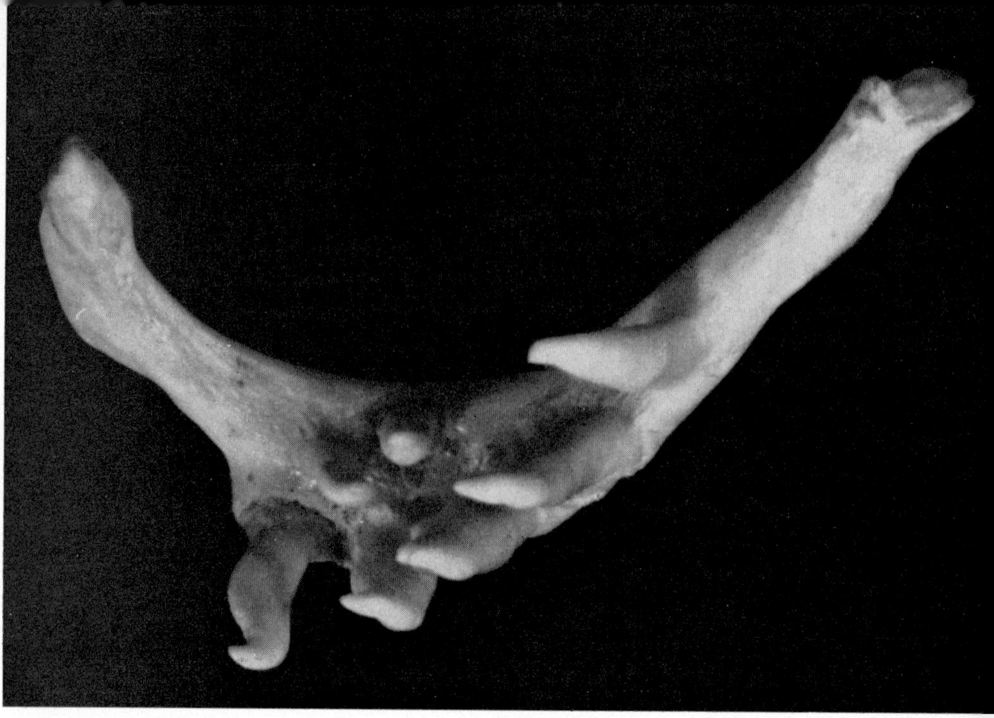

Pharyngeal teeth of chub (above) and roach (below) are certain species identification pointers. The pity is that one has to kill the fish before being able to examine these interesting features of the carp family. The chub pharyngeals helped to prove a fish claimed as a large roach to be a chub. Although the body shape was much deeper and the fins much redder than one expects in this species, the pharyngeals proved beyond doubt the fish to be a chub.

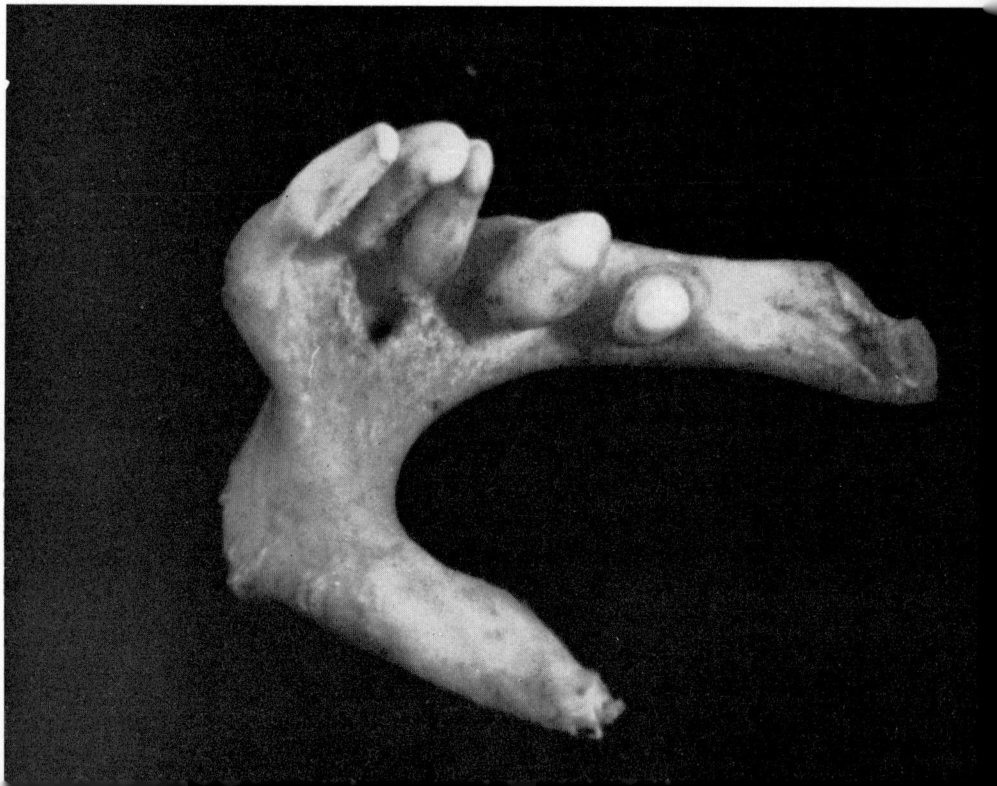

Figwort, Ragwort, Foxglove, Marsh Thistle, Meadow Plume Thistle, Potato and Yellow Flag.

The foregoing are examples of caterpillars which are specifically recommended by experts as killing baits.

While not being a user of this bait, I feel justified in suggesting that any caterpillar which infests trees, shrubs or plants that overhang the water are more likely to prove deadly in their particular vicinity than any subterranean specimens dug up and taken to the water. This would appear to apply particularly to chub, which hover near the surface in wait for such titbits as may fall from overhanging foliage into the water.

It may come as a surprise to some readers to know that some caterpillars are cannibals. Owen S. Wilson, in his *Larvae of the British Lepidoptera*, says:

> . . . cannibals without the paltry excuse of hunger, for they will seize and devour their own or any other species in the midst of abundance, and in a state of nature.

For these diversions may I put in the plea that they are at least interesting.

Hooks should just penetrate the skin, the grub being free to wriggle.

Hooks for use with larvae of this kind should be small, very sharp and of fine wire, to ensure that the animal receives only the smallest possible puncture. Large hooks and clumsy hooking will disintegrate them. They are best when freshly gathered and will not live long in captivity. A supply of the food-plant upon which they are found will preserve caterpillars for a few days.

FLIES (NATURAL) –   –   And other waterside insects.

FROGS –   –   –   –   Used dead. They should be smallish.

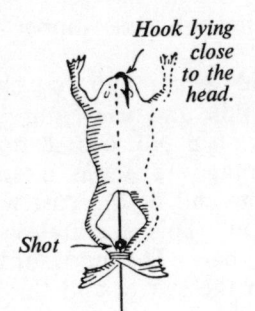

Hook lying close to the head.

Shot

Kill a small frog and attach a large round bend hook by passing a baiting-needle through the mouth and out at the vent. Tie the legs in rear to the line with fine nylon, above a shot pinched on the hook-link as illustrated. The hook-link is attached to the cast through a sufficiently large (specially tied) loop. Fish with a suitable fly-rod making long casts. This is a method I have not employed, but it is killing in the hands of an expert.

The late and great Mr. G. E. M. Skues having read the foregoing, wrote:

I see you have no experience of the use of the small frog. I had a few week-ends on the Ouse near Huntingdon and St. Ives years ago, fishing in this manner.

The small frog was fixed on the hook much as described by you and was cast from a bait with a thin silk line on a stiffish greenheart fly-rod of about 11 ft. with a stiff split-cane tip, so that the frog hit the water with a flop.

The line was greased to float for about three or four yards, beginning about a yard above the bait.

If there were chub about they generally took at once, if undisturbed by the boat, they were detected taking by the draw of the floating line.

Sometimes the hook came away with the bait mangled by the chub's throat teeth, but the fish were generally securely hooked. On one of these occasions fishing with my brother we caught half a dozen from 2½ lb. to 4 lb. in weight.

Seeing another angler bank-fishing as we left the water, we asked him if he could use our chub—he said he could and as we handed them over remarked that 'They would weigh in proper at the Club tomorrow.'

It would appear that to be an angler is not *sine qua non* to be a sportsman.

CRAYFISH TAIL – – Boiled crayfish tail is regarded as a deadly bait for chub, especially in waters where these crustaceans abound. The remainder of the crayfish is mashed and used as ground-bait. I have not used this bait, but have no doubt it is worth trial.

GRASSHOPPERS – – Special hooks are obtainable whereby these and other insects are clipped to the hook without injury, for use alive.

GUDGEON – – – Small, used alive. Hook through the upper lip only and use a single not a triangle hook. Excellent early in the season.

MINNOWS – – – Live, hooked through the upper lip only.

MACARONI – – – This is a splendid winter bait for chub. Par-boil it in milk and use from ½ in. to ¾ in. lengths on a No. 6 or 8 hook. It is an advantage to serve a small link-swivel at the end of the cast when fishing macaroni. This facilitates the renewal of the bait. The hook-link is unshipped from the swivel and the line threaded through a length of macaroni, then the link is hitched up again. It sounds troublesome but is not so in practice. A supply of macaroni chopped

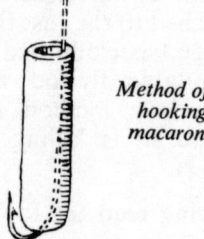

Method of hooking macaroni.

into pieces about ¼ in. makes a useful ground-bait.

(Some anglers use triangle hooks size 10 to 14. I prefer the single.)

I have referred earlier to 'Mona' of pike weight-scale fame. He made a careful study of baits, believing that certain foods were only acceptable to fish at particular times of the year. One of his successful concoctions was:

MACARONI – – – This he boiled lightly, then steeped it in melted butter to which a small quantity of cheese parings and a pinch of salt were added. The bait was for use during the months of July and August.

Mr. Ernest J. Barrow, writing of this 'fantastic bait' in the *Fishing Gazette* of 3rd February, 1945, said: 'This I have tried and have met with success when all other baits failed.'

MAGGOTS – – – Much improved if fed on cream cheese.
SHRIMPS – – – Sea or freshwater, boiled or alive.
SLUGS – – – – The large black species is excellent for specimen chub.
SNAILS – – – Water or land, taken from their shells.
'SNOWBALLS' – – – Chub will sometimes take those big white berries which appear in the autumn — children call them 'Snowballs.' They grow on a spindly shrub; you will doubtless know them well. The official name is 'Snowberry,' *Symphoricarpus albus, var. laevigatus,* Chevin shows a liking for them, especially where such a bush overhangs a stream and these berries fall into the water, but not exclusively in such a place by any means. These berries are bouyant and it is necessary to fish them with a largish hook and a shot close to the bait. A friend who fishes the Dorset Stour swears by 'Snowballs' for

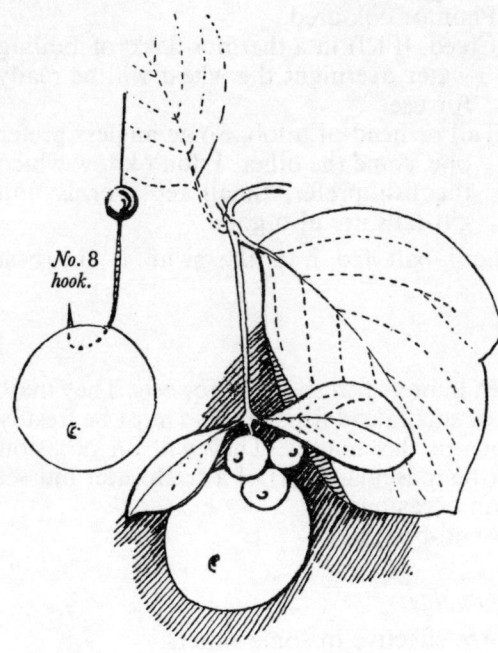

No. 8 hook.

chub—they are always worth a trial. Ground-bait with bread and bran. If the chub don't take them readily turn to another bait. But if they do, look out!

STRAWBERRIES   –   –   Small and ripe.

WASP GRUBS   –   –   Steamed or gently baked to toughen.

WITHY GRUBS   –   –   Found in September on trunks of Elm trees.

WORMS   –   –   –   Medium sized lobs or the tail of a large lobworm.

To these may be added artificial flies: Alder, Badger, Black Gnat, Black Palmer, Red Tag, Soldier Palmer, Brunton's Fancy, Coachman, Cochybondhu, White Moth, Zulu. Chub may also be taken on small pearl spoons, metal spoons, plugs, etc. and spun natural fish. Again bread, bran and middlings with a little of the hook-bait—or inferior hook-bait in clay balls makes food ground-bait.

DACE—*Leuciscus leuciscus.*

BARLEY   –   –   –   Creed—see Wheat.

CADDIS GRUB   –   –   Stripped of its case.

ELDERBERRIES   –   –   Fresh or preserved in a 5 per cent solution of formalin.

HEMP SEED   –   –   –   Soaked overnight. Then simmer till seeds begin to burst. (See p. 67.)

MAGGOTS   –   –   –   Plain or coloured.

WHEAT   –   –   –   Creed. If left in a thermos flask of boiling water overnight the wheat will be ready for use.

WORMS   –   –   –   Tail or head of a lob. Some anglers prefer one, some the other. I don't know which the fish prefer. Small red worms and gilt-tails are also good.

Small quantities of the hook-bait fed into the swim is the best ground-bait.

EEL—*Anguilla anguilla.*

Few anglers except specimen hunters fish specially for eels. They may, however, be taken on worms or small dead fish. The fish must be freshly killed. Eels are very fastidious in this matter. They will on occasion take live baits. The 'tongue' (the muscular foot) of a freshwater mussel (see Roach) is also effective on occasions.

Worms may be used as ground-bait.

GRAYLING—*Thymallus thymallus.*

BEETLES   –   –   –   Are effective in some waters.

MAGGOTS – – – Plain or coloured.

WORMS – – – Small red or gilt-tail well scoured in moss.

Grayling are essentially quarry for the fly-fisherman. Wickham's Fancy, Red Tag, Orange Bumble, Duns, Dark Needle, Fog Black, Steel Blue, Green Insect and nymphs. Such lists are almost illimitable, but local practice or your own views will help you to make a suitable choice.

A few loose hook-baits fed into the swim is the best ground-bait.

GUDGEON—*Gobio gobio*.

BREAD PASTE – – Small pieces must be used.

MAGGOTS – – – Natural or coloured.

WORMS – – – Small portions of red or gilt-tail worms. Blood worms.

No ground-baiting required but periodic raking of the bottom is very attractive to these fish.

PERCH—*Perca fluviatilis*.

LIVE BAITS – – – The fry of perch, dace, roach and minnows. The latter are in my view second only to the fry of their own species when they are obtainable. Small frogs, see Chub.

SPINNING – – – Pearl and various metal spoons. Natural fish on spinning flights. All spinners should be small.

No ground-bait is required or advised for perch. Some anglers say the sinking of a sealed bowl of minnows causes perch to congregate. I have not tried this experiment but have no doubt it would prove effective under certain circumstances.

PIKE—*Esox lucius*.

DEAD BAITS – – – Fish of all species. Herring used with paternoster or ledger tackle.

LIVE BAITS – – – Small pike, perch, dace, roach, gudgeon frogs, indeed almost any living creature of the water.

SPINNING – – – Any dead fish as mentioned above on one or other of the scores of mountings. Artificial spinners for pike are legion, among the best are bar spoons, Wagtails, Plugs, Phantom Minnows, etc.

There is room for a great deal of ingenuity and interesting winter evening employment in the home construction of spinning flights for natural baits and artificial spinners. Both are easily lost and both are expensive.

ROACH—*Rutilus rutilus*.

As roach are such a popular quarry and so catholic in their taste for various baits, I will offer the reader a rather wider choice in this list of baits for *Rutilus*. For convenience also I have arranged the various baits under class headings.

BREAD PASTE   –   – This should be made up in a piece of clean rag at the waterside, using the water in which you will fish as a moistening agent. Bread a day old with the crust removed is ideal. Handle as little as possible.

Biscuit –   –   – Make up as above but add flour as the crushed biscuit is worked into a paste, to obtain a right consistency.

Cupping   –   – This is made up from a mixture of day-old bread and bran. Add water as necessary and work until the mixture becomes glutinous. When used on the hook this bait flakes off and is very attractive. Its great drawback is the oft-repeated need for rebaiting. Always worth a trial in quiet waters.

Coloured pink paste is sometimes and in some waters attractive to roach. The addition of a little cochineal to the paste will produce the desired shade. A little cochineal goes a long way. For yellow shades mix in either chrome, custard powder or saffron.

PASTES (Scented)   –   – Onion, aniseed and oil of rhodium are sometimes used but are of extremely doubtful benefit. To wipe the slime from a caught fish over your paste is, however, effective. Whether this comes into the scented category I leave to the reader, with the assurance that it is much more effective than the three former scents.

Hemp   –   –   – Paste made with the water in which hempseed has been boiled is effective in waters where hemp is fished. Ground and scalded hemp seed mixed with bread paste is sometimes good also.

Beer   –   –   – Paste mixed with beer is also good.

Pastes may be sweetened with sugar, honey or golden syrup, but this is of doubtful benefit. Flour and banana made into a paste is quite good if a semi-sweet paste is desired.

BREAD CRUST   –   – This hook-bait stands in my view in a class apart, especially for winter fishing. It can be prepared quite easily at the waterside. Cut the bottom from a day-old tinned loaf. The slice should be half crumb and half crust. Soak this in river water for a few minutes, then place it on a clean dry cloth to soak out surplus water. Place on a flat surface and cut it into dice of about $\frac{1}{4}$ or $\frac{1}{2}$ in. square. Thrust the hook through the crusty side when baiting. A more elaborate method for home preparation is described earlier and is better, because the pressing advised toughens the cubes in such a way as to make them hold the hook much better.

When using paste or bread crust on the hook, a mixture of scalded and well-pulped stale bread with ground rice and middlings makes a good ground-bait. This should not be made any stiffer than will ensure it breaking up as it sinks to the bed of the swim, and should be as fine in texture as to constitute little more than a thick cloud.

CEREALS   –   – – Creed wheat, barley, malt and rice. Prepare overnight in a thermos flask.

Ground-bait as above, or a few loose hook-baits cast into the swim occasionally.

FRESHWATER MUSSELS   – Roach may be taken on the tongue-like portion of freshwater mussels. Remove the tough yellow part at the root and fish the ledger tackle.

Cut up the residue of the mussels and mix it with bread and bran, or bank clay, for use as ground-bait. I have not used this bait, but it is held that the only other fish which will take it is the eel.

LARVAE   –   – – Maggots (gentles) plain or coloured. These should be meat-bred and well scoured in bran (not sawdust). The chrysalis (red) is sometimes killing when fished on the surface. Wasp grubs, baked or steamed gently until they are sufficiently tough to be hooked without breaking up.

Caddis grubs freed from the shell are very killing.

Meal worms are useful when fishing a mill-tail. Ash grubs from rotten tree bark. Caterpillars, earwigs, grasshoppers, beetles and freshwater shrimps may be included under this heading, though not larvae. Almost any insect of the waterside is good.

MISCELLANEOUS

Cheese –   –   – Either as paste or in irregular knobs of suitable size is sometimes good. The cheese must be soft.

Currants   –   – Of the small black variety, but they must be fairly soft. These make a good hook-bait when hemp is used as 'feed.' The use of hemp in this way should be very sparing.

Occasional small pellets of cheese cast into the swim will serve as ground-bait.

Finely mashed greaves placed in balls of bank clay make good ground-bait.

Hemp Seed –   – Prepare the seed for the hook by placing it in boiling water overnight. In the morning it will be sufficiently split for use. If not, the slightest second boiling will suffice. This is a clean, handy and quite harmless bait. Elderberries are good hook-baits used with hemp as 'feed.'

A few seed only should be used as ground-bait. Large quantities spoil rather than aid hemp-fishing.

Bread flake –   – Simply pinch a piece of new bread on the hook.

Ground-bait as with crust and paste.

Snails   –   –   – Removed from the shell. Either fresh water or land snails.

Small slugs.

If snails and slugs are used as hook-baits, occasional small quantities of the hook-bait chopped up may be used as ground-bait or 'feed.'

Roach will, of course, take household flies, bluebottles, etc., and ARTIFICIAL FLIES.

Among the most useful are Alder, Black Gnat, Silver Sedge, Sweep, Aquatic Spider, Brunton's Fancy, Coachman, Wickham's Fancy and Zulu.

WORMS   –   –   –   Worms of many kinds are acceptable to roach. Lobworms, either whole or the tail only. A complete lobworm should only be used when large roach may be expected, otherwise the tail is sufficient. Small red worms used singly or in twos or threes are good in some waters.

Blood worms, the tiny larvae of one of the mosquitoes, found in the mud of some ditches, are deadly but difficult to use. A number 18 hook is necessary for these little worms. Docken grub is sometimes killing, and always worth a trial.

Brandling or gilt-tail worms used singly or two or three together are good. And 'Cow-dung Bobs,' those small red worms found under cow-dung are not to be despised as lures for roach.

When fishing worms one may either enclose a quantity in clay-balls and use these as ground-bait or chop some worms and cast the pieces into the swim.

Marigold petals have been used with success, but not by me. Other unusual baits are the white pith from rushes growing at the water's edge and pieces of mushroom.

While travelling the Southern Railway system (now part of British Rail) and fishing with J. W. G. Tomkin during our work on *Fishing in the South*, I learned that wood-lice (found under stones, under the loose bark of dead trees and in a score of other places) are favoured by some Medway fishermen as a bait for roach. They call them 'pea bugs' and contend that the males are no use because they ball up when touched, but that the females, which remain flat, are first-rate baits.

I have some doubt of this alleged method of distinguishing the sexes, as some species are unable to ball themselves up completely. There are several species of wood louse, but the common slaty-blue ones are generally used. Comparatively little has been written about these interesting animals, but in their excellent manual, *The British Woodlice*, W. M. Webb, F.L.S., and C. Sillem give the following list of local names which may be useful:

... 'sow-bug,' 'lucre pig,' 'carpenter' and 'chiselhog' (Berkshire). Dr. Fernie gives a number of others: 'Thrust-louse,' 'tiggyhog,' 'chislip,' 'kitchenboll,' 'chiselbob,' 'lugdor,' 'palmer' and 'cudworm.' ... The same writer notes that in the eastern counties they are known as 'old sows' or 'St. Anthony's hogs,' while the Welsh call them 'little grey-hogs,' 'the old woman of the woods,' or 'grammar-sows' grammar signifying a little shrivelled-up old dame. Other names are 'socchetre,' 'church louse' and 'chinch.' So you have plenty of choice.

Greville Fennell, writing of fishing in the Thames (about 1825), says:

> To get on board a ship discharging timber was a great boon; for there, as the deals and battens were thrust out of the portholes, countless wood-lice would fall into the water and would attract shoals of fish which were only too eager for the coveted luxury to examine closely the baited hooks.

RUDD—*Scardinius erythrophthalmus.*

The baits suited to the capture of rudd are so akin to those enumerated for roach that repetition would be tedious.

Dry bread (floating) moored near rudd haunts will nearly always attract these fish. They sometimes feed on the bottom with roach, when the same ground-baits as used for *Rutilus* are advised.

TENCH—*Tinca tinca.*

BREAD PASTE –	– As described for roach. It has often been declared that a flavouring of coal-tar in the paste adds to its attractiveness. It's worth a trial.
GENTLES (MAGGOTS) –	– As for roach, etc.
WASP GRUBS –	– Gently baked or steamed to render them tough enough to stand up to being placed on the hook.
WORMS – –	– These are the baits *par excellence* (for tench). I prefer a well-scoured lawn worm. Brandling or gilt-tail worms are also good.

Prior ground-baiting is advisable where possible. Tench are shy. A sprinkling of chopped worms mixed with bread and bran is a good ground-bait.

It is hoped that this résumé of some of the best baits for our various coarse fishes will prove useful at least to those of limited experience. Any repetition which is necessitated for the sake of immediate and direct reference I ask the reader to excuse.

CHAPTER XXXIX

MATCH FISHING

IT is some years since I wrote what follows, for inclusion in a collection of essays published by Messrs. Milwards Fishing Tackle, Ltd., then of Redditch, under the title *Anglers' Angles*.

I could not write anything better now as an introduction to this chapter; so I obtained the kindly permission of Colonel H. G. V. Milward, T.D., D.L., to reprint it here. This is the way of it:

Were I told of a more gripping, varied and democratic sport, pastime, recreation or hobby—as you will—than coarse fishing, I should indeed be sceptical; but, were this possible, I would at my time of life steer very clear of it. Odd you may think, to avoid an opportunity for enjoyment and relaxation as such a wonderful sport would afford. But is it?

Some fifty years' experience finds me still toying with the fringe of this most versatile form of fishing; what time then would remain for study of an even more mutable sport? No! With all its intricacies and puzzles give me coarse fishing, which, in one or other of its forms, is such as can be followed by the simplest of folk with unflagging keenness throughout a long lifetime.

Aristocrats and artisans, bishops and burglars and so through the alphabet to Zoroastrians and zanys, are gripped by the fascination of watching a float, tending a ledger, spinning a lure and casting a fly for coarse fish. If I were told of a sport more fraught with differences of opinion regarding methods, tackles, aye, even the politics and etiquette of the pursuit of coarse fishing, I could not believe my ears.

One has only to con the correspondence columns of the angling Press, to find coarse fishermen in fierce argument on these subjects; and yet I'll wager that could the protagonists meet in the flesh, they would be the first to offer hospitality to one another in the 'local.' They are a wonderful band these 'bottom-fishers!'

Izaak Walton wrote of coarse fishing as 'The Contemplative Man's Recreation,' and thought in terms of lone anglers who plied their art, craft or whatever one may correctly call this coarse fishing, in contented isolation: and those who adhere to these ends still, of whom there are many, have come to be known as 'pleasure fishermen.'

Could fishing of any kind be other than a pleasure? How then, came this strange title?

We are told that 'circumstances alter cases, just as noses alter faces,' and so it was, that with the growth of thickly populated industrial areas, fishermen living in these districts found that through industrial pollution and over-fishing of the few waters near at hand, facilities for angling diminished. The fish which they were able to catch in their local mill dams, pit flashes and canals became few and very small; and better fishing was far distant, in places to which neither their time nor their pockets would allow them to journey.

These facts gave rise to a very natural question. If there are no rod-benders what can be wrong with pitting our skill against each other to catch the greatest number of small fish? There being nothing apparently amiss with this suggestion, individuals competed, then clubs were formed; and later came the affiliation of these clubs into associations and a great body of organised anglers came into being. These anglers are in the main 'match fishermen,' and the welding of these into large organised bodies, has benefited thousands by making possible the provision of comparatively cheap transport and better fisheries, which would otherwise have been denied them.

It is these organised 'match fishers' who delight in feverish competition for whom speed and rhythmic dexterity in filling a keep-net is paramount, who coined that strange appellation 'pleasure fishermen.'

On the one hand then we have the lone 'pleasure fishers,' who regard solitude and the rustling of wind in the reeds, the song and sight of birds and the glint of light on the water, a part of the joy of a pleasant day's fishing, and who be it said, while they like to catch fish, are in no wise dismayed if they do not. On the other are their gregarious brethren of the angle, who fish in breathless competition by the hundred and at times by the thousand, spread out over miles of river bank.

And why not either or both. You may ask? Why not indeed? Therein lies one of the coarse fishermen's greatest problems.

The number of both 'pleasure' and 'match' anglers grows relentlessly all over the country, but does the available fishable water increase similarly? Does it? Is there room for them both? At the time of writing the answer is *nearly*; but the overlap has started.

To accommodate large contests, vast tracts of fishing are being bought up every season, by clubs and associations. All too often these fisheries are thereafter denied to unattached pleasure-fishermen and sometimes even to local anglers who have fished them for years.

From this complaint, which affects the whole gamut of coarse-fishing, it is but a short step to the only possible safeguards of both interests, the rights of which are no more than equal.

The first of these may be stated simply, i.e., the cultivation of a generous spirit of give and take, in respect of the use of all waters which are at present available.

The second safeguard which is more complicated in its details, is within easy reach of anglers as a whole. Every drop of clean water in the land should be populated with the right species of fish, in direct proportion to the amount of fish food which the water in question can provide. If this is to be accomplished both club and unattached anglers will need increasingly to turn some of their attention from fish catching to fish rearing. You want an example, if any? What of the famous Dagenham Lake in Essex, where pisciculture and angling go hand in hand, with magnificent results?

The other and final safeguard is without doubt to support with hard cash and plenty of it, all and every organisation which is devoted to the active suppression and eradication of pollution.

'Factories or Fish?' is an outmoded shibboleth, which in far too many cases has supplied the readily gripped excuse for commercial enterprise to foul our waters needlessly.

Devices and methods of rendering effluents innocuous are at hand, and must be used if our national heritage of pure water, without which there can be no good fishing, is to survive.

Be you 'pleasure' or 'match fishermen, skilled or a novice, if there are no fish there can be no fishing; and unless and until anglers *to a man*, pit their forces against pollution and unreasonable water extraction in deadly earnest, this sport is in daily jeopardy.

Having delivered myself of these, to me and for you, all-important facts, let us consider Match Fishing, match fishermen and their ways.

Being a man of peace, I am unwilling to make any statement which might disquiet either 'match' or 'pleasure fishermen.' This sentiment must not, however, prevent me expressing considered opinions without fear or favour.

What manner of men are these match anglers? As a body they are a grand lot of good sportsmen who like to add an extra gamble to the element of chance which attaches to all fishing.

Were there no prizes in the offing many of them would not fish at all; and for the odd few, the prize would seem to take precedence even over the game.

In a greater or lesser degree they are all accomplished fishermen; and there are those so expert that they would appear to be able to conjure fish out of an empty wash-hand basin.

This is emphasised by the fact that 'The Old Firm' will sometimes offer '100 to 1 bar four' at a match.

Good match anglers are admirably painstaking in both their pre-match preparations of tackle and bait and in the undivided assiduity with which they fish. Their accuracy is casting and skill in manipulating their tackle is consummate; and the slickness with which they strike, swing in and unhook their usually small quarry and deposit it in the keep-net, must be seen to be believed.

Their adroitness in adapting their methods to the prevailing conditions of wind and water; and when necessary changing either their tackle or tactics to meet an altered circumstance is exemplary.

A good match angler is an incredibly versatile fisherman for whom no amount of trouble and care is too much to attain a place in the prize list.

In short they are prototypes upon which in a more leisurely way many 'pleasure fishermen' would do well to model their own fishing procedure.

By now you may be wondering what these men have which good 'pleasure fishers' lack. The answer is nothing except prizes, sweep money and when possible a wager with the 100-to-1 boys.

By the way, it would seem that one of the most universally known 'pleasure fishermen' of all time succumbed to the temptation of a wager on his fishing prowess.

Was it not Izaak Walton himself who wagered that he would catch a large chub?

> . . . only one, and that shall be the biggest of them all; and that I will do so, I'll hold you twenty to one, and you shall see it done.

That he did in fact catch such a fish we know, but whether Venator accepted the bet and paid out remains a mystery.

Against these the 'pleasure' men can set the joys of freedom of movement at will and comfortable unhurried fishing. Match anglers on the other hand are as a rule 'pegged down' to a given swim, where they must stay win, draw or lose, to the end of the contest. And their motto must be based on 'time is the essence of the contract.' Seconds are vital to success and fishing in a match can be real hard work! Hence perhaps the appellation 'pleasure fisherman'; and from the pegging down system there can be no doubt that we have the match man's phrase 'the luck of the draw.' This, of course, derives from the draw for fishing 'pegs' or positions, that may be either good, bad or indifferent from the angler's point of view.

If you harbour any misgivings as to the reality of the influence of 'the draw' on the probable results of a match, look at it this way. Given hundreds of anglers at 10 yard intervals ranged along the banks of a river, do you think it likely that there will be a shoal of fish waiting to be caught opposite each competitor, or even that there will be fish near enough for all of them to attract fish into their swim even by the most skilful ground-baiting? If not you must admit the element of luck that creates some champions and frustrates others. Yes 'the luck of the draw' can defeat consummate skill.

If you are toying with the idea of taking up match fishing the foregoing brief sketch of the human consideration involved, will I hope be sufficient to enable you to make a decision as to how you prefer your reward for angling, i.e. pelf or pleasure? That is the question, the answer must be yours. Some of both may be?

Organisation

Under this heading I think preference should be given to the annual contest which is organised by the National Federation of Anglers, a body which now has a membership of over 300,000. This match which was first fished at Pangbourne on the River Thames on the 15th October, 1906, is now organised on principles derived from over fifty years' experience and may therefore be regarded as an exemplary model.

Before detailing its *modus operandi*, however, let me make this important interpolation.

The National Federation was founded in 1903 to promote measures for the improvement of the law as applied to freshwater fishing; to fight pollution, to safeguard the rights and privileges of anglers; to develop common fishing waters, etc., etc. And it is still a matter of perplexity to the Federation's Officials that while this fact is little known, their annual match is a matter of common knowledge and interest in the angling world. I have more than a suspicion, that a desire on the part of clubs and associations to acquire the right to compete in this contest is all too often their sole reason for seeking admission to the Federation. This however avails such applicants nothing and is resisted sternly by the N.F.A.

Now to the ways and means of this 'National Angling Championship' the all embracing sound of which title is somewhat misleading as it applies only to members of the Federation.

Prior to 1972 the 'National' was fished as one huge match on the second Saturday in September each year. Teams of twelve anglers were involved, with twenty yards between each angler. This, on a simple arithmetical consideration, gives a stretch of river required of some 13 miles. There are comparatively few rivers which offer so much water of an acceptable consistent character from a match fishing point of view. Among the waters that have been selected for the 'National' venue are the Witham, Trent, Welland, Severn, Huntspill, King's Sedge-moor Drain, Nene, Bure, Thurne, and of course, the Thames. There are few other waters which offer the facilities suitable for this major freshwater fishing contest, but all that has now changed. The National Federation of Anglers, early in 1972, issued a brand new set of Match Rules, to take effect from January 1 that year. These rules altered completely the conception of the 'National' as has been loved and recognised since the first match on the Thames in 1906. No longer is it to be a one-off match, fished at one venue. To quote Rule 3, the National Championship will be in future fished in divisions, depending on the number of associations in membership of the N.F.A. and the matches will be held in each region of the N.F.A. in rotation, but any regional council may waive this right if it so desires.

Those of you who are familiar with the divisions of the Football

Association (and who is not?), will be able to understand the complete metamorphosis that the National has undergone. The new rules say that the maximum number of teams in the first division shall be no more than 80, and the remaining associations in the Federation which are eligible to compete shall be formed into a further division or divisions. The soccer pattern is further copied, and promotion and relegation will operate throughout the divisions, ten up and ten down. The new rules are long, but there are a number of points which from an organisational point of view are essential, therefore I feel many readers interested in the very specialist field of match fishing will find them interesting. Club Secretaries will find them perfect as a basis upon which their own club match rules can be founded.

Match Rules of the National Federation of Anglers

1. The National Federation of Anglers shall organise the National Championship and any other competitions upon which it may decide. The Elected Officers will appoint a National Match Committee, which will be responsible for supervising the arrangements for N.F.A. competitions, and the selection of representative teams.

2. Entries will be accepted for the National Championship from one team of twelve plus 3 reserves, from Associations subject to the following conditions:

   (a) That they have been in membership of an N.F.A. region before 31st December in the year prior to the Championship Match.

   (b) That they have paid their N.F.A. fee by March 31st for the year the Championship Match takes place.

   (c) Associations not represented at the Annual Conference for three successive years, except new members, shall not be permitted to enter the National Championship Match until represented at the Annual Conference.

   The names of team members and reserves to be submitted by dates to be notified, and the entrance fee shall be paid to the Central Secretariat. All Associations submitting teams for the National Championship who have not paid their proper dues, including transport fees, by the appointed date shall be debarred from competing in that year's match. Any angler submitting his name, or knowingly allowing his name to be submitted in any way to an Association for inclusion in their team will not be eligible to be considered by any other Association or team, for the Championship to which his submission refers. The expenses of the National Championship will be limited to the amount received from the entrance fees of the competing teams, and any surplus shall be paid in to the general funds of the N.F.A.

   No angler shall be eligible for membership of an Association team in the National Championship unless he is permanently domiciled

in the region in which that Association has its permanent headquarters, except by permission of the two regional councils concerned.

3. The National Championship will in future be fished in divisions,
depending on the number of associations in membership of the
N.F.A., and the matches will be held in each region of the N.F.A.,
in rotation, but any regional council may waive this right if it so
desires.

The maximum number of teams in the First division shall not be
more than 80, and the remaining associations in the N.F.A. and
eligible to compete shall be formed into a further division or
divisions. Promotions and relegation shall operate throughout the
divisions, with 10 up and 10 down. A team not competing will
automatically be relegated. The waters chosen to be fished in the
Championship matches should be closed for fishing for 5 days
prior to the match, if practicable, but in any case to all competitors
from midnight the Sunday previous.

4. The National Championship shall be a 'pegged-down' competition,
pegs to be not less than 20 yards apart, or more where practicable.
The draw for positions shall be made so that there is one member
of each team in the first section and a similar procedure adopted for
subsequent section. The draw shall be made in the presence of the
team captains. The section draw will be made by the Officers or
other nominees of the National Match Committee. Section cards
for each team member will be placed in envelopes together with a
map of the water and sections to be fished, sealed, and drawn by the
team representatives.

No weight cards will be used to record competitor's weight. Each
competitor shall be responsible for ensuring that the correct weight
of his catch is recorded by the section steward on the section
record sheet.

Any competitor changing his section or transgressing official
arrangements or rules will be disqualified, and no replacement
competitor will be allowed. The signal to commence and cease
fishing will be given by the President or his nominee.

The duration of the National Championship will be 5 hours. Team
changes must be notified in writing before the team concerned draws.

5. Each competing team will be required to provide up to 2 stewards
with scales if necessary, but in any case there shall be not less than
9 stewards for each section. The stewards will examine all containers
carried by competitors prior to the match at their pegs and sign
their section cards after this inspection.

They will do their utmost to prevent spectators approaching or
interfering with the competitors. No bait may be given to any
competitor during the match. Peg numbers to remain in position
until the match is over.

6. Competitors on being drawn must proceed to and from their pegs only by official transport, and receive no further assistance after boarding the transport. (Any disabled competitor may have assistance, only on the written authority of the match committee.) They must not on any account groundbait the swim, wet a line, plumb the depth or disturb the water other than to wet groundbait before the starting signal. They shall not wade at any time other than to position keep-nets under the supervision of a steward. Every competitor must fish from within one yard on an imaginary line between his peg number and the water. On flowing water he will fish from his position in the direction of the flow as far as the next peg. On still water he may fish as far as half the distance between his peg and the pegs on either side. Where competitors are drawn on opposite banks the limit of the swim will be the line midway between each bank. The competitor will restrict his activities completely to these boundaries. Neither his person, his tackle, his baits or groundbaits may intrude into his neighbours' swim.

7. A competitor shall have in use only one rod, one line and one hook at one time, but may have other rods and tackles assembled for use in a position behind him, *providing that no such other tackles are baited*. Any bait, subject to local rules, may be used except live or dead fish, spinning baits or artificial lures. All groundbaits may be thrown in by hand, or by use of catapults, throwing sticks, swim feeders and bait droppers, but no other mechanical means of projecting groundbait is allowed.

8. Competitors must play and land their own fish. Competitors will cease fishing at the finishing signal, but may be allowed no more than 15 minutes to land fish hooked prior to the finishing signal. All fish are eligible for weighing-in except salmon, trout and crustaceans. No competitor may leave his or her peg except for the calls of nature.

   All competitors will remain at their pegs until details of their catch have been recorded on the section sheet by the steward, even if they have caught no fish.

9. Competitors must use a Keep-net of not less than 8 ft. in length with a diameter of not less than 15 in. in circular nets, or of a size not less than 15 in × 10 in. in rectangular nets. Competitors must if practicable, keep alive all fish caught which after being weighed must be carefully returned to the water by the scalesman. If for any reason competitors cannot keep fish alive, the stewards shall have the power to weigh in during the course of the match and return the fish to the water.

10. No competitor may have his catch weighed in who has litter lying on the banks of his swim. The individual weight of each competitors catch will be recorded to the nearest quarter of an ounce on standardised scales.

11. Referees shall be appointed who will adjudicate on the authenticity of any fish weighed in or on any other controversial matter which may be referred to them by the National Match Committee and the Referee shall have the power to disqualify the offender. In the event of any competitor contravening these rules the National Match Committee will have the right (subject to endorsement by the National Executive Council) to suspend the offender from participation in any N.F.A. events.

12. Any objection must be made in writing and lodged with a member of the National Match Committee, or a Referee, or Senior Section steward within one hour of the end of the match. Irregularities which are brought to notice at a later date may be dealt with only by and at the direction of the National Executive Council.

13. The result of the team competition in the National Championship shall be determined on a points system. The top weight in each section shall receive one point, the second highest weight two points etc. In the event of any angler or anglers failing to catch fish they will receive one more point than the lowest recorded weight in their section. Absent and disqualified anglers shall receive the same number of points as there are teams in the match.
    In the event of more than one competitor recording the same weight in the same section, those competitors will each be awarded equal points, i.e. one point more than allocated to the previous highest weight in that section.
    Therefore if 3 competitors tie for positions 6, 7, & 8 having equal weight, all would receive 6 points, the ninth competitor would receive 9 points and so on.
    The team with the lowest number of points will be declared Champions.
    In the event of a tie on points the highest aggregate team weight shall decide the issue.

14. The holders of the trophies shall, upon presentation, give a guarantee for their safety, and shall deliver them in a clean and satisfactory condition to the Secretary-General of the N.F.A. by the morning of the following National Championship in good time for them to be displayed.

15. All these rules are subject to River Authority Bye-laws.

And what kind of catches do these experts achieve at the 'National'?
The best team weight to date (February 1959) was 136 lb. 15 oz. 1 dr. by Sheffield Amalgamated A.A. on the River Huntspill and King's Sedgemoor Drain in 1955. J. Carr of this Association was the individual Champion with 68 lb. 2 oz. 1 dr; and the total catch of 99 teams that competed on this memorable occasion was no less than 4,036 lb. of fish!
On the other hand the lowest weights in this contest were recorded

in 1913 when twenty-two teams competed on the River Dee, at Chester. The Nottingham Association won with a total catch of 2 lb. 15 oz.; Mr. W. Gough of Nottingham was the individual champion with 1 lb. 14 oz. 8 dr. of fish and it is not surprising that no record was kept of the total weight returned by all teams on this occasion.

From the records before me it would seem that only one angler has won the individual N.F.A. National Championship twice. This distinction was achieved by the great angler the late J. H. R. Bazley, a Leeds schoolmaster. He won it first in 1909 while fishing for the Leeds Amalgamated A.A. at the Dyke, Newark, with 2 lb. 2½ oz. Then in 1927 fishing the Middle Level Drain at King's Lynn, he took 16 lb. 5½ oz. of fish to become the National Champion for second time. 'Baz' as he was universally and affectionately called has become a legendary figure in the annals of Leeds anglers; and that he was among the foremost fishermen of his day, both 'match' and 'pleasure,' is beyond dispute.

Having so said, I quote his pungent description of a match angler in action:

> His accuracy in dotting the bites and the dexterity with which he unhooked the fish, re-baited and got to business again, were amazing. It was tense quick work and a terribly hot day. The perspiration dropped from his nose and chin as time drew near.
>
> Not until the four hours were up did he pause to take the handkerchief from his pocket to wipe his flaming face. If I remember rightly, he had 168 gudgeon in those four hours—an average of 42 per hour—in the end he won fairly comfortably.

Are you surprised that the expression 'pleasure fisherman' has become common parlance?

Match men's methods

I have said already that where actual fishing ability is concerned match anglers have nothing on good 'pleasure anglers' and I adhere to that view. There is, however, one marked difference which is, I think, in favour of match men. They are meticulously thorough in every detail and I think take greater care in the preparation of their gear, baits and what have you, than is taken by 'pleasure fishermen.' For them the predominant factor is the need to weigh in more fish than anyone else and this I'm sure fathers their extreme care in every detail.

They consider carefully the venue. Is the water fast or slow? The tackle, baits, ground-baits and tactics for fishing a canal, would for example be quite different from those selected for use in a fast river; and they act accordingly.

Will long casting be the order of the day or will one be able to trot the stream from the rod point? Such considerations will as likely as not determine whether a revolving drum or fixed-spool reel will be used and if in doubt a match angler would certainly carry both.

Regardless of such considerations, however, match men always fish as fine as conditions will permit. If a single shot, a tiny ducker float and a gossamer line and cast are adequate, you may be sure that your match men will be using just that kind of gear. But if good bream come into their swim it will only be a matter of seconds before they have changed to more adequate tackle than was necessary to deal with the small roach, dace, etc. which had been their only patrons till the bream arrived. In short a good match fisher is always energetic, versatile and flexible, studying continually to suit his gear and tactics to the prevailing circumstances of quarry, water and weather conditions. Many 'pleasure fishermen' would do well to emulate this characteristic.

Most match men are addicted to the use of ultra small fine-wire hooks, and there is little room for doubt that this accounts for more bites and indeed for the collection of more fish when the fish are small bleak, gudgeon, etc. It is however equally certain that many a match winning whopper has been lost as the direct result of the use of a tiny hook. The smaller the hook and the finer the wire, the more easily will it tear away from its hold in a good fish.

You may wonder why small hooks account for more bites than larger ones. For what it is worth my opinion is that the smaller the hook the lighter it is and consequently it allows the bait to move more naturally, i.e. more as an unattached bait would move in the water. I may be wrong about this, but I am satisfied that the sight of a hook does not perturb fish. They just do not know what a hook is.

This question of hooks brings me to the very important matter of shotting, which could be the subject of a quite substantial book. But suffice it here to say that good match anglers have reduced the weighting of the business end of their tackle to a fine art in respect of both the amount of weight used and the positioning of the shot. Careful study and experience are their guides; and as the old saying has it 'experience is an expensive teacher but it teaches its lessons well.' There is in other words no short cut to the mastery of this most important aspect of all bottom fishing; and there is no rule-of-thumb which eliminates the need for experiment, careful observation and perseverance.

This applies also to the preparation and administration of ground-baits. It would be manifestly ludicrous to throw 'fog dust' into the Hampshire Avon or weighted cobs of bread and bran into a streamless canal. Good match anglers are acutely aware of this and apply their knowledge unfailingly. If, moreover, there is any doubt as to whether their 'peg' on any given water might be either fast or slow, they do not neglect to equip themselves with the necessary alternative ground-baits to meet either circumstance.

Little and often is generally speaking their motto for ground-baiting and accuracy in placing it *and fishing over it* is for them an axiom. By the skilful application of their ground-baits they can control the movements of any fish in their swim to a quite surprising extent, even vertically. Loose ground-bait used sparingly will bring fish up and more solid heavier ground-baiting will keep fish on the bottom. I remember reading in one book of ground-baiting methods for leading fish away from neighbouring competitors. Whether one should do that or not is a matter for individual decision, but I am told 'all's fair in love and war' and as some big matches come into the category of war to the death, perhaps it is quite an ethical procedure, and particularly so if one's adjacent competitor has not the know-how to prevent it, in which case it would presumably serve him right.

Although match men refer to ground-bait as 'feed' they take every care that it should be a lure only and at the very best but an inferior feed, when compared with the hook-bait. A good instance of this is exemplified by the match man's practice of using 'squats' (small inferior maggots) as ground-bait; and polishing large hand-picked gentles in bran for use as hook-baits.

In this connection whether colouring maggots has any beneficial effect must remain a matter of opinion. Some swear by and some swear at coloured gentles.

Most match anglers pin their faith on maggots as hook-baits, but bread as either cubes, flake or paste, wheat, etc. are used not infrequently. Whichever is selected for a match it has the maximum care in its preparation and not a few competitive anglers carry a number of change baits. As I have said no amount of trouble in respect of detail is too great for these fellows. This applies and is always demonstrated at the waterside. You have only to see how a match 'crack' arranges his tackle and baits. The handle of his landing net is always within close reach of his most accustomed hand. The mouth of his long-necked keep-net is so placed that an unhooked fish can be slipped into the net without the remotest risk of it falling back into the water; and all this with the minimum of movement and effort.

His ground-baits, hook-baits and miscellaneous tackle items are in orderly array, a place for everything and everything in its place. Practical neatness is essential to competition fishing and can be of great assistance to 'pleasure fishermen' many of whom would be well advised to put it to the test.

How often for example have you sought high and low for your disgorger, so long sometimes that the luckless fish was dead before you found it. Why not try the Post Office pen idea, i.e. attach it to a button-hole with a piece of line or string?

Oddly enough I have progressed thus far without mention of that all important item the rod. While some match anglers have a number of rods I think that most of them have a favourite with the use of which they are so at home that they and the rod are one entity; and I am certain that this is the ideal. One factor in this connection is however most important, namely, that your rod must be suited to your physique. Providing that it is so constructed that it strikes instantly, is of suitable length, and is light enough for you to use for hours with the minimum fatigue, that is the match rod for you.

There is nothing really mysterious about this match-fishing business and whatever you do don't fall for any suggestion that the most successful 'cracks' have any unfailing nostrums or secret killing baits. They mix their ground-baits and prepare their baits with common sense and they use them with knowledge born of experience. It's as simple as that, bar 'the luck of the draw' which can either play into the hands of a comparative novice or mar the best efforts of an expert.

I think it only fair to stress that to meet the various hazards that face him, a consistently successful match angler exhibits greater fishing skill to catch fish under match conditions, than the angler who is footloose and fancy free. And even if he is 'water licked' (unsuccessful) he will be found at the next match full of hope. This match-fishing calls for characteristics in its followers which are both vocational and fanatical in some respects.

If you contemplate taking up match-fishing, first be sure that you have the fundamentals of angling, which I have tried to explain in preceding chapters, well ground in. Then, if possible, make friends with one or two 'dab hands.' You will learn their arts, or is it crafts, more quickly that way than any other.

You may have expected me to go into detail as to ground-bait recipes, shotting methods, etc., etc.; but in my view these are so multifarious to meet the unending circumstances for which they are intended that a separate book would scarce contain them all. The way to become a winning contest man is the hard way and this chapter is intended merely as a match-fishing taster.

Much has been said about 'experts' and 'cracks' in the foregoing. But what is a fishing expert?

Is he necessarily just a catcher of many fish? I have always felt and still feel, that the most enviable form of angling expertise is to get the greatest interest, personal satisfaction and thrill out of fishing in any of its phases.

Which of us in later life, be he 'pleasure' or 'match' fisher, can place his hand on his heart and say that he compares favourably in these respects with small boys?

CHAPTER XL

'NOTA BENE'

A FEW reminders of the easily overlooked essentials may well make a useful tailpiece of this work.

N.B.—There are comparatively few waters where you have an *incontestable right* to fish.

Fish may not hear in our sense of the word, but they are very sensitive to bank or boat vibrations. Knock your pipe out on your hand, friend, and wear rubber-soled shoes in a boat.

Fish most certainly see and no man knows how much or how clearly they see. Don't wear white jackets or tennis shirts in the summer when fishing and expect to do well. Keep your shadow off the water. Take all possible cover and don't move jerkily. All so elementary I know, but watch the average fisherman at work, and you will soon see that the reminder is justified.

Remember the function of ground-bait is to attract and hold fish in your swim—not to feed them. Make up and administer ground-bait with this in mind and your battle is half won.

A float is but a necessary evil. To serve its threefold purpose of suspending a bait at a given depth below the surface, carry a bait to otherwise inaccessible parts of the water and indicate to the fisherman any interference with the bait; it should be the smallest suited to the prevailing water conditions. The smallest float which will do the work in hand is always a wise choice.

A float can only be sensitive when its diameter at the point where it emerges from the water is small. The more slender a float is at that point the more sensitive it will be.

The stability or steadiness of a float is governed by the size of its underwater body and the depth at which the body is below the surface. Within reasonable limits the larger and more deeply sunk the body is the more stable is the float.

Heavy shotting is not in itself a grave disadvantage. One must remember, however, that some fish dislike quantities of lead mixed with a hook-bait.

If the water you are fishing is fast and interspersed with ribbon weed (like many stretches of the Hampshire Avon), abandon low shotting; and spread the shot on the cast. This will facilitate its passage between the weeds and minimise hang-up.

Shot are used not to cock a float, which is only an incidental function, but to carry a bait down to the fish and hold it there. The smallest number of the lightest weight which will do this is the best shotting to use.

Floats should be as streamlined as possible.

The more buoyant the material from which a float is constructed the better. Balsa wood, for example, is better than cork, because a smaller piece of balsa will suspend the same weight.

Fish as fine as you dare on all occasions. The less visible your gear the more likely it is to deceive wary fish; but fish suitably rather than ultra-fine, you will catch more fish in the long run.

Don't use too small hooks; their hooking power is small and their holding power even less. There is no virtue in using a No. 18 when an eleven hook will hold the bait and the fish much better.

Fish as near to your quarry as you can without frightening the fish. The less line you have out the more control you have over it. The shorter the line the quicker the strike.

Half the art of fishing is to know where the fish are and when. No amount of study of this subject is too much.

Only those fishermen catch fish whose bait or lure is in the water.

To catch fish is greater than to kill them. Please don't kill fish for killing's sake.

Never allow a fish to gasp to death in your creel or on the bank. If it must die dispatch it expeditiously; a small priest or any empty bottle will do the trick.

The late Sir Herbert Maxwell, Bart., F.R.S., put it like this:

> ... Fishes ... extract (from the water) oxygen necessary to their existence by means of branchiae or gills. Let these organs once get dry, and the animal perishes of suffocation just as certainly as a lung-breathing creature will do if kept under water.

Never, never, never permit this!

Versatility is one of the good fisherman's most important attributes. The expert is always ready to change his tactics to suit prevailing conditions. A slavish adherence to one style of fishing is a great mistake.

Study the depth and speed of the water before putting ground-bait into a swim. Your ground-bait is useless if it does not fall along the path of your hook-bait and reach the bottom where your hook is at work and *vice versa*.

Always be ready to learn from others and to accept local advice and methods. But do not follow either blindly. You *may* know more than the locals. A process of trial and error is always wise when time permits.

Prepare your baits with the same care as you bestow on your tackle.

Water is the arch enemy of fishing tackle. Dry your rod and reel at once when you have finished fishing. A drop of oil is a godsend to a reel.

Keep a list of the various items you will require for any particular type of fishing. By this means if you fill your bag or creel with the aid of your list, you will avoid the dreadful chagrin of arriving at the waterside (miles from home) and finding you have left your reel behind. It has happened scores of times. The same list will enable you to make sure that you have not left anything on the river bank or in the boat when you 'pack up' at night.

It's an idea also to paint items white which may get mislaid amongst long grass. They are much easier to find, especially in failing light.

A rod painted any dull matt colour errs on the safe side. Glint from a highly polished rod will put fish down under certain circumstances.

Always hang your rods up tied loosely in the bag. Leaning them up tends to warp the best of rods, and tying the bag strings tightly will twist some rods like a dog's hind leg.

Clear your rod rings regularly of any accumulation of dirt and line grease. Details of this kind make all the difference to the efficiency and longevity of your tackle.

Speaking of fly-fishing tackle reminds me that, while you may be filled with respect, admiration, even awe, of the profound entomological knowledge displayed by some anglers, such knowledge may find itself in sharp conflict with the art of presenting a fly. Better, I think, be an artist with a rod than an encyclopaedic bungler. A combination of both is, of course, ideal, but if you are puzzled by the huge numbers of flies, etc., don't let them worry you. Study to present a few well.

The successful pike-spinner's creed is spin low and spin slow.

If you are contemplating a day's fishing, make up your mind for which fish you will angle. Pack the gear for that type of fishing and be content. It is a great mistake to take a forest of rods, etc. No man can fish properly with more than one rod at a time.

Light rods, reels, etc., are always most comfortable to use. Weight is a silent destroyer of a day's pleasure, particularly if sport is not brisk.

A little adhesive tape is an excellent companion when fishing. There is nothing better for effecting a temporary repair to a broken rod top.

Landing nets and keep nets should be dried after use as religiously as lines, rods and reels. Many a man has had the mortifying experience of seeing fish disappear through the rotten meshes of a landing or keep net.

It is a good idea to place a suitable stone in or attach a permanent weight to the bottom of your landing net to ensure it sinking when dry. Many a fish has owed its freedom to an obstinately floating net.

When moving from place to place with your rod set up, carry it with the point behind you.

Remember D'Oyle Hemingway's dictum: 'Big fools lay their rods upon the ground for bigger fools to tread on.'

Your personal comforts are very much your own affair, but an ample light rubber or plastic mackintosh is worth its weight for dryness.

Play a fish quietly out of the swim. Skull-hauling and allowing a fish to flap on the surface puts the others down and is the mark of a tyro.

Certain wind and weather conditions are not auspicious, but don't be put off—'have a go.' Some surprising catches have resulted from persistence in the most adverse conditions.

It may be very inconvenient, but it is usually more productive to fish all day with the wind in your face, especially in still water.

Don't stand about on the bank behind a well-concealed angler. He won't appreciate you as an audience. The camaraderie of the sport can easily lead you into this error. Sheer admiration is another cause. But please don't do it.

A change bait is always worth carrying. If the fish will not take one they will quite often accept another bait or lure.

Never handle a fish with hot dry hands; you may injure it by doing so. Dip your hands in the water first. The slime on a fish protects it from disease, acts as a lubricant as it moves through the water and keeps it waterproof. A fish denuded of its slime will become waterlogged and die.

Disgorgers are the most elusive items in a fisherman's equipment. It's a good plan to tie your disgorger to a buttonhole with a suitable length of string.

Always carry a torch when winter fishing. Dusk soon becomes darkness and . . . where is it?

Always lower weights or anchors gently into the water. The splash of a weight or the rattle of a chain over the side is sufficient to scare any self-respecting fish for hundreds of yards around. Nowadays, when almost every water is 'caned' fish are for the most part very self-respecting.

Anglers in moving boats catch few fish. Give a swim a real trial before moving to a new pitch.

Precision when casting a spinner is an art well worth great effort to acquire. The precise caster catches more fish and loses fewer spinners.

Never lay your reel down on sandy ground, and if you do so inadvertently, clean it thoroughly on the spot and re-oil. Grit is death of a good reel.

Preserve as far as possible a right angle between your rod and line while playing a fish. This ensures that your rod is doing its work and lessens the chance of a break considerably. The usual advice is 'keep your rod point up.' It may, however, be held to the left or right and parallel with the water with the same effect. It is not always possible to keep the rod point up.

Retrieving a spinner is not mere winding in. Study to give your lure a lively or irregular movement through the water in simulation of a sick or wounded fish.

Fish don't know what hooks are; you need not be afraid of your hook being visible to the fish.

Please do not remove the spiny dorsal fin from a perch before using it as a live bait. It is a ridiculous practice which injures the bait needlessly and causes it to work feebly. Pike have no means of removing this fin before pouching a perch—and pike are fond of perch, dorsal fin and all.

Prospects are not good when the air is colder than the water, or when the water is very cold.

Always try to play a big fish from a sitting position; hundreds of specimens have been lost through the angler showing himself unduly and causing a 'fright bolt' at the psychological moment.

If you make a reel-box or other container for tackle, file off the edges and corners, that will save holing your tackle-bag.

Most books on angling drone this piece of elementary advice, to such an extent that I had contemplated its omission by way of a change. But no! I must say it. Keep your hooks needle-sharp. Sharpen them at home and take time off to resharpen them at the waterside. A fish-hook cannot be too sharp. And while you are at it file off some part of any barb which is too long. Doing this will become a habit which you will never regret forming. A small piece of carborundum is all you need.

Finally, let us consider the future of angling. It is now a sport actively followed by millions, with not a by-line fan among them. Everyone takes his rod and tackle to the water, whether it be still or running, and 'does his own thing' either in the company of his friends or alone. The amount of water-side available to each man dwindles as his numbers mount. Therefore we must cherish our heritage with all the powers at our command before 'progress' and 'civilisation' with their attendant horrors of pollution both industrial and sheer criminal lunacy from 'water lovers'—and that includes followers of our own sport—leave the angler with nothing but memories of what once was a sport.

Since *Angling Ways* first edition appeared, a new body has been formed, called the National Anglers' Council, and the best way to describe its aims is to allow it to speak for itself. It says: 'the N.A.C. is recognised by the Minister for Sport and the Sports Council as the responsible body representing the whole of the sport of angling.' Its objects are:

a. To co-operate with its members in encouraging the promotion and development of the sport for angling in England and Wales amongst all sections of the community.

b. To co-ordinate and put forward the views of all bodies and persons concerned with the sport of angling in England and Wales in any negotiation or on any other appropriate occasion.

c. To formulate and review an Anglers' National Policy.

The National Anglers' Council does not seek to govern the sport in the sense of laying down rules, e.g. for size limits, tackle, allocation of water. It exists to improve the status of anglers in negotiations with the Government, to increase the supply of water for angling, and to protect the interests of all anglers against the ever increasing threats of encroachment by other sports or pastimes. In one short sentence, this body protects the future of angling. My recommendation to all who have the future of the sport at heart is to join. Membership is open to individuals as well as organisations, and the address of the secretary is: National Anglers' Council, 17 Queen Street, Peterborough, Northants. A pound a year is all you need find—and how much do you spend on maggots in twelve months?

The special threat of pollution, although very much the concern of the N.A.C., can also be fought by the Anglers' Cooperative Association. This gallant body happily takes on those juggernauts of industry who care little in general for the local stream except insofar as it accepts filthy effluent and without fuss takes it away downstream. That fish life is killed and the water unfit for anything is unfortunate, so long as the profit margin keeps constant. So this is the other body you must support, for it can mean the difference between water holding fish and water unable even to support the humble water snail. The address: Charles Wade, Director, The Anglers' Cooperative Association 53 New Oxford St., London W.C.1.

INDEX